THEOLOGICAL

TRANSLATION FUND LIBRARY.

VOL. XXVIII.

EWALD'S

COMMENTARY ON THE BOOK OF JOB.

COMMENTARY

ON THE

BOOK OF JOB

WITH TRANSLATION

BY THE LATE

DR. GEORG HEINRICH AUGUST VON EWALD,

Professor of Oriental Languages in the University of Göttingen.

TRANSLATED FROM THE GERMAN

BY

J. FREDERICK SMITH.

Wipf & Stock

PUBLISHERS

Eugene, Oregon

Wipf and Stock Publishers
199 W 8th Ave, Suite 3
Eugene, OR 97401

Commentary on the Book of Job
By Ewald, Georg Heinrich
ISBN: 1-59244-822-4
Publication date 8/26/2004
Previously published by Williams and Norgate, 1882

THIS translation into English of the late Professor Ewald's work on the Book of Job, the third part of his *Dichter des Alten Bundes,* has been made on the same principles as that of his work on the Prophets of the Old Testament, which has appeared as volumes ix, xii, xviii, xxi, and xxvi of this series. The translator has considered it his duty, in this as in the former case, to faithfully observe the fundamental principles on which the great interpreter of the Hebrew Scriptures performed his task of reproducing as closely as possible the minutest peculiarities of his Hebrew authors, even at the cost of German grammar and idiom. Real students of Ewald would not thank an English translator for the attempt to improve upon him. On one point only has any concession been made to English popular taste. The Hebrew proper names in this volume appear, with the exception of יַהְוֶה, in their traditional English form. This slight departure from the author's practice of transcribing these names in their Hebrew form can hardly be regarded as the violation of an essential principle of his Commentaries.

The references in this volume to other works of the author's have been made as explained in the "Translator's Preface" to the first volume of the "Prophets". The §§ of his Hebrew

Grammar, which in the German of this volume of the Poets of the Old Testament are those of an early edition, have been made to correspond with the paragraphing of the last editions of that work. The first edition of this Commentary has generally been compared with the second and last, from which this translation is made, and important differences between the two have frequently been noted.

J. F. S.

CONTENTS.

INTRODUCTION:—

TRANSLATION AND COMMENTARY:—

THE BOOK OF JOB.

INTRODUCTION.

1. THE THOUGHT OF THE POEM.

It is easy to see from the first glance at the book that the poet is making the evils which afflict mortals the subject of his consideration. He found the view which had prevailed from of old down to his own times already self-contradictory, and he attempted a profounder solution of the conflicting principles. The successful accomplishment of this task, however, required as its condition the most distinct conception of the contrary notions themselves.

1. According to the notion which descended even to Christian times (John ix, 2 compared with the ancient evidence Num. xxvii, 3), the dark and grievous ills which befall man are the corresponding consequences of special sins. They are primarily the consequences of the sufferer's own sins, but in exceptional cases, where the measure of calamity appears out of proportion to the particular sufferer's guilt, the causes of it are traced back to his parents or earlier ancestors. But in every case the ills are regarded as a consequence of personal sin. Nor need it create surprise that the ancient world possessed at the first no tried and valid notion as regards the causes of human ill. The idea of evil, ill, is of such a wide and indefinite nature, the causes of it are both so various and so concealed, that even after long experience and close examination it remains difficult to present a satisfactory theory of it. As long as natural evil, that is evil which is involved in the very creation and con-

stitution of the world, is not distinguished from personal evil, or from what is properly wickedness, and as long as men in their personal capacity are not more strictly looked upon as raised above merely external evil and wickedness which has not touched them personally, it will be impossible to attain to a view of evil in its relation to man which will be in all respects satisfactory. As long as the above conditions of such a view are unfulfilled, the best, and, as far as the simple feelings of early religion are concerned, the most natural view is that above referred to, which arose in the most distant antiquity. This was a conception which early antiquity embraced with affection and reverence, which was subsequently held for a long time, and which must always retain a certain justification in less elevated and more confined spheres of thought, inasmuch as it contains a certain amount of truth. For every ill of the great undistinguished multitude of ills which befall a man, in whatever way it may have arisen, in any case always powerfully provokes serious consideration, and in the first instance compels him to abandon his customary indifference and to seek the less obvious causes of the calamities which he so painfully feels. In that case, what will he more naturally think of than his sins and ill deserts? For the unsophisticated mind feels profoundly that it is from sin that disturbance, confusion, and suffering proceed. In this way natural evil also becomes a moral one to him who is conscious of such a disturbance and disorganisation within, and the wickedness of others with which he has connexion by ties of blood or family appears justly to reach him in its consequences. As long as the consciousness of human imperfection and of the magnitude of guilt has not been aroused with sufficient force or clearness, this way of looking at the undistinguished mass of evil is not without reason or usefulness. Every fresh calamity snatches men from their natural indolence and confused thoughtlessness, and every hard or severely felt blow of that kind is like the wave which is meant to impel the ship of the soul, as it is still contending with the troubled billows of ignorance, towards a calmer and fairer port. As thus in the case of men generally the recognition of the terrible nature of guilt in all its magnitude must become clear and vivid before they can in return overcome its terrors, so the men of early antiquity were confronted by the undistinguished aggregate of evil in all its forms in order that the truth of human guilt might be brought out most sensibly and painfully. And that nation of antiquity which experienced and felt most vividly all divine truths in this respect also passed through the profoundest experiences, although in a greater or less degree the feeling, that calamities are the consequences of sin, pervades the whole of antiquity. So natural and powerful was this feeling in those ages that it was felt by everybody in that stage of human development, not only by individuals who were themselves the immediate sufferers but also by those who were merely spectators and contemporaries.

Primarily, however, by the immediate sufferer himself. He feels most directly the irresistible assault of mysterious suffering, whether it be the burning fever of a violent illness or some other peril threatening complete destruction. Assailed by the most painful sensations, experiencing nothing gentle, mitigating, alleviating, he believes that instead of the former gentle, quickening divine breath, the value of which he now for the first time fully recognises, he endures the wrath of God, xvi. 9; xix. 11; xxx. 21; Ps. xxxix. 11, 12; Lam. i. 12; ii. 1, 3; iii. 1; iv. 11; that he feels His indignation entering into him x. 17, that he grievously and helplessly falls under His enmity xiii. 24; xxx. 21. This feeling seeks expression by means of the most varied figures. The unhappy sufferer feels as if his sufferings were an indignant, chastising hand, with which God clutches him and which rests upon him heavily and without cessation, i. 11; ii. 5; xiii. 21; xix. 21; xxiii. 2; xxx. 21; Ps. xxxviii. 3; xxxix. 11. The cruel pains of his calamities appear to him like those caused by sharply pointed and deeply penetrating arrows and missiles of all kinds, vi. 4; Ps. xxxviii. 3; Lam. ii. 4;

iii. 12. Their incessantly repeated and increasingly violent attack appears to him to be like that of a whole host of armed and fierce assailants, who continually march up with ever fresh forces to storm a fortress, relieving each other by turns, x. 17; xvi. 9, 12—14; xxx. 12—15. And the solitary, frail mortal is set up as it were to be the obnoxious aim of all such incessant attacks, vii. 20; xvi. 11; Lam. iii. 12, and must probably at last succumb as if shamefully prevailed over by the proud enemy who seeks to entrap and to insult the poor unfortunate, xiv. 20; xix. 9, 10; xxx. 19; Lam. iii. 4. All this appears, in consequence of the burning fire which he feels raging within, as if it were at the same time inflicted by the most indignant enemy, as if the arrows which penetrate him were poisoned vi. 4; xxx, 27, and wrathful glances from God went through him without ceasing, vii. 19; xiv. 6; xvi. 9; Ps. xxxix. 14. On account of this overwhelming burden and torture, attended by the paralysis of all his energies, the sufferer feels himself irrecoverably handed over to a higher power. At one time it seems to him as if shut in on all hands he could find no exit, as in trackless horrible darkness iii. 23; xix. 8; Lam. iii. 7, 9; or as if he were in rigorous confinement where he may not move or stir, vii. 12; xiii. 27; xiv. 16; Lam. iii. 7; or as if entangled in a net and caught in snares xix. 6; Lam. i. 13. At another time, when the danger threatens and rages more violently, he seems to himself to be sinking as if forcibly overwhelmed, carried away by a vast flood, Ps. xxxviii. 5; xlii. 8; lxxxviii. 8, 16—18; lxix. 1 sq. (a figure not used in the Book of Job); or as if hunted and run down by a raging lion, x. 16; xvi. 9; Isa. xxxviii. 13, or even a still more terrible case, as if pursued by the violence of a storm, hurled on high, dashed in pieces, ix. 11, 17; xiii. 25; xxx. 22. Now although these feelings and similes could not have arisen unless from the very first the more or less distinct forboding and terror of the divine wrath had existed in the background, this terror nevertheless only becomes truly powerful and definite in the course of such calamities and pains. It is in his mysterious afflictions that the poor sufferer thinks he finds the proof and evidence of the divine disfavour and hostility (*I know* that Thou will not acquit me, says Job, ix. 28; x. 13; xxx. 23). Thus the trouble is twofold, possessing the whole soul and filling it with the darkest terrors. All the afflictions which are either actually endured or threatened and dreaded become thus precisely so many images of anguish and alarm to the confounded soul which is labouring under the delusion of the divine wrath; boundless dismay, horrible despair, is added to the physical tortures of the body, destroying every consolation, iii. 24, 25; ix. 11, 15—20; xxiii. 16; Ps. vi. 7, 8; xiii. 3; lxxxviii. 16. Whilst he supposes that he feels most painfully the glance and hand of his angry God, he must still feel on the other hand that God as the glorious, kind and gracious One has withdrawn from him and appears to stand afar off with His face turned away, xiii. 24; xix. 7; xxiii. 8, 9; xxx. 20, 21; Ps. xiii. 2; x. 1 sq.; xxxviii. 15. And although with every new and unexpected stroke he experiences afresh the wonders of the divine power, this power is nevertheless simply dark and terrible in this case, ix. 11 sq.; x. 16. This dismay, this ceaseless foreboding terror, is finally the more intense in proportion as the consoling and cheering prospects which the ancient world entertained regarding the gloomy Underworld, or Hades, were few; from it there seemed to be no possible return, and dread of the death of the body, and of being compelled early to enter the Underworld, was great. So that a man, whom such a calamity befalls before the satiety and weariness of old age, although in the moment of maddening pain the quickest death seems the one thing to be desired, vi. 8—13; vii. 15; xiii. 14, can yet at other times pray pitifully for at least a brief respite before the last breath is drawn, vii. 16, 19; x. 20; xiv. 5—12; Isa. xxxviii. 10—13.—And if the man who is thus afflicted is conscious of no definite grievous sin, it will still appear to him in the midst of all these conceptions, as if his incessant pain tortured and compelled him to reflect and in penitence and submission confess transgressions the commission of which he cannot recall. His sufferings become a painful instrument of torture with which God enquires after his sins, x. 6, becoming constantly more intense in proportion as he makes resistance (as in fact by the impatience and rebellion of the sufferer his sufferings increase) ix. 12—20, 34; x. 16, 17; xiii. 21. The final punishment, the end of the process of torture, death itself, appears to be irrevocably determined, and God, delaying and yet constantly bitterly punishing, merely meditating amidst the interchanging severe torments upon the manner of the certain impending death, xiii. 15, 26; xiv. 17; xxiii. 14. In such circumstances the thought of God's omnipotence is itself a burden and a terror, because a mortal (even should he innocently fall) appears unable to deliver himself in opposition to omnipotent decrees, inasmuch as beyond God there is no appeal, but He is the almighty and at the same time the highest judge, ix. 2—20, 30—33; xxiii. 6, 13, 14; xxx. 18.

However the spectators and contemporaries also behold in such sufferings a sign of the divine punishment of the sufferer himself: his misfortunes are an unfavourable witness not to himself alone, xiii. 27; xvi, 8, but also to his fellowmen. The alarming sight of such sufferings, which sometimes provokes disgust even, combined with the consciousness of possible participation in similar sin and punishment, excites even in the kindly-disposed and considerate friend the suspicion, that the sufferer is paying the penalty of equally grievous sins. The ordinary, pusillanimous and selfish man carefully turns away, or even insults and mocks the sufferer, not blushing to charge him with false crimes. As the poor man's afflictions increase, the confusion and error of such spectators grow, and nothing causes the sufferer deeper pain than this suspicion which he meets with from his fellowmen, this narrow-minded treachery by which he finds himself isolated or betrayed, this cruel scorn with which he finds himself so bitterly persecuted,

ii. 9; xii. 4; xvi. 7 sq., 10, 20; xvii. 6; xix. 22; xxx. 1 sq.; Ps. vi. 8; xiii. 3 sq.; xli. 6 sq.; xxxv. 11 sq.; xxxviii. 12 sq.; lxix. 5 sq.; lxxxviii. 8, 9, 19; Lam. ii. 15, 16; Isa. xlix. 7, liii. 3, and many other passages. The most friendly and calmest of the spectators cannot refrain from urging the poor man to do profound penance at least, and they insist vehemently on confession of committed sins.

The ancient languages also point by the forms and usages of many words to ideas of this kind as generally prevalent. Thus נֶגַע is a *stroke* of God, an affliction of the body intended as a punishment; and how deeply the ancient Hebrews felt that the ideas of guilt, punishment, and suffering were interchangeable, is shown by several words which convey all these meanings, as עָוֹן, for instance, denoting properly what is wrong, a transgression, guilt, but also the mysterious sufferings connected therewith, Ps. xxxviii. 5; by חַטּאת and פֶּשַׁע *transgression, sin,* the consequences of wrong-doing, the *punishment,* or the suffering, are at all events often expressed, Ps. xxxix. 9, rather than the wrong-doing itself, on the supposition that the latter implies the former. Nor, indeed, can any one deny that a profound and eternal connexion subsists between sin and suffering, as much as between divine right and salvation, as the ancient nations, but particularly the Hebrews, surmised in such a grand and severe manner. It is only the form under which they conceived this connexion to exist which is confused and mixed with error in the above popular conceptions.

2. For that view may fairly well suffice as long as human life remains in its first simplicity, but not as it grows more complex. With the progress of the collective life of the race, men's relations to each other become by degrees very complicated. The individual and separate households get interwoven with the prevailing order or disorder of a great community; the individual so often suffers without corresponding personal fault under the sufferings of the whole community, or bears alone even the guilt of a whole period, the consequences

of the errors of many centuries. As thus the disturbance of the simple equilibrium between suffering and personal conduct becomes increasingly painful, that ancient view of the calamities of individuals as the consequence of their personal sins also receives perpetually more and more injurious shocks, inasmuch as experience so often and so decidedly contradicts it. This rift in the ancient notion, moreover, widens still further in another direction. The idea of guilt, which has been brought to greater perfection under this notion as its outward integument, becomes itself a means of its dissolution. For when that early delusion fully roused and aggravated the consciousness of guilt, it necessarily met with its end precisely as it attained this object: just in proportion as the heart has become softened and obedient, it has also become the more able to escape from its own darkness and errors. When once the idea of the true extent and the real magnitude of the personal guilt of mortals has become quite clear to the mind, it will turn with all the clearer perception and courage to the recognition of what does not strictly constitute a part of that guilt, and resist more and more decidedly the universal validity of the ancient belief. Men learn to put in opposite scales the measure of their sufferings and the measure of their possible transgressions; and in the case of the individual who suffers so severely but cannot with the most minute examination discover anything which completely answers to his afflictions, there arises from that early delusion a host of doubts and troubles xiii. 26[b]; Ps. xxv. 7. And then, on the other hand, God himself is the being who is full of kindness and mercy, and as time goes on is more and more inwardly and cordially felt to be such. If that is the case, wherefore shall the sufferer not hope for relief from the mercy and salvation of God? For, indeed, mercy must be the predominant characteristic of God, and the Creator seems to be necessitated to treat his creature rather with love than with the desire to destroy it, x. 3, 8; xiv, 15. In the midst of the growing confusion and the increasing universality of misery, the certainty and necessity of the indestructible divine mercy as the only salvation come more and more into the foreground: and when once this conviction has grown powerful, it turns primarily against that ancient belief, which has become a delusion and superstition, as its dangerous antagonist.

It is true that at first the endeavour was made to maintain both of these contradictory views, inasmuch as the sufferer, though still oppressed by the feeling of the divine wrath, nevertheless prays to be chastised not beyond measure but rather to be pardoned, and while he wrestles with his affliction gathers from the idea of the divine mercy reasons with which to excite God's pity. And as a fact noble souls which can discover such reasons, succeed thus in getting comfort for the moment*. The contradiction between these two ways of regarding God,—as the hostile unjust tormentor, xxvii. 2, and as the highest judge from whom at all events no final wrong can be expected, xiii. 9; xi. 16,—the poor man seeks to overcome by thinking of God as only at present hostile, xiii. 24; xiv. 16; xxiii. 3—17, and so putting forth his utmost strength he wrestles to feel that He is once more inclined to him. But notwithstanding there still remains an oppressive, unsatisfied feeling, inasmuch as this solution of the contradiction involves on its part much that is not clear and intelligible. And as the times grow increasingly complicated, as the life of the more conscientious gets constantly more troubled and toilsome, the hold of despair gets stronger, it becomes growingly difficult within the region of that ancient delusion, notwithstanding the thought of the divine mercy, to attain to lasting satisfaction. Even in cases where a noble power of faith contends with despair and aspires to victory, we soon see notwithstanding at one time how the utmost effort to escape the fear of the divine wrath and the mockery of cruel persecutors, Pss. xxxv; xxxviii; lxix; cix., succeeds only with difficulty in overcoming and assuaging

* See my Commentary on Ps. vi. 13.

the bitter, almost scornful, contemplation of the frailty of human life and endeavours Ps. xxxix., and at another time the most melancholy longing for salvation, pining almost in vain in a last effort to find comfort and deliverance, closing with a mournful outlook, Ps. lxxxviii. If in such a case the affliction nevertheless afresh surprises the poor man who is not at all conscious of such great guilt, and he sees himself disappointed as regards the peace which should follow his innocence and the hope arising from divine mercy, is it not possible that at last pure despair may prevail and its source—that ancient belief—be turned against itself in fierce indignation? As a sufficient reason for such great wrath is not felt, the fear of that wrath becomes a dread of all divine leadings and providences in general, and the one thought which ought to bring comfort and hope to the sufferer—the thought of God—is changed into an image of terror.

But this possible error does not reach its climax until the personal sufferer turns his dazed and dimmed eye from his own individual calamities to the consideration of the great world to find there its full confirmation. The man that is conscious of such perplexity and confusion within his own soul, such emptiness and desolation, discovers also very quickly calamities of a similarly excessive character in the world around him; indeed, he simply finds there things which answer to his own mood and experience. How many seem, on the one hand, to suffer most profoundly though no great personal guilt can be proved or presupposed in their case! On the other hand, how prosperous often is the powerful sinner who defies all law and order! If man's external fortunes are to serve as an index for the judgment as regards the divine favour, in such cases does not everything in the present world appear to violate all order, and does not experience teach the exact contrary of the early belief—the adversity of the faithful and, which is the most distressing, the apparently complete and lasting prosperity of the violent and lawless? ix. 22—24; xii. 5, 6; xxi. 6, 7;

xxiii, 14; xxiv. 1—25; comp. Pss. xlix, lxxiii. And if it is sought to excuse the outward prosperity of the wicked by the supposition, that at all events his sons would nevertheless have to suffer for it, is that really a righteous retribution proportionate to the dignity of God and of the human person? xxi. 19—21; comp. v. 4. On the contrary, are not the sons of those who suffer innocently sharers in their parents' misfortunes from no fault of their own? Do not many follow the seductive example of a prosperous sinner? xxi. 32, 33. In general, where is the mighty and manifest intervention of God as judge which the early belief maintained?—Whoever in this general confusion under which the world seems to be suffering feels himself involved and overwhelmed with no light or succour from within or without, must naturally either sink into a state of gloomy and oppressive dread, in which, overwhelmed by the burden, he resigns all collected thought, or, if he remains too strong to give way to such cowardly fear, must rise up boldly in warm indignation against the confusion itself and Him whom he regards as its ultimate cause. For the mind of a healthy, intelligent man cannot comprehend such a prevalence of wrong, inasmuch as it is a contradiction of his own nature. The dark unresolved enigma torments and teases him most painfully. And if such an impossible, yea, preposterous state of things appears to come even from God himself, and thus to force itself upon his attention, man possesses still the marvellous power and desire to turn with a Titanic daring against Heaven itself, to call to account the Omnipotent One regarding that which is to his mind so inexplicable, and not to tremble even in the presence of an angry and threatening God! He who is thus driven by the dark storm of doubt and perplexity is more likely to sacrifice the ancient faith altogether with all that might be true in it, and a single individual may find it easier to combat the universally prevalent, or even the sacred, notion, than that he should from consideration for it betray a true experience which contradicts it and faint-heartedly pay homage to the dark obscurity. And if God and all the powers of the world endeavoured by means of the ancient doctrine to deprive him of his conscious innocence, he could only all the more boldly in the midst of all dangers defend the hereditary faith itself against (the external) God, the outward world.

But justly as the violated moral feeling revolts against the ancient delusion and in a short time inflicts upon it incurable wounds, this method produces no salutary result, but immediately nothing but increased perplexity, growing trouble. Thus we have, on the one hand, a delusive faith grown to a superstition, and on the other, the same faith simply converted into its contradictory, doubt and denial degenerated into unbelief! On both sides misconception: for both still depend upon external appearances, without having grasped the whole and the heart of the matter. Nevertheless amid these painful mental throes the higher truth may at last come to light. Contradictory views when most strained and decisively brought out conduct readily to the clearness of truth. When doubt has been fully developed, it soon proves its own destruction; under the ruins of it and the ancient faith there is already lying secreted the purer truth which is so anxiously longed-for and the want of which is so painfully felt, and unexpectedly a favouring wind calls it forth at the right moment.

3. This correct view proceeds from the recognition of the fact, that outward evil as such is not at all necessarily the consequence and punishment of the sins of the individual, that physical evils such as earthquakes, pestilences, on the contrary, befall both good and bad no less indiscriminately than physical benefits (comp. Luke xiii. 1—5; Matt. v. 45). On the other hand, outward evil which has its origin in human wickedness, e. g. oppression and cruelty, can although it affects the guilty most painfully, at the same time just as easily fall upon the innocent also. Evil as something outward, visible, and physical holds therefore no true inward relation whatever to

the personal merits of man, inasmuch as the most guilty may sometimes enjoy what is apparently the greatest prosperity and the most innocent may for the moment bear the most painful and humiliating suffering. It can, however, never destroy the immortal spirit of man. The divine design of the evil which befalls a man must therefore be altogether different from that which the ancient belief supposed: evil must be intended simply to raise and bless him by arousing his spirit and compelling the exercise of its profounder energies. For when it meets him as an enemy, it really arouses simply his hidden energies, the unused infinite treasures of his soul, to the endeavour to overcome it, and points the inexhaustible immortal spirit to its own dignity and power. But this spirit as it rises to the struggle, and partially or in the end wholly overcomes the dark, and disturbing view, becomes conscious of its own greatness. It is in this struggle and victory that man becomes a partaker of the divine life, a truly free man and a ruler. So that evil assumes even a necessary place in the divine order of the world, and where there are the most and the greatest evils there also is the possibility of the most glorious victory and the highest happiness. It follows therefore that evil must befall all without distinction, and if it were merely the temptation, or the danger of the idea of erring, which had to be overcome, the most innocent would be obliged to pass through this fiery trial; just as, on the other hand, the most guilty is at all events in any case warned and as far as is possible for him summoned to get free from his guilt. And should the sin of parents and ancestors exert considerable influence upon their children and descendants, the spirit is notwithstanding so fresh and capable in each young member of the race that it can annihilate all earlier evils and return to the eternal divine mercy, comp. Deut. xxiv. 16; Jer. xxxi. 29, 30; Ezek. xviii. 1 sq.; John ix. 3. As accordingly trial successfully withstood and pain happily overcome are no longer evils, outward evils do not become really evils until they are inward, whether this takes place by means of the evil of a sin which is rooted in the heart, inasmuch as the heart which is oppressed thereby is inclined to regard every evil which is added from without as related, or whether it takes place by means of the false notion of outward evil as a simple divine punishment. In the first case, the confusion of the inward evil, the evil conscience, with the external one, is put an end to by the destruction of the inward evil; in the latter case, the mistaken notion comes to an end of itself by the shining forth of the pure truth as the noblest gain of the conflict with the evil itself, since the latter in this conflict of man with it must gradually reveal its own nature more and more distinctly, and as the false spectre of evil flees, the idea of true moral evil becomes so much the plainer and more certain.

Is this so, there then naturally follows as a general principle for the person actually suffering, that he can overcome evil, without fear and despondency, simply by the assurance of the immortality of the spirit and of all other divine truths, by patience and fortitude in true faith and trust, and by the clearer knowledge of himself which comes through suffering, while by the contrary, particularly by the conception of evil as simply the punishment of an angry God and by the gloomy fear and perplexity which arises therefrom, he only makes evil really dangerous and the burden of it most oppressive.—And for the spectator follows the principle, that he may not be alarmed at the outward bugbear of evil and its more repulsive features, that he may not judge hastily and narrowly concerning its mysteries, nor impute to the sufferer some sin and prepare confusion by which both the suffering itself is made more painful and even the good intentions and the desire to comfort of the sympathetic are frustrated.

This thought in all its truth, according to the grounds and deepest sources from which it is necessarily derived, it is the design and aim of the Book of Job to illustrate and magnify. At the time of the writing of the book it was without doubt a new thought, which here for the first time finds its worthy and fully qualified apostle, but did not obtain general acceptance until a considerably later period. So greatly must the poet have outrun his age. We already meet in this book with the same fundamental view of evil which is subsequently briefly and forcibly established in the N. T. and will last for all time. But here we see it as it is still wholly new in the struggle of its discovery, wrestling with its own inner necessity, in all the freshness of its genesis and formation. By this the book receives a peculiar charm and special importance in comparison with the later and more concise expressions of the same truth. If we wish to see the terrors and dangers of the opposite errors in a vivid light, if we desire to experience on the other hand how glorious and refreshing the pure truth is and how necessarily it springs out of its contradictions, we must weigh well what this book contains from beginning to end. Only in this one respect does the thought appear to be not quite fully brought out: we do not find here the idea of the eternal duration of the spirit in the same uncommon force with which it prevailed in later times. If subsequently, amid still greater errors, a multitude of martyrs bore testimony with their blood to the truth, that for an advanced faith even the greatest of outward evils—death itself—must lose its ancient terrors; if in the N. T. the highest example is given of divine victory over death; there is here, on the other hand, less ease and familiarity as regards these ideas, and Job has to contend much in order to get the first foundation of a certain hope in the immortality of his soul and of his just cause. This is, it must be allowed, the mark of an earlier and simpler view of life, and the ancient horror of death has not in this case been yet completely overcome by the act of an innocent death. Still, on the other hand, it is clear that the thought of the book has no validity whatever if it cannot find the basis of its certainty in the immortality of the soul. For how can outward evil be overcome completely to the very end save that the soul maintains the struggle with it to the end and is conscious that even by the loss of the last outward good—life itself—it will not perish? The new thought of the book tends by its very nature to this truth as that wherein it attains for the first time its own perfect power and clearness of view. And from this consideration alone we may infer that this constituent portion of the thought of the book could not be wholly wanting. But this truth appears here as only desire, surmise, and intuition struggling with difficulty and aspiration out of lower views, as a final outlook and necessity which only follows from the whole thought of the book and all along remains somewhat in the distant background: hence rather a hope than a fact. See xiv. 13—15; xvi. 18, 19; xix. 23—29; comp. the already more deeply feeling and stronger utterance of it Ps. xvi and xlix. More closely considered, even this has in a certain respect its advantages, inasmuch as thus in the case of this particular truth also, which is the farthest off and highest of the whole book, we witness its throes as it were and its first birth, and feel how painfully and yet how necessarily and imperatively it forced its way out of the ancient trammels. When a truth for the first time comes to light, shooting forth in its first young impulses, it is always most easily recognised as regards its just claims, whilst later it often seems to luxuriate too rampantly and is easily again misunderstood. The Book of Job has the merit of having prepared for the profounder views of evil and of the immortality of the soul and of transmitting them as fruitful germs down to all subsequent times.

2. THE MATTER OF THE POEM.

The poet's design was not to express the thought of his poem hastily in the winged brevity of a lyric, as though he were still carried away by the first powerful feeling and by the magnitude of the truth; neither was it his design to present it nakedly as a simple doctrine or as a precept and direction. But the thought lies from the very first so profoundly and also so calmly in the poet's soul that he feels urged to present it in a complete form from all points of view. The thought therefore shall be unfolded and established as necessary not merely out of the heart of the poet but rather out of the light of life's past experiences. It shall emerge from its own deep foundations, in the serious conflicts with its contradictories, and everything which seems to create and mould it, its contradictories from both sides, the various stages and advances of truer views—all this must in its proportion and everything in its own manner and its proper force appear and cooperate, in order that the indestructible higher truth may finally proceed from it all as the conclusion and necessity. Without doubt this is a higher grade of poetry, when the inward fire which the true thought has kindled in the poet has the power of self-denial and self-restraint, whilst the calm and brightness which on that very account prevail none the less in the poet look down upon and artistically describe in peaceful contemplation the sway, the struggle and the victory of this thought in the world, so that that first fire is only the hidden warmth with which the poem and its art are aglow, and which in turn rekindles itself in the breast of every contemplator of such a finished work. Here we have most closely united an inner life and an outer form, the warmth and inwardness of feeling with the vivid realisability and truth of the calm course of everyday life, the impulse of personal hope and higher endeavour with the certainty of divine necessity; the thought of the poem is precisely thus perceived in its profundity as well as its prevalence and power in the world. The Drama (for this kind of poetry belongs generally to the drama) includes within it not only lyric, but also the opposite of it, epic poetry.

As the thought has to be unfolded and proved in this manner, its poetic quickening and embodiment is necessarily sought for from history: but in this wide field nothing immediately presents itself to the poet so suitable as a narrative from hoar antiquity. On the one hand, on account of the peculiar elevation, solemnity and sacredness of a narrative from such a region; the poet feeling such reverence in view of the loftiness and divine truth of the thought to be represented that he prefers to accompany it into a region by the purer air of which he feels himself beneficially quickened and his thoughts brightened. On the other hand, on account of the poetic freedom of treatment which is allowable in the case of a legend of early antiquity, the more or less scattered elements of which, as they have been preserved to memory, receiving from every successive narrator a new connexion and peculiar form, whilst most readily submitting to fresh handling under the plastic art of a poet. As the dramatists of ancient India and of early Greece chose their materials from mythological sources, so to the poet, who is conscious of the power and vocation to give poetic life to that genuinely Hebrew thought, materials presented themselves from the antiquity of the Hebrews in the widest sense, which though not so mythological were yet legendary.

As such plastic material the poet chose the tradition of Job's sufferings and deliverance. For least of all can it be seriously doubted, that the story of Job which is here handled, is not described by the poet for its own sake as in the stricter sense history, but only serves as the material for the energies of the creative spirit of the poet, and is intended as the foundation for the artistic working-out of the leading thought to be presented. For the work of the poet is not so much a history of Job as of his sufferings and his deliverance, and of the latter only so much is described as is required for the working-out of the thought of the poem. But whatever serves this purpose is wisely selected to meet the laws of artistic proportion. Just as this art, as dealing unrestrainedly with the details according to its own designs, determines the general arrangement of the entire book, as will be subsequently shown, so it pervades it in every minute detail, to such an extent that hardly a single word is put down without its artistic propriety and suitability in the place it occupies. When, *e.g.,* the poet gives to Job before his calamities seven sons and three daughters and afterwards restores to him the same number; when he describes Job as living 140 years after his deliverance; when he presents every detail which the proportion of the whole work requires him to touch upon after the manner of such general proportions and relations—how is it possible to avoid seeing that the story itself has become poetic and artistic under the hand of the poet? And if we had simply the appearance of Satan and the speaking of God, that would be of itself sufficient proof that the every-day level of history must not be looked for here, but a somewhat common material, in giving form to which the poetic thought constructs for itself its own higher, that is, purely divine history.

But on the other hand his unformed material cannot have been simply invented by the poet. For the invention of a history from the very first, the derivation of a person, who is at the same time intended to be regarded as historical, purely from the brain of a poet, is, as extremely forced and unnatural, so entirely foreign to the antiquity of all nations that it only gradually commenced in the later periods of an ancient literature and is met with fully developed only in modern times. The ancient literature of the Hebrews does not contradict this observation. Although in the feeble final growths of its ancient trunk, in the books of Judith, Tobit, the historical accounts are derived simply from the reflections of the poet, even in the case of the chief characters and events, in the older books there is no trace of this species of literary art; nor was there any necessity for it at an earlier period, inasmuch as a poet who was less removed from earlier antiquity could without difficulty draw from the fullest legendary stream, whilst in the case of later generations this source failed with the course of time. The poet who wrote the Book of Job, however, lived at a time which still remained in many ways in living relation with the views, customs, and traditions of the early antiquity which was then disappearing with its peculiar characteristics. From which circumstance alone it may be confidently inferred, that the poet was not called upon to create the material of his work, but that a happy glance into the treasury of the legends of antiquity must naturally conduct him to the man whose history was most akin to the special thought which occupied his own mind.

The less legitimate, therefore, the question is, whether the work of the poet as we possess it contains history or fiction, as if a third thing were not possible, or rather the case, with all the greater urgency does the other question at once arise, what then did he find as ancient tradition ready to his hand? How much did existing legends present to him? For it is only when this point has been more particularly determined, that the degree of freedom with which the poet handled his material and his own peculiar property in it, can be fixed. It is true that the answer to such a question is very difficult, particularly in the case of this book, inasmuch as in other cases of a similar nature in the Bible it is not easy. For a completely satisfactory prosecution of such an inquiry presupposes a rich store of related legends of the most various ages and localities. If the same legend can be traced through several directions and halting-places in the course of its travels, it is possible to determine more particularly how it has been gradually transformed after its first separation from its source, and what fresh changes have been made in it at each of its resting-places. Such abundant literary remains as we have from ancient India or Greece, often supply in conjunction with the other remains of antiquity sufficient assistance in this respect for such inquiries; whilst in literatures which are more meagerly preserved, as the Biblical literature of this class, a legend appears very often standing quite by itself, preserved in one form only, although it may already have passed through many. Accordingly it is only when the inquirer has previously gained experience by the study of the plainer legends of more perfectly preserved literatures that he can successfully deal with the scattered fragments of legends in more limited literatures. The legend of Job is now found recorded amongst the older books of the O. T. in this Book of Job alone, and we have neither an early, nor a late, account of him which may not be referred back to our book. For all that is elsewhere found regarding Job turns out on closer inspection to have been derived from this book, or subjoined to it. And accordingly the memory of Job would have probably wholly perished, if our poet had not preserved it in this book by immortalising therein an imperishable thought together with this ancient hero. But now that Job has most gloriously risen from the grave through the poet's mind and art, thus immortalised he lives henceforth a second life, as a light to others, which is evidence of the profound impression which the immortalised Job of our poet produced upon the centuries which immediately followed this spiritual resurrection. Job, as the poet describes him, is first mentioned Ezek. xiv. 14, 20, then more at length in the book of Tobit, particularly ii. 12, and James v. 11. But soon the endeavour prevailed to know still more of this Job than the poet had thought well to say, and accordingly his history passed through a second process of development, partly by means of the annexation of other narratives to those of this book in order to supplement them, partly by means of a free continuation and embellishment of situations which had been already described in this book in brief outline; which two sources of alterations may be regarded as generally the chief causes of the formation of apocryphal narratives. The first is found especially in the Greek addition to the Septuagint at the end of this book, where the innocent but vain attempt is made to connect Job, who was not found elsewhere in the patriarchal legends of the O. T., with the Idumean king Jobab, Gen. xxxvi. 33, 34, based partly upon the similarity of the names, which is however great in the Greek but not in the Hebrew [1], partly upon Uz as Job's country, which could be

[1] איוב, Ἰώβ; יובב, Ἰωβάβ.

reckoned as belonging to Edom acc. Gen. xxxvi. 28 [1]. The second kind of continuation, when a later distant re-narrator had the courage to further develop the poetic form and resuscitation of the history, is met with in the Koran [2], where several passages of Job's life are freely expanded, without our being able to discover any other ultimate source of them than this book before us; for the things which the Arabians narrate of Job are based in the last instance simply upon various passages of the O. T. book, and it is in vain to search in Arabic for special oral or written sources [3]. Although we can thus

[1] Zerah who is named as the father of Jobab, Gen. xxxvi. 33, is also then compared with the descendant of Esau, ver. 13, and a fresh basis for comparison therein discovered; מִבָּצְרָה, which could not well be regarded as Job's city, had to submit to serve as the name of his mother, Βοσόρρα. The Greek augmentor ventured also to add to the number of Job's years before his calamities, and to conjecture that the Hebrew book had been translated from the Syriac, i.e., probably the Idumean.—Tolerably early a variety of such detailed narratives regarding Job's fortunes must have been written, how his wife was called Rachma, the daughter of Joseph, etc.; see *Catal. cdd. syr. Mus. Brit.* p. 111; *Itinerar. Hierosol.* p. 587 ed. Wessel.; *Journal As.* 1845, p. 174. The additions found in part here and there in the LXX, particularly ii. 9 and at the end of the book, comp. with Aristæus in *Euseb. Præpar. Evang.* IX. 25, are probably merely fragments of such a narrative.

[2] Sur. xxxviii. 40—44; xxi. 83, 84.

[3] There are in the Koran two legends of Job peculiar to it: as he prayed to God for help, it is said, a cool spring broke forth at his feet, with which he washed himself free of the burning heat of his disease (this appears to have been derived from xxix. 6); and again, it is said, that after his complete restoration he gently chastised his wife at the divine command (inferred from ii. 9; xlii. 8). These legends, which the Koran only briefly indicates, and some others, which where they differ have undoubtedly come from impure sources, are narrated by the Mohammedan Chroniclers more at length, see at present in their most lengthy form in *Tabari's Annals* p. 263—276, ed. Dubeux (where a *city of Job* in Basan, p. 273, and the names of his children, p. 276, are specially noteworthy), Abulf. *Hist. Anteisl.* p. 26 sq.; see also Sale's *Notes on the Koran.* The name Ajjûb, or Ejjûb, frequent in the Mohammedan writers, was not first introduced by the Koran, as several Arabians of the centuries immediately preceding Mohammed were named after the ancient Hebrew hero (see the particulars in the *Zeitschrift für die Kunde des Morgenlandes* III. p. 234): but many Biblical names were similarly naturalised in these centuries among the Arabians. Thus every trace of Job in Islam belongs to the multitude of Biblical histories that

follow the narratives concerning Job from this book of our poet down into late times, on the other hand, all external evidences fail us when we attempt to pass beyond the book itself, the work of the poet alone remaining to assist in the examination of the question of the amount of raw material that descended to the poet from earlier times. And if this question is a bold one, it cannot nevertheless be evaded, and on closer inquiry admits, in general at least, of a tolerably satisfactory answer. The work of the poet itself, when strictly examined, displays its various sources, or the points where the poet freely creates and where he was under greater external restraint.

1. The name Job is not one first coined by the poet. His procedure in case he wished to coin names required for his purpose, may be inferred from the names of Job's daughters, xlii. 14: for though he forms these names simply because he needs them in order to supply briefly with them the proof of the perfect beauty of these daughters, on that very account he coins them with a meaning which is easily perceived to suit his purpose. A similarly transparent, only slightly veiled meaning, is, however, not to be found in the name Job, as there are neither any traces of it elsewhere in the O. T., nor can any plain derivation of it be found in the Hebrew tongue. The name may perhaps originally, like most very early ones, have had its origin in the life of this hero, as a concise expression of his chief characteristics, as the world remembered them[1]: still, the poet has plainly received it from tradition,

found their way to Mohammed only through the medium of indirect sources of various kinds.

[1] It is difficult to find the one correct derivation of the word אִיּוֹב. So much is clear, the root אוב, as a softer form of חוב, שוב, denotes *to turn*, and also *to turn inwardly, to return*, آب hence אוֹב إيّاب *a bottle, belly*, so called from the notion of turning into itself, morally *conversion* from ܬܘܒ, and also, with a dialectic difference, *to turn against others*, whence in Hebrew אֵיבָה *enmity*. אִיּוֹב as the designation of our hero, would therefore most suitably denote a man,

and can hardly have regarded even once its etymological meaning as significant, inasmuch as he does not apply it at all as contributing to his purpose. Similarly, the names of the three friends bear no relation whatever to the main idea of the book, or even to the special character of any of them as it is described in the book. From whatever legendary source the poet may have derived these three names[1], it is at all events certain, that they were actual names which did not first originate at the will and in the art of the poet. On the other hand, the manner in which the name and the entire idea of the hero would spring from the thought of the poem, is shown by the words Tobith and Tobia, Judith: names which have a perfectly intelligible meaning in Hebrew, and the veil of which may be easily withdrawn by any one who follows the poetical thought of the book in which they occur.

2. The hero is removed into a particular country, Uz, or according to the pronunciation of the LXX *Ἄυς*. The determination of its position is reserved for future inquiries: in the Bible the ancestor of Uz is in the first instance reckoned to belong to Syria, as a son of Aram, Gen. x. 23, undoubtedly because Aramaic was spoken there; but in the second instance he is reckoned more particularly amongst the sons of Nahor, or the relatives of Abraham, Gen. xxii. 21; or he appears too, because

who after sad despair, turns within himself and by that act turns to God again: for, in fact, in this consists the highest idea of the history of this hero, xlii. 6; and we may without difficulty suppose that Job's memory in general was preserved in this form in ancient legend. The conjecture of some moderns, that איוב denotes properly the man hated, treated as an enemy (by God), which would be a name in the highest degree indefinite, inexpressive, and indeed (inasmuch as the chief idea, *God*, would be absent from it) wholly obscure, is much less appropriate, the only recommendation of it being really the prejudice in favour of a Hebrew derivation.

[1] The first of the three, Eliphaz, is an old renowned Idumean name, Gen. xxxvi. 4, 10, 12, which the poet undoubtedly chose because he wished to have a famous ancient sage out of Edom. Bildad and Zophar must equally have been actual names from early legendary history, of which we have simply now lost the trace; there is no possibility of discovering a figurative meaning in them.

the country was at last, if perhaps only partially, subjugated by Edom, as a descendant of Edom's, Gen. xxxvi. 28[1]. According to this, it lay therefore, as the Greek addition to the LXX says, on the confines of Idumea and Arabia, that is, bounded on the south by Idumea, on the west by Judea, on the east by Arabia; on the north lay probably Bashan, with which it is even confounded if the Mohammedans mean to describe the country of Job[2]. After another fashion, this country is also made to belong probably to northern Arabia, as the southern boundaries of Syria and those of northernmost Arabia run very much into each other, and the Arabians extended themselves continually in this direction; according to this geography, Job is reckoned amongst the children of the East, i.e. the Saracens, i. 3, comp. Gen. xxv. 6; Judg. vi. 3. Further Uz has no renown in the legendary history of the Hebrews, either as a country or a people; it is, on the contrary, plain that the land first acquired a certain name through this book, and if

[1] Or reversely, and with equal truth, Uz is called the native land of Edom, Lam. iv. 21.

[2] See above p. 22 and Abulf. p. 26; Josephus also, *Ant.* i. 16. 4, places the country towards the north-east. The Arabians know nothing of a land Uz; it is a question whether their name عيص, for Esau, contains a reminiscence of Uz, and is on that account so greatly altered from Esau. For it is certainly allowable to raise the question, whether the names Uz and Esau are not ultimately related and only two different formations of one primitive name. I have some time ago expressed elsewhere the view, that the name Uz was originally identical with Esau, i.e., at first denoted the same uncultivated land (and people) which was also called Esau. To this the expression Lam. iv. 21 in particular plainly points, and that it is legitimate so far as the letters of the words are concerned follows almost from what is remarked *History of Israel* I. p. 234 (I. p. 336). The various localities and small countries to which the name Uz was subsequently further attached, appear therefore simply as remnants of a land and nation which in primitive times, at all events, must have extended far beyond the country usually called Idumea; and perhaps the small country intended in the Book of Job may have been that which, as late as Ptolemy, is specially named Ἀισῖτις. It is, however, unmistakeable that the name appears in the Book of Job precisely as a very ancient one, and that only after it had thus become so famous again is it used Jer. xxv. 20 in conjunction with Edom, ver. 21, and also applied in another manner Lam. iv. 21.

at the time of Jeremiah it was exceptionally more spoken of, Jer. xxv. 20, Lam. iv. 21, the explanation according to all the peculiar circumstances is, that the name at that time had again become more current by means of this book. It does not appear, therefore, why the poet should choose a name which was so little renowned and almost forgotten in his time, unless he had been induced to do so by an ancient legend concerning Job.—Similarly, the three friends whom the poet thinks well to introduce are described so definitely as regards their native country that we are compelled to suppose that he has borrowed the names of these men and of the places of their extraction from early legends. The better known Idumean city, Tæman, is everywhere closely associated with the name of Eliphaz, Gen. xxxvi. 11, 15: although it is very probable that the poet selected an Idumean as the first and oldest friend of Job simply because this man, according to the poetic requirements of the book, must be the wisest of the friends, and wisdom at the time of the poet was regarded as specially indigenous in Edom and particularly in the city of Tæman[1]. Shuach, whence the second friend came, is, according to Gen. xxv. 2, a small clan between Palestine and the Euphrates, probably, according to Gen. xxv. 2 and Job ii. 11[2], north-east of Uz. Naama, the home of the third, is met with elsewhere as a city of Juda, Josh. xv. 41[3]. Although, therefore, it will appear further on, that the poet in the first instance interwove this group of three friends, who come from the south, the north, and the west to Job, into his book, because he could not dispense with them in carrying out its idea, the particular men and places themselves cannot nevertheless

[1] Comp. *History of Israel* IV. 193 (III. p. 696).

[2] It is true Burckhardt's *Syr.* p. 623 refers to a mountain شيحان in ancient Moab, but the name of it is rather to be compared with that of the early King *Sihon* of that district.

[3] The better known name of the *Minites*, which is uniformly substituted in the LXX (see *History of Israel* I. p. 240 sq. (I. p. 344), can only have arisen from confusion with another name, as Aristæus (in Eusebius' *Præpar. Evang.* IX. 25) still wrote Μανναῖος.

have been arbitrarily invented, but must have been found existing here or there in ancient legend.

3. In addition to other commoner calamities which pure poetic invention could put forward, there is a very special and rare one placed upon the hero, which the poet makes to surpass all others, as the chief calamity and most violent and persistent pain, and to pervade the entire drama. Although it is at first, ii. 7, called simply a bad boil covering the whole body, in the course of the book it is so often and so plainly more particularly touched on that the most attentive readers of all ages have observed that the poet borrows his description from the worst of skin diseases, the elephantiasis, which is in general one of the most distressing, wearisome, and commonly most incurable of maladies. At the beginning violent itching of the skin, ii. 8; next the transformation of the healthy skin into one covered with loathsome boils, which now gather and run and then get hardened again, the skin thus becoming cracked, scaly and rigid, in many places thickening as if it were an elephant's hide, vii. 5; the gradual emaciation of the body under the disease often of many years duration, xvi. 8; xix. 20; xxx. 18; the fetid breath, which often of itself, even if the disease were not known to be contagious, frightens everybody from the presence of the diseased person, xix. 17; lastly the constant inward agony of the sufferer night and day as he feels his breathing oppressed and fears suffocation, vii. 4, 13, 14; xxx. 17,[1]—all these are unequivocal indications that the poet really intended in the whole course of Job's severe affliction to describe this one as the greatest and last of those which affected his body[2]. Now, the reason why the poet se-

[1] Hence sufferers from this disease often desire to commit suicide, see Abdias' *Hist. of Apost.* VII. 15.

[2] A medical view of this disease, which is met with in all the hot countries of Asia and Africa, though of infrequent occurrence and also varying with its localities, will not be expected here. But we may remark, that as far back as the accounts of the Job of our book reach, elephantiasis is named as his disease,

lected precisely this uncommon calamity before all others, seeing that he could just as well have supposed a number of others, and the reason why he adheres through the whole book to this one with such great tenacity, showing such lucidity and vividness in his descriptions, as if he had been compelled by some external necessity not to depart from it,—this is most easily explained if he was most particularly here led by the legends about Job. For the motive does not lie in a mere poetic or artistic necessity; and the book of Tobit may here again serve as a counterpiece to assist us to perceive that the material of the Book of Job has not been throughout invented. And no one qualified to judge will maintain, that just as modern poets must carefully preserve throughout the situation, even of invented characters, which has once been adopted, so likewise the ancient poet would have been helplessly bound by his own arbitrary supposition: such equivocal art, in which often the highest skill of modern poetry shows itself, was wholly unknown to early antiquity, particularly to the ancient Hebrews, as we shall further see subsequently in the case of this book.

This is, however, everything that we can certainly say the poet had received from legendary tradition: it is not possible with our present means of inquiry further to lift this veil. Plainly the poet was bound, by the force of the legend which he found the most suitable for his purpose,—to the names, the

Orig. *Con. Cel.* VI 5, 2; Abulf. *Hist. Anteisl.* p. 26 (*ǵudâm* i.e. mutilation, inasmuch as the extremities fall off in the end through this disease); comp. J. D. Michaelis *Einleitung ins A. T.* I. p. 57—65. If it is desired to see how true the descriptions in the Book of Job are, the lamentations of a noble Arab afflicted by it may be compared Abulf. *Ann. Mosl.* t. II. p. 266, 2, 3.—The Syrians and Arabs probably also call it the *lion-disease* on account of its terrible nature, see *Catalog. codd. syr. Mus. Brit.* p. 65. The Hindoos call it *kushtham* i.e. falling-off, like the Arabic word, or the black leprosy in contrast to *çvittri* the white, Man. iii. 7; and they deem it an hereditary punishment from God. W. Ainslie describes it from his personal observations, in the *Transactions of the Royal Asiatic Soc. of G. Brit.* Vol. I. p. 282—303. Comp. also Bruce's *Travels;* and *Déscription de l'Égypte, état mod.* t. xiii. p. 174 sq.

country, the age, and the main features of the history of his hero. But every early tradition which has not yet received a less yielding shape by its later fortunes is extremely fusible, impressible, plastic. We may, therefore, equally well suppose that the history of Job received new life and a more fixed form at the hands of our poet, inasmuch as he recoined and ennobled it by means of the higher thought which he had to expound. Whatever the actual personal history of Job may have been, it was not by it alone that the poet was moved and inspired; but clearly the poet's soul, already filled with the great thought of the poem, sought in tradition his material and found in the legendary story of Job what was most suited to his purpose; so that the Job of olden times rose again in the light of a later and more advanced age as a mirror and instruction for it.—But in that thus the thought and the material of its embodiment coincide in the attractive presentation of the truth, the more modern time supplying its deeper feeling and warmth, the ancient time its elevation and calmness, the poet is conscious in the midst of his own most personal effort of being at the same time supported and elevated by the greatness of the antiquity which he in turn ennobles with his thought. Job is to him no mere semblance, no mere creation of the imagination, but a true hero of the hoar past, whose history shines forth before him only in the brightness of a new truth so gloriously that amongst the numerous traditionary legends of antiquity he selects precisely it alone, and that the material freely chosen in turn assists and moulds his thought.

The question raised by recent commentators, whether Job is not a purely allegorical person, and his sufferings merely figurative, is accordingly frivolous. That would be pretty much as if it should be supposed that the diseases of the Philoktetes of Sophokles were allegorical and were thus understood by Sophokles. Even Pss. vi., xiii., xxxviii., lxxxviii., the descriptions of physical sufferings are not to be taken in a figurative sense: how much less in this book, whose fundamental thought does not at all depend on such details of the description. All the particular calamities and lamentations of Job are to be taken historically in the sense of the legend, accordingly in conformity with the poetic purpose of the book: but the sense of the poem itself is expressed only by the whole work, and in this respect the material is very properly to be distinguished from the peculiar idea and aim of the poet.

3. THE ART OF THE POEM.

The task which the art of the poet has to accomplish is, to combine this material with the thought, before explained, in such a way that neither shall receive undue prominence but both cooperate in the production of a work of beauty. The poet may neither lose his individuality in the matter he handles, by delineating anything of importance in the history which would be unsuitable or superfluous to his thought, nor, on the other hand, laboriously put forward the thought, as if this did not of itself proceed from that treatment of the material which was suited to it. The thought must permeate and control the material, while the material must be entirely submerged in the thought and lend itself to the latter simply as its convenient and pleasing garment. If both thus cooperate, with the progress of the treatment of the subject in this animated and vivid form, the deeper, secretly moving thought, will in its various members successively come out more clearly, and permit itself to be surmised in its truth and necessity with increasing completeness, until with the end of the poet's utterance it shines forth in its fullest brightness. The thought as it lives in the poet's own soul from the very first, thus retreats outwardly into the background, like a light which flashes forth simply from within, of which with wise restraint only so much shines through in the course of the work as the development of the adopted structure of the members in each instance requires, until at the end all rays combine in one bright light, and out of the finished, beautiful, outward form the soul dwelling within shines forth more distinctly than it could have done had it not created for itself such a beautiful body as its visible and enduring representation.

This task, we maintain, the poet has fulfilled most satisfactorily, although following simply his own individual impulses, without painful toil or scrupulous adherence to a modern rule of art. But since this is not easy for us at once to understand, we must now show more particularly in detail, how the poet brings together by an inseparable bond the thing in question, or the thought, and its representation, or Job's history: for it is in the true combination and fusion of these two things that the stage of art which here bears the sway displays its highest powers.

As the thought is intended to be put forward in a concrete and living illustration, the antitheses in which it successively advances become visible in certain prominent persons, who come at the provocation of the obscure question at issue into contact and embroilment, until the confusion and embarrassment begins gradually to work its own destruction, and with the complete solution of the enigma a general reconciliation also takes place. The point was, therefore, to procure perfectly suitable, clearly defined characters to represent these antitheses, who would contribute by an inward necessity to the progress of the thought, and then to cause them, according to their various powers, to go through their respective ranges of mental conflict in mutual relation to the development of the action. From this *plan* and its *working-out* follows of itself the corresponding *division* and memberment of the whole work.

I. The poet must call into action three dominating powers: with regard to dark mysterious suffering, unbelief and superstition must enter into conflict with each other, until on their mutual destruction true faith follows. Therefrom result three essentially different representative characters, or personated antitheses, by the contact of whom the action of the poem opens, and reaches the point of dramatic entanglement, which has then to find its solution. These three characters, not more, result therefore, as a fourth antithetic element is not conceivable; and not less: although it is possible that one of the three antitheses should resolve itself into several separate persons. These three, as the poet with wise selection determines, are Job, the three friends, God.

1. Job the mortal hero, the person in whom the whole action centres, represents the part of despair and unbelief, raging against heaven itself in his madness, appearing dangerous and terrible as any Titan inflamed in burning rage against the Gods. However, this is not a despair which springs from an ignoble source, which indeed no true poet can desire either to glorify or to excuse. On the contrary, it is a purely human, noble despair, generated not in an evil but in a good conscience, not by great and destructive personal guilt, but by a painful enigma of life, the puzzle of which so powerfully oppresses and perplexes the mortal who is not prepared for it nor as yet able to meet it. That is, Job is a true model of manly godliness as it grows conscious of its foundations, a man who in his ripe manhood can without vainglory boast that he has not from his youth up committed even lesser sins, xiii. 26; xxxi sq., who therefore bears the most extreme calamities for a long time with the noblest resignation and fortitude, because he feels himself strong in his innocence, i. 20—22; ii. 10; yea, who in the midst of the frenzy of most intense pain and in the outbreak of terrible despair has retained from the hidden treasures of his past blameless life so much wise self-possession that he never wholly forgets the grandeur and necessity of integrity, and even defends it against all sad appearances to the contrary most heartily with the language of happy personal conviction and experience, vi. 10; xiii. 16, 23; xvi. 17, 18; xxi. 16; xxiii. 10—12; xxvii., xxix—xxxi. When notwithstanding such nobleness of life and strength of a pure, fearless conscience, and notwithstanding the clear conviction in the midst of his calamities that he is innocent before God and joyfully awaits and desires his judgment, x. 7; xiii. 3, 16—19; xiv. 15; xvi. 19; xix. 25 sq.; xxiii. 10, 17; xxvii. 6; xxxi., he is nevertheless seized and more and more completely carried away in

his despair by the force of an unbelief which defies Heaven, the cause of this is to be found simply in the fact, that the noble, outspoken man, at the time when he is surprised in his integrity by his calamities, still shares the general comfortless views of antiquity and particularly the delusion that mysterious suffering announces the wrath of God. This is a superstition which he can for a time permit to sleep, but inasmuch as it remains lurking in the background, when aroused and provoked by an unexpected occasion it soon breaks forth vehemently, and is transformed, in conflict with that diametrically opposite feeling of innocence, into unbelief: for unbelief is superstition already come to light but not yet overcome and resolved into pure truth. On the one hand, he believes that he suffers the wrath and punishment of God as if he were guilty; on the other, he knows that he is certainly innocent, but is again in the peace and happiness of this consciousness disquieted by apparently the plainest, most undeniable proofs of the divine punishment and by the accusations and attacks of men based thereon; with a pure conscience he hopes in God's graciousness and kindness, and yet is again most profoundly perplexed and troubled by his own hard lot of continued and increasing painfulness, and still more by the like apparent injustice and wrong state of things which seem to prevail throughout the world. Thus assailed from the most opposite sides, seeing the ancient superstition shaken by a new, stronger and more certain experience, and still discovering as yet no clear truth in the place of it, a tremendous despair must take possession of him. Then, as he does not understand in God the calamity which he feels bound to regard as a suitable divine punishment of wickedness, and as he struggles in vain to find human insight and consolation, he is compelled to turn in wild vehemence against God, against Him who created such a painful enigma, impetuously urging its solution, even passionately, and, as it seems, defiantly rising up against the God who created such an incomprehensible and indeed preposterous state of things. He is thus led astray by passion to the most inconsiderate assertions, though all along simply jealous for the divine righteousness and really moved by the force of the purest self-consciousness. Integrity, when called upon to sacrifice its one peculiar possession—a clear, happy conscience—for the sake of an opposing view, however sacred it may seem to be, prefers with self-denial to throw away with indignation and maddened daring everything which is opposed to it, as the consideration of mankind, the prevailing views, laws and experiences, the God of outward nature Himself should He seem to set Himself against it, evil and good, falsehood and truth, whatever appears hostile to it, before it sacrifices itself and the one firm, certain, inalienable truth which is clear at all events to it. For integrity is for the individual the one sole firm, certain, and inalienable thing which can turn even against a beclouded Heaven with a giant's energy, vii. 11; ix. 22 sq.; xiii. 13 sq.; xvii. 8; xxiii. 15—17; xxvii. 2—7. On that account, therefore, even this despair, though to be lamented and indeed dangerous, inasmuch as a weaker man might easily quite succumb to it, is not without hope and the possibility of deliverance in the case of Job. For in the agitated raging sea of pain, doubt, bitterness and deepest calamity, when everything is in most violent commotion and turned upside down, it is precisely the consciousness of his integrity, which is by this very resistance strengthened and fortified, that must increasingly become conscious of itself as the only immovable rock, around which all lost possessions may again collect and new nobler ones may gather. His pure soul is thus violently assailed and brought into such severe struggles only in order that it may in the first instance be thrown back upon itself and give up every untrue and frail hope. When this has been done further advances will be possible. It can then go on to discover its own immortality and certainty. From the new clearness of view thus obtained, it is possible both to correct the indiscretions and exaggerations which had escaped him in the heat of the struggle, as well as readily to acknowledge the ultimate and most difficult thing as soon as it is revealed, namely, the higher view of mysterious suffering and divine leading, the want of which had been the sole cause of such heavy trouble. When this higher view is revealed, everything at once finds its reconciliation and adjustment, and the brave spiritual contender is most signally rewarded with the truth which he so zealously sought and surmised but so seriously suffered the loss of when in human haste he missed it, he being as zealous and sincere a recipient of it as he was a searcher after it. As Israel by contending with God obtains for himself a holy divine blessing [1], so Job passes through a long and severe conflict with the God of outward nature Himself, in order finally to begin as a regenerated man a new higher life, after he has by toil and distress achieved the divine revelation so fervently longed for. For it is precisely the divine promises and truths which have to be won at greatest cost. God, as He at first appears in the outward course of the world, confronts man in order to reveal Himself to him to the extent to which he by conflict forces from Him His secrets; and if the gain and the rest cannot be obtained without some profound agony and penances for the human rashness and warmth, inasmuch as every spurious and impure element mixed with a noble endeavour must be again separated from it, the final victory is nevertheless all the more remunerative. And thus the aim of the poet in projecting the picture of this noble hero was to show, that though even the noblest man of perfect integrity may sink into the most terrible despair, he need not nevertheless necessarily succumb, but victoriously attains, after the greatest pains and dangers, the higher truth and blessedness, which as soon as they have once been reached by one man must become the common possession of all who behold this model. So that in the mind of the poet the one

[1] Gen. xxxii. 25, comp. *History of Israel* I. p. 357 sq. (I. p. 512 sq.).

man Job, suffering, contending and triumphing, is intended to become the representative of the whole race as passing through similar sufferings; on which account Job is in this poem the principal person in whom everything else centres. All the various opinions and endeavours in the matter of the enigma are arranged with reference to him and powerfully affect him as the person most immediately concerned; and although he represents chiefly unbelief, he has still properly not wholly got free from superstition, as, on the other hand, he stands in closer relation to the true faith than appears to be the case, and as soon as ever this is revealed, without compulsion, willingly following his own perception, he appropriates it, and resigning all former errors remains faithful to it ever after.

2. The friends represent nothing but the early faith as it has already become a delusion and superstition. This faith is from its nature that which more commonly prevails, which seeks to maintain itself with emphasis and earnestness against every innovation and variation. With profound insight the poet introduces several friends in contrast with the solitary Job. Unusual calamities and unusual experience are the lot of but a few; endurance under unexpected trials and steady resistance of current narrower views, founded upon fresh and certain experience, is still more uncommon; but most uncommon of all is the hero who successfully brings out triumphantly a new truth which is still weak and little understood. Accordingly the poet must bring forward Job alone, without human help or stay, as every great truth can at first by one man only be felt and defended so keenly and powerfully that the one acts decisively for all. And although in a smaller degree many may have experienced the same and have similarly risen up like Job against it, as indeed the poet makes Job plainly say as much in the course of the conflict, xvii. 8, and makes him more and more contend for all who suffer like him, iii. 20; xii. 5; xxi. 6 sq.; xxiv. 1 sq., Job must nevertheless alone by himself wage the whole conflict and refute the antiquated

views by means of his own personal experience, which is peculiar to himself in this degree. On the opposite side stands the great multitude with its prepossessions, consciously or unconsciously combatting the man that revolts against them. The poet accordingly causes the representative personality hostile to Job to divide into a number of separate persons, bringing forward three old sympathetic friends of Job, who on visiting him and considering more closely his misfortunes soon become his opponents. These three men, whom the poet was the first to require for his purpose, have scarcely been borrowed from the early legend of Job, inasmuch as they are only distantly connected with it: it suffices to suppose that the poet brought them together from other scattered legends. In this instance it was necessary that they should differ from each other merely in respect of their age and mental characteristics. Eliphaz, the first, is the oldest, xv. 10, and most experienced, iv. 8, 12; v. 3; xv. 11, who always takes precedence of the others as the model and umpire, and contends with superior dignity and weight more forcibly than any of them. Bildad, the second, possesses, on the contrary, less adroitness and resource, although not without a certain acuteness in judgment and well-meaning cautiousness. The third, Zophar, as the youngest and most easily excited, begins most hotly but is all the sooner exhausted: We must look upon Job, according to the poet's conception of him[1], as a man of ripe middle age, as older than Zophar but considerably younger than Eliphaz, and accordingly of about the same age as Bildad. But the views of these three are the same. Really the most honest, well-intentioned men, not less animated by the strictest ideas of the divine exaltation and righteousness than by the most fervent abomination of all human wickedness and wrong-doing, they are still, on the other hand, so completely possessed by that ancient delusion of outward evil being a necessary punishment

[1] And according to the plain indication xlii. 16.

from God of the former sins of the sufferer, that they are unable to see anything beyond it. Their rigid twofold proposition is, that surely no man can be chastised by God on account of his godliness, that therefore if a man is chastised it must be on account of his sins, xxii. 4, 5. Living in this belief as their most sacred conviction, they are accordingly compelled to presuppose in the case of every sufferer without distinction blame and sins as the cause of his sufferings, whether he is conscious thereof and has actually committed them or not. And the sufferer with whom they sympathize they can only urge to humble himself, by repenting of and confessing his guilt, whether it is visible or not. If he refuses thus to humiliate himself, either from actual obduracy or because he is unable to discover his guilt, they are obliged to condemn and discard him as obdurate. If they are asked for their reasons, they have no profounder one than, "the fact is, man is such a frail creature, occupying a place far beneath God and the celestial beings, that, inasmuch as he sins continually, indeed lives in sin as in his element, he cannot accordingly be punished enough, and suffering is part of his nature; from which condition there is no other escape than that, whenever a calamity befalls him, he must implore and regain the divine mercy by confessing his guilt and humbling himself", iv. 18—21; v. 6, 7; xv. 14—16; xxv. 4—6. In this way the friends of Job were no doubt accustomed to humiliate and mortify themselves, or, which is the same thing, they sought by endless external sacrifices accompanied by a number of prayers to avert every actual or threatened calamity. But all this is based upon a low idea of man, which gradually developed itself in such an exclusive way in Mosaism, until at last it became a fundamental principle of the Pharisees. If, however, sin is such a part of human nature that it is in it a necessity, indeed the proper element of man, under the power of which he must bow himself, this nature would be not simply bad from the beginning and without the possibility of future amendment (a supposition which is contradicted by the history of the creation itself), but strictly speaking every calamity would in that case be, as a consequence of the (after all necessary) sin, an unjust infliction of God. So that this sad, mournful view refutes itself, if there were not already the plain example of such an innocent and blameless sufferer as Job to contradict it. On that account, because it cannot be logically thought out, this reason is not found to meet the requirements of the friends; but their readiest, more obvious argument remains the ancient tradition and experience which appear to favour the above view, inasmuch as they teach, that it is only the wicked who suffer severely and perish without deliverance, while their momentary prosperity is without duration. Hence the friends also dwell particularly upon this, iv. 8; v. 3; viii, 8; xv. 17—19; xx. 4; xxii. 15. But every external reason of this kind is valid only as long, in any case, as experience does not plainly contradict it: even the least trying experience of the contrary overturns it, although it may have been so long considered valid and sacred. How, therefore, can the friends successfully contend with such arguments against Job, whose perfectly blameless life flatly contradicts all their experiences and opinions? How can they hope to reduce to submission the man who is not conscious in himself of the least stirrings of an evil or troubled conscience? Before the revelation of the higher truth comes to him, Job unconsciously goes with them in the first half of their view, namely that suffering is a divine punishment; but the second half, that it is a just punishment for corresponding sins, he is obliged from the very first to deny, and can never allow it without giving up himself and honesty and virtue. The contention must therefore be unequal, inasmuch as Job is not only well acquainted with the ancient superstition, on the basis of which alone his friends speak, but has also to his advantage the wholly opposed and much more deeply felt experience of which they know nothing. He, as knowing both the principle and its contrary, fights with double weapons, whilst they simply defend the ancient delusion, which does not hold in Job's case, and to free himself from which he has already made the commencement, though it may be unconsciously and uncertainly as yet. If they also try to touch Job's conscience in the most pointed manner, making threatening descriptions of the certain final overthrow of the wicked in order to terrify him, asking whether he alone thinks of arraigning and upsetting the eternal divine justice, viii. 2; xviii. 4; xxii. 4, all these attempts must glance aside from him, because his conscience is clear and he is compelled to deem otherwise than his friends of the divine righteousness, who think that every calamity is a righteous penalty for sins and that to submit in this sense to suffering is to acknowledge the divine justice. Inasmuch, therefore, as the opposite of everything which they maintain can be thought and asserted in the same outward, superficial manner, they can only introduce worse confusion into the contention, not help to smooth and settle it. With reference to the question under debate, they judge even more partially and unjustly of God than Job, supposing that He sends to every man suffering only according to the measure of his sin, which neither Job nor God Himself, xlii. 7, can ever allow. Starting with the best intentions, they are soon compelled, inasmuch as they gradually come to regard Job simply as an obdurate sinner, to change their attitude towards him into one of severity and hostility, thus simply increasing the sufferings which they meant to assuage. The sole service they render is, that without intending it they by their opposition and blindness, on the one hand, provoke unbelief in such energy, perfection, and self-consciousness that superstition must be dumb before it, and, on the other, drive the sufferer to that inward possession which was at first hidden from him and which has remained unconsumed in spite of all outward calamity. This inward possession is the good conscience which he now first discovers to be his highest good and holds fast when it is about to be taken from him; and by it he confounds his opponents and wins the victory at last. It was, therefore, the object of the poet in describing the three friends to show, how greatly superstition misconceives the truth and how little it can overcome unbelief, which is already a step in advance of it.

3. God is the revealer of the truth, the author of the nobler faith. He who occasioned this enigma must also solve it for the weal of mankind, or cause men to take closer glances into His nature and His glory; as indeed Job very clearly in the midst of the storm of calamity and passion sees to be necessary, but desires in vain to bring it about by his vehemence, xiii. 3 sq.; whilst God as the plain, gentle revealer will not stoop to man until he, putting aside all earthly passions and confusions, raises himself simply to Him. Therefore the poet, with his whole being occupied with the divine idea, represents God as from the first constructing in heaven the enigma, whether a godly man can suffer though blameless and yet remain faithful, in such a way that the reader may beforehand see at all events the possibility of such a thing happening in harmony with a true idea of God, whilst in the present case it depends on the terrestrial, human participant in the problem to what extent this possibility shall become a reality by means of his personal cooperation. But as regards the earth, God cannot appear upon it to explain, decide and reward, until the human sufferer, already in fact conqueror in the struggle as between men, inwardly prepared and rendered competent to penetrate the last veil, draws near to Him in pure longing and hope. The appearing of God then supplies simply the outward completion and confirmation of that which is already inwardly accomplished and necessary. A fleeting moment, but one of immeasurable significance, brings the longed-for pure truth forth from its depths, and no sooner does it appear than at once all still remaining errors are scattered with irresistible force. The inmost mind of God comes forth plainly and distinctly in this enigma, that it may never again be lost among

men but go on to establish ever greater good. And as the poet can represent in the patriarchal age God Himself as appearing personally in all His greatness and strength, he obtains thereby the happiest opportunity of describing the purest and most striking revelation of the higher truth which it is here intended to magnify. If superstition became silent before unbelief, so the latter in turn is silenced before the true faith, as in every question so particularly in that regarding integrity. To show this is the aim of the poet in his description of the divine revelation.

II. In that these three dominating principles are brought into contact by the enigma which has to be solved, and mutually, according to their respective views and forces, attract, throw into confusion, and finally come to terms with each other, we have the working-out of the poem corresponding to its plan, or the complicated action of the drama in the development of which the thought is itself incarnated and explained in all its parts. It is an enigma of actual life which it is intended to solve and disclose. If the proper persons and circumstances are at hand amid which it must actually originate and only after it has been solved disappear, the details assume their proper form of themselves by higher necessity, the first apparently insignificant commencement already involves the end, and the most violent collision of the opposing principles only promotes more rapidly the final solution.

1. The action is twice commenced, more remotely in heaven, nearer at hand on the earth, because the question regarding guilt or innocence and its potency or impotency concerns not merely men but also the divine kingdom and all divine truths, indeed in the higher sense is an affair of His who has His choicest delight in the world of men and by the glory of men is Himself glorified. Now, inasmuch as the exceedingly grand capacity and power of man to suffer blamelessly and to overcome the outward evil and attain higher blessing by the integrity thus attested, has in God an eternal possibility and

inner truth, it must also at some time come to light as actual fact and outward truth. And when thus the divine idea becomes actual human history, it cannot lie beyond the range of the divine will and work to inflict upon the most blameless man the heaviest afflictions; inasmuch as in the case of each concurrence of suffering and blamelessness in the world (and this collision will never be wholly absent), the eternal divine purpose simply aims at pointing man to the peculiar power which lies dormant within him of overcoming the evil under which he suffers and the incitement to wickedness which is therein hidden, and at raising him by the victory over it. Hence the poet's magnificent description, how God in the celestial council suspends over Job on the occasion of the calumny of Satan the heaviest sufferings, not with an unfriendly intention, nor with the foreknowledge that he must necessarily succumb to them, but continually in watchful love and in the conviction, which though not expressed is evidently strong, that such a valiant combatant as Job will finally prove faithful in utmost extremities. Thus the reader is at the same time initiated beforehand into everything by the celestial scene, and is able to anticipate by this glimpse into the divine mind the necessary course of the entire action.—But upon earth, where this divine intention is as yet wholly veiled, where what is possible shall first be realised by the cooperation of man, there is opened, on the other hand, a field for doubt and conflict. For such a case has hitherto been unheard of amongst men, that a completely blameless man should suffer so severely. And what conflicts does a new both painful and unusual experience occasion before it is properly understood and favourably accepted? At first Job endures for a long time the heaviest and extremest inflictions, remaining true to himself; since it contradicts all his previously received principles to set himself against God even in the dark, hard enigma of life. But the enigma remains in the background, the still unsolved perplexity merely retreats to permit itself to be surprised and called forth by a lurking opportunity. As such an opportunity the poet very suitably chooses the arrival of the old friends for condolence. For before a friend the wounded, pent-up heart opens itself readily and without suspicion; the desire to hear comfort and condolence elicits feelings and lamentations from the breast, which would otherwise, when carefully restrained, have never betrayed the real condition of the unfortunate sufferer. Thus for the first time the so long repressed complaint is freely poured forth: despondency bursting its fetters breaks out the more violently, not indeed in a rejection of God Himself, but still in an execration of life which leads to a subdued complaint regarding God's dark providences. But thereby not only has a perilous commencement of self-bewilderment as regards divine things, and at last of a contemning of God Himself, been made (the evil which lurks in the outward evil), but the friends also, instead of perceiving Job's whole meaning, are thereby strengthened in their suspicion, that Job suffers on account of serious sins, since instead of showing repentance he even still continues to utter such hard things concerning God as if he desired to dispute with Him. In all directions therefere is the conflict opened up.

2. But, first of all, superstition, as the antagonist most immediately concerned, which feels itself painfully struck at, must oppose itself to the unbelief which has thus risen against it. Thus arises the merely human conflict, which, as the complete truth is found on neither side, becomes as passionate, complicated, and wearisome as all earthly conflicts upon which the pure light does not shine. Whence it follows that the immediate general result can be simply, that the weakness of both sides is evidently brought out, and though the old ideas must give way to the new, delusion to certain experience, superstition to unbelief, yet the latter, together with the former, still remains without true illumination and complete satisfaction with regard to the real matter of the conflict.

The positions of both sides are at the beginning of the conflict the following: the friends, having heard Job's complaint, maintain, (1) man may not speak against God, as if he were juster and wiser than God, because (2) general divine justice is never in default, but always expresses itself at some time in a terrible manner towards all sinners. In these two propositions, which are perfectly true in this general form, the friends hold therefore positions which cannot easily be taken: they have here strong defences from which they can make attacks and behind which they can retreat: they have here their advantage and their strength. But together with these two propositions they maintain also (3) the principle, that calamity is never unattended by guilt, so that whoever speaks on account of calamity against God and the divine righteousness betrays himself *ipso facto* as guilty. This latter is their weak, dangerous position, by which their former positions are again rendered insecure. For as this third proposition does not in the least accord with the case in question, upon which the entire conflict is based, they get constantly in danger of falsely applying their excellent general truths. The advantage which they possess on the one side, they lose on the other; indeed, what they have of the truth must by constant diversion to false issues fall under suspicion, their best weapons must gradually get blunted. They are like orators who say much that is good and true, only it is not true and appropriate for the case in point. The more they are compelled therefore by the course of the contention to deal precisely with the particular case at issue, the more they must get wrong and lose their way. At first, it is true, the advantage seems to be wholly on their side; inasmuch as starting from a good intention and relying upon the doctrines of antiquity generally, they meet Job with quiet confidence, with unbroken ranks, relieving and supporting each other repeatedly. Moreover, every assailant has always an advantage, how much more these men as assailants of a sufferer who is so low and despondent as Job. Still, the assailant has but to retreat at one point, and his entire cause may easily be lost, and woe to him if because he cannot defend the weak position, he must also surrender his secure ones to the assaulted opponent who has become an angry assailant!

At first Job is much less favourably situated. A blameless man, when thus seriously suspected or severely accused, will often blush at once to refer to the perverse and foolish charges, and the more innocent he is conscious of being, the less will he hasten with the defence of his innocence before fellow-mortals. As if he considered it beneath him, Job never speaks to his assailants simply to justify himself sedulously and scrupulously against their veiled or open reproaches; he prefers so far to expose himself even to the most unsparing sallies. Thus exposed, he further endures, all the more, great pain at the wholly unexpected attack and, as it seems to him, perfidy of his friends. It is the addition of this trouble to all his previous calamities which adds the climax to his woe and renders a calm defence so difficult. On the other hand, so far as the views and positions asserted are concerned, Job has (1) the great advantage, that from his own personal experience he can positively know and conscientiously maintain most firmly, that calamity is possible without guilt. That which is the weak and obscure side of the matter in the case of his opponents is in his case the strongest and plainest, and as in fact everything in the whole contention really depends on this central position, he must from the very first be in possession of the chief truth which is in this matter decisive, the truth which they so wholly fail to see that they stoutly maintain the exact opposite of it. But, again, because Job, still partially blinded by the old delusion, does not as yet at all comprehend this truth, under the birth-pains of which he suffers, as actually and justly based in the nature of God, but on the contrary expects God will not permit the innocent to suffer, he is exposed from the beginning to the danger of falling into great errors and shocking assertions, on account of his own greatly troubled state of mind and in respect of the course of the world. As innocent, suffering, therefore, as he thinks unjustly, he may in his impatience be easily led astray—(2) to dispute generally with God, not merely endeavouring to get reasons which might avail to move Him to take pity, but also calling Him to account vehemently, indeed, apparently defiantly, which rashness attains its climax in the actual challenge of God to appear and to give judgment. And going still further, taking a wider view of the world generally, he may even—(3) question the presence of the general divine righteousness in the world, and maintain the exact contrary of a connexion between happiness and innocence as prevailing in the world. These are the two dangerous propositions by which Job is about to surrender the general truths which his friends were in possession of and which he himself must have maintained in calmer moments. They are propositions which had lurked covertly in his troubled soul from the commencement of his calamities, but which could only gradually by the violence of the contention and the spirit of contradiction assume such a terrible power within him. Indeed, they may at last become even opposing positions and weapons against his friends, for the purpose of expelling them from their firm positions; because if really outward prosperity or adversity is to be the guide of the judgment concerning innocence or guilt, then, according to the undoubted experience of the adversity of innocence, these propositions can be with equal justice used for attacking the friends, just as they constantly apply their truths falsely in Job's case. But if these propositions had really been uttered by Job as his truths, particularly the proposition against the divine justice, there would have been opened for him at last the broad road of endless error, of a complete fall, of denial of God Himself, since no one can in calm judgment fail to see, or even deny, the divine justice without denying God Himself. His own integrity, which Job will defend and protect before all things, is in extreme peril and is but a step removed from its fall, save that his conscious adherence to right is too great and powerful to permit it ever wholly to desert him in the course of the contention, even in its most extreme bewilderment and perplexity. The more, therefore, Job confines himself alone to his own case and his consciousness of pure integrity, and the more closely he is compelled to consider his own case, the greater gainer is he, whilst by that very means and to an equal extent his opposers are the losers. Notwithstanding all dangers and errors, Job possesses precisely in the special case which occasions the contention, and still more in the consciousness of his integrity, a secure foundation and basis of departure which cannot be wrested from him; he may go wrong in the human contention, but it is only the more certainly to recover himself.

As now the positions assumed by both sides are from the very first so totally different, that they only accord in the mutual misunderstanding of the enigma to be resolved and its different false applications [1], in that Job also fails to see his case as clearly as is needed, although he is better acquainted with it than they, there can only follow from the encounter in the first instance a constant increase of the misunderstanding. It is true, the friends display at first much caution and forbearance in conformity with their disposition: and Job, as though he foreboded the sad danger of mutual provocation and exasperation, at first shuns the commencement of the real contention, asks for friendly consideration, vi. 28—30, and avoids for a long time speaking directly against his friends, ch. ix. But nevertheless the contention advances inevitably to the point of violence: if the friends only distantly hint at Job's guilt, his inmost feelings are roused; if in his indignation or pain an ambiguous or hard word escapes him, their suspicion is increased. Thus they come into collision with each other and get wider apart without meaning it, simply compelled by the

[1] The friends: calamity befalls the guilty as punishment; therefore he may not speak against God—. Job: calamity befalls the blameless as punishment; therefore he may very properly—.

growing misunderstanding neither side can give way; because the one defends the ancient, sacred belief, the other, his good conscience and human right. The most angry and difficult contention has been kindled, in which every point must be fought out to the last. Still, it is also possible provisionally to foresee as the end, that it is rather Job who will at least survive the conflict and conquer in the contention with his fellow-mortals. First, because he personally quite well knows not only what the friends allege, but also much more, and precisely what is here decisive, namely, the truth, that a blameless man may suffer severely; and, next, because he possesses in addition the infinite treasure of a good conscience, a power which grows in the conflict with immeasurable independence and energy, which, the more the endeavour is made to dim and darken it, the less does it suffer any darkening,—which, when exasperated and injured, reacts against its enemies with a keenness which was not anticipated. The friends seek to deprive him of his good conscience, in that they urge him to confess a sin which he really cannot charge himself with, thus to perplex his pure conscience and make him surrender it; and he himself in the heat of the conflict comes into the tremendous danger of wholly losing his clear self-possession and speaking against the sacred voice of his inmost conscience. But all the more powerfully in the end his conscience rises up against all that is hostile to it, and becomes at last, since it is the one certain and perfectly true thing in this contention, the sole victor and judge, as far as it can end and settle the human part of the conflict without the new revelation which must fully remove the enigma.

When carefully considered, there follows from these primary positions and principles of the two parties also the complete plan of the necessary course of this contention, with all its possible movements and vicissitudes. The assailants, it is true, possess in their mind in reserve from the first the three primary truths which constitute the strength and the weakness of their positions, and are unable to surrender any one of them, because they conceive human life in general, and Job's case in particular, simply in the light of the closest combination of all three truths: but they are not obliged to give equal prominence to each of the three on every occasion and in every situation of the contest. On the contrary, as Job's half-despairing half-querulous complaint had led them first to suspicion, and they hope at the beginning to be still able to save him, they advise him (1) first of all to abstain from such rash and defiant words, calling him seriously but kindly to repentance, and permitting the hard fate of the wicked to appear only in the background. If they thereby attain nothing, they can (2), by placing as they proceed their second truth in the front and bringing forward the general divine righteousness, then seek to touch his conscience by terrible descriptions of the frightful ruin threatening all the wicked, as if they regarded him as already semi-obdurate and lost. Finally, if neither this severe measure prove efficacious, they can (3) accuse him openly of the greatest sins, which they cannot, it is true, strictly prove by evidence, but presuppose as certainly committed, thus unambiguously and unsparingly applying their third principle, that calamity is never without guilt. This is the necessary line of progress which their attack takes. The assailant must, if he will not retreat when an assault has not attained its object, cause necessarily a still more pointed and merciless assault to follow, until at last he puts forth all his resources, even the residue and reserve of forces, which at the commencement of the contention he had imagined he should never be obliged to bring out. Twice this line of advance recurs; the first time more by the way, less perceptibly and abruptly, though essentially the same; iv. 2—v. 7; viii. 2—19; xi. 6: but the second time at length, very plainly and pointedly, iv., v., viii., xi., xv., xviii., xx., xxii. When they have thus not shrunk, led on by the growing heat of the conflict, from expressing the utmost that they can say, and nevertheless have not subdued the object of their attack, they are evidently compelled as completely exhausted to think of a retreat and hold their peace; their first confusion and exhaustion becomes a total defeat, even a retreat is cut off from them if they are determined not to surrender.

Whilst the assailants thus perform their movements in but a somewhat limited space, to the man attacked a much larger field is open: he can defend himself, make the attack, and withdraw in safety from the attack to his original position:—

(1) He can defend himself by showing, as he adheres with increasing emphasis to his integrity, that he has the justest reason to complain on account of the undeserved mysterious sufferings which have befallen him, as vi. 2—13; xvi. 6—17; xix. 6—22; xxi. 4, 5; and this remains to him a powerful stay which cannot be wrested from him, because it is exactly suited to the present case. But although he may thus defend himself by reference to the present case itself, or at the same time complain with increasing bitterness of the harshness of his friends as they (intentionally) fail to perceive his innocence, vi. 14—27; xvi. 4, 5; xvii. 4, 10—16, what avails even the most emphatic and sincere defence against the want of intelligence of his opponents, who, when all is said and done, are determined not to let go the proposition of their experience and faith, that calamity is never without guilt? In vain does Job endeavour repeatedly by every possible means to get them to see his innocence. At the very commencement, he seeks to enlighten them with an affectionate appeal to their consideration, vi.; he puts before them in agonising despair, how terrible a thing is the persecution of a blameless man, xvi., xvii.; he tries finally, in the profoundest grief, to touch their conscience and to supplicate their compassion, xix. But all is in vain; precisely the truest and deepest words of suffering integrity are in this case unintelligible to the friends; they discern in them only evidences of the growing audacity and the rashness of the sufferer! If therefore Job meant all along to confine himself in his answers to the defensive, he would inevitably be at

last overthrown, inasmuch as integrity, particularly in its own defence, is not such a material, palpable thing that it could make its defence by openly showing itself. He must therefore, even in self-defence,

(2) assume the offensive, when this at length becomes a necessity. He must attack the first two principles of his opponents, because from the basis of these their firm positions they perpetually defend their assertion regarding calamity as the sign of guilt. But as regards the question of Job's guilt or innocence, it is wholly impossible they should come to an understanding; neither can Job venture a successful attack on behalf of his innocence, so long as the opponents believe in his guilt on the ground of their two general propositions, supposing he must be guilty because he speaks against God and the divine righteousness, and threatening him with God's appearance and His retributive justice. They thus compel him at last to turn these dangerous weapons with which they attack him against themselves: by their blind opposition they call forth the evil spirits which from the very first lie dormant in the sufferer, in order that these spirits, when they have become powerful by the provocation, may turn against themselves. For certainly Job has to some extent a right thus to retort upon them. A truth, when falsely applied to a particular case, can precisely on the basis of that case be reversed. If it is maintained, that man may not speak against God and fail to perceive the divine righteousness, *because* innocence cannot suffer, then the man that nevertheless actually suffers though innocent (therefore according to the early belief contrary to justice), will be in a position to speak against God and to doubt the divine righteousness, in defiance of all who call in question his innocence; and the man who is closely pursued by his opponents will, almost against his own will, be at last driven to this as his only way of escape. It is not simply Job's fault, that when both unfairly and blindly attacked, he at last presents his uncouth aspect alone, thus likewise losing his self-possession.

If the opponents desired early in the contention, as fearing their own weakness, the approach of God in judgment against Job, xi., how much more justly and courageously can the man, who is now persecuted even by his friends without a cause, appeal to this judgment on his own behalf, and eagerly turn this weapon against themselves, using this opportunity to get a moment of respite? xii.—xiv. Nor does this blow remain without its consequences in the case of the friends. For although Job pays dearly for this rashness, since, inasmuch as God does not appear, he for the first time feels himself wholly abandoned of God, inexpressibly miserable and cast-down, still neither do the friends, confounded by such unlooked for rashness, venture ever again to invoke such a judgment; they are compelled to think of other lines of attack. And if the friends then tenaciously maintain the general proposition, that the sinner is according to the divine righteousness always unprosperous, with the implied meaning, that the unprosperous man, *e.g.*, Job, is always guilty, of course Job must at length, as soon as he takes a closer view of this stronghold, perceive the terrible reverse-side of this opinion; since the mere outward appearance, which the friends follow, teaches also the exact opposite of it, that the sinner may be (at times) very prosperous, the godly man very unprosperous, just as may be most plainly perceived precisely in the present case of the pertinacity, bordering on cruelty, of these fortunate friends towards the unfortunate sufferer. If they present to him a completely onesided, false picture of the divine righteousness, he is naturally compelled, inasmuch as it does not answer in the least to his immediate experience, to discover the exact opposite of it from his point of view: for he would only too gladly adopt the picture which his opponents present; because, if it were true, he would as innocent necessarily be made prosperous immediately. But since he is both conscious in himself of the exact opposite and also perceives it in the world, he is compelled in deepest bitterness and perplexity of soul to call in question this divine righteousness described to him. Without intending it, his discourse becomes the keenest attack upon the no less pertinacious than one-sided assertions of the friends, xxi., xxiv. But if the opponents are thus in their firmest positions shaken, thrust through, and if not convinced yet brought to silence, by the reckless attacks of the sufferer, which they had not looked for, so that Job is now able as conqueror to review the entire situation with greater calmness and circumspection, he must at once perceive, that he cannot permanently retain these weapons with which he combated and overcame his opponents. For if there were really nothing in the world but wrong, he would himself have no longer any ground for complaint regarding his present personal misfortunes, nor for life at all: with the deliberate denial of divine righteousness generally, all human reflections and endeavours must be annihilated. Either Job proceeds still further upon the dangerous course (in which case there is nothing for it but to deny God himself, as the friends believe he will do, and has already done in secret); or he must now cast off the appearance of being capable of that, and must all the more necessarily do this in conformity with his own conscience, inasmuch as precisely in the course of the contention he has become conscious, with a strength never dreamed of before, of his integrity and its grandeur. For during the growing confusion of the limited views of mortals, there has already in secret been stirring and attaining clearer consciousness the superhuman energy, which can alone preserve the despairing sufferer from wholly sinking and hinder the conflict from ending in mere altercation and exasperation. While Job at first, before the attack of his friends, did not at all clearly and consciously recognize the infinite treasure of his integrity, by means of that attack he is conducted more and more forcibly, and then more and more consciously, to it, and learns to value a possession which he had hitherto overlooked. The more his opponents seek to deprive him of it, the more intimately he gets acquainted with it and the more stoutly he defends it. The voice of his integrity has made itself heard, gently at first, vi. 10 *c*, then with greater power, ix. 21, quite early speaking out most vehemently, when the moment came to wrest from the opponents the appeal to God, xiii. It is true, that by this unreasonable, half-defiant appeal the zeal which had been awakened was greatly quenched, and the hope as it is here conceived was destroyed: but in the midst of the worst confusion of this conflict, when he regards himself as wholly cast off by men and God, his good conscience rises all the more absolutely by its own indestructible force and clear conviction above all that is wrong and enigmatical in the present: the soul recognises its own unending duration, xvi. 19; xix. 25—29. This inward certainty and pure self-reflection, which thus germinated unobserved in the midst of the fiercest storm of all his calamity, can now all the more spring forth wholly unhindered, as Job has just now again experienced in his own case in this conflict the wealth and grandeur of integrity and already foresees, although as yet but dimly, a final deliverance. The dark, dangerous proposition of the reign of unrighteousness needs only to have been plainly brought forward in all its force, to be in this loftier and calmer frame of mind for ever abandoned. Accordingly Job has

(3) a secure retreat from the attack and the victory. As a brave victor, who has after all never become unfaithful to God, and who has now become conscious of his own powers, he can at last draw the conclusion from the contention—'no one will again deny that calamity may exist without guilt'; and Job will never permit himself to be deprived of this doctrine and actual result of the contention; indeed, he can grant the misery of the wicked, of which so much is made, because he is entitled to expect a better lot;—although to himself it is still not clear, *how* suffering integrity is in itself possible and a divine arrangement. At last the clear consciousness of himself and his integrity, after it has long been overwhelmed by the billows of melancholy and despair,

breaks forth in full splendour as the enduring fundamental principle, expressing for him, in an abiding form and in calm patience, that which is certain to him and still uncertain in God, and closing the conflict as between himself and his fellow-men not merely truly victoriously but also consciously and modestly, xxvii.—xxviii.

It appears from this, that the turning-point of the whole conflict and the commencement of the decision of Job's good cause, takes place at the point, which is at the same time the climax of the complication of the contention, when the friends appear outwardly to have the victory and Job appears humanly speaking to be doomed to perish, xvi.—xix. The last human hope has just been snatched from him, which he had resorted to after the perception of the unfaithfulness of the friends. God, for whose appearance he had so zealously and courageously prayed, xii.—xiv., has not appeared, the most agonising prayer is not heard: everything in which he previously believed he had a stay has perished; and bitterly deceived in all his hopes, he seeks in vain for some conceivable external support and help. But this profound humiliation and disappointment was not uncalled-for, in order to completely destroy all the elements of his previous superstition, to which he still so firmly adheres, and to direct him to the true eternal possession. Forsaken of men and of the God of the outward world in whom he had hitherto believed, he must nevertheless learn to retain and to protect his good conscience by looking to the hidden God within and the immortality of the soul. If every fragile support disappear, the imperishable one is all the more clearly recognised. Thus where already complete ruin appeared to prevail, there arises from the mysterious depth of his soul, when driven into its inmost, holiest consciousness, a new, living, indestructible truth; as a flash of lightning, the light of the pure clear intuition shines through the ancient darkness, and for the first time the true, inward strength and hope springs up, towering above all times and vicissitudes, xvi. 19; xix. 25—29.

On that account the gain of this highest moment can never be again wholly lost. Amid the final spasms of the word of the friends, who do not comprehend such a spiritual elevation, when Job also pours forth the last residue of the dark thoughts which are stirred by his opponents, the noble sufferer exhibits after all already an unlooked-for calm and confidence, as if he felt that God, though it might not be till after the death of the body, but not weak men, would be able to help him, xxi. 2—6; xxiii., xxiv., xxvi. And immediately he returns with growing conviction, after the defeat of the opponents, to that profounder consciousness, and closes with marvellously strengthened powers xxvii., xxviii. Job's inward power grows, therefore, under all circumstances from stage to stage, whilst that of his opponents irretrievably declines, and at last the unfavourable vicissitudes also promote his advantage. He, left to himself, passing through such profound sufferings, combats each opponent whenever one of them speaks, never wholly flagging, and not one of his speeches falls short of its adverse predecessor in point of inward or outward force and finish. He is always original and inexhaustible, whilst his opponents proceed vigorously a few steps, just at the commencement of each fresh encounter, soon flag, and getting impoverished, repeat their words with but little variation. If he several times in succession positively scorns to answer, following more his own reflections than the charges and will of his opponents, vi—vii., ix—x., xvi—xvii., xix., yet in a single powerful speech he amply supplies subsequently everything that had been omitted and replies to three adversaries at once xii—xiv., xxi. He leaves nothing allowable and noble untried, to arouse even the compassion of his unfeeling opponents, both at the first and again in the thickest of the fight, vi. 28—30; xix. 21, 22, and resorts to severe measures only when compelled to do so. Thus concealed or openly, on the defensive or the offensive, always making victorious progress and gaining even by apparent losses, from being the suspected, persecuted, insulted sufferer, he becomes the daring, invincible hero, the wonderful teacher, xxvii. 11, of those who endeavour to correct him, the vanquisher of all the superstition which has prevailed till that time.

On Job, as assailed but invincible, more and more victorious, depends, therefore, the true progress of the contention in all its successive steps and stages: instead of being urged on by the assailants, he soon urges them on much more than they him. They take up a position against him: he compels them to seek another by finally destroying it and occupying it himself. They are obliged continually to seek a stronger and more decisive position if they expect success; and in fact Job's increasing daring and apparent impiety justifies them in becoming more and more pointed and decisive, inasmuch as they find a confirmation of their suspicion in this conduct. When he has in vain invoked God, they are obliged to deem him mad; when he has plainly called in question the divine righteousness, they must look upon him as manifestly impious. Thus on both sides everything is brought to the most decisive point. But if at last they cannot maintain the third most extreme and decisive position which was possible (see p. 50), they must suddenly find their strength fail them and the victory is incontestably Job's; for the friends have but three different positions corresponding to their three main truths. On each occasion Job does not make any great haste to attack; since warding off the enemies' blows better becomes him who is as sorely troubled as he is innocent, and for the noble soul the attack is resorted to only in self-defence. The two first times, accordingly, he leaves his adversaries to speak without properly paying them back in their own coin and provoking them by intentional attacks. The first time, he avoids every irritating word towards his friends and proceeds simply in complaints toward God, compelled by his sadness, vi—vii., ix—x.; the second time, he is less able to bring himself to do this, xvi—xvii., xix.; it is not until the third and youngest opponent declines nevertheless to leave him in peace, that he replies by an attack, and the first time, when the point is the coming of God to judgment, with a sharply irritating contradiction, xii—xiv., the second time, in connexion with the question of the divine righteousness, rather compelled by the profoundest anguish to opposition, xxi. Thus three times the oldest of the three friends, the one to whom it may soonest be left by his colleagues also, is forced to assume a new position, which the two first times the two subordinate friends maintain, the first time making also an important advance, but the second time only a little. But as the contention has thus been carried much too far to permit of an understanding and reconciliation, Job, not provoked by the unconcealed reproaches, remains by his two former attacks which have not been answered, xxiii—xxiv., but, in order to put an end to the contention which has become unprofitable, he smites the second speaker who is scarcely able to utter a few words, xxvi., with such crushing superiority to the ground, that the third does not venture to speak again, and Job rising instead of him, can now for the first time declare his innocence quite triumphantly. The entire contention as carried on between these men passes, therefore, through three phases, which, inasmuch as the three friends speak each time in their order, may also be called its three revolutions or advances. The first advance is on both sides an attempt, in which everything, all that is dark as well as all that is clear, is first brought into action, but everything gradually more and more into perplexity and complication. The second advance presents the highest point of complication, when Job appears outwardly as already lost, whilst his deliverance is preparing in secret. The third advance completes Job's victory. The first two advances serve to bring out the two dangerous thoughts of Job, his resentful discontent regarding his own calamities which becomes at times a challenge to God, and his indignation at the apparent injustice prevailing in the whole world; until these two thoughts, precisely because they have been made perfectly clear, are set aside before they obtain complete ascendancy. It is at the end of the third advance, after the exaggerations and passions on both sides have spent themselves, that these thoughts are overcome by that party in the conflict which, notwithstanding all reprehensible wanderings and errors, was nevertheless right in the present matter, and possesses, morever, a good conscience, and this result which has been brought home to the mind in the contention and trouble can make itself freely felt and remain alone dominant, in that the victor in the contention with men regards himself as vanquished by God, xxvii.—xxviii.

To make a brief resumé of the whole: As between the human representatives of it, the contention proceeds in the following three antitheses, in which also its three advances and phases appear:—

The three friends maintain that a man may not

(1) speak against God, because

(2) the universal divine righteousness is never at fault; for

(3) calamity is never without guilt: so that whoever on account of calamity speaks against God and divine righteousness, *ipso facto* betrays himself as guilty.

Job on the contrary maintains:

(1) Calamity, it cannot be denied, is possible without guilt; therefore the blameless man, *i.e.*, the man suffering unjustly, may and must, in spite of those who try to deny that clear fact,

(2) speak against God, in order to challenge Him to a defence and the restoration of justice *(end of the first advance)*, and if nevertheless justice is not restored,

(3) call in question the general divine righteousness *(end of the second advance)*.

But still, speaking against God and calling in question the divine righteousness, is after all when carefully considered, not merely useless and confusing but even impious when done deliberatily and persistently, and if done in passion for once, the godly man will not continue it in his deliberate moments. Therefore, with a full acknowledgment of the divine majesty and universal justice, the original proposition,

'Calamity is possible without guilt't, is still valid; but how it is so, that remains after all a divine enigma, modestly to be acknowledged but still always painful in the extreme *(end of the third advance).*

This is the course of the contention together with its necessary limits.

3. Thus it is true that by the result of the contention between the mortal participants therein the enigma has not as yet been solved on earth. Those on the one side have been wearied out; the one representative of the other side has been rendered wishful by the merely negative result, not yet perfectly satisfied and enlightened. So all long for a higher wisdom coming from another source. Even to Job, though he is victorious over men, a still more exalted victor must approach, One whom he has in fact already begun to anticipate and in silent humility to desire to see draw near. Everything that has gathered turbidly and dark around the question has been cleared up; the merely onesided, passionate conceptions and aims lie destroyed as victims of the conflict. But not until now that the real question itself is quite closely approached, does its true darkness appear, to scatter which all past human wisdom has proved unavailing. It is only a new revelation which can here supply the deficiencies of the ancient views and illuminate what was to them impenetrable darkness. And in fact the friends already early invoked this new revelation, xi. 5, and Job at first desired nothing more intensely, indeed, challenged it with vehemence, xiii., but at last perceived with deepest pain the futility of a desire so presented, xxiii.: for the hidden truth does not come when thus called for with defiance and in persistent folly. Now for the first time, when Job has attained to all the calm reflection of which he is capable, does the longed-for revelation become perhaps possible.—Still, the course of this weary contention has by no means been fruitless; on the contrary, the solution has been in secret thereby

prepared for. For, in the first place, all lower conceptions are now on the way to be completely exposed, because they have been shown to be weak and unsatisfactory. Superstition, if not convinced of the contrary, has been reduced to silence in any case, and has been perceived most plainly to be insufficient. Unbelief, after it has vainly tried everything possible to it, has perceived, just as it was victorious, its own insufficiency and of itself begun to rise to the inkling of a higher truth. In that the passionate, almost defiant speech towards God, as if He did injustice in the present case, and the empty despair regarding the general wrongness of the world cease, the mind turns with all the greater inwardness, intelligence, and collectedness to the calm, although intense, confiding manner of regarding the particular case in question, hoping the eternal divine truths may not fail even in this darkness, and perceiving that when this darkness is dispersed, the divine righteousness will approve itself similarly everywhere. But what is still more, integrity has only now perfectly stood the test of practical action by resisting the most perilous mental trials under all extremest pains. Job has neither surrendered to superstition, thus sinning against his better knowledge, nor resigned himself so far to the threatening unbelief, that he ever let God Himself and the divine truths go; since, on the contrary, in every instance where this danger specially beset him, and most of all as soon as he had clearly perceived it, he started back with horror. He went wrong in his conceptions, but never in intention and action, and so in the midst of his calamities, when the attempt is made to deprive him of his integrity, he has become fully conscious of this infinite good, and now, as a victor amongst his fellow-men, he stands upon the threshold of higher insight. How vastly he has been the gainer by the conflict in point of self-knowledge and stable conviction, is shown by nothing more plainly than the comparison of the discourse which kindles the strife, iii., with that which closes it, xxvii —xxviii.: the first is deficient in clearness and dangerous, while the second is admirable, and if not wholly clear is yet tending towards clearness. All the vicissitudes intervening serve only to mediate between these antitheses and the avoidance of that danger. At last the calamities of Job, which are at first completely dark to human view, begin of themselves even to catch a brightening light. Inasmuch as they have not been able to destroy Job's integrity, it may already be surmised that they are no real inward calamity, no punishment from God, but the opposite of it; and after he has learnt this by experience, Job is thereby alone prepared for this higher insight. Accordingly there is in fact nothing further wanting than the advance to the closing revelation of the pure divine voice, which reconciles and glorifies everything, to that awful moment when the last veil is drawn aside, in that heaven and earth meet together and what in heaven was eternally prepared is consummated upon earth.

After, therefore, Job having turned away wholly from his friends, without any defiance or any sullenness as regards the world in general, quite collected and worthy of himself, serious and modest, has in grief compared together his former prosperity, now so wishfully asked for again, and his present vast misery, and at the same time most solemnly with animated certainty protested from the purest soul his innocence (and that now for the first time with such calm composure, full consciousness, and definiteness); after he has thus, exhausting all human power in agonising, holy zeal, uttered to God alone everything that he can say of a longing, painful, purifying nature before higher enlightenment has come, not violently calling forth the divine decision, yet with repressed longing desiring it, drawing forth his whole inner man with great sincerity and cordiality, xxix—xxxi;—when all this has been done by Job, at last God Himself appears, not as an enemy and not calling Job to account for some former sin, but in order to deliver the brave contender, if he has suffered himself previously to be warned and enlightened by the higher truth.. No complete deliverance can come as long as Job has not completely released himself from the bonds of delusion, *i.e.,* until he perceives that he hedges up the way to knowledge and deliverance by speaking against God and the divine righteousness. For during his calamities and temptations he has suffered himself to be misled to thoughts which alone hinder the solution of the enigma; thoughts which he has, it is true, already begun to abandon, but has not yet clearly enough perceived to be wholly false, nor sincerely enough repented of. It is always true, that the light of the divine truth does not appear without at the same time bringing to light and removing more deeply concealed defects in what is humanly devoid of blame and sin. So in this case, it cannot appear without first cancelling certain defects in him whom it has come to deliver and exalt, and when he has been wholly purified from them then nobly to reward him. And it is always true, that man never contends with God in order that he may enter in His secrets without at the same time carrying away as conqueror at last some scars as marks of the divine superiority and traces of the mortal struggle, Gen. xxxii. 26[1]. Now, inasmuch as Job had previously sinned in two respects, first, in that he spoke at all against God, and next that he spoke in particular against God as judge by calling in question the supremacy of righteousness in the world, God accordingly now challenges him twice to contend with Him, demanding whether he is determined really to continue the one or the other form of speech against Him Who now not only makes Himself known as the strict judge and ruler, but also as the infinitely wise arranger of the universe, as the marvellous restorer of justice, as the revealer of His full glory? And as Job, having seen the purest light, submits in humility before a glory which has now become fully revealed, xxxviii. 1—xl. 14; xlii. 1—6, as he stands pure before God and has put away even the small spots which human haste and perplexity during

[1] See above p. 35.

his suffering had brought and left upon him, God at last gives him the noblest opportunity of obtaining satisfaction from his three friends, namely, the opportunity of interceding for them; and for himself, God gives him deliverance from all the evils which have befallen him and the noblest reward, in that his prosperity becomes greater than it was before his calamities. And thus the higher belief is established, that integrity may suffer, indeed, but going forth from its trial with steadfastness and victory, then first attains its true reward, having arrived at true self-consciousness and higher knowledge. The dark enigma is nobly solved on earth to the glory of God and man. The end of the drama refers back to the beginning. Considering the example of Job and the enigma which is now solved, henceforth every one may overcome like Job, without having like him to contend so severely with superstition and to suffer so perilously from unbelief.

The common supposition that it is the poet's purpose to show, that man cannot penetrate God's plans and therefore does best to submit in his ignorance to everything and without complaining, has not been derived from an accurate knowledge and a clear survey of the book. If the book went no further than from ch. iii. to ch. xxviii., it might be possible to regard that supposition as not improbable, although the thought would then be bad enough and unworthy, much as it may commend itself to many in these days. However, the fact is, the plan of God is revealed in the book, in the form in which every prophet reveals it; and Job is not blamed by God because he wished to penetrate the divine plan. No more weight ought to be attached to an incidental remark of Goethe's [1] than to such

1 The remark of Goethe's referred to is to be found in his review of *Lavater's Predigten über das Buch Jonas*, one of the early reviews contributed by him to the *Frankfurter Gelehrte Anzeigen*. It is simply: "In the Book of Job the proposition, God's providence is unsearchable but nevertheless always great and worthy of admiration on account of its issues, was undoubtedly the manifest main purpose of the author." Tr.

an endless number of other superficial opinions regarding the meaning and aim of this book.—If others actually suppose that the book is confused and its thought not well worked out, they simply betray the fact, that they have not understood it either in detail or as a whole.

III. The human portion of the contention, occupying the principle part of the main body of the book, proceeds therefore by three stages, in such a way that, although in this part of the poem speeches alone are found and neither fresh persons nor great outward events are introduced, nevertheless the question itself upon which everything in the end depends makes thereby regular and proportional progress, and the proper solution is of itself insensibly prepared for from the midst of the complication of the question as it reaches its climax. The entire poem accordingly falls into five perfectly distinct and yet most closely connected parts. And if the poem, according to what we saw above [1], intends by its very plan to supply the answer to its question in a corresponding illustration of it taken from the midst of human life, or in a *Drama,* the true development of such a drama cannot be more correctly presented than is done in these five parts. For they are just the same five stages as those in which an important action in a human life must naturally unfold itself and advance to its satisfactory conclusion: *first contact of the various conflicting elements, complication, climax of the complication, commencement of the solution, solution.* The complication, or entanglement, of the question follows of itself from the introduction of it with its various conflicting elements; and in that this complication advances to its climax, through all the profoundly agitated aspects and torn-up recesses of the question, in order that the most hidden and apparently most impossible elements of the case may be forced to develop themselves and come to light, the commencement of a solution is prepared for by the new possibilities and

[1] p. 17.

energies which come to light, under a progressive destruction of the errors. The solution itself actually comes as soon as the necessity which is at first completely hidden can at last get wholly free from its impediments by the destruction of even the last errors. This will always be the outline of the plan and development of a true drama; and inasmuch as it is involved in the nature of the thing itself, the Greeks were not necessary to teach it. But as early as in this Book of Job it appears carried out with such perfection and ease, both in the details and the whole poem, that our admiration of the work can only be increased as we rediscover more correctly its perfections in this respect. Every part and every detail is most compactly put together, with the first foundations the whole execution of the work is already clearly provided for, there is nothing redundant and nothing defective, everything is in its place, and in its place it is in all cases the right thing and just what is required.

Compactly and necessarily as the larger and smaller members of this drama all hang together and present themselves by every indication as the authentic work of the poet, with equal certainty and plainness the two pieces of the present book which are not included in the action of the drama, the speeches of Elihu, xxxii—xxxvii., and the description of the two animal-monsters, xl. 15—xli. 26 (A. V. ver. 34) do not belong to the original work. This conclusion which is explained in detail below, I established as early as 1828 [1]; and nothing has been said in reply which can be substantiated by the truth of the case. But only a serious misconception of the whole book could mislead several moderns to conjecture a want of connexion, or another hand, in the case of ch. xxvii and xxviii. Similarly, the so-called prologue, i., ii and the epilogue, xlii. 7—17, have had suspicion cast upon them without any just reason: for these prose passages thoroughly harmonize as regards their material and thought, style and art, and language also (as far as prose can be like poetry), with the ancient poetic book, and everything that has been urged to the contrary is either pure misconception or of no importance. The transposition of certain verses in ch. xxxi and xxxviii has only been erroneously proposed. Whoever has really understood the book, will, we hope, as often as he reads it over again and with closer attention, find this judgment regarding primary or later pieces in it confirmed, just as I have found nothing since the year 1828 to alter in this respect.

[1] In the *Theol. Stud. und Kritiken,* Vol. II. p. 767 sq.

Throughout the whole poem there runs, as has been said, a single, closely interwoven, sharply defined action, based upon its great thought. However this drama was not intended by the poet for actual performance on a stage. Whether or when, therefore, the action, in simple narrative, or in the elaborately presented speeches of the persons taking part in it, is meant to advance may be gathered from the relation of the particular description to the fundamental thought of the book: where the latter requires a closer inspection of the dangers, stages, and grounds of the higher faith, the simple thread of narrative then gives place to the broader web of the elaborate discourses of the persons engaged in the action. Nothing can so clearly, so instructively, so inspiringly conduct a reader into the inmost feelings and thoughts of integrity as it wrestles with calamity, with God and the world, into the soul of the restricted, antiquated, helpless faith, into the full all-surpassing grandeur of the divine mind when it reveals itself, as elaborate discourses from each representative person exhausting the reason of the matter. It is not so much rapid disconnected dialogue, such as is used in the bustle of common life, which is appropriate here, where the most serious subject is treated in its dignity and difficulty by the representatives of differing views, who are of their respective classes the worthiest and wisest, and each of the longer discourses is like a wise, well-considered, sententious proverb [1]. On the contrary, the vast preponderance of purely spiritual matter, combined with the desire and capacity of the poet to give it exhaustive utterance by means of its proper instrument, the human-divine word, must cause the decided predominance of the calm, profoundly penetrating development of the action by means of elaborate discourses. As soon, therefore, as the action comes to the first decisive moment, which gives rise to a course of development the end of which cannot be seen, this profoundly

[1] מָשָׁל xxvii. 1; xxix. 1, comp. xiii. 12.

penetrating mode of treatment commences in a discourse which calmly further pursues its way, ch. iii.; and it is only a little before the end, after the whole spiritual matter has already been completely treated in an uninterrupted tournament of thought and oratory, and the final result is necessarily at hand, that the continuation of the action in simple narrative again suffices, xlii. 7—17. But while thus the flow of discourse proceeds in all directions, carrying forward the action of the poem at first imperceptibly and soon very perceptibly, the less important accompaniments of the main action also advance with it, inasmuch as it receives everything into its stream as it is all along predominant. To much of a subordinate nature which takes place in the meantime there is, however, only incidental reference made, *e.g.,* that according to the intention of the poet, the disasters of Job are further increased by the cowardly mockery of inferiors, becomes plain xvii. 6; xxx. 1—10; that the three stages of the contention, as is of itself probable, are meant to be distributed amongst successive days, appears from the hint let fall xxiii. 2.[1]

As accordingly the art of the poem *as a whole* is brought to perfection by the judicious arrangement, accurate working-out and compact jointing of the whole, no particle of it being in the wrong place, there being nothing redundant or deficient, nothing detached and without easy transition and preparation, nor anything without effective reference to what went before or what comes after, so also *in detail* the poet's art is all along the skilful mistress of his material, determining its destination and form in conformity with the requirements of the thought which has in each instance to be illustrated. The greatest variety of description, style, manner of presentation, is required in matters of detail by the general arrangement of the poem: the poet knows how to present in every case the most varied things at their proper places, so as to meet the

[1] See on this point the further remarks in the *Tübinger Theol. Jahrbb.,* 1843, p. 753.

requirements made by his work as a whole, without ever losing himself in the details, or treating any detail too feebly or too elaborately. The raving and all the misery of despair, no less than the peace and blessedness of better knowledge, the pungent, castigating speech of him that instructs from good-will or threatens from provocation, no less than the agonizing complaint, ending in woeful grief, of him that is bowed-down, the helpless exhaustion of him that is vanquished, no less than the exultation and pride of him that is deeply afflicted and yet not compelled to succumb, the passionateness and precipitancy of man, no less than the gladness of God, shedding its serious but smiling rays over everything, and the glory of God,—all this the poet represents attractively and adequately. It follows of itself from the entire form of Hebrew poetry, that the speeches of the persons of the poem, when they at a longer or shorter length, rise to a poetic height, may at the same time be broken up into strophes; but it is needful to remark that the poet approves himself in this respect also as a rare master [1]. But even the prose, where it is introduced, is worthy of the poet and bears his impress. The prolixities and repetitions of the friends too, in the second stage of the contention, though not of themselves very pleasing, only cast a shadow which all the more heightens the effect of the rest of the poem. It is only a little too clearly that we hear the voice of calamity in the century of the poet coming from the long, mournful descriptions of the confusion and wrongness of the world, ch. xxi. and xxiv., as if the poet had himself delayed as long with it as possible and had at last been compelled to give it vent in the most gloomy passage of the poem. But how powerfully does Job immediately rise against it with recovered heart, xxvi sq., and how sublime also is the close, for which everything great and surprising appears to have been preserved. Moreover, everything is free from all trace of constraint, without any laboured

[1] The treatment of this matter which I have given in the *Jahrbücher der Bibl. Wiss.* III. p. 116 sq., appears below more completely worked out in detail.

artificiality, manifestly the easiest, most unforced effusion of a lofty poet-mind and of his unfettered art.

On account of the peculiarity and complete originality of this poem, it is therefore difficult to assign it a place in Greek poetic art. As regards its matter and purpose, the book, as is evident on the face of it, is the most sublime didactic poem of the Bible: but it appears more difficult to say what it is as respects art. Still, when more closely considered, the book, leaving out of view adaptation for the stage which has not here been made, belongs, as we saw p. 17, to the drama, and, if it is desired to give it at least an approximate Greek name, cannot properly be described otherwise than as the divine drama of the ancient Hebrews[1], since it is not only unique of its class in the O. T., but is also distinguished amongst all books by the peculiar art as well as the deep feeling and sublimity of its matter. If, however, in point of simple truth and freshness particular thoughts of many other pieces of the O. T. may compare with this, on the other hand, the art which in it makes such successful efforts in a subject of such magnitude and with such a high degree of perfection is quite peculiar to it. This book supplies us with the greatest thing that the Hebrews accomplished in poetic art, in the way of a masterly handling of a given material and immortalising a thought. Accordingly it has subsequently, if not as a whole (inasmuch as for this the requisite knowledge was very often wanting) yet in certain parts of it, been admired and imitated by many great poets, particularly has this been the case with its opening, which is more easily understood. This is not the place to examine the question whether Goethe's Faust can be compared with this book or not: it is, however, plain enough that its brilliant prologue would not have been what it is without the Book of Job.

With what ease the poet is able to handle his material appears also in the fact, that he draws a sharp distinction in outward respects between the time of early antiquity, which his material requires him to describe, and his own later age, and takes care to avoid every unsuitable confusion of them. It is true that he does not by any means, like our modern poets, pedantically make a point of keeping up the antique colouring in every smallest point and of carefully avoiding the appearance here and there of the age of his real contempor-

[1] Inasmuch as several writers, since the appearance of the first edition of this work, have made a great ado at this view of mine, I may here just remark, that to Leibnitz also the book appeared to be "operatic"; as was recently remarked from a manuscript in Dr. Schmidt's *Zeitschrift für Geschichte* 1847, Mai, p. 436.

aries. On the contrary, as his design is after all really to instruct his own age, he does not scruple to let traces of it clearly shine through the artistic veil, yet always at the proper place, where it has no disturbing effect on the whole poem and appears naturally to suggest itself. If in the midst of his own maddening pain Job cast a glance also at the large number of others who like him suffer for no fault of their own, and then illustrations of calamities suggest themselves such as only the experience of later times could present in such a manner, ix. 24; xii. 23; xxi. 7 sq.; xxiv. 2—17, he uses in such cases the language of one carried away by the higher flight of imagination and surveying all times, describing evils in striking examples such as were in the actual time of Job already about to arise. And if the poet sometimes, as the exception, puts into Job's mouth [1] the Mosaic divine name Jahvé, though he usually, when he makes the old men speak, uses the pre-Mosaic names אֱלוֹהַּ, אֵל and שַׁדַּי, these are the most sublime passages in Job's life and discourses, where the ancient hero, who according to tradition worshipped like Abraham the true ancient God [2], as if suddenly moved by the purest spirit, thus early gazed quite into the glory of the God of Moses; which exceptional use of the name Jahvé, thus introduced at the proper place, is very effective. There are also some figures borrowed from a later time, such as the frequent one from the customs of writing and sealing, xiii. 26; xiv. 17; xix. 23, 24; xxxi. 35, 36; xxxviii. 14. But where simple narrative and the connexion of circumstances require an antique description, at the commencement i. ii., at the close xlii. 7 sq. and elsewhere, there the genuine colouring of the time of Job, that is the time between Abraham and Moses, is everywhere very faithfully preserved, so

[1] i. 21; xxviii. 28, where אדני = יהוה. Further xii. 9, where however אלוה is probably to be read, as some MSS. do.—Where the poet simply narrates, there is nothing in his usage to hinder him from employing the name Jahvé, i. 2; xxxviii. 1; xl. 1, 3, 6; xlii. 1 sq.

[2] Comp. also particularly xxxi. 26—28.

that it can be seen that the poet well kept up the difference of times when anything depended upon it. Historical examples are borrowed only from the primitive and patriarchal world, as xviii. 15; xxii. 15, 16.

The question may be asked, whether the poet has not at all events in the delineation of subordinate circumstances of the action now and then forgotten himself? With regard to one circumstance in particular this question may be raised. According to i. 18, 19, comp. xlii. 13—15, Job loses *all* his children at the very beginning of the tragedy; but according to the correct meaning of the words xiv. 21; xvii. 5; xix. 17, 18, he still has children at a later stage of his calamities. This discrepancy cannot be removed by the supposition that the narrative at the commencement, i., ii., and at the end, xlii. 7 sq., is by another author: for this supposition is supported by no other reason (as we have seen); and moreover, there is the further fact that according to viii. 4, xxix. 5, comp. xxi. 11, the author of these verses presupposes the destruction of Job's children. If the contradiction should be regarded as irreconcilable, we should still not be compelled on that account alone to lay upon the author any great blame. At all events Goethe (Gespräche mit Eckermann, vol. III. p. 155) maintains on another occasion, that a great poet may very well for once forget himself as regards unimportant details, as Shakespeare has done in Macbeth, Act i and iv., in reference to the question whether Macbeth had children or not; as a fact, this discrepancy in Macbeth has not been removed, as Tieck's remarks on Act iv. do not at all meet the case. Neither in the Book of Job is it enough to suppose, that Job means in his speeches by his sons really his grandsons, as the latter were in any case still quite young according to xix. 18, and as it may be supposed that probably some grandchildren escaped the destruction of the sons. For even that only some of such grandchildren were left to him is when well considered but little accordant with the sense of the whole poem; and, moreover, these sons are expressly described, xix. 17, as of his own body. However, when we remember that the poet describes Job as a man of the same kind as Abraham, or a similar patriarch, he could very well give to him, particularly in his later age after his wife had grown old, some children by a concubine; and these children could as easily be passed over without mention in the brief narrative of ch. i., as the few scattered servants which Job still possessed according to xix. 15, 16, notwithstanding that his servants were slain acc. i. 17.

ON THE DATE AND THE HISTORY OF THE BOOK.

For the discovery of the name and other personal relations of the poet, the more particular indications are now wanting. There is hardly another piece in the O. T. by the same author: with regard to Ps. xxxix., which would most naturally claim to be compared, see my *Commentary on the Psalms in loco.* It is a natural supposition that the poet was inspired to undertake the work by some personal experience: but the historical evidence is wanting which would carry us beyond supposition. Neither is it possible to fix the date of the book other than approximately by centuries. For as a deliberate product of poetic art this book did not originally proceed so immediately from the definite circumstances of a particular time as did the prophetic and most of the simple lyrics; and such circumstances can the less be presented by it in palpable indications, in proportion as the poet, by letting go his time, has consistently carried through the illustrations from distant antiquity required by his materials. Nevertheless, the poet plainly wrote his book for contemporaries who were prepared for and intensely desirous to hear its doctrine. The old faith regarding evil must already have been most profoundly shaken by contrary experiences and unbelief have taken deep root; for without such precursors the thought and design of the book cannot be comprehended. Accordingly it cannot have been written in early antiquity, when the simple faith was still quite valid and satisfactory, Ex. xx. 5; nor at the time when undaunted courage still contended successfully with what was unsatisfactory in the ancient view, as in Pss. vi., xiii. But from the eight and the seventh century B. C., the perplexing confusion of personal and national relations and circumstances was so greatly increased that it might quite well rouse the poet to seek a solution of the enigma of the time: the detailed proof of which belongs rather to the general history of the nation and of its literature than to this place. If the despair of the faithful had risen to the manifestly undue height of Ps. xxxix., and the cry for help had become so urgent as in Ps. xii., all the conditions were supplied which the poet needed for conceiving and working-out the conception of his work. One sees also in the background of this poem the picture of such extraordinarily disorganised, calamitous times as precisely the centuries above-named were for Israel[1]. On the other hand, the poet appears to be one of the first whose mind arose out of that perplexing confusion to this elevation of pure insight and advanced hope. For we see him still struggling with the higher part of the thought, and the greatest truth which has to be here presented is so far from being anything long since made out and ready-to-hand that it breaks forth in this book as something quite new and fresh from its first source. That which is the consequence and teaching of this book appears already in a more fixed and final form in Pss. xvi., xlix., and lxxiii., as if the higher hope had further developed itself by the simple progress of the times. If in this book the view, that children ought not to suffer for their parents, makes itself felt in painful struggle, as if it were only just seeking to get clear to itself, xxi. 19—21, by Jeremiah and Ezekiel (*ante* p. 13) it is already announced with forcible brevity as a proposition which cannot be denied, as also the whole manner of the discourse of Ezekiel's on the divine righteousness, xiv. 14 sq., xviii., appears like a result of our book. But, again, without doubt that steadfast faithfulness unto death, which, according to the piece on which is founded Isa. liii., the martyrs under Manasseh exhibited[2], was still not historically known to the poet. Similarly, the truth which is forcibly presented in

[1] ix. 24; xii. 4—6, 23; xv. 28; xvii. 6—9; xxi., xxiv. The fire of burning sympathy with which the poet really refers to the disastrous calamities of his own time and of contemporary Israel, to the ruined condition of the ancient kingdom, the rise of a *tyrannis*, the intrusion of foreigners (xv. 19), and the commencing deportation of the nation into captivity, often flashes quite suddenly from the midst of the speeches of the heroes from an olden time.

[2] Comp. *History of Israel* Vol. V. 207 sq. (IV. 715 sq.).

that chapter and in the whole of the great work "Isa." xl—lxvi., as the climax of all higher views regarding evil, namely, that the true servant of Jahvé suffers *for others,* and indeed for the guilty, in order that the divine kingdom may spread in ever wider circles, is not yet touched upon at all here. Putting all these things together, it will be found most probable that the poet lived not long after Isaiah, towards the end of the eighth or the beginning of the seventh century, when the northern kingdom was destroyed, the southern, Judah, suffered under various disasters. It is unfortunate that we know but little of the history of these first years under Manasseh.—This conclusion is confirmed by a comparison of the later portions of the present book with the earlier ones. The speeches of Elihu, as will appear below, show a time considerably further advanced, which had already made a much closer acquaintance with the truth which the poet had previously experienced. According to all other signs also the distance between the different pieces of the book is that of a century, or even of two. If therefore the later additions were written in about the second half of the sixth century, as may with probability be supposed, the date of the book is brought by that fact considerably earlier than the time of the Babylonian captivity.

Other indications do not appear to contradict this supposition. A number of unusual poetic figures and conceptions appear to unfold themselves in this book like a new world. From which fact the question naturally arises, whether they all appeared here for the first time in Hebrew poetry, and whence they originated? In consequence of the limited extent of the O. T., this question is often difficult to answer quite precisely, particularly as this book (except the Canticles, which is again of such a very different character, in that it does not admit of sublime and lofty figures) is the only one belonging to the class of artistic poetry in the strict sense, in which therefore almost alone the poetic conception of the Hebrews regarding the visible and invisible world with a certain conscious purpose are presented at length. To mention a few of the most important things in this respect, the book contains

(1) many very unusual representations and pictures of terrestrial things, as of plants, viii. 11; ix. 26, of animals, xxix. 18; xxxix. 1 sq., of mining and precious treasures of the earth, xxviii., of the marvellous edifices of men, iii. 14. We see also that a very large knowledge of the more distant wonders of the earth must have reached the poet, which is not conceivable without an active intercourse between the nations; but we must regret that we are often imperfectly informed as regards the precise nature of the dispersion of such knowledge or traditions. Several figures appear to be borrowed from Egyptian things, iii. 14; viii. 11; ix. 26. However, it would be hasty to infer from that fact, that the author, as in this respect a fellow-sufferer with Jeremiah perhaps, wrote his book in Egypt, inasmuch as many Egyptian and Ethopian characteristics were known in Palestine, Isa. xviii. 19, and the two chief pictures which can be cited in favour of such an inference, of the Nile-horse and the Crocodile, xl. 15—xli. 26 (A.V. xli. 34) are from a later hand. It appears, however, to be certain that all the figures of this kind might very well be well-known at the beginning of the seventh century.

(2) A great number of astrological traditions and figures, as well as of conceptions of other celestial wonders, distinguishes this poet, by which he often trenches upon the mythological region, as iii. 8; ix. 9, 13; xxv. 2, 3; xxvi. 12, 14; xxxviii. 7, 31—33, 36. It is worth further inquiry where legends of this kind were first formed and made current. The Hebrews were certainly the furthest from being the originators of such first elements of a mythology, since everything mythological which is found amongst them was preserved or spread simply in spite of Mosaism. Yet traces of mythological elements are decidedly met with amongst them as early as the eighth century, since Rahab occurs Isa. xxx. 7, the Seven Stars and Orion

even as early as Amos v. 8, whilst the simple herdsman Amos will be furthest from using new figures in such matters.

(3) Most remarkable are the conceptions of angels and Satan which are peculiar to this book. The Satan, as he is described i., ii., is, it is true, as regards his love of tracking and punishing among men what is wicked or suspicious, quite the subsequent evil spirit: but with all that similarity, what a great difference is at the same time discernible! Subsequently, when these conceptions had been fully developed under the influence of the religions of Eastern Asia, we see the Satan at the head of a great empire of spirits, and between him and the empire of the good spirits an infinite and impassable gulf fixed, so that scarcely in the earliest ages of the creation is the possibility yet presupposed of the origin of this gulf. But in this book not only does Satan enter alone, without attendant hosts, into the divine Council-Meeting, and appears still as independent and self-sufficient only to a very limited degree, but the entire empire of superior spirits has not as yet got into this irreconcilable separation. On the contrary, the spirits generally are regarded as such as can go astray in spite of all their elevation, just as the visible heaven notwithstanding its unearthly splendour is yet dull and impure in comparison with the purest light iv. 18; xv. 15; xxv. 4—6. And the mythology tells not only of great revolts on the part of the higher powers, but also of how stern judgment was held over them, so that not one even of the mightiest of heaven is able to withstand the true God, but all serve Him in peace, ix. 13; xxi. 22; xxv. 2, 3; xxvi. 12, 13, comp. v. 1. This conception of the variable moral condition of the higher spirits occupies a place midway between the ancient Mosaic conception, according to which the angels have no separate, personal will whatever, and the later view, which strictly separates good and evil in the innumerable hosts of spirits also, but makes the first angels of God all good and without error. As this phenomenon of the book cannot on closer examination be

mistaken, it points to a time when the ancient conceptions of the realm of spirits, undoubtedly not wholly without the influence of foreign religions, were undergoing their first transformation and assuming new forms, when unfaithful spirits and a spirit which secretly sought and willed evil, were spoken of, while, on the other hand, they were not yet so completely transferred into a separate realm of an entirely different nature. From the description of a prophet of the ninth century, 1 Kings xxii. 19—22, to that of this book, i., ii., which is in some respects so similar, there is, it must be allowed, an important step, in that the name and the idea of the Satan appear for the first time in this book; but from this description to that of Zech. iii. 1, 2, where Satan and angels of God contend concerning a man and Jahve speaks to Satan only in anger, there is again a scarcely less important step, because that separation between good and evil in the realm of spirits appears here as already completed; and from what is here said regarding resisting celestial powers, that which is said by a later prophet "Isa." xxiv. 21, 22 differs in an important degree. Similarly, there occurs here for the first time the prayer to higher spirits as intercessors, v. 1, a thought which arises as soon as ever the realm of spirits is conceived as taking shape more freely; but this thought is in our book far less rigid than subsequently. And whilst later poets and prophets shrink from introducing God immediately, or even as appearing on the earth, this poet does not scruple to make Him appear and speak to Job. We can therefore come to no other conclusion than that the author of this book occupies a place midway between ancient and late conceptions, and lived at a time when that which became the prevailing view was still thoroughly malleable and modern.

The language and orthography of the later pieces of the book conduct to a time when the Aramaic peculiarities were creeping in already to a considerable extent: but the language and orthography of the earlier pieces show scarcely any marks of a commencing decline, *e.g.,* the more abbreviated orthography

ריִשׁוֹן, viii. 8 [1], instead of רִאשׁוֹן; רִיעֲכֶם, vi. 27, instead of 'רֵעַ, and nothing whatever which a poet of the first half of the seventh century might not have written, since the name קְדֹשִׁים "saints", v. 1, for the angels of God, occurs again Zech. xiv. 5 in a piece which was certainly written before the dissolution of the kingdom of Judah. The fact that many words rarely found elsewhere occur here, is simply one of the numerous indications that nothing else by this poet has been preserved, probably also evidence that he did not write in Jerusalem. But if some words appear here for the first time which subsequently became common in the later language, the reason for that is rather to be found in the general relations of the Hebrew poetic language.—The high stage of the art of the book was neither possible in the earlier centuries, when Hebrew poetic art was only commencing its course of development, nor is it very easily conceivable in the later centuries when poetic art generally declined gradually, and most of all the higher art needful for the production of greater creations and works; neither is such a compressed, pithy style of discourse as prevails in this book found subsequently in longer pieces.

Lastly, the observation of the outward condition in which this book is found in the series of the books of the O. T. points to the same age. It is true, to conclude from the extreme purity of the copies in which the book came into the Canon, it appears not to have been much read for a long time: but on the other hand, it must be remembered that this purity is owing to the fact that the poet must himself have provided for it in his original manuscript.[2] Still, the traces of the book being read can to some extent be followed. Of the Psalms of the third period some refer back very plainly to this book, just as Zech. i. 10—14; iii. 1, 2; vi. 5 presuppose the descrip-

[1] Comp. רִיאשׁוֹן, xv. 7: an orthography which is also found in Sacy's *Correspondence des Samarit.* p. 103, 1.

[2] According to the remarks, *History of Israel* IV. p. 286 (III. p. 821 sq.); see further below.

tions of ch. i., ii. as long known; צָבָא, "Isa." xl. 2, is borrowed from vii. 1, or at all events originated about the same time[1]. If Ezekiel mentions Job in company with Noah and Daniel as a model of a godly man (ante p. 21), it can only be, when all circumstances are considered, because our book had made that hero once more famous[2]. The book must have been known in Ezekiel's time and much read. In the Book of Jeremiah, with whose tone of mind this book accorded extremely well, and still more in the Book of Lamentations, there is much reechoed from it[3]. On which side the employment of the words is original cannot in this case be a matter of doubt. Ps. lviii. 8 reminds us of iii. 16; Ps. lxxii. 12 is almost exactly repeated from xxix. 12: and thus it is not difficult to show that this book accordingly dates as far back as the beginning of the seventh century[4]. Reversely, passages can be quoted which show that earlier authors were before the mind of the poet, as the expression "he that walketh over the heights of the sea", ix. 8, is formed probably after the simpler form Amos iv. 13[5], and the whole verse-member xiv. 11 after Isa. xix. 5[6]; although the poet continues to be very markedly distinguished from the later artistic poets, who borrow their chief excellences from the ancient writings.

[1] See *History of Israel* IV. p. 208 (III. p. 716 sq.).

[2] The relation of Daniel to the readers of that time is a distinct question which must be answered elsewhere. See now *Prophets of the Old Testament* V. p. 169 sq. (III. p. 312 sq.).

[3] As Jer. xx. 14—18 from iii. 3—26; xv. 18 from vi. 15 sq.; xvii. 1 from xix. 24; xlix. 19 from ix. 19. As regards the *Book of Lamentations*, see *ante* p. 3 sq., and comp. in addition how the words Lam. iii. 38 are only a slight echo from Job ii. 10. In all such cases the most decisive point is the multitude of the signs of the use of one book in another.

[4] As regards the still earlier Book of Deuteronomy, see the remarks in the *History of Israel* I. p. 127 sq. (I. p. 186); as regards Prov. i—ix., *ibid.* IV. p. 220 (III. p. 733).

[5] In this case also the most decisive thing is the accumulation of indications: xviii. 16 further reminds us strongly of Amos ii. 9; xii. 15, of Amos ix. 6; and the reference to the constellations is similar in both writers. The connexion of the words even in xxvii. 16 appears to have been taken from "Zech." ix. 3.

[6] Comp. also the continuation Isa. xix. 13, 14 with the repetition Job xii. 24, 25.

The book came into the Canon undoubtedly somewhat late, after the subsequent additions to it had also been written a considerable time, and the name, date, and circumstances of the earlier poet had long been lost to memory. On that account many readers of the centuries subsequent to the formation of the O. T. down to our own times have believed that Job himself was the poet, or at all events that the book was written in very early antiquity by Moses or a similar holy man. Or it has been conjectured that the original language of the book (as if it were written by Job himself) was not Hebrew, perhaps the Idumean or the Arabic. However, all such suppositions are wholly groundless, inasmuch as they have sprung ultimately from confounding the hero with the author of the book. Many readers have in recent times suffered themselves to be so far misled by these errors that they cannot make the book late enough, and bring it down at least into the Babylonian exile. But they thereby overlook partly the great dissimilarity that exists between the earlier and the later pieces of the book, and partly their judgment with regard to many points of it is in other respects insufficiently instructed. When, *e.g.*, the false derivation of the word שָׂטָן i., ii. from שׁוּט i. 7, was rejected, but at the same time the absurd assertion was made, that the Satan appears here exactly as he is met with later, even the little amount of truth, however much mixed with error, was then lost again. A completely reliable proof of the view of the age of the book above offered belongs, however, rather to a treatment of the entire course of general ancient Hebrew Literature: it was intended here simply to supply briefly some of the leading marks of it. Further details have been given in various places of the *History of Israel.*

That this book was much read as early as the seventh century B. C., appears from the evidence referred to a short time ago. And how greatly its beauty early produced all kinds of imitations and continuations of it, we shall see below, when we come to consider the two considerable pieces which were subsequently inserted into it. But originally the poem must have been written and distributed abroad in very good copies: for even yet the text, particularly in the original portion of the book, is comparatively very pure, a point carefully to be noted in connexion with the question of the sense of somewhat more obscure passages[1].

[1] Accordingly there is no reason for supposing that many emendations of the Hebrew are necessary. The passages are rare where a few small errors may have crept in, as vi. 14, 21; xii. 13; xx. 11; xxii. 23; xxiii. 2; xxix. 7; xxx. 12, see also below on xxi. 10. The error which could most easily arise through the fault even of early copyists, would be the omission here and there of a verse-member or a whole verse.

I. THE FIRST STAGE OF THE DRAMA.

OPENING OF THE CONTENTION.

1. Job's life and character, ch. i. 1—5.

With reference to this, simply what is absolutely necessary; particularly that which is of importance for the course of the action, namely, how Job was no less prosperous than god-fearing; everything put with individuality, yet only so as to meet circumstances which are generally suitable. Of those two aspects of Job's life, the prosperity and the piety of it, however, it is the last which is the more important for everything that follows: it is put forward at the very commencement, and at the end, vv. 4, 5, it is returned to with the additional detail appropriate here, how carefully Job watched over the purity and blamelessness not only of his own life but also of his whole house, presenting sacrifices annually, even on account of the sins which his grown-up children might possibly have committed in secret. So that the calamities which followed naturally befell him wholly unexpectedly, inasmuch as he had, according to ancient belief, done all that was humanly possible to avert divine punishments from his whole house. But since, as will subsequently appear, all such customary religious works are insufficient to avert the calamities, the insufficiency of such works may in any case be inferred from the result.

i. 1 There was a man in the land of Uz, whose name was
Job: the same man was blameless and upright, godfearing
2 and departing from evil. And there were born to him seven
3 sons and three daughters; and his possession was seven
thousand head of sheep three thousand camels five hundred
yoke of oxen and five hundred she-asses, and a very large
household: so that the man was greater than all sons of the
4 East.—Now his sons went often and made a feast, at the
house of each on his day, and sending they invited their

It appears from the corresponding passages ver. 8, ii. 3, that the conjunctive —וְ before ירא אלהים, ver. 1, is not much required: for the first two adjectives are simply explained more accurately by the last two, as the integrity of the heart תם necessarily implies the fear of God, uprightness in action the avoidance of evil. Thus the four words together supply the plainest definition of perfect piety.—As the occasion when the children of Job, who as might be expected from the example of their father were in other respects blameless and living in perfect amity (xlii. 15), might have sinned, the poet chooses, vv. 4, 5, the annual festive gatherings [1], which the sons, who had already grown-up and were living in various directions around their father's abode in separate houses, kept in common, and where the boisterous pleasure might easily on an occasion get the better of the generally prevailing seriousness and break the bonds of the habitual earnest habits. For it must be remembered that the degree of stability in divine things which Job presupposes in the case of his sons is not that to which he supposes himself to have attained, upon which godliness is no longer a command and compulsion, is not a thing which might be lost, say in a moment of intoxication. If it is asked more particularly of what kind these seven feasts were, after the passing-by of which Job brought an expiatory offering, the birthdays of the brothers might be thought of, as if each one had kept his birthday in his house. Yet as the seven birthdays must have been spread more over the whole year, it is not easy to see why Job did not always make sacrifices immediately after each of them; neither would it in that case be said "when the days of the feast were ended", as if all the days were connected, but something like "when the days of the year were ended" would be said. It is therefore much better to suppose that the ordinary annual feasts of joy are intended, particularly the autumn feast which was much observed in ancient times, or again the feast of spring, all these feasts generally lasting a week, so that exactly one day fell to each son for keeping the feast in his house according to the order of seniority, which is confirmed by ver. 13. With regard to בית איש יומו *in the house on the day*, *i.e.*, in the order, *of each*, see §§ 300*b*, 278 *b*.

[1] That is, not the simple daily meal, but special banquets are plainly intended, as appears from the words and the general meaning of the description.

5 three sisters to eat and to drink with them. But when the
days of the feast were gone by, Job sent and atoned for them,
early in the morning bringing whole-burnt-offerings according
to the number of them all. For Job thought that perhaps
his sons had sinned and bidden God adieu in their heart.
Thus did Job all the time.

The reason for such a careful reference to the place and succession of the feast, does not appear until vv. 13, 19. Moreover, as the sons had each time to come together from their different houses in that one to which the turn fell, the description begins with their *going (they went and made a feast)*; and because their father did not keep the feast with them, he *sent* each time to them after it, to cause them to come and be atoned for, since the person to be purified might not be absent from the sacrifice, Lev. iv., vi. 17—23; vii. 1—10; the zeal with which Job did this, is shown by the added clause *early in the morning*. With regard to the variation of the expression in cases where frequent repetition is described, vv. 4, 5, see § 342 *b*.

2. Job's heavy and heaviest calamities, determined upon in heaven, carried out on the earth, as yet without becoming dangerous to him, i. 6—ii. 10.

Mysterious calamity, the cause of which is to the earth an enigma, must fall upon Job who is so completely blameless. Yet it is mysterious only on the earth of that time; for in the presence of the pure divine light, where all scattered rays converge and whence they proceed, the clue to this enigma cannot be lost in the darkness. But for the reader, who must from the first behold under the pure light of heaven the real commencement of the action of the drama, in order that he may comprehend its necessary development, and, standing above the mortal sufferer, follow his history, the poet at once draws back the celestial curtain and lets him glance into the holy of holies, as far as the veil may be withdrawn thus early in the poem. Job is, it is true, given over by God Himself to his sufferings: but not by the malicious God, or the God who is angry with him, but by the God who knows and loves him, the compassionate One; by the God who is at first, as it were, loath to let him suffer inasmuch, as He does not desire the suffering as such and Job's destruction, and yet must necessarily cause him to suffer. For Job's godliness has not as yet passed through the fire of purification, and that God Himself cannot hinder. Indeed, the man to whom the greatest measure of strength and prosperity has been granted must also contend the most painfully. If just now, within the limitations by which he has hitherto been surrounded, he seems to stand most securely and really so far to deserve all divine approval, he is immediately sent forth to new and perilous struggles, that it may appear whether as conqueror there also he can more firmly hold his earlier attainments and succeed in gaining fresh and higher ones. The preparation for these perilous struggles accordingly is made in the celestial counsels. Jahvé in the divine council-chamber mentions with pleasure his servant Job to the Satan who ferrets out everything bad or suspicious and gladly inflicts evils. Jahvé refers to Job as a servant against whom this Satan can produce nothing. But the enemy with wicked cunning seeks to throw suspicion upon him, as one who is godly merely for the sake of prosperity as an earthly advantage. Inasmuch as the suspicion has once been raised, and appears not without foundation, as judged by possible, and indeed probable, human weakness, Jahvé can do no other than permit the trial which the Satan desires, were it for no other reason than simply to put the Satan himself to shame. Keeping silence as regards the issue, yet not saying or thinking that the godly man must succumb, prescribing to the trial its limits, Jahvé dismisses the Satan with full power. We fear as men for Job and await with intense interest the issue, but taking a deeper view anticipate the possibility, indeed the certainty, that he will not succumb, and that evil together with the Satan will in this case only serve as the instrument for the promotion of goodness itself. That which is thus prepared for in heaven finds its fulfilment on earth within its prescribed limits, save that what in heaven is clear is on earth veiled, and is only painfully felt in its effects, especially as the Satan spares no pains to bring decreed calamities upon Job with surprising suddenness and severity. And yet the temptation to impatience, despair, confused thinking, and folly is withstood by the brave man whom God distinguishes by the name of his servant, and who does not disappoint the divine hope. He shows the noblest resignation and submission, maintaining, both from voluntary personal impulse as well as under the derision and provocation which he has to bear, the truest moderation under suffering and resignation under bereavement, although his calamities all the time continue to be dark and mysterious to him, and though accepted in humility are still regarded and borne as a positive evil sent by God. As therefore Job is thus brave and great, thus steadfast and faithful, the advance of this entire stage of the action is twice repeated: preparation in heaven, mysterious suffering on earth, patience and steadfastness standing the trial; all this is twice repeated, only with accumulating force and pressure. The first trial takes from him all his valued outward possessions together with his children; the second, the last outward good which outweighs all the rest, his health, by a disease which both creates disgust and threatens life itself. The first time his patience has simply to contend against himself; the second time, with the despair of the only being on an equality with him in his house remaining to him, his wife. He remains faithful, therefore, to the uttermost in that stage of religious life upon which he had hitherto moved.—All this is described, though only in a rapid narrative, with truly poetic vividness and perfection. The inapproachable dignity of Jahvé, though engaged in a consultation after the fashion of men, the alarm and surprise of calamities accumulating in rapid succession, the genuine human resignation of the godly man, can hardly be pourtrayed more forcibly than is done in these few noble lines.

6 And it came to pass on the day the sons of God came to
present themselves before Jahvé, and there came also the
7 Adversary in their midst. Then said Jahvé to the Adversary:
whence comest thou? and the Adversary answered Jahvé and
said: from ranging through the earth and from going about
8 through it. Then said Jahvé to the Adversary: hast thou
set thy attention upon my servant Job? for there is not like
him in the earth a man perfect and upright, godfearing and
9 departing from evil. And the Adversary answered Jahvé and
10 said: doth then Job fear God for nothing? surely Thou hast
set a fence around him and around his house and around all
that he hath, hast blessed the work of his hands, and his
11 herds spread abroad in the land; but only stretch forth Thine
hand and touch all that he hath, verily to Thy face he will

i. 6—12. היום as a transitional form, in cases where an event of a single day, occurring in a space of time formerly mentioned, is intended to be referred to, means *the day* = the time, then, or *on the day*. *Sons of God* is an ancient name for the celestial beings subordinate to God, Gen. vi. 2, particularly used when they are described as occupied in heaven (as in this passage, xxxviii. 7 and Ps. xxix), whilst when they are employed on the earth they are called angels. Like the magnates of an earthly realm before their king, they must *present themselves* at certain fixed times before Jahvé, in order to hear His inquiries and commands. If in the answer of Satan, ver. 7, the emphasis is laid on the word *earth*, an antithesis to other worlds might be found in it, as if he also ranged through the moon also, *e.g.*; but this would be quite opposed to the ideas of the ancient world, and it is plain that the emphasis is simply on the fact that Satan does not now come back from some commission in particular, such as inflicting upon the earth some great calamity, but only from a general expedition into all quarters of the earth, in order to come upon something of a suspicious nature somewhere or other. שוט בְּ־ expresses merely a rapid ranging-through, התהלך בְּ־ the cautious and attentive movement in all directions, which is no less desirable; both words together are required to supply the complete idea of a rapid but at the same time observant journey through the earth in all directions; although either word alone would on an occasion suffice. Vv. 9, 10 said with great craft: No wonder that Job fears God, since God so carefully protects him; probably therefore he does not act from pure love, but only for the sake of his reward and advantage, in order to be thus protected in future. Evil spirits which everywhere presuppose nothing but mortal weakness always draw such inferences, and not without a certain justification as long as they have not been refuted by experience. *To thy face*, quite openly and boldly, not merely secretly in his heart, as ver. 5; comp. ii. 5; xiii. 15; xvi. 8; xxi. 31 with xxi. 14; xxii. 17.

12 bid Thee farewell! Then said Jahvé to the Adversary: see
thou hast all that is his; only upon him lay not thine hand!
13 And the Adversary went forth from Jahvé's presence.—And
it came to pass on the day whilst his sons and his daughters
were eating and drinking wine at the house of their first-born
14 brother, there came a messenger unto Job and said: the oxen
were ploughing and the she-asses were feeding at their side,
15 then the Sabeans invaded and took them, smiting the man-
servants at the edge of the sword; and I only escaped alone
16 to tell it to thee. While he was yet speaking, there came
another and said: Fire of God fell from heaven, set on fire
the sheep and the manservants and consumed them; and I

i. 13—19. As the valued outward possessions of Job consist, acc. vv. 2, 3, in children and four kinds of flocks and herds, together with the servants corresponding to them, the poet here suitably distributes everything in such a way, that at first three calamitous blows carry off all his flocks and herds together with his servants, the she-asses being easily connected with the oxen, ver. 14, while then there is added to these three, as the fourth and most painful calamity, the loss of all his children at once. Further, inasmuch as for these four calamitous blows four different visible causes and instruments must be put forward, the poet again interweaves the four cases so appropriately that he derives the first and third from human, the second and fourth from celestial causes. In the first pair of cases he makes the men act as robbers, and in the first instance, ver. 15, the Sabeans, the marauding part of that northwestern Arabian tribe, the other part of which was engaged in trade (vi. 19, comp. Gen. x. 7, 28; xxv. 3), who made their attack from the south; and then, ver. 17, the still more warlike Chaldeans, who fought in a more orderly fashion, from the northeast, whose mention here seems to disclose a writer belonging to the first half of the seventh century; when the Chaldeans became once more powerful and soon after founded a new dominion in Babylon by Nabopolassar (see *History of Israel* IV. p. 254 sq. (III. p. 778 sq.); of causes from the higher regions, from the welkin, the poet brings forward first, ver. 16, a fire of God, or a sudden sultriness and burning heat, which may in a moment, as by a divine blow, slay large masses of animals and men, whether it be a shower of brimstone or the Simoom (the poet makes his picture simply after ancient legends, not according to his own personal observation, comp. Ps. xi. 6; Num. xi. 1—3; xvi. 35; 2 Kings i. 10 sq., also Lev. x. 2 compared with ix. 24); then ver. 19, he brings forward a mighty wind coming from the immense Arabian desert, which can easily overthrow a lightly-built house on the fringe of the desert, comp. Matt. vii. 27, Wellsted's *Reise zur Stadt der Chalifen* p. 211 sq. But in one respect all four calamities must again be alike, that they destroy everything completely in one day, so that from each set of victims only a

17 only escaped alone to tell it to thee. While he was yet
speaking, there came another and said: The Chaldeans ap-
pointed three bands, rushed upon the camels and took them,
smiting the manservants at the edge of the sword, and I only
18 escaped alone to tell it to thee. While he was yet speaking
there came another and said: Thy sons and daughters were
eating and drinking wine in the house of their first-born
19 brother, and behold a great wind came from beyond the
desert and touched the four corners of the house, so that it
fell upon the children and they died; and I only escaped
20 alone to tell it to thee.—Then Job arose, rent his garment
21 and shaved his head, fell down and worshipped; and said:

Naked went I forth from my mother's womb,
and naked I return thither:
Jahvé gave and Jahvé took away;
let Jahvé's name be blessed!

22 In all this Job sinned not and gave to God no offence.

single messenger of evil escapes, and Job is meant to be overwhelmed with surprise and driven to despair by the calamitous tidings which always close with the same terrible refrain. That also increases the surprise, that all this happens during the first day of a festive meeting of his children, ver. 13, accordingly before his children could as he thought need atonement for their sins, vv. 4, 5; and with that the poet then found at the same time a good opportunity to describe the destruction of his children all at once, ver. 19. A certain uniformity in the four repetitions produces a good effect in the description; hence probably עֹד (Gen. viii. 22) must be read ver. 18, as in the other instances, instead of עַד, which shorter word however may also possibly indicate duration, at all events its use is very similar viii. 21; Neh. vii. 3, comp. § 217 *e*. *At the edge of the sword*, or *according to the sharpness of the sword*, vv. 15, 17, is an ancient form of expression for to slay murderously after the usages of war. To attack *in three bands*, or companies, ver. 17, is an ancient war stratagem, in order quickly to surround and overpower the enemy, Gen. xiv. 15; Judg. vii. 16, comp. 1 Sam. xi. 11. *From beyond the desert*, v. 19, therefore blowing from the most remote end of the desert over its entire face with increasing violence.—i. 20—22. The customary signs of mourning are immediately followed by higher reflection and the resignation of all these possessions as merely outward and dispensable, which are to be received with thankfulness to God and to be resigned without murmuring against Him. *Thither*, into the mother's womb, but in this case, of course, into the general and the last womb, mother-earth, comp. my note on Ps. cxxxix. 13—15; repeated almost verbally

ii. 1 And it came to pass on the day, that the sons of God came
to present themselves before Jahvé, and there came also the
Adversary in their midst to present himself before Jahvé.
2 Then said Jahvé to the Adversary: From whence comest thou!
and the Adversary answered Jahvé and said: From ranging
3 through the earth and from going about through it. Then
said Jahvé to the Adversary: Hast thou set thine attention
upon my servant Job? for there is not like him on the earth
a man perfect and upright, godfearing and departing from evil;
and still he is holding fast to his integrity, and nevertheless
thou hast misled me against him to destroy him without cause!
4 And the Adversary answered Jahvé and said: Skin for skin;
5 and all that a man hath giveth he for his life: but only
stretch out Thine hand and touch his bone and his flesh:
6 verily, to Thy face will he say to Thee farewell! Then Jahvé
said to the Adversary: see thou hast him; but save his life!—

after this passage Ecc. v. 14. תִּפְלָה is properly what has a bad smell, or a bad taste, comp. vi. 6, hence disgust and the object or cause of it, offence, xxiv. 12: till then Jahvé had found in Job a sweet smell, a delight, and neither now did this cease, since Job thus far did nothing bad to destroy it; comp. similarly באש Ex. v. 21; 1 Sam. xxvii. 12; 2 Sam. x. 6; xvi. 21.

ii. 1—6. Jahvé's language, ver. 3, is touchingly compassionate, as if it already repented Him almost thus to have destroyed, *i.e.*, reduced to the most lamentable condition, the hero without any fault of his *(without cause)*. But Satan is not the kind of being to permit himself to be moved by pity to anything good: in his cunning he knows how once more to cast suspicion on Job, representing his steadfastness as a thing not to be surprised at, inasmuch as he still has in his physical health a possession which is equal to all outward gifts of fortune and for the sake of which he would gladly resign the latter; but if this last, chief good also should be taken from him so that he had every moment to dread death, he would certainly lose his patience. „*Skin for skin*" is a proverb which does not occur elsewhere in the Bible, the meaning of which however, as one skin is as much like another as one dead piece is to another, appears on the surface, and is in this connexion sufficiently clear: like for like, the one for the other. It is simply an exchange which Job seems to have made: for as at the time of misery he was obliged to fear that he should lose all his possessions, that one thing has remained to him which alone outweighs all the rest, which the loss of the rest has first taught him to prize so highly that he feels himself fortunate to be able to enjoy this one all the more. Therefore the trial has only been partial, and now is the time when, if directed against the one highest and last possession, it can attain its purpose.—That in

7 And the Adversary withdrew from Jahve's presence and smote
8 Job with an evil boil from his foot-sole unto his crown; and
he took him a potsherd to scrape himself there with, sitting
9 in the midst of the ashes.—Then said to him his wife: Dost
thou still hold fast to thine integrity? Bid God farewell
10 and die! But he said to her: as one of the foolish women
speaketh speakest thou; the good too we receive from God
and the evil shall we not receive? In all this Job sinned
not with his lips.

the midst of his profoundest mourning he must scrape his skin, ii. 7, 8, shows that the poison had worked only too effectually.—The woman appears, ii. 9—10, as elsewhere in the O. T., as the more easily seduced half. But she is already so faint-hearted that she scornfully reproaches Job with his patience and faithfulness. For nothing can be more scornful than the words: Thou who under all the undeserved sufferings which have been inflicted upon thee by thy God hast been faithful to Him, even in fatal sickness, as if He would help or desired to help thee who art beyond help,—to thee, fool, I say: *Bid God farewell* (who will not deliver thee from death as thou believest)—*and die!* nothing else remains for thee now than, compelled by death, to say farewell to God, whom thou art so slow to let go, and at the same time to the upper-world! if thou hadst been wise sooner, thou wouldst not have put vain hope in God. But Job only advises her not to speak as *one of the foolish women, i.e.*, the heathen women who live in ignorance of divine things and represent folly itself in misconceiving the true God, in that heathen can depart from one God whose powerlessness they have perceived to another, but not the person who has known the true God. *Also* the good we accept if He send it, although perhaps we did not deserve it; and not the reverse, without which even that premised case could not exist, the evil? גם is correlative. The more Aramaic verb קִבֵּל does not occur elsewhere in this book, although in other respects the language of the prose pieces, as has been partially shown, has the greatest similarity with that of those in verse; it occurs here for the first time in prose, although it may not be inferred from that fact alone that the book is of a very late origin, since it is found as early as Prov. xix. 20.

3. Arrival of the friends and the first outbreak of bitter complaint, ch. ii. 11—iii.

If Job hitherto, in the accustomed relations of his house and in his consciousness of being master of them, did not sin against God even in word, much less in deed, as the narrator twice so significantly remarks with reference to future complications, i. 22; ii. 10, he now falls into the danger of this from a quarter from which he least expected it. Three friends come of their own accord to bestow compassion and comfort on the sufferer; and greatly shocked at the first sight of the calamity which they found unexpectedly severe, they mourn with him the customary earlier part of the period of a visit, doing honour by profound silence to his vast grief. In the presence of such sympathetic friends, the wounded heart is opened and gives vent without suspicion to all its bitterness and doubts, really only in order all the more deeply to call forth the comfort after the balsam of which it thirsts. When accordingly the time of the solemn silent visit is past and the matter can be approached more closely, Job is at last overcome by the force of the loud lamentation and breaks out almost against his will into words which only permit the one aspect of his inmost feelings, the dark aspect, to be divined, while he is all the time seeking comfort and light. But therein he takes the first insufficiently considered, dangerous step, which can draw after it serious and bitter consequences. First, because he presupposes in the case of his friends an insight and disposition such as they probably do not possess, so that his hope to get in this way comfort from thence is frustrated. Secondly, because with the partial, one-sided conception and expression of his trouble and perplexity, he for the first time gives up perfect self-control and sober reflection, and ventures out into an unknown, stormy sea, where he may easily, from simple despair of life and a faint complaint at the fortunes of an afflicted man, in the end be carried so far as to reject the divine truths and God Himself. He puts himself into the power of despair, which is human and so pardonable, but none the less dangerous.—For when the long repressed pain is able at last to break out freely, it will pour itself forth all the more vehemently and unsparingly; and precisely there where the agonising restraint was first broken, will the ultimate outburst be the more terrible. Thus in this speech also, in which the whole accumulated despondency of Job finds for the first time free course, the despair of life only gradually subsides from the utmost vehemence to greater repose, until at length, still with its mystery unrelieved but with its force exhausted, it gives way to grief and his agitation finds an end again in groans. At first, therefore, the accumulated burden of his despair, which can hardly explain its own cause, rushes forth in the mad execration of the day of his birth, iii. 3—10; next, since after all actual birth cannot be undone, his despondency, growing gradually calmer, changes into the desire at least to have died immediately after birth and into the seductive reflection, how pleasant rest would be to the miserable sufferer in that place which is the end of all pride and all disquiet of the guilty and the innocent alike vv. 11—19; finally, inasmuch as this wish is also vain and there remains nothing but the actual burden of unalterable wretchedness, the speech leaves that description of the rest of death, in the attractive picture of which the poor sufferer's imagination revelled in vain, and, becoming somewhat more vehement again, turns to the closing question, for what purpose then, if it must inevitably be accepted, was life given by God to the suffering, who desire nothing more intensely than death, and for what purpose particularly was it given to Job, who suffers he knows not why, can find no rest, and constantly fears and meets with fresh calamities? with which complaints the speech mournfully concludes, vv. 20—26. Towards the end the agitation which had subsided in the middle again increases, but in such a way that, with the growing reflection upon the true, unalterable condition of misery, the languishing complaint gets the upper hand and the boundless despair, which storms at the commencement, only issues in dull groans, remaining without light or relief; for it is in the end explanation and comfort which the complaining sufferer alone seeks to draw from his friends. His despondency is also as yet confined to the misery which he has himself experienced: at the end vv. 20—22, there is scarcely a glance at more general human misery, previously introduced by vv. 18, 19; and as if the despair as yet shrunk from bringing God within the range of its complaints, it is only at the end ver. 20, that it barely ventures to hint that He himself is the cause of the misery. Thus timidly does the despair make its first appearance: it scarcely permits us to divine how much it conceals within its abysses; it still has a dread of its own dark consequences, and nevertheless presents a sufficiently dangerous first appearance which is really more dangerous than the reality.

11 Then the three friends of Job heard all this evil which had
come upon him, and they came each one from his place,
Eliphaz the Temanite and Bildad the Shuhite and Zophar the
Naamathite; and they agreed together to go to compassionate
12 and to comfort him. And lifting up their eyes from afar but not
knowing him, they lifted up their voice and wept, rent every
one his garment and strewed dust upon their heads towards
heaven; and they sat down with him on the earth seven days
and seven nights, whilst none spake to him a word, because
iii. 1 they saw that his grief was very great. After this Job opened
his mouth and cursed his day; so that Job answered and
said:

ii. 11—iii. 2. After receiving the tidings, they first go to seek each other, probably following the action of Eliphaz, and then agree to visit him in company. On their arrival they see him, it is true, in the distance, because as a matter of course and as the LXX add in explanation at ver. 8, he was carried as a leper from the house into the open air, Lev. xiii. 46: but they do not recognise him, because his appearance had been so completely changed; hence the first violent expression of the first vehement mourning, ver. 12. But good manners required then, in the first instance, that they should sit mourning in silence the first week of their visit by the side of the mourner, because according to ancient custom the friend that came on a visit from a distance had first to make himself perfectly familiar with the family, rejoicing or mourning with it for a week, Gen. xxix. 14; Ezek. iii. 15. In all this therefore the friends acted quite irreproachably. עָנָה iii. 2, *to reply*, generally to speak upon any definite solicitation, ἀποκριθείς, Matth. xi. 25.

Let the day perish on which I came to be,
  The night which said: a boy is born!
Let that day be darkness:
  let not God seek it from above,
    nor a ray beam upon it;
let darkness and gloom redeem it,
  let cloud encamp over it,
    let terrors of a day scare it!
That night—dimness take it hence!
  let it not rejoice among the days of the year,
    come not into the number of the moons!
Yes, that night let it be unfruitful,
  come into it no rejoicing;
let them ban it the day-cursers,
  those that are skilled to stir up the dragon!

1. vv. 3—10. The whole day, the νυχθήμερον, or the light day in particular and still more the night following, as the real time of his birth (for this the poet could suppose without difficulty), is the object of the curse, day and night being at first thus named together, ver. 3, then in the detailed description the day is cursed vv. 4—5, and with twofold vehemence the night, vv. 6, 7—9: for the agitation the cause of such a horrible curse cannot be somewhat more plainly mentioned until the end, ver. 10. The indignation desires to have the day wholly annihilated, ver. 3; yet inasmuch as it nevertheless returns annually as a birth-day, the indignation, explaining itself more fully, demands only a total darkening of it, so that to that intent it appears wholly to perish and is marked as a black unlucky day and goes by dreaded, empty, desolate and joyless, as though it were not *(dies ater, nefastus)* [1]; let also the night be barren and without the joy of birth, lest another should again be made by it as unfortunate as Job, ver. 7 (comp. vv. 3, 10): even the enchanters shall make that night a disastrous, black unfruitful one, ver. 8, in accordance with the use of such magic spells met with elsewhere, Num. xxii—xxiv. However, the blackest darkness, which is the chief thing in the detailed description, cannot be painted strongly enough: while the special cursing of the day keeps to the darkness, vv. 4, 5, the longer curse of the night passes in the middle of it to other thoughts, while it begins and ends with the idea of darkness, vv. 6, 9; and as from the very commencement the first ray of dawn shall be wanting to

---

[1] It is well known that the Romans had this superstition in a strong degree: and a direct consequence of it is the custom, which is still, or was till quite recently, found in Madagascar, *e.g.*, of killing at once children born on certain unlucky days of the year.

dark be the stars of its twilight
  let it wait for light—in vain,
    let it not behold the eyelids of the dawn:—
10 —because it shut not the doors of my belly
  and hid not trouble from mine eyes!

Why died I not from the womb
  had I escaped from the belly—and departed?
wherefore hastened the knees to meet me,
  and why breasts, that I should suck?
For then should I, having sunk down, be at rest,
having fallen asleep, then were there rest for me—

the day, as if God did not concern Himself at all in His bright elevation about it and let it perish in unpitied gloom, ver. 4, so at last the black, starless night shall wander for ever without being enlightened by morning stars or scattered by morning-dawn, ver. 9: on the contrary, darkness shall take possession of day and night as their property, vv. 5 *a*, 6 *a*, the darkest most fatal clouds and other horrors (*e.g.*, eclipses of the sun) that can ever terrify a day, shall overtake it, ver. 5 *b. c.* The unusual word כמרירי, ver. 5, the first letter of which Massorites and ancient translators mistook for a preposition, must be pointed as a substantive of colour כַּמְרִירֵי § 157 *a*: כמר, Heb. and Aram. denotes not only *to scorch*, but also to *burn*, *to get black*, كمد (ד = ل = ר) as well as جمر being related. When the execrators of the day, ver. 8, are described as possessing the daring and skill to arouse even the dragon, this additional clause must have a meaning which accords with the chief clause; and since לויתן occurs always (except xl. 25, as will there appear) in a mythological sense, we are thereby induced to suppose, that we have here a myth similar to the Hindoo myth of the Râhu, according to which the eclipse of the sun and of the moon comes from a dragon which has coiled round them, which therefore magicians are able to rouse or again ban and drive away.—It appears from the case itself and from the transition to vv. 11 sq., that the night is here always not that of the conception but of the birth; and the immediate addition of *a boy* of itself proves that הֹרָה is in poetry the same as נוֹלַד.

2. If he must then be born, wherefore did he not die immediately after his birth, but was born alive and received and preserved with affection vv. 11, 12. For had he died at once, he would now have rest at the hand of death, no less than the mighty ones of the earth who were once so rich and proud, whom nevertheless all the laboriously gained marks of their pride and splendour now profit nothing; or rather, since after all he desired not to have been brought up but to have been at first born dead, he would now be as those abortions which come not at all to the light of day, but are forthwith sent down into the darkness, vv. 13—16; it is only in the lower-world that all toil

with kings and councillors of the earth,
who built for themselves Pyramids,
15 or also with princes, rich in gold,
who filled their houses with silver;
or, as a hidden abortion I should not be,
like children who have never seen the light.
There the wicked cease from raging,
and there rest those exhausted of strength;
altogether the prisoners cease from toil,
never hearing the voice of the slave-driver:
small and great is there the same,
the slave free from his lord.

and torture cease, both in the case of the violent and slave-holders who torture others on the earth, and of those who are tortured (to whom Job belongs), vv. 17—19. The longing for death which springs from weariness of life, which can here be expressed at length in the speech as it gets gradually calmer, and the attractive picture of the rest of the underworld, coincide here in an unusual way and form in combination the most melancholy conception of terrestrial things: those which are on the earth most widely separated, the proud mighty ones, who seek in vain to cling fast to the earth by splendid buildings and treasures, and such despairing wretches as Job are there equal; and in the end those who torment others and the greater host (יַחַד ver. 18) of all classes of tormented ones, there find rest together. It is as if the tormented Job himself found alleviation in contemplating this picture and pursued it with eager pleasure. As now the end of this middle strophe is connected with the third by the mention of the tortured, so the beginning, ver. 11, starts directly from the end of the first, ver. 10, in that the most impossible thing of all is given up—the not having been born—and the question is put, why then did not death follow immediately on birth, *e.g.*, by miscarriage (ver. 16), but father and mother, or nurse, met him with protection and nourishment: for the knees, ver. 12, can in this connexion only be those of the father to whom the child is first presented to be acknowledged. As regards עַתָּה, ver. 13, *now*, if the case were as has been said, accordingly = then, comp. viii. 6; xiii. 19 with xi. 15. The word חרבות ver. 14, was explained by ancient translators as חֲרָבוֹת *swords*, by the Massorites apparently more passably as חָרְבָ֫ *ruins;* but neither explanation meets the case: *to build ruins* would mean to restore ruined places, which would not be suitable here, the ironical explanation to build erections which would after all become ruins again at last, is not suggested either in the words or in the sense of the passage, since here it is only the splendour, that is to no purpose in the underworld, which must be described, a splendour which the powerful in possessions of the earth get with much toil, and which they may really possess in this life, only that death forcibly separates them from it, so that in the end it is useless to them, comp. ver. 15. There is therefore not much room to doubt that the word is not Hebrew and is derived from the

20 Wherefore giveth He to the sufferer light,
life to the bitterly troubled,
who wait for death—in vain,
search for it more than for treasures,
who rejoice unto exaltation,
leap that they find a grave?—
to that man whose way is hid,
who is hedged round about by God?
Surely for my daily bread cometh my sighing,
and as water flowed my complaints:
25 for before somewhat I trembled—forthwith it overtook me,
and that which I dreaded, it cometh to me;
never have I rest, never quiet, never peace,
nevertheless raging cometh.

Egyptian word pyramid, *hyrama* (hyraba) having a softer first letter than pyrama, comp. هرام and de Sacy's *Abdollatif*, p. 292 sq.; אַרְמוֹן, on the other hand, a word which does not occur in the Book of Job, appears to have an entirely different origin, see *History of Israel* II. p. 6 (II. p. 4), III. p. 486 (IV. p. 36). Vv. 17—19 is pervaded by the antithesis of the tormentors and the tormented in such a way that the first alone are described ver. 17 *a*, and then the latter separately ver. 17 *b*, ver. 18 *a*, and finally both together ver. 18 *b* and ver. 19, but in general and particularly towards the end the tormented and their happiness is made more prominent. Everything is thus explained reciprocally, especially the raging of the powerful wicked ones, ver. 17 *a*, by ver. 18 *b*; it is true that the torture with which they in their lawless raging torment others, ceases again for themselves to be a toil only in death: only the antithesis in this place requires us primarily to think of the tormenting aspect of this raging as it afflicts the vast number of miserable victims. It is otherwise with the raging, ver. 26, which comes upon the unfortunate sufferer against his will, not originating in his will, like that of the wicked. With regard to הוּא, ver. 19 *a*, comp. § 314 *b* and *Jahrbb. der Bibl. Wiss.* III. p. 221.

3. Vv. 20—26. The last strophe reverts to the question why life is given to the suffering, who prefer to search for death as for hidden treasures (vv. 22 *b*, comp. ver. 15; death like treasures coming from the bosom of the earth, Pluto god of both), and who finding a grave are filled with exultation: the question here repeated is confined to Job, who is so involved in calamity that he cannot see his way, ver. 23 (comp. xix. 8), to whom sighs and tears are instead of eating and drinking, ver. 24 (comp. Pss. xlii. 4; lxxx. 6), because he is in constant dread of fresh calamity, vv. 25, 26. On לִפְנֵי *for, instead of,* = *like*, see § 217 *b*, *History of Israel* IV. 27 (III. 472).—Comp. with vv. 3—9 Abulf. *Ann. Mosl.* tom. I. p. 236 not. ad tom. I. p. 131, tom. III. p. 758, tom. IV. p. 560, Schol. Hariri p. 310, *Dschami's Jusuf und Suleika* p. 137, Rosenzweig's edition.

II. SECOND STAGE OF THE DRAMA.

FIRST ADVANCE IN THE CONTENTION.

CH. IV—XIV.

But the friends do not comprehend these sighs after consolation, still less the apparently disconsolate despondency and the rising storm of despair. On the contrary, as they from the beginning presuppose in their hearts that Job is not innocent, this open expression of his complaint, which in a subdued form is already directed against God even, is to them plain witness against him and his guilt. They therefore begin their well-meant warnings, and in this first advance of the contention, where they have the full advantage, they proceed boldly and rapidly in the declaration of their three principles, driven to it the more by the to them incomprehensible resistance of Job. Eliphaz seeks to show him, that neither he nor any man may speak against God; Bildad already insists more pointedly upon the divine righteousness in opposition to him; Zophar finally, thus early desiring openly the judgment of God, lets drop with little concealment his conviction, that Job suffers much less than his sins deserve: yet herein they all agree, notwithstanding this increasing warmth of feeling and severity of language, that they still cherish the best hopes of Job's deliverance, as soon as ever he exhibits sorrow and repentance instead of such inconsiderate, godless speeches. Therefore they all conclude their speeches with the most attractive pictures of the salvation which was still certainly to be expected on repentance. Thus at the end they sweeten the serious and bitter exhortations which they believe it their duty to make, in order to entice their friend by flattering and consoling pictures also to that acknowledgment of guilt which they desire:

this position, first taken up by Eliphaz, is maintained faithfully by both those who follow him.

Yet such an ingredient of moderation, which is easy to the fortunate friends, is much more difficult for Job. He has been painfully deceived in his hopes of his friends; and, moreover, constrained by their opposition to hold fast and defend the despair into whose power he has now once surrendered himself. Thus the danger which he had summoned up in his former speech, now first bursts upon him with overwhelming force. A vast region of sore confusion, doubt, despair, and unbelief opens up before him. Will he not wholly lose himself in that dark, unknown land? It is true he succeeds in preserving at the beginning a degree of composure which must astonish us in his situation. As if himself foreseeing that the contest provoked might have the worst consequences through heat and bitterness on both sides (vi. 28—30), and moreover neither being in a mood nor deeming it necessary to defend expressly his innocence, he is satisfied at first with simply showing the necessity of his complaint and pointing out the cruelty of his friends (vi. 2—30). When he is a second time and more sharply attacked, he constrains himself again not quite to attack the friends, though he seeks to measure himself with them; and as he considers the divine righteousness which they magnify, he is profoundly moved and at last incapable of being terrified by the terrors which they depict (ix. 2—x. 2). But when the youngest of the friends, making almost too dashing an onslaught, not only lets fall an unveiled reference to Job's sins, but also desires thus early an appearance of God and His judgment, he then at last, unable longer to endure such growingly unfeeling attacks, himself assumes the offensive. He confidently measures himself with them, wresting from them, in the exultant consciousness of his integrity, their appeal to God's judgment, and using it with overwhelming force to his own advantage. Indeed, he now challenges and vehemently desires the divine judgment, even much more boldly than they, xii. 2—xiii. 22.

And because the friends say nothing which could really ameliorate or put an end to the complaint and the despair to which he had given utterance before this contention, he again at the end of his speeches, as the power of his despair is still so unbroken and only increases by the confusion of the contention, falls back into it again and again, and so makes wider and deeper the abyss of sorrow and depression the more the friends seek to cover it up by the wrong means. The end of his speeches is therefore generally still more than the other parts of them the exact opposite of the notions of the friends. Whilst they endeavour to close each speech with joyous prospects, his discourse issues again and again in a gloomy elegy which stirs to indignation, and closes with the prospect of certain death. Thus both parties involuntarily get farther and farther from each other, even before the attack which Job at last makes, in the third reply, completely annihilates this first position of the friends.

Accordingly this first advance in the contention serves to bring out all the turbid and the transparent parts, all the powers and truths of this contention, in order to lead them all, against the will of the contending parties and yet necessarily, to successive higher stages of development. It is true that both parties at the commencement of their contention still see more clearly than they do subsequently in the climax of its confusion; as, indeed, both parties open the contention without any evil intention. The friends anticipate at the beginning, that the issue of the matter will be glorious through the mercy of God, as they have hitherto heard nothing but good of Job, and cannot, therefore, as long as they look at everything with moderation and without prejudice, properly presuppose a very serious, mortal offence, v. 8, 17—26; viii. 7, 21, comp. iv. 3, 4. And Job quite properly anticipates that he shall stand as innocent before God and put the friends to shame, xiii. 7—17, comp. vi. 10 *c*. The true anticipations of both sides are confirmed by the result, xlii. 7—9, 12: whereby the poet obtains a fine opportunity to permit an inkling of the issue of the whole drama to appear remotely at the very commencement, and to connect more closely all the scattered threads of his extended fabric just where they tend to separate. But this partial clearness on both sides at the beginning is soon dimmed by the much stronger tormenting obscurities, is soon overcome by the rising passions. The absence of the higher truth brings both into constantly increasing misunderstandings and perplexity, which at last become so great that the contention cannot be further continued in this way and in this position of the friends. The evil consequences for Job are in the end as follows: in the first instance, increased provocation of the friends who are openly attacked, and in their first position damaged and beaten; more remotely and more seriously, the degree of actual temerity by which he suffered himself to be overtaken, in that, after he had already, ch. ix., held a perilous soliloquy regarding the divine righteousness, he at length, ch. xiii., boldly, and almost presuming upon his imagined right, challenges God to judgment, by which he acts against his better feeling and commits an offence against the divine majesty. It is true that he now reaps the unexpected advantage, that he ameliorates his own melancholy depression by the outpouring of his complaint and brings forth his gloomy ideas in order that they may appear in their true light, but especially that he is compelled more and more to call to mind the forgotten treasure of his integrity and is by force thereby driven to a hope which cannot be lost, whilst ch. iii. he did not as yet at all call it to mind, vi. 10*c*; vii. 20, 21; ix. 15—22, 30—35; x. 7; xii. 4; xiii. 3—23. However, even this solitary support to which Job can cling, by the aid of which he remains even unconsciously strong, is at last greatly weakened thereby, that when he for the first time grasps fully and warmly the thought of his integrity he is at the same time, in consequence of the remaining darkness which still enfolds him, carried away by the thought itself so as almost defiantly to challenge God to judgment, ch. xiii. So that at last, with a dim recollection that after all God will not appear on such a challenge, he is overtaken by unutterable despair; and for the first time, letting go all present and temporal things, he is surprised by the thought of a desirable deliverance that may be possible for him even after death, xiv. 13—15. With the last thought the prospect of a wholly new consideration is opened, the consideration of the immortality of the soul and its certainty, the addition of which to the consciousness of integrity is the only way by which true patience can be prepared for and the final victory obtained.

1. ELIPHAZ AND JOB.

a. ELIPHAZ. CH. IV., V.

In the sense above explained Eliphaz here first undertakes to correct Job according to his best notions. He is, it is true, already fully convinced of Job's guilt, and speaks to him as a teacher with superior assurance, like a friend of acknowledged large experience, as to one who is in error. Still, he speaks, particularly at the beginning and at the close with great caution and forethought, in order to say what is necessary with as much tenderness and consideration as possible. This first speech, therefore, embraces many and various points, quietly exhausts its matter, and is arranged with unusual art. It is so put that the zeal of the cautions man of years to quench at the very beginning the kindling fire of defiance of God and to show the necessity of repentance, by a kindly yet serious and severe treatment, is perceivable. In that the most earnest admonitions are reserved for the middle of the discourse, the first part of it leads up to them with superior tact: with a tentative and gentle touch, it compares cautiously Job's former conduct with his present state of mind, and as it were repels the unfavourable suspicion which the comparison suggests while permitting it nevertheless to appear; it appeals to Job's own knowledge, until insensibly the speaker's boldness grows, and at last when he has become vehement, like a storm which has grown out of a gentle wind, he thunders forth the truth, that according to his experience it is only the wicked that irremediably perish as overtaken by God's wrath, iv. 2—11. The full weight of the earnest revelation and higher insight, which the speaker presents as his principle in opposition to Job, having been thus prepared for, comes iv. 12—v. 7, the principle, that weak man, as impure before God and therefore destined to suffer, ought on no account, unless he will involve himself in the most grievous sin and punishment, to get angry with God. And after Job has been severely chastised by the application of this principle, though in a veiled and cautious manner, Eliphaz finally in the third part, v. 8—27, makes the transition to a gentle, kindly conclusion, hoping from the divine grace and miraculous deliverance the best for Job, who has been chastised by God for his good, who may be delivered by Him from all evils so as yet to find the happiest end. The more bitter the medicine of the middle of the speech was, the sweeter and more pleasant is the effect which this conclusion, with its promises of possible deliverance, endeavours to produce; however, not so as wholly to conceal the most serious admonitions which form its basis.

iv. 1 Then answered Eliphaz of Tæman and spake:

1.

Will it vex thee should one venture a word to thee?
yet to restrain speech who is able!

1. iv. 2—11, in two strophes. In these strophes the growing assurance of the speaker must be noted, increasing from the most gentle manner as he at first makes his appearance until it becomes at the end the boldest and most outspoken utterance, beginning as the soft breathing of the wind and ending as an overwhelming tempest; the intermediate stages are very skilfully arranged. At first the most diffident commencement, undertaken at the call of duty, ver. 2; then the surprised comparison of the previous endeavour of Job to comfort all the despairing with his present inconsolability when his turn comes; with which

Surely thou hast put many right,
  and slack hands thou wast wont to strengthen,
the stumbling thy words upheld,
  and bowing knees didst thou confirm:
5 now that it cometh indeed unto thee—and it vexeth thee,
  it reacheth unto thee, and thou art dismayed?
is not thy religion thy confidence,
  thy hope—the integrity of thy ways?—

Remember now, who ever being innocent perished?
  and where have the upright been destroyed?
as far as I have seen, they who plough iniquity
  and sow disaster, reap the same;
at the breath of God they vanish,
  at the storm of His wrath they pass away:
10 the lion's roar and the growler's voice
  and the teeth of the young lions—are struck out;
the old lion perisheth without prey,
  while the grown-cubs of the lioness are scattered.

comparison the unhappy question can with difficulty be repressed, whether then religion (יִרְאָה, comp. xv. 4) and innocence (in case he possess it, as is to be desired) is not his confidence? vv. 3—6; finally, as the boldness of the speech has rapidly grown with this surprising question and its scarcely repressed expression of suspicion, the admonition to Job, to remember the ancient truth which has been forgotten only in the perplexity of the present moment, that righteous men were never destroyed (therefore neither has Job any thing to fear in case he is righteous), but on the contrary, at least according to the experience of Eliphaz, the guilty only suffer for their sin, vanishing without remedy before God's anger and losing all their previous rage, the sad picture of an old lion perishing miserably, deprived of his own vigour and even of his children's assistance, while his roaring and teeth lose their terror! vv. 7—11. Thus the discourse constantly grows most energetic when the certainty of the overthrow of the wicked is touched on, to set which in a terrible light is its object, in order thus to terrify Job at first, in case he also, as Eliphaz simply shrinks at present from openly saying, should in some way belong to the guilty. Ver. 2, נִסָּה is another orthography for נָשָׂא: but it is very remarkable that even after the weak הֲ of interrogation the clause with the perf. can be parenthetically inserted in such a way that the principal verb, to which the interrogation immediately belongs, does not follow before the end in the imperf., strictly: *whether*, supposing *a word to thee has been raised* (ventured) = if a word—*thou wilt take it amiss?* a construction which is somewhat easier with the stronger

2.

But unto mo a word stealeth,
  and mine ear caught a light sound thereof,
when visions of the night bring dream-thoughts
  when deep sleep is fallen upon men;
a terror had come over me and trembling,
  and thrilled with terror all my bones—
15 and before me a spirit presseth
  —the hairs of my body grow stiff
it standeth still—I discern not its appearance
  an image before mine eyes!
    a whispering voice I hear saying:

combination הֲלֹא, ver. 21, comp. iii. 11; and if the imperf. presupposes simple possibility, the perf. before it may insert parenthetically the action which must necessarily be conceived as having already taken place, which must have happened if the action of the imperf. should occur, iii. 13; xxiii. 3, 10, comp. § 357 *b* [1].—Ver. 5 כִּי denotes the surprised application: how strange that thou, when once thy turn comes, art too weak and exhausted! Ver. 6 the וְ in וְתֹם is the *vav conseq.*; because contrary to the customary order of the first member the predicate was placed first, the subject is thus more emphatically connected and is itself made more prominent: *thy hope*—with regard to it—*it* now, is it then not *thy innocence?* comp. similar uses of the וְ xv. 17; xxiii. 12; 2 Sam. xxii. 41. § 348 *a*. Vv. 10, 11 translate the hearer as by magic to the scene and moment when the old lion which has become superannuated and weak (perf. ver. 10), deprived of his voice, whose roar was so terrible, and of his young sharp teeth, now perishes in want, whilst his children also abandon him, scattering themselves and founding their own houses.

2. iv. 12—v. 7. As Eliphaz believes that he has obtained his superior insight even by means of an oracle (for as the ancient tradition, which must shortly be referred to, itself teaches, that which man cherishes latently and dimly in his heart, may in light and sound come to him from without, at certain moments taking more palpable and firmer shapes), he first prepares suitably

---

[1] In the "additions and emendations" which the author placed at the end of the second edition of his work, the following withdrawal of the interpretation given in the text occurs. "The similar case ver. 5 is in favour of this treatment of תלאה as the verb of the principal clause; and the word does not occur anywhere else. Sinco, however, according to v. 27 also, Eliphaz begins in the name of all his friends, it is after all better to take נסה simply as follows: '*shall we venture a word to thee quod aegre feras, which thou takest amiss?*'" Tr.

"Is man before God righteous,
or before his Maker a man pure?
Surely even in His servants He trusteth not,
in His messengers placeth error:
how then they who dwell in houses of clay,
whose foundation is in the dust,
who are destructible as the moth,

for the great importance of the oracle itself by a solemn description of the awful moment of its revelation. This is done in order to translate Job beforehand into the mood of extreme awe and expectation in which he himself had received and been deeply impressed by it, and in which Job must again hear and receive it, vv. 12—16. He then quotes the oracle itself, vv. 17—21, and draws from it inferences with regard to Job's situation, v. 1—7. The introductory historical delineation, vv. 12—16, is really executed with a master-hand for the production of the designed effect. It is meant to be a dream-oracle, because such oracles (*e.g.*, according to the Book of Genesis) were most frequent in the patriarchal age, and because the poet is unable here to give to Eliphaz a clear, luminous oracle from the highest God in broad daylight, such as he must reserve for the end of the book, xxxviii. 1 sq. For the truth which Eliphaz communicates is much less extensive and significant: to him steals in the night merely an individual spirit, although it may also reveal some true things. Nevertheless precisely the limited, mysterious, semiopaque nature of such an isolated, partial revelation possesses the greatest charm for the man that has not yet made the acquaintance of a higher one. Just as for Eliphaz the bit of truth of which he has been the recipient must have the highest importance, only that he, who has as yet so imperfectly penetrated the outward covering of the pure truth, is also very dependent on the covering and begins with the description of it. Accordingly he delineates with awe-struck recollection the picture of the profound repose of mysterious night, when the gentle celestial voice can make itself more audible to man as he has withdrawn within himself but has been aroused by dream-visions; how in that hour a spirit appeared to him, already at a distance making him tremble at its approach, then coming nearer with an increase of his awe, at last standing still as if it desired to speak (comp. 1 Sam. iii. 10), yet all along not directly recognisable, hovering before the eye of his mind like an image, until its gentle spirit-word is heard as if borne by sighing breezes. In this description everything is most effectively managed; particularly fine is the description of the impalpable form of the spirit, which is plainly noticed and yet again remains unknown, inasmuch as it is the characteristic of spirit that it makes itself felt, as if it had a fixed, palpable form and irresistible outward existence, while again it cannot be seized and grasped as a material body, but flees as soon as the attempt is made to sensibly lay hold of it, just as finally also it disappears again without leaving behind any outward sensible traces. And this most vivid picture is sketched

20 from morning to evening they can be beaten in pieces,
without intelligence they perish eternally,
their inward sinew is torn asunder,
yea! they die away at once—without understanding!"—

by the poet with a few grand strokes. For it is quite obvious that with vv. 12, 13, the same thing has already been briefly said that is then, vv. 14—16, further worked out; and שמץ, ver. 12, the soft, gentle word which came as by stealth (גְּנֹב) to Eliphaz, is explained ver. 16 by דְּמָמָה וָקוֹל: a *whispering*, as of the gentlest zephyr, a revelation of the subtle spirit, 1 Kings xix. 12, *and a voice*, at the same time audible, accordingly a subtle whispering spirit-voice. The word שמץ, difficult as regards its root, occurs here and xxvi. 14 only, and its meaning in both passages is evident from the context: it appears originally to signify a *whispering*, ψιθύρισμα Sym., with which שִׁמְצָה Ex. xxxii. 25, malicious joy ("Schadenfreude") derision, ἐπίχαρμα LXX, is very well associated as the secret whispered suggestion of the evil which is desired. To this corresponds شَمِتَ to feel a malicious joy in another's calamity, the primitive root seems to be therefore سَمْسَمَ to hasten, to be hasty, then شَمِصَ to speak hastily, with which a whispering is easily connected. But after the introduction ver. 12, the next verse, ver. 13, at first describes simply the mysterious working-time of the spirits: when wandering thoughts arising from night-visions, *i.e.*, when thoughts and imaginations become active through dream-visions in deeply sleeping man. In what more particular time Eliphaz received this oracle, whether some years, or only some days before, he leaves unmentioned as superfluous: for it is at the present moment as vividly before his mind as if he were just now hearing it, so that he begins in the present tense: *but unto me a word stealeth*, but in this uncertain state of mind I hear a decisive word, which must here be explained just as I have received it.—The real assertion of the oracle is made quite at the commencement, ver. 17, to the effect, that a man cannot on any account regard himself as more righteous and blameless than God, which he nevertheless does when, more openly or more secretly, he makes accusations against God: the rest, vv. 18—21, is simply a subsidiary proof of the main assertion based upon a comparison of the superior spirits and weak man. If the celestial servants (angels) do not appear as quite pure before God, so that He does not absolutely trust in them in His commissions to them, but presupposes error (תָּהֳלָה from תהל = שלה, Arab. ضَلَّ, also ثول) as possible in them, how much less (אַף, ver. 19, § 354 *c*) can weak, frail men appear as pure and deem themselves so, who inhabit earthen bodies like fragile houses of clay, having their roots in the dust itself as their foundation (Gen. ii. 7; iii. 19); who are therefore as easily even as the moth to be destroyed (ידכאום

v. 1 Call then! will any one answer thee?
and to which of the holy ones wilt thou turn?
but the fool resentment slayeth,
and the hasty indignation only killeth!
I myself saw a fool take root—
yet I cursed his pasture forthwith;
his sons are far from weal,
and put down in the gate, without a deliverer:

"which men crush, or can crush", are able to be crushed), those miserable creatures who are smitten to death (must die) from morning to evening, *i.e.*, often in the course of a single day (comp. Isa. xxxviii. 12. 13), in the morning alive and well, at evening a corpse ["morgen roth, am abend todt"], and as soon as the weak, hidden sinew, or the thread of life, is rent (ver. 21 *a*, vi. 9; xxvii. 8, comp. Ecc. xii. 6; Isa. xxxviii. 12), are immediately surprised by death—without wisdom, inasmuch as the mass of men are overtaken also by death in the same stupidity, unintelligence and folly in which they had lived. The last point serves almost involuntarily to give Job a strong reminder, as if the spirit led the speaker precisely to close the mournful description of proud man, who is yet so weak, in such a manner as would make it most suitable as an admonition to Job, to the effect, that he must see to it that he does not die like the multitude without wisdom. With emphasis, therefore, this thought is expressed twice at the end of the last two verses, מִבְּלִי מֵשִׂים "without any one giving heed", no one paying attention, is equivalent to וְלֹא בְּחָכְמָה, "and not with wisdom", without it; comp. further in explanation and confirmation xxxvi. 12; Prov. x. 21; v. 23. The last three verses, therefore, without a break all describe man, and in this case intentionally only from his weaker and lower side, which exclusively engages the attention of this speaker.—The inference from this oracle, v. 1—7, how infatuated it is for frail man to murmur against God, warmly passes, therefore, immediately with great boldness to an application to Job, though nevertheless soon cautiously resorting again to general truths and experiences and closing with calm earnestness. How infatuated, therefore, to complain against God, since the angels also, if Job should think of appealing to one of them, would with the consciousness of their position as regards the Highest One not receive a complaint of this kind; on the contrary, such murmuring and complaining as this, by which the fool simply wears himself out, is of so little use that it can only be regarded as a mark of a wrong state of mind, of a sin, and it can only be said, that discontent and heart-burning [*Groll und Eifern*] slay the unreflecting fool, vv. 1, 2. A fool may very well seem for a time prosperous and even firmly established, but without fail his desert overtakes him and his whole house: as Eliphaz formerly, when he made the acquaintance of such a man, was not deceived by his outward prosperity but immediately (פִּתְאֹם here as Num. xii. 4) foretold with abomination his final

5 he whose harvest the hungry eateth
  and taketh it even out of the thorns,
    after whose possessions the thirsty pant!

For there groweth not out of the dust disaster,
  and from the field there springeth not suffering:
but man is born to suffering,
  as the sparks fly up on high!

punishment, which has now come terribly enough, inasmuch as his sons, still suffering for their father, are unable to obtain any justice, since the men who were long oppressed by the father now, after the overthrow of this tyrant, rob and destroy, as in hunger and thirst, his and his sons' property, restrained by nothing, even should they have to get the corn, which had been vainly stored, from the midst of prickly thorns and thorn-fences (צַמִּים appears to be a sing. adj. from צם = צָמֵא, if צְמֵאִים = [צמאים § 73 *e*] is not rather to be read; the suff. ־ם in חילם refers directly to the sons, or the whole family, of the tyrant, comp. the contrary xxxi. 38 sq.). This example also, although Eliphaz had really met with this experience elsewhere, is so put that, like the corresponding former one, iv. 8—11, comp. xx. 10, it can have reference to Job, vv. 3—5.—For, considering the matter quite generally in conclusion, let not man proudly exalt himself nor deceive himself as to his own nature; since calamities together with their cause, sin and evil, do not originate *without* man, as herbs spring from the earth, so that man might be able to annihilate by his own will that which accidentally originated without, just as he could extirpate weeds in a garden; but, on the contrary, they spring up within himself and are most intimately connected with his entire nature, so that he is as necessarily born to bear suffering as it is the nature of sparks to fly upwards. In this way the speech returns in the assertion of the weak and humble nature of man to iv. 19—21, but in such a way that Job is plainly given to understand how greatly he sins against the order of the world and the proper nature of man when he murmurs and repines. The language is here undoubtedly very brief, yet the strophe is probably as the last intentionally abbreviated; and the brief addition of the comparison ver. 7 *b* by the simple *and*, which is elsewhere rare in this book, xii. 11; xiv. 19, comp. xxxiv. 3, is thereby explained [§ 340 *b*]. [1]

---

[1] In his last work *Gott und die Bibel*, Vol. II. p. 293 note, the author gives the following addition to v. 7. "According to all indications בְּנֵי רֶשֶׁף belong to the primitive and well-known mythological figures of the ancient world which a poet might use. After it has now been shown (comp. the *Göttingische Nachrichten* 1872, p. 572—586), that רֶשֶׁף or רֵשֶׁף existed as the Phœnician Apollo, the most suitable sense of these words seems to me to be, "But Sons of Phœbus fly too high and then fall all the lower", with an allusion to the reckless flight and corresponding lower fall of Phaethon and others of that kind." Tr.

3.

Nevertheless, I will turn unto God,
and upon the Highest set my expectation:
Who doeth great things, unsearchable,
and wonderful things, not to be counted;
10 Who giveth rain over all the earth
and sendeth water over all the pastures,
to raise the abased on high,
that the mourners may rise to weal;
Who breaketh the plots of the crafty
that their hands do nothing wise,
Who taketh the wise in their craftiness
so that the counsel of the artful is precipitous,
—in the day they grope in darkness,
as if it were night, they feel about at midday—:
15 so He rescueth the destroyed out of their mouth,
and out of the hand of the strong the helpless,
and hope cometh to the bowed-down,
wickedness shutteth her mouth.

3. But after Eliphaz has thus overthrown every earthly hope and all human pride, he rises all the more freely and eloquently to the higher necessity by resort to which man can overcome the lower physical one. That higher necessity is the divine power and mercy, which, as working marvellously but everywhere bringing forth that which is good, even chastises simply in order to bless. And as Eliphaz himself has hope from it for Job still, so he endeavours to inspire him with the same confidence. After he has, therefore, at first lauded it in general, as the divine grace and power which helps the bowed-down and is absolutely wonderful, vv. 8—16, he passes with a surprising effect to Job, who also is really only chastised by it in love, and by suffering himself, therefore, to be warned by divine chastisement and returning to the divine life (by repentance), may hope that having been constantly delivered from all dangers, he will yet enjoy the most prosperous and delightful life, vv. 17, 18—26. Eliphaz then leaves all this, as the well-considered judgment of the friends, to Job's most serious consideration, ver. 27. The praise of the divine work, vv. 9—16, is first established in general, ver. 9, then in detail from both the world, vv. 10, 11, and human life, vv. 12—16. But in connexion with human life it is not without a purpose mentioned, that all human craft and cunning are put to shame before the severity and the light of the divine management of affairs, and they who suppose themselves to be the most astute suddenly grope about helpless at midday as if it were dark: an example which Job with

Yea happy is the man whom God chasteneth:
  the correction of the Mighty One despise not!
For *He* woundeth and bindeth up,
  He smiteth and His hands heal.
In six straits He will deliver thee,
  in seven also evil will not touch thee:
20 in hunger He redeemeth thee from death,
  in war from the power of the sword;
when the tongue scourgeth thou art hidden,
  and fearest not desolation when it cometh,
at desolation and famine wilt thou laugh,
  at wild beasts fear thou not:
for with the stones of the field is thy covenant,
  the beasts of the field are at peace with thee.
So thou wilt find that thy tent is secure,
  and surveying thy pasture miss nothing,
25 and find that thy seed is numerous,
  and thy offshoots like the herbage of the earth;
thou wilt come to the grave with white hair,
  as a ripe shock is carried home in its season.—

his fancied wisdom will do well to lay to heart! But in both spheres, the world and human life, the divine activity, marvellous and perpetually new as it is, follows simply the object of alleviating calamity and delivering innocence from the persecutor (since the rain, *e.g.*, prepares fruitful crops for those in famine, the craftiness of the violent, which involves and destroys itself, must in the end always give way to the victory of innocence); so that the simple sufferer (who is neither quite innocent nor yet completely lost), whom the purifying, correcting, but not as yet the destroying, power of God touches, is rather to be pronounced happy, because precisely as warned thereby and casting off the evil, he may again be healed by Him who wounded, vv. 17, 18. Ver. 15 מָחֳרָב must undoubtedly be read instead of מֵחֶרֶב, which is here quite out of place; the former is a rare word which the Massorites did not understand: the figure is taken from the prey of wild beasts which a good shepherd rescues from them (1 Sam. xvii. 35). As "six" or "seven", ver. 19, is only a round number, precisely the same number of evils are not named vv. 20—23; instead of the pestilence, which is usually named as a fourth calamity with famine, war, and wild beasts (Rev. vi. 8), there appears here an evil which becomes very dangerous only in countries that have outgrown a simple state of things, namely, secret defamation, called here the scourging of the tongue, of which, however, there is much said in the Psalms and Proverbs. So far is thy condition from

Behold, *this* we have searched out: thus it is;
hear it, and thou—consider it for thyself!

being hopeless that then even the stones which render the field unfruitful, and still more easily, the wild animals which burrow in and turn it up, appear to be kept away as by a covenant of peace with them, that they may not hurt thee, comp. Hos. ii. 20. The word כֶּלַח, ver. 26, and xxx. 2, is what is overripe, shriveled up, dried, accordingly the most advanced age, to be compared with قلحم, قحل (and تَقَحَّم), قهل, كهل, Koran, Sur. iii. 41; v. 109, in Ethiopic ልቀ, comp. ኀልቀ, belongs to the same root; hence it is appropriately connected in a simile with the shock of overripe corn, which is carried to rest at the right season into the garner.—Strophes of considerable length, consisting of 9 verses each, are here quite obvious, as ver. 27 forms simply the conclusion; but between these two large strophes there is a single verse, ver. 17, at the rapid transition of the thought, such a verse not being infrequent in the book subsequently.

b. JOB. CH. vi., vii.

And what shall Job now say definitely in reply to this speech, the partly open and partly concealed meaning of which he at once plainly enough perceives and follows? Shall he at once defend himself against the accusations hinted at? But it is precisely the man who is conscious of being most free from such charges that makes least haste to vindicate his innocence; who indeed feels a deep repugnance against meddling with such unpleasant things, which he does not even altogether understand. Accordingly Job is still too conscious of his dignity and his moral elevation to expressly defend himself, or even in any way to take up the contention. Only incidentally there escapes him, with a certain emphasis, the recollection that he has never resisted God, vi. 10 *c*. On the other hand, in proportion as Job feels bitterly this unexpected conduct of the friends as the disappointment of his hope and as unfaithfulness towards himself, and in proportion as he feels that thereby the measure of his calamities has got full, do his pain and despondency rapidly grow. His despair, cruelly thrown back upon itself and compelled to justify itself to itself and the world just when it sought relief, recovers from the hard blow only to become, with new energy, all the more dark and gloomy. It is true that higher wisdom and reflection still occasionally flash through this assault of fresh despair. Having a presentiment that the storm of gloomy feeling may easily lead him to still more inconsiderate words (the only sin of which he is conscious, and of that only as the product of his suffering), he desires to keep down the contention while it is still only rising, modifying the few hard words of melancholy, which he is compelled to utter to shame the friends, by a kindness which condescends to requests and the expression of readiness to repent. But the despair, which is as unseemly as it is vainly resisted, has already become too powerful not to increase and be carried to greater lengths, although it may fear further steps. This anxious suspense, this wavering between reflection and the desire to return and repent, on the one hand, and an unmanageable, growing despondency, on the other, with the victory of the latter, constitutes the chief peculiarity of this speech, which in its position at the head of the planned conflict produces a decisive effect on all that follows. The overwhelming power of despair, to which Job succumbs although he resists it in the presentiment of its mournful consequences, obviously pervades the speech. And since the despair from which Job had started, ch. iii., must accordingly maintain first its own justification only against itself and the friends, in order to advance still further when it has retired into itself, the speech falls into three parts:—(1) the first look round after such a painful blow, as if the unrestrained utterance of complaint and repining, having met with opposition from without, must first be justified again to itself by recalling the tremendous calamities which no one could patiently bear, vi. 2—13; (2) the word to the friends themselves which could not be wholly avoided, mournful, beginning severely but at the same time beseechingly, not in order to refute or to defend, but simply seeking to avoid further contention of this kind, growing almost against the speaker's will somewhat bitter but immediately changing again to the tone in which it commenced; lastly, since what had to be said to others is finished, (3) a recurrence to the soliloquy of despair, or the undisturbed advance of it in its own territory, in that now particularly the toil and moil of weak, shortlived man is lamented, whom, surely, God, as the kind and gracious One, ought rather to forgive than to punish so severely even an actually committed mistake, vii. 1—21. The three parts are not therefore of equal length and proportions: but, as the way to the speaker's own situation is with vehemence made through opposition, they gradually increase in extent and fulness, so that the third is the longest and the calmest, the first the shortest and most full of effort and agitation.

vi. 1 And Job answered and said:

1.

Would that *weighed* were my resentment,
and that my suffering were together therewith raised with the scales!
for now—heavier is it than the sand of the sea;
—therefore my words prattle amiss!—
For the arrows of the Most High I endure,
the heat of which my spirit drinketh up;
the terrors of God beleaguer me.

1. vi. 2—13. This commencement rises slowly but irresistibly from a heavy, oppressive burden to the greatest agitation and vehemence, the more the despair is compelled to bring forward its own justification. At first, vv. 2, 3, the weary desire scarcely gets expression, to see the suffering, which has now become quite unendurable, only measured in its whole extent in comparison with the angry discontent which has now been expressed, ending in a brief presentation of the true state of the case as far as he knows it and as he regards it, that is, in a severe reminder as to the nature and origin of these sufferings: it is from God that he suffers the most terrible, hardly endurable calamities! ver. 4. Must not therefore his complaints be correspondingly terrible, and with indignation cast off the suffering which is presented to him as the result of sin, though he knows he is innocent? vv. 5—7. Indeed, he desires rather

5 **D**oth the wild ass then bray over grass?
  or doth the ox low over his fodder?
is then tasteless food eaten without salt!
  or is there flavour in the white of an egg?
my soul refuseth to touch it:
  they are as nauseousness on my food!—

O that my request might come,
  that God would grant my hope,
that God would—and He crushed me,
  let go His hand—and cut me off!
10 in order that my comfort might yet arise,
  I leaped up in unspared pain!
    —for I never denied the words of the Holy One!

at once to die, regarding the granting by God of this one wish as a pledge of the divine mercy towards the innocent, vv. 8—10, inasmuch as he is deprived of all power of further endurance, vv. 11—13; at which point his despair rapidly increases almost to madness.—(1) The desire that his suffering might *only be weighed* (נָשָׂא to lift = to weigh, answering to שקל, ܡܣܩܠܐ *a balance* from the same root, נטל Isa. xl. 15) together with his angry resentment (with reference to v. 2), forces itself first upon him who alone knows the immense weight of his calamities; on which account it is not so inexcusable if he, as he himself fears, should in the excess of his pain and resentment speak inconsiderately, as he had done ch. iii., and is against his will about to do again; hence the passing incidental remark ver. 3 *b* is very appropriately inserted here at the beginning, comp. ver. 26 *b*. לָעוּ as if from לוּעַ, yet this would have to be equivalent to לעה, لغا, لغي, to prattle, hence to speak as a child, inconsiderately, LXX ἐστι φαῦλα, only too general; comp. Prov. xx. 25.—For, briefly to express the terrible nature of his suffering, from God Himself he endures inevitable, fatal inflictions, marks of a guilt of which he is nevertheless unconscious, horrible things which are presented to him he does not understand why, ver. 4: can it therefore (2) be required of him patiently to accept such things, and must he not be horrified at them, vv. 5—7? Every living creature, animal and man, perceives the difference when pleasant or obnoxious things are offered to it, and expresses itself differently accordingly; the animal that is just in the midst of abundance and satisfaction will not make complaint, ver. 5: but will it be expected of anyone that he should accept tasteless things patiently as if they were good, pleasant food, ver. 6? no, Job, at all events, is from his inmost feeling as little able to accept and swallow these loathsome, horrible things patiently as the unwholesome parts of his food, ver. 7. Thus the figure of presented food runs through vv. 5—7; for

What is my strength that I still hope,
  what my end that I hold out?
or is the strength of stones mine?
  or is my body of brass?
is not my inward help gone,
  sure salvation driven from me?

calamity, pain and misery appears to force itself upon man from without, that he may accept it and appropriate it, absorbing it into his own life, and endeavour no more to shun it as bitter and loathsome. With regard to ריר חלמות the most probable conclusion is, that it signifies the fluid part, the slime (spittle) surrounding the firmer central mass (חלם means firm, sound, comp. خُلْبٌ the marrow of certain things) of the egg, that is, the white of egg which is nearly tasteless and to many loathsome, the meaning given to the words by the Targum. The pron. הֵמָּה, ver. 7, refers to the subject at the beginning, ver. 4, that is, to his sufferings: they, the sufferings, which I must swallow, are as nausea (דְּוֵי from דְּוַי §§ 147, 213 *e* sickness, pestilence, and the nausea which results therefrom) of my food, as a pestilence that cleaves to the food presented to me, which I cannot be expected surely to take patiently! comp. Isa. xxx. 22.—(3) Would that instead death, which has so long been desired by me, might come, vv. 8—10, since (4) all power of further endurance has already been taken from me! vv. 11—13. At this thought his despair becomes vehement to the degree of mad exultation; after the disappearance of all others, the one hope was left, that a near, certain death would end all sufferings, but the last eager desire has remained unfulfilled: o that it might now please God to send him quick death not as punishment and terror but as a boon, and so without delay cut off the thread of his life in an entirely different sense than Eliphaz, iv. 21, had indicated, like one cruelly and yet mercifully crushing him with uplifted hand! in order that he may, surely (§ 347 *a*), enjoy amidst all his calamities the one consolation of knowing their early cessation, not feeling any more dismay and terror at certain death as other men do, but rather doing that which is incredible—leaping and exulting in the very midst of full, unspared pain of death; for he is not conscious of being so bad as that he ought not to ask for further mercy and expect consolation from God, whose words he has never denied, were it only the mercy of a speedy death, the only thing that is now left! with ver. 10 *c* comp. xii. 4; xxvii. 3, 4. The pain of sublime suffering, rising to scornful laughter, can hardly be greater than we find here. סלד acc. to LXX, Targ. and Arab. صلد comp. صلت and زلط to move violently with stamping, to leap, to rejoice most tumultuously; לא יַחְמֹל must be a relative clause to חילה, acc. § 332 *a*: *pain* which *He* (God) *does not spare*, but causes to come in full measure, comp. xx. 13. Job believes, acc. ver. 11, he has neither strength for further patience nor to anticipate an end of such long sufferings which would bring the reward of patience, since he sees

2.

To the despairing love is due from his friend,
[*from the brother compassion to him who is afflicted by God, lest he succumb to his grief*]
and abandon the fear of the Almighty:
15 but my brethren deceived like a brook,
like the bed of overflowing brooks,

death only, if it should be somewhat more distant, at the close of such long and severe sufferings; why then should not death come at once? Therefore ver. 12 answers to ver. 11 *a*, ver. 13 to ver. 11 *b*; with regard to הַאִם see § 356 *a*.

2. vi. 14—30. After the speech has reached this extreme agitation, it becomes somewhat more collected and composed as it passes to the friends. At first the calmest description of the unfaithfulness of the friends, who surely ought most of all to bestow love and consideration upon him that is despairing and exposed to the greatest spiritual peril, vv. 14—21; then, it is true, as Job has realised vividly the ungenerous deed of the friends who have so bitterly disappointed every hope placed in them and he does not now scruple to use deservedly severer language towards them, a violent attack, as in self-defence, cannot be avoided, in order somewhat to alarm the hardened conscience of the friends, vv. 22—27; but nevertheless immediately the most conciliatory, touching and supplicatory language, as of one who really still desires to avoid all contention, recurs, vv. 28—30. The entire passage is accordingly simply deprecatory, dwelling upon the nature of the disappointment which the friends have caused him, as if he were still wholly unable to believe that their accusation was seriously intended. But for the rapid course which the proof now takes short strophes of three verses each are here most appropriate, as in the previous part of the speech.—At the commencement Job places the proposition, that in the nature of things love and consideration (חסד) is due from one friend to another in calamity, who despairs and is thereby even in danger under its influence of forsaking the fear of God, of not thinking and speaking of God so reverently as he ought; a danger to which Job feels himself exposed contrary to his intention, as he had already ver. 3 *c* said and still everywhere in this part of his speech preserves that degree of reflection, comp. vv. 26, 29, 30 (and the imperf. יעזב does not signify that he has already wholly let it go). For what is the service which a friend renders but to approve himself precisely in the greatest peril and to bestow the more love in proportion as the miserable man he befriends supposes in the darkness of divine providence that he receives little love from God Himself; and love enters into the state of mind of the sufferer and helps without provocation and display of opposition. Appropriate as this meaning is here, and plainly as the form of the clause ver. 14 *a* is the same as that of xii. 5, the member *b* does not fit in according to the present

Which are muddy and dark from ice,
  down upon which cometh snow hidden:
suddenly drying up they have vanished,
  when it groweth hot they are consumed from their place.
caravans turn aside their way,
  go up into the desert-country—and perish;

The caravans of Tæma look out,
  the travellers of Sheba inwardly hope:
20 they are put to shame that one trusted,
  they came unto them—and were deceived.—
Thus have ye now become—unto me;
  ye behold the terror—and ye fear!

reading; if the reading were retained, we should have to take ו—יעזב acc. to § 350 *b* as a continuation of לַמָּס *to him that despaireth and . . . . . forsaketh*, but this would be too hard and unusual even in the strained language of this poet, on account of the intervening words מרעהו חסד; we may therefore suppose, for the reasons explained in the *Jahrbb. der B. W.* III. 120 sq., that two halves of a verse have here been left out by an early mistake.—But, on the contrary, Job's friends have, as it must seem to him, bitterly disappointed the just hope of the unfortunate sufferer, depriving him of his last human comfort; like deceptive mountain streams; which at one moment are quite full of water and cause great joy and raise the fairest hope also for the future, but then suddenly dry up without a trace and most terribly deceive the poor travellers, who recalling in their need the former abundance go in search of them by long detours and mustering their last energies, while they nevertheless die of thirst in the barren desert deceived of their last hope. Hence Job paints this expressive picture with special pleasure, thus representing somewhat under a veil most exactly the absolute weakness of the position of the friends. At first, vv. 16, 17, the sharp contrast of the double, deceptive appearance of the Wadîs: at one time their water is quite turbid and dark from the mass of dissolved ice and snow which pours itself down upon them from the mountains as in a blackish stream, but through the heat they are suddenly as if burnt up and vanished to such an extent that they cannot be recognized; hence the perf. ver. 17, in order to represent the rapidly effected transformation, § 135 *a*, 343 *a* יְזֹרְבוּ must be: at the time when = as soon as, they were burned, touched by the heat, זרב = שָׂרַף, צרב, ضرم *to scorch*, corresponding to בְּחֻמּוֹ, *when it becomes hot* (the suff. as neut. § 295 *a*). According to the Massorites' opinion, ver. 18 would be the continuation of the preceding: *the paths of their way turn aside*, no more running connectedly in a full stream, *they ascend into the desert and perish;* yet this is of itself expressed not very suitably: better, therefore,

Is it that I said: "Make gifts to me,
  and from your means make presents for me;
and deliver me from the oppressor's hand,
  and from the hand of the tyrants redeem me"?
Teach me, then I will be silent,
  wherein I erred, declare unto me!

25 **H**ow very sweet are straight-forward words!
  but what reproveth the reproving of yours?
to reprove words even do ye think?
  but into the wind go the words of the despairing!
even over an orphan ye would cast lots,
  and bargain over your friend!—

יִלָּפְתוּ אָרְחוֹת *caravans turn aside their way*, make a wide detour in order in their want of water to get to the longed-for abundant streams, but *ascend into the desert land.* Thus what was at first briefly expressed is described graphically in detail with a fresh commencement, vv. 19, 20, the rich caravans of the most important Arabic trading tribes being brought forward; on account of the sharp antithesis of the acts the copula is not required before בֹּשׁוּ; בטח *he*, in the first instance the guide, had confidence. Generally comp. Hamâsa p. 174. 16; Wellsted's *Travels in Arabia* I. p. 89.—As if himself surprised by the sad truth of this illustration, Job cannot longer refrain from calling his friends to account, as to the ungenerous character of their conduct, nor from making a serious attempt to end by bitter scorn further contention. To go no further, how ignoble is it to tremble just when danger threatens the friend, and to rather part with friendship than shameful fear! ver. 21. (But כִּי = *yes*, surely, does not alone suit the context, and probably כֵּן should be read instead; לֹא would have to be taken as *nothing*, worthless, acc. § 296 *d*, but as this would after all yield no proper meaning in this connexion, it is better to read לִי instead of it). Poor friends thus retreat when it is suggested to them to really sacrifice a portion of their material wealth, *e.g.*, to liberate by a ransom a friend who has been unjustly cast into prison: but has Job demanded anything of that kind from them, he who suffers not from a mortal but from a divine infliction, and therefore requires from friends nothing more than cheap sympathy? vv. 22, 23: he desires from them comfort simply and, as far as he may have gone astray, kindly correction, ver. 24. But if they are prepared really, as it seems, to instruct him, he will gladly, inasmuch as he can value an honest word, submit to their correction; only so severely to correct and pitilessly to persecute simple inoffensive words, particularly when uttered so rapidly and inconsiderately at a moment of unhappy despair, displays a degraded habit of mind which may easily change even into active cruelty towards the defenceless and friends,

And now, may it please you to look upon me!
  to your face will I, verily, not lie!
return now, let not wrong be done!
  and return—I am still right as to it!
30 is there then wrong in my tongue?
  or doth not my palate distinguish faults?

3.

vii.1 **H**ath not man slave-service on the earth,
  and as the days of a hireling are not his?
as a slave panteth after shade,
  as a labourer awaiteth his wages:

vv. 25—27. As winged as his indignation, is here the language of the sufferer; and equally compactly is everything concatenated in the arrangement of the thoughts. נמרץ, ver. 25, must be another orthography for נמלץ *to be sweet*, from the meaning of being smooth, slippery, which is implied in מרץ, מרט; by another way the meaning of being *sick* is also derived from that of being smooth, *soft*, xvi. 3. But *what* does the correction which you give *correct?* evil deeds? but they are not to be found; therefore mere words? (מלים in contrast with deeds xi. 2) do ye mean to reprove them? but the words of a despairing man, such as mine are, go into the wind (viii. 2; xv. 2; xvi. 3), do not at all need reproof. With ver. 27 *a* comp. 1 Sam. xiv. 42; Amos ii. 8; Nah. iii. 10; Ps. xxii. 19; Prov. i. 14; with *b* xl. 30 (A.V. xli. 6).—After the worst has thus been said, at last, vv. 28—30, wise reflection returns with loftier repose and the wish for reconciliation. Just as if he had a foreboding of the lamentable complication of the contention and increase of heated feeling, on his part also, if the friends continue in this way, he requests them beseechingly only to look upon him without prejudice, since he as an honourable man will surely not lie to their faces when he protests his innocence, and believes that he has thus far committed no injustice even in speech, indeed, believes also that he has sufficient taste left to avoid what is unseemly (xii. 11; xxxi. 30). עוד, ver. 29 *b*, must, contrary to the accents, be connected with the following words.

3. vii. 1—21. But defended against outward attack, the despair only sinks inwardly to lower depths, advancing with rapid strides. While previously, ch. iii., as in the passage to which this joins on, Job had complained almost solely of his own calamities, he now includes within the scope of his consideration the whole human race, finding its misfortune to arise from its weakness and misery. Thus proceeding from the condition of the race generally and feeling himself involved in its misery, he lingers now by the consideration of the weary toilsomeness of the short-lived, weak child of earth, who after death never returns again to the sunny Upper World, and the comparison of this brief toilsome life and its end with the divine grace and power arouses bitter melancholy no less than indignation and profound pain. First, therefore,

so had I to inherit moons of wretchedness,
nights of weariness have been apportioned to me.
If I lie down, then I say: "when shall I arise?"
and the evening is made long,
I am full of restlessness until morning;
5 my body rottenness covereth and earth-crust,
my skin waxeth rigid and runneth again.

a melancholy glance at this misery of man generally and particularly of himself, vv. 1—5: but this of itself issues in the agonising prayer that God may take pity on his life before it is lost beyond recovery, vv. 6—10. However, again, this hope has but to be clearly conceived by the hopelessly lost sufferer to immediately vanish from his gaze and give place to absolute despair, yea, to indignation; to what end are prayers and tears? if he is in any case already lost, he will put no restraint upon himself but give free course to the most open speech against God, desiring death instead of such unendurable, endless sufferings of a weak harmless man, and only demanding a moment's rest beforehand! vv. 11, 12—16; but even if he had been guilty of some inadvertences with regard to God as the strict Watcher of men, how weak after all is man and particularly Job as compared with God, that he should not rather expect indulgence from Him, before it is too late, as unhappily in this instance, by certain death, vv. 17—21. Thus this soliloquy, which is most agitated in the second member of it, dies away at last once more in heavy sighs and profound pain, without any other hope than dark death: no other goal is gained by the despair which always increases by its utterance. But precisely in the middle of the long speech the thought takes a sudden turn: accordingly the sudden, spasmodic exclamation, ver. 11, outside the series of the four strophes, each of which has five verses. And this sudden, violent change into the manner of the first speech of extreme boldness introduces into the contention something which is not less new than pregnant with consequences in the comparison of human sin with God's forgiveness; a point which cannot be at once fully worked out, simply because it is here too new, but is subsequently taken up again, x. 2 sq. That is, when the matter is more closely considered, there are in general really but two fundamentally different reflections with which an unfortunate sufferer can occupy himself, either so as to raise himself above his calamities, if he discerns properly the consolation and encouragement which they contain, or so as to sink into despair, if he discerns merely their dark side. These reflections are, first, on the earthly, temporal consideration of the brevity and wearisomeness of human life and the powerlessness of man, and, secondly, the divine consideration of the impossibility that a man can be quite pure in relation to God and of the necessary love of the Creator for the creature notwithstanding. The first reflection still prevails here, as that which is most natural, as it was at first, ch. iii., without the mixture of any other: the second gradually plays a more important part as the whole contention growingly gathers around the question

More fleeting than the weaver's shuttle is my life,
  and is spent without hope.
O remember, a breath is my life,
  never again will mine eye see prosperity;
the eye of my friend will not behold me,
  Thine eyes seek me—in vain!
gone is the cloud and vanished,
  so he that went down into the underworld cometh not up,
10 returneth not any more to his house,
  and not any more doth his place know him.—

So then neither will *I* refrain my mouth,
  will speak in the anguish of my spirit,
    complain in the grief of my soul!

of Job's guilt or innocence; here for the first time it occurs almost incidentally, by way of additional remark, but quite differently x. 2 sq.—(1) A calm description both of human hardship and toil in general and in particular of the constant grievous restlessness lasting through the whole night, ver. 4, of the body as covered which boils, ver. 5; hence (2) a description of the end of this hopeless life, which is so certain and sure to come, if not immediately, ver. 6, comp. ix. 25, which last thought, surely, most naturally starts the mournful prayer to God, to remember the brevity of his life before it is too late, vv. 7—10. The description of the restlessness, ver. 4, is graphic: as early as the evening, on lying down, he cannot get the morning to come early enough, all his wishing for it is in vain! to the sleepless, restless sufferer the evening draws itself out to a terrible length, yea, the whole night is spent in the most agitated restlessness. His skin, ver. 5, is completely covered with putrefying boils, and is nevertheless at the same time rigid and hard, like an earthen crust (comp. جسا to be hard, dry, with גוש *clod*, جَسْوَةٌ hard earth, it being, as the second member explains, sometimes rigid (רגע as in the Arab. and Eth.) and sometimes running again when the old boils gather: comp. Tod's Rajasthan tom. II. p. 327. In the representation of the hopelessness of a return from the Underworld the most touching feature is ver. 8, that then neither the eye of any man now beholding him would see him again, nor would even God Himself, if He would, as Job continues firmly to believe, at some future time (alas, too late!) judge his cause and on that account seek for him, seek for him among the living other than in vain; hence the language also ver. 8 *b* is particularly agitated, comp. ver. 21 *d*.—(3) As the uselessness of the prayer to God is brought home all the more painfully to the sufferer by precisely this expression of it, his despair, which has become complete, now grows vehement and bursts all restraints. If there is no deliverance to be hoped for from God, the sufferer also on his part

Am I a sea, or a sea-monster,
  that Thou settest over me a watch;
if I think, 'my bed shall comfort me,
  my couch shall lighten my complaint',
then also Thou scarest me with dreams,
  terrifiest me by visions?
15 No, strangling my soul chooseth,
  death rather than these bones;
I despise them: I will not live always!
  cease from me, for a breath are my days!—

What is man, that Thou magnifiest him,
  that Thou settest upon him Thy heart
and visitest him every morning,
  every moment triest him!

(בַּם comp. my notes on Ps. lii. 7) will boldly and unrestrainedly let loose the dark thoughts which intensify his trouble; that which is contradictory and tormenting in the thought of God shall be fearlessly uttered! ver. 11. To judge from the incessant, violent pains which prostrate Job, it must be supposed that he is something in the highest degree dangerous, which cannot be sufficiently kept down or closely enough watched, something to which not a moment's rest may be granted, if it shall not do immense injury on getting free. But is he then really such a creature, a sea, or a living monster of the sea, that he is so keenly and violently plagued by God and as it were guarded (comp. xiii. 27), yea, does not even find rest in sleep,—he who is so absolutely weak and harmless? vv. 12—14. No, rather than continue to carry about longer this wretched skeleton, this body which has been reduced to bones (comp. xix. 20), he will seek strangling or death in any form; this body he despises (ix. 21), does not at all desire to live always, as he has already lived too long; therefore at last the wild demand, which he has in vain resisted, escapes him, that God may at least now grant him a moment's rest, as in any case his life is already forfeited and he has no desire to retain it! vv. 15, 16 (comp. with ver. 16 *b* ver. 19, ix. 34; x. 20).—(4) After such a storm the speech at last, vv. 17—21, again stoops to somewhat calmer reflections, as if in justification of such wild despair. Reference to the hidden cause of his calamities—guilt, which had hitherto been passed over unnoticed by Job, is introduced for the first time, as it was the possible dangerousness of a weak man which was just spoken of. The comparison of the possibility of guilt in some form, of the divine goodness and the vast burden of his calamities, conducts him to the following reflection: It may be necessary that God should punish man on account of error, but if this is to hold so rigorously that every smallest mistake is immediately most rigidly

when at length wilt Thou look away from me,
  let me alone, till I take breath?
20 If I sinned in what I do unto Thee, Thou Watcher of men,
  wherefore didst Thou make me as a butt for Thee,
    so that I am become a burden to myself?
and wherefore dost Thou not forgive my sin,
  dost Thou not overlook my guilt?
for—now I will lay me in the dust,
  Thou wilt seek me—and I am no more!

punished by the God who always torments with his severe inspection, surely, man seems neither sufficiently strong and armed against error, nor sufficiently dangerous, to be always treated with such severity and suspicion, vv. 17, 18; and how long will God not look away from Job in particular, fix his severe eye of punishment upon him, leave him not a moment's rest? (*until he swallow his spittle*, *i.e.*, recover his breath, ix. 18, de Sacy's Chrest. Arab. tom. III. p. 259, 2nd ed.), ver. 19. But suppose Job had sinned in his treatment of God and demeanour towards Him (מָה א׳ ל׳ is the accusative to חטאתי), the possibility of which he grants, it being also so easy to be caught in a fault by the strict, constant Watcher over men: but in that case why did God let go all his arrows (vi. 4) at him, as a wanton hunter at an object, or a hated point of attack מִפְגָּע, comp. xvi. 12 and رَمِيَّة Ham. p. 60, ver. 2) lying in his path, setting him up as it were for a butt even, and heaping upon him so many calamities that he is unable to bear himself; and why does He not rather forgive instead of inflicting such terrible punishments which are out of proportion to his strength, before it is too late, as alas it now appears to be, since Job sees nothing before him but the grave! vv. 20, 21.

2. BILDAD AND JOB.

a. BILDAD. CH. VIII.

In the last part of the previous speech Job had almost charged God directly with injustice, at least in his own matter. But thereby he had put into the hands of the friends a fresh and dangerous argument against himself, which Bildad at once uses, since it appears shocking, and, indeed, blasphemous, to suppose that God can be unjust. This is Bildad's only new thought. God *cannot* do injustice, nor accordingly, if human calamities are the divine punishments of the special sins of the sufferer, as Bildad believes, ever punish a man who is wholly innocent: let Job, therefore, take heed in time, that being purified again he may by the divine mercy be delivered, before certain destruction befall him like all those fools who imagine they can flourish without the divine grace as the sap and energy of life. This is Bildad's meaning here, which he, although already speaking more plainly than Eliphaz, presents as yet only in a considerate manner and hoping the best for Job, particularly guarding against the conclusion that he and his friends wished in any way ill to Job and considered themselves as his enemies. And since from want of personal experience he must borrow the best confirmations of his speech from ancient pithy proverbs, he first presents his own view as briefly as may be, vv. 2—7, but then finds in the wise sayings of hoar antiquity the proof of his principal truth, that every wicked man is on the road to his certain sudden ruin, vv. 8—19, and returns in a brief conclusion to his view of the present case and the hope of Job, vv. 20—22. The solemn, serious, weighty voice of antiquity, which is explained in the second part, is therefore in reality the main portion of this speech; and whilst Bildad hardly as yet ventures to speak more severely to Job, there lies concealed in this primitive pithy utterance of wisdom much serious and stern admonition for Job no less than others, which he has to discover and apply; moreover, in respect of its more artistic, florid and yet compressed language, this passage is the climax of the whole speech.

viii. 1 Then answered Bildad the Shuhite and said:

1.

How long wilt thou speak such things,
are a mighty wind the words of thy mouth?—

1. vv. 2—7. After a brief expression of astonishment at such improper, passionate speeches, ver. 2 (like a *violent wind*, very stormy it is true, yet empty as all winds), Bildad immediately asserts, ver. 3, the main truth which he supposes Job had denied, and shows its application to Job. If God does

Will God then pervert justice?
will the Almighty pervert righteousness?
If thy sons sinned against Him,
He handed them over to their own guilt.
5 But if thou wilt seek unto God
and unto the Almighty make entreaty;
if thou art spotless and upright—
surely then will He always watch over thee,
and give peace to thy pasture of righteousness;
so that what thou wast formerly will be a small thing,
and what thou wilt be later, an exceedingly great thing.

2.

For ask now of the former generation,
and attend to the mind of its fathers!
—since of yesterday are we and without wisdom,
a shadow surely are our days upon the earth—
10 certainly, they will teach thee, tell thee,
bringing forth words from their heart:

not make crooked the right, but the divine righteousness, as is presupposed, chastises every man according to the measure of his own sins, the destruction of Job's sons, which has already been carried out, shows just as clearly that they had committed a grievous mortal sin as the present calamities of Job that neither is he wholly pure and can be saved only by humble repentance; and Job will do well to take warning from the example of his sons. Bildad expresses this only in a considerate and hopeful tone: *if*, as thou, surely, wilt not deny, *thy sons sinned against Him*, *then He gave them up*, as justice itself required, *into the power of their guilt and punishment*, and let everyone see therein an example, particularly whoever is near destruction like Job; *if thou*, on the contrary, turnest to God, He will, supposing thou art pure (which is at present hardly the case) *watch over thee*, that no calamity (again) befall thee, and no more show Himself hostile to thy house, comp. v. 17—24, so that even thy prosperous past will appear as a small thing when compared with the much more prosperous future: as also actually happens at last, xlii. 12, though by quite another course of events than Bildad here anticipates. The masc. יִשְׂגֶּה is, acc. § 174 *c*, construed with the fem. אחרית.

2. Vv. 8—19. Bildad first formally introduces the wise sayings of others, vv. 8—10: they contain the wisdom, based upon deeper experience, of the fathers of the former generation, of the earliest patriarchs, who on account of the greater length of their lives alone might be able much more surely to perceive the laws of life, whilst the short-lived moderns are people of yesterday

"Groweth then the papyrus aloft without bog,
shooteth-up Nile-grass without water?
it is yet there in its freshness, not yet to be cut off—
and nevertheless it withereth before any grass:
so is the path of all that forget God,
the hope of the profane perisheth.—
He, whose inward strength snappeth asunder,
whose confidence is a spider's house:
15 he leaneth upon his house—and yet standeth not,
layeth hold on it—and yet endureth not.
Fresh is he in spite of the sun,
over his garden run his shoots;

(תְּמוֹל acc. § 296 *d*) and of little wisdom; hence what is based upon profound insight, what flows also from the rich eloquence of inward conviction and love, ver. 10 (*bringing forth from their heart*, not from an empty heart by mere skill in speech, as xi. 2; xv. 3; xviii. 2, comp. Prov. i. 23). חֵקֶר, ver. 8, is that which is within, the hidden basis and reason, properly that which has to be investigated, in this case therefore the deeper mind, the thought, acc. xi. 7; xxxviii. 16, מחקר Ps. xcv. 4. The principal and most pregnant of these ancient utterances itself, vv. 11—19, conveys the simple thought, that man at once perishes when the true element of life, the one living principle of the divine grace, is withheld from him after the measure of his sin has been filled up, although he may be externally very powerful and apparently protected, which only makes his fall the greater and more terrible. But this is worked out in an extremely florid manner. The figure of a luxuriant, splendidly verdant plant predominates: as soon as water is withheld from it as its element of life, it suddenly and hopelessly withers away, just while it is flourishing in full vigour. The commencement is made with this figure, the most luxuriant plants, those growing in marshes, being taken as examples, vv. 11—13; after the baselessness of the ungodly and all his means has been described in distinct figures, vv. 14, 15, the first figure is returned to with emphasis, only that this time it is rather a luxuriant garden-plant that serves as an example, the figure also insensibly passing into the thing illustrated, neither being again quite separated, vv. 16—19. The division in the whole delineation takes place before ver. 16. First, ver. 11, we are carried by a bold question at once into the very centre of both the figure and the matter: do then papyrus and other rapidly growing Nile-weeds shoot up without water (and man without the divine grace)? let it not be deceived: while it is still in its freshness, shall by no means be yet cut down as ripe, it withereth (if the water is withdrawn from it) even more rapidly than any grass, even the poorest growing in the most unfavourable and driest places: likewise those who forget God suddenly perish hopelessly, that fool who imagines,

firmly about the hill his roots are wrapped,
  stones he parteth from one another:
if He destroy him from his place,
  it disowneth him "I never saw thee!"
behold, that is the joy of his way,
  yet from the dust shoot forth others!"

3.

20 Behold, God despiseth not blameless men,
  and holdeth not firmly the hand of the evil-doer.
He will yet fill with laughter thy mouth,
  thy lips with loud rejoicing,

indeed, that he has strength and courage enough, but is forsaken of all inner strength (פֶּסֶל), precisely in danger, when he must put his baseless and empty inward character to the test, so that it is with him as if the rotten web of his imagination snapped asunder at the slightest touch like a spider's house, instead of sustaining him when he will hold by it to keep from sinking. Just as a green shrub, which spreads over the garden, firmly entwining itself even in the stoney ground and proudly dominating it, before the sun with its burning heat, that is, in spite of it, he may for a time defiantly hold out, but then when he is most defiant, there is inwardly the greatest danger, and as soon as *he* (who, is left undetermined, in the end God, for vv. 18, 19 the thing itself, more without figure, comes to the front) has withdrawn from him the water as his element of life, he falls, without even being commiserated by the home which he had honoured with his splendour, disowned and abandoned by his own place, if he desired to rely upon it (comp. vv. 14, 15, to which the discourse recurs), ver. 18 *b*, comp. vii. 10; Ps. ciii. 16; *that* is the joy of his way, thus changed into profoundest wretchedness! Yet from the dust of a ruined sinner others spring forth, like shoots from a tree destroyed by storm or drought: let therefore every man of a later time take good heed that he is not like the sinners of earlier days who are here described, as if shooting forth from their ruins! which Job may attend to; although Bildad prefers to show,

3. vv. 20—22, the application with some tender consideration. Therefore God does not despise the afflicted innocent man (neither thee, if thou prayest to Him when thus afflicted, vv. 5, 6), just as on the other hand He does not preserve the wicked (nor thee, if thou resolvest to be of their number). But I hope He will yet so bless thee that thy enemies (to whom we do not belong) will behold with shame thy prosperity: nevertheless, it must once more be repeated with earnestness, the house of the wicked is as good as annihilated for ever, comp. xi. 20. As to עַד, ver. 21, see the note on i. 18. יָקוֹט, ver. 14, acc. § 162 *a*; but if the meaning mentioned in *Ewald-Dukes' Beiträge* I. 89, should be further substantiated, the clause *he whose best strength are summer-*

with shame will thine enemies be covered;
yet the tent of the wicked—it is gone!

threads (gossamer threads) would still better suit the structure of the verse-members; modern Arabs call them devil's webs (*Zeitschrift der Deutsch. Morgenl. Gesellsch.*, 1851, p. 98), and the word might seem to be connected with קיץ قيظ *summer.* With regard to בית, ver. 17, see § 217 *g*: חזה is then used in this construction with בין in its primary meaning of *to divide and separate* quite in the local sense.

b. JOB. CH. IX., X.

In vain, therefore, has Job endeavoured to bring the friends to his own way of thinking, in vain has he refused to enter into their manner of regarding his calamities. They proceed simply in their own way with greater persistency, just as if he had not made this endeavour at all. He is unable, therefore, longer wholly to hold back, as he has been repeatedly hard pressed to deal with the meaning of the words of the friends: however, he is still disinclined directly to attack his opponents, the previous shrinking from this step still remaining too powerful. Accordingly, he now goes only so far as to take up the general fundamental thoughts of his opponents for the first time as it were by their extreme points, to take out the truth in their words which he cannot contradict, in order to try how it suits his case. This he does at first without any reference to the bad inferences and imputations of his opponents, and still without the feeling that he must defend his innocence before men; in fact, without retaliating upon them by similar recriminations and provoking them by express direct address and controversy, still preserving more the form of an audible soliloquy. It is, moreover, very appropriate that in doing this he now takes into consideration the speech of Eliphaz alone, partly because he must esteem him much more highly as the older and wiser opponent, partly in order to show that he has from the beginning marked and not forgotten any of the words of the opponents, as may have seemed to be the case. As he thus for the first time, as if compelled to do it, ventures the perilous attempt to enter more particularly into the meaning of his opponents' words and to come down as far as he can from the heights of the matter to their mode of thinking, he must naturally grant what was correct in their words—the truth of the divine omnipotence and of human weakness before God, as indeed he himself knew this as well and can probably describe it better and more eloquently than the friends. But that bald, cold way of regarding this antithesis of divine omnipotence and human weakness, which the friends had broached, admits, in fact, of exactly the opposite inference, namely, that God precisely as the Almighty One cannot afflict a weak man to the very uttermost, while the man is unable in any effective way to resist. This terrible experience is just now made by Job, as he believes, since his pains and calamities are only increased by complaint and rebellion at his undeserved and inexplicable misery, and God seems to correct and humble him the more severely, yea, to threaten him with the terror of certain death, in proportion as he threatens to grow more rebellious against the unjust inflictions. So that, according to a low human way of reasoning, he ought, if he will not further increase the burden of his sufferings, instead of rebelling patiently to expose himself to every humiliation, although he is convinced of his innocence (and of the divine injustice). As, therefore, he experiences most plainly and terribly in his own person the divine omnipotence, which is quite well known to him, precisely in this aspect of it and in this sense of it with which his opponents are not acquainted, he is compelled, instead of fleeing with delight to the thought of the divine omnipotence and human weakness, rather to find in it from the first the deepest pain and bitterest mockery. That which ought to be his help and comfort, becomes the most alarming idea just when he is compelled to consider it; and without intending it, he flings back with scorn and mockery the wisdom which is not simply useless in his case but has been experienced in his own terrible pain: the bitter scorn lies in the situation itself.—But if, from this standpoint, to which his opponents had conducted him, on remembering the bad consequences of further resistance and provocation of the divine wrath, Job ought thereby to be persuaded to bear in simple, silent, unthinking patience his unavoidable, mysterious sufferings, on the other hand, he is compelled by the greater strength of his good conscience again boldly, in spite of all evil consequences, to rise to free unsparing language regarding that which is not to be understood and is contradictory in God. Scarcely has he, under compulsion from without, clearly realised to himself the weakness of even the innocent in a contention with God, scarcely has he looked into the inference, that he would do better to give heed to human fear and hold his peace, when immediately, starting back from the inference and obeying simply the voice of his conscience, he prepares with all the greater vehemence for the most reckless speech against God, and forgetting all outward things sinks back into mad despair. Whilst in the beginning he seemed to tremble at the thought of speaking freely to God (but simply led by his opponents, for a moment giving way to lower considerations, and restraining the mightier voice of his integrity), at the end, when it has become impossible to restrain the pure voice within, he returns with all the more vehemence to it; and whilst at first, without evil intention, he strikes down the whole view of his opponents with a sword torn from them, in biting and yet only righteous and mournful scorn, without openly attacking them, he soon marches as conqueror in his own territory with none to disturb him. Accordingly this speech, which proceeds stormily in tremendous antitheses, is simply contemplative and theoretic, and yet deals hard blows at the opponents whom it does not even once mention, falls into three parts, the second of which acts as a mediator between the other two, which would otherwise be irreconcilable: (1) the scornful admission of the divine omnipotence, as Job had long been acquainted with it and as he describes it in rivalry with his opponents, but also as he experiences it in its terrors precisely for a sufferer, ix. 2—20; (2) the rebellion of the good conscience against the terror of this omnipotence and the reasons for unrestrained speech against God, ix. 21—x. 2; (3) this speech itself, x. 2—22.

ix. 1 And Job answered and said:

1.

Verily, I know that it is so!
and how should man be just before God?
if he desired to contend with Him,
he would not answer Him one of a thousand!

1. ix. 2—20. After the absolute power of God in comparison with that of men has been conceded at once in a brief, scornful word, vv. 2, 3, Job describes that power further in emphatic and eloquent terms, as if in rivalry with his opponents, and in such a way that gives most prominence to that side of it which appears in the outward world, vv. 4—10. But as Job himself conceives the nature of this omnipotence as it is brought to bear upon weak man, God appears simply as a Being who when once He becomes angry can rapidly and irresistibly subdue and destroy even the strongest who may oppose Him. So that much less can Job, the most miserable of men, although suffering from no fault of his own, have any desire to resist Him who, when made angry at his resistance, has the power, as supreme lord and judge, to torment him most terribly, yea, by His terrors to change his just cause into an apparently unjust one! vv. 11—20. Thus with an apparently calm commencement, the speech rises at the end to the wildest commotion and most painful agitation, in proportion as the reference to his own dismal history finds free course.—(1) Vv. 2, 3: that therefore is the decisive point, that God is omnipotent? well, doubtless (אמנם, scornfully, like *nimirum*, xii. 2) I know that myself! and how could weak man, incapable of resistance, get justice in a contest with the omnipotent God? Truly, in that matter Eliphaz has seen the truth, iv. 17! If even man really desired to contend with God (but the desire would probably vanish on reflection! at all events Job is not now clearly conscious of it, but comp. xiii. 3), he would nevertheless be unable to answer one of the thousand questions with which the infinitely wise and powerful God would overwhelm him, in case therefore he should be right, would still not be able to prove and maintain his cause! The first expectation turns out in the end to be really justified, xxxviii. 1 sq., only it has no such bad ending as he now fears.—(2) Vv. 4—10. The elaborate description of the omnipotence of God begins

Wise of heart is He and mighty in strength:
who hath defied Him and escaped whole?
5 He who removeth mountains—they know not
that He overturneth them in his wrath,
He who startleth the earth from her place,
so that her pillars are shaken;
He who commandeth the sun—it riseth not,
around the stars putteth a seal,
Who boweth the heavens quite alone,
and walketh over the heights of the sea;

with the general remark, that it is accompanied by the highest wisdom and skill, so that hitherto no one has provoked God without suffering for it, ver. 4; but then the description remains at first quite unexpectedly by the consideration simply of the external world, vv. 5—10, as if Job were so absorbed in this representation of the Infinite One that he forgot for the time all human affairs and also himself and his sufferings: whilst on other occasions he always speaks primarily only of himself and of the relation of all human affairs to God. But undoubtedly this representation of the omnipotence of God would not have been thus confined to the universe without reference to man, nor have been so marvellously calm, eloquent, and extensive, if it had not at the same time been spoken in rivalry with Eliphaz, v. 9 sq. Hence this passage, in which Job shows that he is in no respect inferior to Eliphaz as regards knowledge and the ability to speak on divine things, forms also a small distinct section of seven verses, closing intentionally ver. 10 as Eliphaz began v. 9. At the same time, it is quite in harmony with Job's present state of feeling and his reflections, that of all the wonders of the universe he selects rather the shocking and terrible ones which reveal the divine wrath, and only quite at the end briefly refers to the others. First, the terror of the earth, the sinking of entire mountains in a moment (*they know not* = unawares) and the earthquake vv. 5, 6; then the terror of the heavens, eclipse of the sun and tempests, vv. 7, 8; lastly, of a more general nature, the wonders of the stars and the innumerable host of other wonders, vv. 9, 10. This appears to be the most correct way of regarding the details. נטה properly *to stretch along*, *to bow down*, ver. 8, is accordingly, as Ps. xviii. 8—15, to be understood of the apparent bowing, stooping, of the heavens in a heavy tempest; after *He alone* has let down the immense weight of heavy clouds from their elevation, He marches as the Mighty One, wrapped in the clouds, over the heights, calming or rousing the billows of the sea which is agitated from beneath; Am. iv. 13; Mic. i. 3 describe similarly Jahvé's march in the heaving tempest hanging over the heights of the earth. If נטה were taken in the sense of *to stretch out*, *expand*, acc. "Isa." xl. 22, it is true that the word "alone" would suit that meaning very well: we should then see Him stretch out alone the great, wide tent of heaven. But the figure of stretching out would have to be

who created the Bear, Orion and Pleiades,
  with the chambers of the south;
10 who createth great things, wholly unsearchable,
  wonderful things, not to be numbered!

Lo He goeth by me—I see Him not,
  presseth through—and I observe Him not!
lo He seizeth—who will stay Him?
  who will say unto Him, "what doest Thou?"

God stayeth not his wrath,
  under Him stooped Rahab's helpers!—
How then should *I* answer Him,
  choose my words against Him!

more definitely indicated, and the second member is too unfavourable to that meaning. Ver. 9 the figure of a tempest might be carried still further, if עשה were understood not of making, properly to thicken, condense, but of darkening (which is also really a thickening), comp. עשה and غشي: yet in that case it would be used with עַל, as xv. 27, and the chambers of the south, containing the hidden constellations of the southern heavens, are already covered and do not require to have this done; moreover, it is rather to be expected that something of a more general nature concerning the divine omnipotence should follow here, preparatory to the very similar close in view, ver. 10. As regards the Great Bear, Orion and Pleiades, see below on xxxviii. 31, 32.—But from this almost too discursive description the speech now returns (3), with the greater haste, in increasing agitation and most rapid turns of thought (hence in five small strophes of two verses each), to its main object, and at first, vv. 11, 12, passes by the easiest transition from the description of the universe to that of man, indeed, of the speaker himself, in his relation to this omnipotence. As with fear everyone in distress that knows Him thus must every moment expect and bear all things from his omnipotence; and as if Job felt Him as in the wind coming upon and passing through him, invisibly and yet through dread and terror sensibly enough, he exclaims, making himself an example of all unhappy sufferers, with a terrified voice: there! He passeth by me and I see Him not! yea, more than this, thus coming up he can seize a poor creature and cause his quick death (*e.g.* by sudden terror, by lightning, by a rapidly fatal disease), no one being able to call Him to account. In brief, therefore, ver. 13, God carries out with a strong hand what he has once in anger determined upon, He under whose mighty hand the most powerful defiant creatures submitted in former times, discovering too late the vanity of resistance. It follows from this connexion that עזרי רהב are not merely helpers in general, but notorious ones from experience and story; and since Rahab is everywhere a mythological

15 **I** who, if I were right, I should not answer,
no, to my opponent I should supplicate,
if I called and He answered,
I should not believe that He heard my voice:

He who in the storm would set upon me,
increase my wounds without cause,
would not suffer me to take breath,
but fill me with bitterness!

Is the matter of the strength of the mighty?—"behold!"
or is it of justice?—"who will summon Me?"
20 if I am right, my mouth will condemn me!
am I blameless—He maketh me crooked!

name of a sea-monster (even when it is used of Egypt), we must suppose an allusion to an ancient tradition, according to which a monster, which had once with all its allies been overcome by God, was by way of example fastened as a constellation in the heavens, where it now shines for ever proclaiming to the world its vain resistance of God; the LXX have here and xxvi. 12 quite correctly χήτα τὰ ὑπ' οὐρανόν; Κῆτος, Πρίστις, Balena, Bellua, Pistrix, are constellations (see Eichhorn's *Biblioth. der Bibl. Lit.*, VII. 593). Similar things were told of several constellations, of Orion also; and as just before, ver. 9, other constellations were mentioned, it was natural to refer here to something of the kind.—If therefore (the speech continues, ver. 14, with increasing haste advancing to its chief object) not even the superhuman, mightest beings could withstand Him, how much less shall *I* (supposing even it should come to a judicial conflict between us as regards my guilt or innocence) be able in judgment to reply to Him, carefully and anxiously selecting (because in great danger the choice is the more difficult) my words *against Him! I*, vv. 15, 16, the weakest of mortals, I, who if it came really to a trial, should after all from fear not defend my undoubted right, but should supplicate to my own opponent (since He is at the same time my Supreme Lord) that I might be spared any defence of myself; even supposing the case that He answered to my call and came to judgment, I should for fear scarcely believe that He really heard and answered it! vv. 15, 16; *against Him*, vv. 17, 18, that infinitely powerful One of marvellously unerring aim, who if I attempted to contradict Him would as invisible in the storm (vv. 11, 12) charge upon me (snort upon, שׁוּף comp. שׁאף), so that I should be compelled to tremble and feel new pains, although for no fault of mine own; He who would not suffer me to have a moment's rest, but would heap upon me bitter experiences enough (such as I have already in sufficient abundance)! And generally, finally, vv. 19, 20, since in Him the highest Potentate and Judge meet in one person, how can even the most innocent meet

2.

Blameless am I! I will not know myself,
will despise my own life!
it is all one! therefore I say:
the blameless and the wicked *He* destroyeth!
If a scourge slayeth unexpectedly,
He mocketh at the despair of the innocent;
the earth is given into the hand of the wicked,
the faces of their judges He veileth:
if not,—well then *who* is it?

Him? if the point is the possession of strength, in that case He cries, *Behold!* I am here, what wilt thou do? (comp. the equally short and abrupt אַיֵּה *where—?* xv. 23); or of right, in that case he cries, who will summon Me, call me before the tribunal? since surely He must be more powerful than I. Accordingly Job foresees that if (which he does not doubt) he were in the right, still his own intimidated, tied tongue would instead of defending him rather confuse and represent him as guilty, that though innocent he would still be perverted and put in the wrong by Him!

2. ix. 21—x. 2. But scarcely has this picture, that he would from terror deny his innocence, presented itself clearly before his mind, than with indignation he starts back from it and now before all things holds fast his integrity and fearlessly maintains it even against God (whom he now plainly enough regards as its opponent), looking beyond all the evil consequences of the free and bold confession. The consciousness of integrity, even when it does not clearly feel God on its side, is still more powerful than all fear of the future, since it is the most certain and the most immediate blessing: it has the strength even to turn against Heaven, if it appears hostile. When from a low human view of things, it ought to keep silence from fear of the wrath of God, it turns precisely then all the more boldly and recklessly against him that will cast doubt upon it, even were it Heaven itself, despising even the most evident mortal peril. Thus in this case Job, who has, after brief reflection, fallen into the most violent state of agitation and indignation, maintains, shrinking from no peril were it even that of losing his life, his innocence and consequently the injustice of God, which he believes he sees in the world also, as he here for the first time throws out rapidly this terrible thought of the general perversion of right upon the earth, vv. 21—24. Becoming somewhat calmer, he enumerates to himself the reasons, borrowed from his own outward condition, which can compel him, even according to a lower way of thinking, to unrestrained speaking against God, vv. 25—28. Then as he is just about really to speak against God the thought flashes upon him like lightning, that by such an outspoken charge against God he would really be committing a grievous sin, but this hesitation he rejects with still greater rapidity, because an attempt to obtain justice

25 And my days are fleeter than a runner,
  they are already fled, not having seen any good,
have glided away like ships of reed,
  like the eagle which darteth upon prey.
If I think: "I will forget my complaint,
  will let go my looks and seem bright!"
then I am horrified at all my pains,
  —I know that Thou acquittest me not.

in the ordinary course would (according to what was said in the first part of this speech) after all be fruitless, vv. 29—33. So that, therefore, regarded from this moral aspect of it even, the reason which seemed previously to recommend to him fear and silence, becomes now on the contrary a reason for reckless speaking (for what then has he left to lose? does not he who is already past hope do best to exercise as lông as he lives the one act of a free conscience, fearlessly to reveal one truth?); and finally he desires, at last once more as a man looking round him before he actually speaks against God, at least meanwhile not to be overtaken by the punishment of the God who is perhaps thereby suddenly made angry, not to be hindered by the divine terrors, vv. 34—x. 2 (as then in fact he is not hindered, and accordingly God does not after all proceed so cruelly as he feared). So terribly does the whole meaning of the first part of this speech become reversed in the second: and spasmodic as is the very commencement, ver. 21, once more precisely in the middle, ver. 29, this hindered stream rises in vain to a gentle outpouring, so that ver. 29 (like the verse above vii. 11) stands as a single disconnected verse between two strophes of four verses each.—(1) Vv. 21—24. With the most vehement fervour Job exclaims at the beginning in contrast with ver. 20: *innocent am I!* this truth, this feeling, I will not let go, boldly I assert it regardless of my life even; *it is all one*, it is a matter of indifference, whether I live or die, the innocent not less than the guilty *He* destroys, who is here not further named from dread and also from wild despair; ver. 21 *b* corresponds therefore to ver. 22 *a*, and reversely. If this severe utterance appears too hard, Job proves it, besides from his own example, also from the world around. First, ver. 23, thereby, that a suddenly occurring public calamity, *e.g.*, a pestilence, does not spare even the innocent in the midst of their despair (מַסָּה, comp. vi. 14), but mocks at their sufferings, which is at least as clear as what Job's opponents said—that no outward calamities befall the innocent, v. 20 sq. Second, ver. 24, by pointing to the extensive sway of a powerful sinner and of the judges of the earth who are as if smitten with blindness by God Himself, examples of which may be very general in certain times[1], and the truth of which none can really deny. As this experience hurls to the ground the whole of the wisdom

[1] Comp. my Commentary on Ps. xxi.

I, I wish to be guilty!
wherefore then do I weary myself in vain?

30 If I wash myself even in snow,
and cleansed with soap my hands,
yet Thou wouldst plunge me into the pit,
so that my clothes would make me loathsome.
For not a man is He like me, whom I could speak with,
that we should come together in judgment;
no daysman is between us,
who might lay his hand upon us both.—

of his opponents, Job might pursue it still further to their disadvantage: but now, as his purpose is rather to maintain his own innocence, he lets this ready argument go again, closing rapidly, *if not*, as has just been said, if God does not do that, *well then who is it?* can it be denied that this puzzling, shocking phenomenon must ultimately come from Him?—(2) Vv. 25—28. After such a hasty, bold utterance regarding the great wrong which comes from God Himself, the speech becomes somewhat calmer, in the contemplation of his own personal condition: only that this very thing also soon leads once more to the same daring resolve to speak freely against God. Surely, my young life has already hopelessly passed away, without my having seen happiness, flown as rapidly as a ship which is seen most quickly passing by and soon disappearing, or like an eagle which darts in a moment upon its prey, vv. 25, 26 (אֵבֶה is undoubtedly a reed, out of which the lightest, quickest boats were made particularly for the Nile, see my note on Isa. xviii. 2 [1] (*Prophets of the Old Testament* Vol. II. p. 247); and it is really so absolutely useless to determine to console myself with the future, since as often as I purpose to keep still, to give up my complaint and wretched looks (פנים in this sense of bad looks 1 Sam. i. 18, comp. ver. 6), I am immediately reduced to terror again by the force of my pains, yea, to the terrible certainty of never finding mercy before the omnipotent God, vv. 27, 28.—(3) But if I speak thus shall I not be guilty of a sin? Away with such a scruple, for this reason amongst others, that precisely this reflection upon guilt or innocence must moreover make me wholly hopeless! I, precisely as an innocent man, *should like* to become guilty by speaking freely against God, to make myself guilty, as it is considered, in the defence of innocence! (ver. 29 *a*) for what purpose then is the vain endeavour to defend myself in the regular course, say, with cautious, humble words? If I most

[1] Upon the Euphrates and Tigris also boats made of woven bulrushes were used, see Layard's *Discoveries* p. 552. The word itself, it is true, is still obscure as to its origin, like the corresponding أَبَاعَةٌ.

Let Him remove His rod from me,
  and let not His fear terrify me!
35 then will I speak, not fearing Him!
  for of such things I am wholly unconscious.
x. 1 My soul is weary of life:
  I leave my complaint free course,
    speak in the trouble of my soul!
say unto God:

plainly set forth my innocence, washed myself perfectly clean from all charges (ver. 30, comp. Isa. i. 18, 19; xliii. 26), He would nevertheless (precisely in consequence of His omnipotence) so confound and terrify me again that instead of appearing clean I should seem to myself and others the most filthy, to be covered to loathing with apparent spots and sins, as if He had plunged me into such a foul pit that my clothes, my impure exterior, made me an object of universal loathing, vv. 30, 31 (see the contrary xxix. 14, and comp. vv. 30, 31 with ver. 20), because He is at the same time the supreme lord and umpire, and the struggle would be so unequal that I could not after all answer his reproaches and incriminations, although innocent of them, could not therefore purify myself from black spots; as is here, vv. 32, 33, briefly repeated from vv. 2—20, but with quite another purpose.—(4) Prepared on such grounds for free, reckless speaking against God, but at the same time still fearing in the terrible commencement or in the course of such speaking either an unendurable intensification of his sufferings, or even a sudden shock of terror, a sudden overwhelmingly alarming appearance from God on account of fresh provocation to wrath (as in reality growing, unmanageable despair easily increases simply the terror and misery), he still desires at first rest, at least during his speech, and desires this with a vehemence proportioned to his sense of the injustice of the treatment which he, the weak, innocent mortal suffers from Omnipotence (and as a fact he afterwards soon overcomes the feeling of terror, finding God more gentle than he feared). Accordingly with fresh emphasis, and yet connected with vv. 32, 33, *Let Him remove* from me His rod, the burden of His pains, and let not His terror, *i.e.*, a terrible manifestation of Himself, confound me! (a demand which recurs in a milder form in the same connexion xiii. 21), then I will speak without fear, *since I am not so* (that I ought to fear Him from a bad conscience) *with myself*, know myself, x. 13; xv. 9, comp. vi. 10, on the contrary, am certainly conscious of my innocence, ver. 21; I am really, moreover, quite tired of my life under such an ignoring of my integrity, x. 1 *a*, as had been said at greater length shortly before, ix. 21, 22, 25—28, and as is here only briefly reiterated as belonging to this connexion. Therefore, follow what may, I will now lighten my profound grief by means of free, uncontrollable utterance against God (comp. vii. 11), x. 2 *a*.

3.

Condemn me not,
show me wherefore Thou contendest with me!
Doth it become Thee to oppress,
to despise the toil of Thy hands,
whilst Thou shinest upon the counsel of the wicked?
Eyes of flesh hast Thou then,
or dost Thou see as men see?
5 are then Thy days like men's days,
or Thy years like those of a man?
that Thou inquirest after my guilt,
and searchest after my sin,
although Thou knowest that I am not guilty,
and none delivereth from Thy hand?—

3. x. 2—22. The discourse with God alone thus introduced is occupied, in accordance with the previous subject-matter of this entire speech and the end of the foregoing special speech against God, vii. 17—21, principally with the thought of guilt, which Job cannot discover in himself, but which, as it seems to him, he must, under torture and compulsion from God, nevertheless confess, whether true or not, the case being as if a powerful earthly tyrant should from some cause seek to compel an unfortunate creature by tortures and sufferings of all kinds to make a confession. But against this idea of God, the profounder conception of Him, as not merely the absolutely omnipotent but also the all-wise and all-good, who cannot proceed so cruelly with his own creature, makes an indignant protest: accordingly in the conflict of these various feelings, now of strong indignation and then of calmer grief and mourning, there arises a despair in the whirl of which Job sinks continually deeper. At first, after a vehement beginning and brief exposition of the whole enigma, the question, how the hard treatment of Job harmonises with the divine omniscience and exaltation? vv. 2—7; then the melancholy reflection, how the Creator can be so enraged against His own noble work, so determined under all circumstances, whether it is guilty or innocent, to destroy it, an entirely new thought of great force here, which is dwelt upon at greatest length, vv. 8—17; finally, as the possibility of a remedy nowhere appears, a fresh, stronger outbreak of despair with the repetition of the demand of vii. 16, that at least a short period of repose may be granted to the hopeless one who is so soon to go down into the Underworld never to return! vv. 18—22. The new and the magnificent aspect of this speech appears in the middle portion of it: hence of the four strophes (each of five verses, for half of ver. 2 belongs to the previous part) it occupies two.—First, the unqualified demand, *condemn me not!* since I am not conscious of guilt; *make me to know wherefore Thou con-*

Thy hands formed and made me,
  round about together—and shouldst Thou destroy me!
remember now that Thou hast formed me like clay,
  and unto dust wilt Thou make me again?
10 Dost Thou not cause me to flow like milk
  and curdle me like whey,
clothest me with skin and flesh
  and interweavest me with bones and sinews?
Life, favour hast Thou shown unto me,
  Thy care hath preserved my spirit:

tendest so severely *against me* without any cause! Then the exposition of the whole case, ver. 3: *is it well in Thee* (the force of טוֹב xiii. 9 also), does it become Thee as God, *to oppress*, yea, *to despise* by destroying without any cause *Thine own work, whilst Thou* (וְעַל־ is a circumstantial clause, acc. § 341 *a*) sendest Thy light and salvation *upon the wicked*, as experience has shown, ix. 22—24. The first of those two acts which seem unworthy of a God, the oppression of the innocent and weak from whom the stronger will force the confession of some guilt by means of tortures of all kinds, is then, vv. 4—7, further considered. Such a way of acting is expected, it is true, from either a short-sighted and ignorant being, who needs the aid of torture to extort the confession of what he does not know but only suspects; or from a being who lives but a limited period, and must therefore hasten to revenge on the suspected offender the wrong which he supposes he has suffered, and at all events, if he has not yet confessed, to keep him a prisoner under still severer torture. But is God then so short-sighted and ignorant, or as short-lived as a man, He who surely knows everything, accordingly Job's innocence, the Eternal whose power and punishment none can escape?—(2) Can the Creator destroy without cause His own work, formed with such skill and toil, man, as the potter his work of clay? This is said at first in general terms, vv. 8, 9 (*together round about*, the whole body therefore with all its numerous members on all sides); then the contrast is brought out more sharply, vv. 10—12. On the one hand, the most marvellous and gracious care in the creation, vivification, and preservation of the human body, from the time of its most secret origin, with its wonderful growth and artistic structure, vv. 10, 11 (comp. Ps. cxxxix. 13—15, Koran, sur. lxxxvi. 5 sq.; because the wonder of this is now so vividly present to Job's mind, he uses here the present tense) unto the special gift of life and its preservation through the numerous dangers of youth to the present, ver. 12. On the other hand—(3) that which wholly contradicts this, together with all this an incomprehensible purpose of a merciless, absolutely certain, destruction of this work, a purpose which has only so lately been plainly revealed, but which must have always been secretly in the divine mind, and now first appears to Job as too certain, ver. 13. This divine determination to destroy him, from

And yet Thou didst hide *this* in Thy heart,
—alas, I know that *this* is Thy mind:
if I sinned, Thou wouldest watch me
and not acquit me of my guilt;
15 if I were in the wrong, then—woe to me!
if I were in the right, I must not lift up my head,
filled with disgrace and seeing my shame!
and if it would raise itself, then Thou wouldest hunt me as a lion,
wouldest show repeatedly on me Thy wonders,
wouldest bring new witnesses against me,
wouldest increase Thy displeasure with me!
changes and hosts against me!—

which he sees no escape, he now depicts, vv. 14—17, most vividly in a picture without a ray of comfort, dwelling in it upon his whole relation to God. God appears to him as a cruel tetralemma, a merciless fourfold net, by which a man must in any case in one way or another be involved; for he believes that God, (1) if he should commit by mistake a small offence (the possibility of which he does not wish to deny vii. 20; xiii. 26), has in that case determined to watch him as closely as possible, in order not to let even the smallest mistake escape unnoticed, but to torment him until he should perish, ver. 14, comp. as regards שמר vii. 12; xiii. 27; (2) if he had done wrong (which he must solemnly deny to have done before these sufferings came upon him), then he must, as is due, be punished, but also (3) if he were right, he must appear as a guilty man, not dare proudly to lift up his head, although in the midst of undeserved disgrace, although satiated with shame (comp. vii. 4; ix. 18) and with his own eyes beholding his humiliation (accordingly רֹאֵה as part. must be read instead of רְאֵה; the Massor. appear to have regarded it with שְׂבַע as an imper. in an abrupt appeal to God, *satiate Thyself with shame and behold my suffering!* cease to treat me so shamefully! But this is against the context, since the circumstances in which he must not hold up his head have to be described); and if nevertheless (4) this so profoundly insulted, innocent head, unable any longer to endure the insult, should raise itself proudly, as is the case now when Job speaks, He would, angry at his resistance, send afresh the most severe and bitter afflictions upon the weak, innocent creature (just as Job now feels the attack of new pains after this rash speech), hunt him as a lion, reveal Himself in His wonders repeatedly upon him by new and marvellous sufferings (ix. 10), bring up against him new afflictions as constantly fresh witnesses of the divine wrath, like the constantly fresh relays of forces in the siege of a fortress! (comp. xvi. 8, and particularly xix. 12, 13; יִגְאֶה is voluntative in the protasis, all the following verbs voluntative in the apodosis, in which way a more passionate conditional sentence is produced, comp. § 357 *b*, and my *Gramm. Arab.*

And wherefore didst Thou take me from the womb?
I ought to have died, seen by no eye,
have become as if I had not been,
have been carried from the womb to the grave!—
20 Are not few my days? let Him cease!
get from me! that I may be bright a little!
before I go and return not,
into the land of darkness and gloom,
the land of thick-darkness like midnight,
gloom and disorder,
so that it getteth light as at midnight!

II. § 750). The last member of the four alternatives he elaborates the more, as he feels most painfully precisely this dilemma. But if thus in all conceivable cases of behaviour there is not one which brings any benefit, and least of all precisely that one which is most worthy of a noble, innocent man, what remains? in that state of things must not—(4) the most uncontrolled execration of life once more get the upper-hand (vv. 18, 19 briefly repeated from iii. 11 sq., the imperfects express that which *ought* to have happened, acc. § 136*f*; כאשר לא הייתי is exactly like كأنّك ما كنت *as if thou hadst not been* thou wilt vanish, Humbert *Chrest. Arab.* p. 39 last line), and the vehement desire yet in his few remaining days of life to enjoy at least a little repose, getting free from the incessant torment, ver. 20, comp. vii. 16 (contrary to the view of the Massora, which recommends the imper., the third person יָשִׁית, יֶחְדַּל is here more appropriate when used of God, because towards the end the direct address to God gradually ceases), before he goes down for ever into the Underworld, with the horrible picture of which this speech also closes. Inasmuch as it is the land of darkness, it is also the land of disorder and confusion, where no one who is accustomed to light, order, and a clear outlook can feel at home; and although there may be there also a slight alternation of day and night, it is nevertheless when it gets light there as dark as midnight on the earth: how great therefore is the darkness of the midnight there! שִׁית מִן־, ver. 19, comp. iv. 20; vii. 19, properly *to turn his attention from some one.*

3. ZOPHAR AND JOB.

a. ZOPHAR. CH. XI.

As Job's speeches thus become increasingly unadvised towards God and exasperating, and also increasingly confident and lengthy, so that it already appears as if all men must hold their peace before him, the youngest of the friends, who, according to the good manners of those times, would have done better to remain silent, ventures under the provocation of such speeches to come forward against Job, in order, in his bold and tumultuous manner, with one blow to end by a wholly unexpected, authoritative word the entire contention. He has not at his command like Eliphaz a personally received oracle, nor like Bildad the wisdom of the ancients: all the more, as the most youthful of the three, he relies upon his own perception and skill quickly to check the conflict which has already grown so hot. If in the previous speech Job had thrown out the idea of appealing to the judgment of God, but had immediately relinquished it, Zophar may now imagine that he will not a little surprise him with the direct expression of the wish, that God may appear to rebuke and correct the man whom men seem unable to bring to an admission of his guilt and to modest silence. And this is the important and only original thought in this speech. So confused and beyond human management is the contention already, that thus early the decision of God, which follows indeed at last, though quite in another form than men expect, is desired. It is, however, first desired by that party in the contention which is in general the weaker and now for the first time shows its own weakness and helpless perplexity. But in the appeal to God it must also for the first time be briefly but openly expressed, that Job has actual sin upon him, and, as Zophar imagines he has correctly observed, still more hidden than open sin, so that he is as yet leniently punished by God, ver. 6 *c*. Quite at the beginning, after an expression of brief astonishment at Job's speeches, he comes out with his new wish, vv. 2—6, then, in order to warn Job the more emphatically by means of the suggested idea of the divine judgment, he sketches an eloquent description, in a calmer tone, of the impossibility that a man should be able to stand successfully a conflict with the divine wisdom and power, vv. 7—12, and returns finally, after the manner of his predecessors, to the expression of hope for Job, which is, however, already very conditional and reserved, bringing forward once more the guilt of Job and appending still more seriously than Bildad a brief earnest word regarding the hopelessness of the wicked, vv. 13—20. Thus even the closing word promising hope in the speeches of the friends gets gradually more and more ambiguous: Eliphaz appends scarcely a slight warning, v. 27, Bildad already briefly introduces into it the opposite of hope, viii. 20*b*, 22*b*, Zophar appends a word, ver. 20, which already appears as an outpost of the host of similar hard threatening words, ch. xv., xviii., xx.

xi. 1 Then answered Zophar of Naama and said:

1.

Shall the flood of words not be answered,
  or a man of talk be in the right?
Thy boasting putteth men to silence,
  so that thou mockest, put to shame by none,
and saidst: "pure is my doctrine,
  and I was spotless in Thine eyes!"

1. The words which are put into Job's mouth, ver. 4, give rather Zophar's brief summary of all the previous speeches of Job: since he, the person attacked, spoke more like a teacher than a repentant learner, it seems to Zophar as if he considered both his doctrine and his life were quite impeachable before God. Both assumptions, particularly the first, incense him, so that he immediately desires the revelation of God, to convince Job by the display of perfect wisdom and knowledge, that God still *causeth* much *of his guilt to be forgotten*, *i,e.*, punishes him far less than he deserves according to strict justice. For it is true enough that his whole misery consists as regards its source in defective knowledge, inasmuch as the man that has but *half* knowledge only too easily applies wrongly the few and imperfect things which he really perceives, and believing that he is in possession of all the wisdom he requires is led astray into confusion and passion, because the outward facts do not correspond with his erroneous view. To this extent Job actually suffers from half-knowledge. But Zophar, presupposing wickedness in Job, does not simply recognise this fact, but goes on falsely to suppose that Job suffers himself by this half-knowledge to be misled to discover simply his innocence and to over-

5 But O that God would but speak,
  that He would open His lips against thee,
and make known to thee the secrets of wisdom,
  how doubly strong it is in understanding:
    then know thou, that God overlooketh to thee much iniquity!

2.

Wilt thou sound the depth of God,
  or mount to the height of the Almighty?
high as heaven!—what wilt thou do?
  deeper than the Underworld—what dost thou know?
longer than the earth in measure,
  broader is it than the sea!

look his numerous hidden and serious sins. So at the end, ch. xxxviii sq., God does really reveal the secrets of his wisdom, and Job learns to perceive the imperfection of his knowledge, but not that he is a sinner. The clause כי כפלים לתושיה, ver. 6, contains an explanation of the predicate of תעלמות חכמה, acc. § 336 *b*: *He revealeth to thee the secrets of wisdom, how*, namely, it is *double*, as strong again, *in best understanding*, as all thy present wisdom which lets thee suppose thyself innocent: what Job therefore at present knows can only be half-knowledge, and accordingly confusion and perplexity. As regards the clause מי יתן אלוה דבר, see § 329 *c*; with regard to the imper. consec. ודע, which might be called the *imper. futuri*, see § 347 *a*.

2. Vv. 7—12. Or wilt thou really contend with God's wisdom and power, and make thyself acquainted with Him as judge? but wilt thou, consider it now, attain to His wisdom, sound the depth (on חקר see the note on viii. 8) of God or scale His highest summit, *i.e.*, discover His perfect, unsurpassable wisdom which is as deep as it is high? that wisdom which is like God Himself all-embracing, as high as the inaccessible heavens (*heights of heaven* is only a concise accusative of measure, but in this place is also according to the context a predicate, so that it is allowable to say instead *heaven-high*, as in the similar instance xxii. 12) and deeper than the dark Underworld (xxvi. 6), just as it also embraces the whole earth and extends beyond it, longer than the outstretching land, broader than the vast sea, so that before it nothing is too high, too dark, too distant, since it consists in the constant, unwavering comprehension and knowledge of everything, vv. 7—9. Ver. 8 and ver. 9, therefore, the predicates refer back to the last thing which is here described, wisdom, ver. 6, inasmuch as it is implied ver. 7 in חקר and again particularly in the fem. תכלית; for ver. 9 it is undoubtedly more correct to read מִדָּה, acc. § 288 *c*, instead of מִדָּהּ, which would have to be derived from a form מַד,

10 He presseth past and shutteth up,
holdeth court:—and who will hinder Him?
for *He* knoweth well the sinful people,
He hath seen the wickedness, before it perceiveth it—
and so a silly man is made sensible,
a wild ass born afresh as a man!

3.

If *thou* wilt raise up thine heart
and spreadest out to Him thine hands:
—hideth thine hand iniquity, put it away,
let not wickedness dwell in thy tents!—

with the suff., which does not occur. Therefore, since the highest power is also associated with the highest wisdom, and the latter receives its truth only by means of the former, it is obvious, that if He comes to judgment attended by this wisdom and power, the sinner who is suddenly overtaken by Him with irresistible might, be he never so stupid and determined to hear nothing of his own guilt, becomes by the revelation of the highest wisdom at once wise, and docile and well-behaved, although he may be as impetuous and wild as a wild ass (xxxix. 2—8, comp. Gen. xvi. 12), through the power which accompanies that wisdom: a single moment in this case transforms the whole man into another being; which is manifestly said not without reference to the restive folly of Job, vv. 10—12. In such a manner Zophar seeks here at the same time to turn what Job had said ix. 11 sq. into the exact opposite of its proper meaning. The arrival of the judge for judgment is in this case a driving past in a rapid storm, *pressing through*, as Job had already said ix. 14; the arrival of the judge is followed by the *shutting up* of the person accused of a serious offence, that he may not escape during the trial; then the הקהיל, or admission and summons of the people to hear the trial, since the proceedings were always public, therefore the actual opening and holding of the court, Ezek. xvi. 40; xxiii. 46. The apodosis begins plainly only with ver. 12, since ומי ישיבנו with ver. 11 form parenthetical clauses. The paronomasia נבוב ילבב might be rendered the *headless* (hollow) man becometh *heedful*, intelligent.[1]

3. Vv. 13—20. The condition, sincere repentance and confession, ver. 13, must be immediately, ver. 14, afresh more emphatically conditioned by another one which is in point of fact earlier, the removal of all previous unrighteousness. As the happy consequences of the fulfilment of these conditions appears (1) a new, cheerful, confident courage, ver. 15, so that Job will no more be compelled to bow down his head in humiliation on account of anything un-

[1] Ewald's German representations of this paronomasia are: "so wird leicht ein *leerer* Mann *gelehrt*", and "der *hohle* Mensch wird *hell*." Tr.

15 then indeed thou liftest up thy face without spot,
wilt be firmly established and without fear!
but *thou* wilt forget the trouble,
as waters gone by wilt remember it.

And brighter than the noonday riseth prosperity,
the darkness will be as the morning:
thou hast confidence then, because there is hope,
thou wilt, looking round, still lie down securely,
take repose alarmed by no one,
and many will flatter thee!
20 But the eyes of the wicked fail,
refuge hath perished from them;
and their hope is—to breathe out the soul!

worthy, as he had complained x. 15; but his confident courage will only be completely possible (2) by a constantly increasing prosperity which will inspire confidence, vv. 16, 17, a prosperity so great that on account of it his calamities will be forgotten like something that never returns, just as water which has once flowed past cannot flow back again, a time of great splendour when even the darkness should it come, will be comparatively bright like the morning (the opposite x. 22); and thus (3) there comes a rest not to be disturbed by any danger, vv. 18, 29, in that on examining his affairs he can always cherish hope, ver. 18, and no one dares to disturb him in this peace, since on the contrary all flatter him, ver. 19. חָפַרְתָּ cannot here come from הפר = חמר *to be ashamed*, vi. 20, as this yields no meaning which suits the context; but it is from חָפַר in the signification *to spy*, to examine, which is very frequent precisely in this book, iii. 21; xxxix. 21, 29: for though the prosperous man pries into, and examines his circumstances, he can, inasmuch as he misses nothing, always lie down in calm security, as a similar idea occurs v. 24; the copula is left out before לבטח תשכב, in order to give greater emphasis to the apodosis. The phrase ver. 19 *a* originates from such ancient figures as Gen. xlix. 9. But in contrast with all this there comes at last, ver. 20, the dark picture of the opposite, how the wicked man with the same necessity perishes irremediably, how to no purpose his eyes fail with longing and grief (Ps. vi. 8) and he has no hope but death! xxxi. 39.

b. JOB. CH. XII—XIV.

But that which was intended, according to Zophar's calculation, to surprise and subdue Job, touches him so little that it can be at once employed as a victorious weapon against

Zophar himself and all the other opponents of Job, and instead of humbling him serves to raise him for the first time above his melancholy and perplexity. In reality, why does he who can to some purpose boast of his innocency, and indeed of his acquaintance with God, vi. 10; ix. 21; xii. 4; xiii. 16, require to submit to the charge, that he is still punished far less than he deserves according to his guilt, or to the charge, that he suffers at all on account of his sins? and to the charge from these men who are about more and more to ignore the truth of his case and to harass the poor sufferer almost without any more mercy. Indeed, in his present state of confusion, in which he now still firmly believes that God treats him at present in any case unfairly, just as amongst men a tyrant may oppress the powerless, he is compelled even to suppose that the friends falsely imputed sin to him simply in order to flatter the tyrant, just as men are often unfair towards the unfortunate in partiality for one whose power and splendour dazzle them, xiii. 8. But, on the other hand, he cannot really think that God would forever take injustice under His protection, because this would be opposed to the idea of God, neither, therefore, the mysterious wrong under which he seems to suffer, nor the evident wrong which the friends are guilty of. Accordingly, scarcely have the opponents carried their suspicion of Job's integrity to its extreme point, and imagine that they will prevent his escape precisely through their appeal to a divine judgment and their desire for its approach, when the hardly pressed man, now on closer reflection, without regard to his previous, vague shrinking from the step of an appeal to God, ix. 2—20, immediately without hesitation seizes the one resource open to him, namely, to appeal to God on his own account and to retaliate upon his opponents as they deserve with their own accusation; and this resource he avails himself of with all the boldness and energy which come from a good conscience. This constitutes a step of decisive moment, which must bring the entire contention another stage onwards as regards all who take part in it. But the consequences of it are most immediate and perceptible in the case of the opponents. Whilst Job has hitherto made no direct attack upon them as regards their arguments, and seemed even to be unable openly to contend with them, he now wrests their own sharp weapons from their hands in an open attack upon them, and having become in self-defence an assailant he makes up with one blow for all past deficiencies. For as he now takes up for the first time openly and with full intent the offensive, he brings to light the entire character of his opponents, their professedly superior wisdom no less than their false accusations. . He finds the former is by no means great, but only very ordinary and low, and that the latter must bring down the stern chastisement of God in judgment upon them instead of upon him. This line of attack is managed with such scornful superiority of knowledge and rebuke, that the opponents, beaten on all hands and seriously wounded, perplexed and astonished, are compelled to give up their previous position. For the moment, a less obvious but far more important advantage which Job derives against his will from the simple progress of the conflict is, that he comes by it to consider more closely his invaluable possession—his integrity, and for the first time with growing consciousness, sometimes sad (xii. 4), sometimes proud (xiii. 16), defends himself by it against dangerous attacks, yea, rises above his former self and his despondency, hoping for the victory of his good cause. While just before, ix. 2 sq., he had still not ventured to assert his good conscience before God, except in vague fear or despair, he now surveys everything more calmly and already begins faintly to cast off the old blind fear. Notwithstanding, the reason for this act of challenging God is still wholly perverse, and Job permits himself to be led astray into passion by a dangerous experiment which is contrary to the majesty of God. For the danger, which is here latent from the beginning, of openly speaking against God, is at this point, where

He is violently, and with a certain degree of defiance, challenged to appear, where an open, solemn accusation is directed against Him, xiii. 23—28, brought completely out, and so far the friends were certainly right in warning Job to beware of greater recklessness. Hence this speech, which as far as it is directed against the friends is a true model of lucidity and quiet force, contains nevertheless from the very first some expressions of troubled despondency, xii. 4–6, is then, the nearer the challenge to God draws, more and more pervaded by the old despair, xiii. 14, 15, 20, 21, and at last, since after all, as Job soon perceives, God does not appear at his summons, falls back into the same despair with which all the previous speeches had closed, xiv. 1—22. Still, the consciousness of innocence cannot have been so powerfully stirred permanently in vain for Job, and already at the close, when all earthly hopes disappear, he is surprised by the question regarding the eternal duration of innocence and of the soul, by that question which, when more closely pursued, opens up a wholly new realm of hope and which points at this place with infinite significance to what has to follow subsequently.—As therefore the challenge to God must be the centre of this speech, it having been prepared for by the attack upon the friends, and issuing in complaints and despair, it falls into the three parts: (1) the attack upon the supposed wisdom of the friends, which is useless to Job, ch. xii.; so that he determines (2) to turn to God instead of to them, to whom they cannot turn, xiii. 1—22; (3) the complaint to God, xiii. 23—xiv. 22.

xii. 1 And Job answered and said:

1.

Yes undoubtedly! *ye* are people!
and with you will wisdom die!

I. Ch. xii. Attack upon the knowledge of the friends: for the attack upon their accusation, if presented at the commencement, would hardly be successful on account of their infatuation; neither could Job make it, since his innocence

I also have a head as well as you,
I do not fall below you:
and *who* doth not know such things?—

A laughing-stock to his friend must I be,
one who called to God and was heard:
a laughing-stock is the just, the godly man!

is not a thing which can be outwardly demonstrated. The attack upon their wisdom, however, can be perfectly well made; and if the friends are represented as people without such tremendous wisdom in comparison with Job, there is thereby a shadow cast upon their accusation also, since the ignorant most easily make false charges. And with regard to his guilt or innocence, if Job then determines to turn immediately to God Himself, he is excused, indeed, he is entitled to do so. Relying upon some general propositions regarding the divine power and wisdom, they had attacked him with increasing vehemence, particularly had Zophar just done this, xi. 6—12: this basis of reliance he now wrests from them, by showing that he knows such propositions much better than they, in order that he may then, himself relying upon them, call for God's judgment with greater propriety than they. The proposition concerning the righteousness of God, which the friends had previously touched on, ch. viii., he still passes over in his refutation, because they have not as yet driven him to extremities, and just now the thought of being able to come off victorious against them by this very righteousness of God flashes through him as a sudden light. But the opinionated use which the friends make of the power and hidden wisdom of God he here puts to shame with a proud superiority, by showing that as regards a knowledge of that wisdom and power he is probably able to compete with each of them; and after the first scornful expression on this point, vv. 2, 3, he is, it is true, somewhat overwhelmed by gloomy displeasure at the unworthy treatment which he has to bear and at the lot of the whole world, which now so naturally appears to him as horribly dark, vv. 4—6; but remembering the whole purpose of this speech, he returns immediately, with prevailing calmness, to the matter with which he had commenced, and shows, after the proper introduction, vv. 7—12, in a magnificent oration, how well he can rival the friends, yea, surpass them, in point of knowledge, vv. 13—25.

1. Vv. 2, 3. Scornful from displeasure: Verily, I must really suppose that *ye* are people, and that beside you there is nobody else, because you make it appear as if you knew more than everybody else and as if when you die wisdom will die with you: you fools, to whom I have no need to yield in any respect, and who have no right to boast of your knowledge in comparison with mine! נָפַל מִן־ to fall, on examination to become smaller than—, only here and xiii. 2.

2. Vv. 4—6. But before he sets about producing the proof of this, the profoundest displeasure threatens to seize him in consideration of this wholly

5 To misfortune scorn in the secure man's thought!
scorn waiteth for those whose foot is tottering;
peaceful tents are to the devastators
and security to them who make God tremble,
to him who bringeth God in his hand.

Yet ask but the beasts, that they should teach thee,
the birds of heaven, that they should tell thee;
or think to the earth, that it should teach thee,
and let the fish of the sea recount to thee:

unworthy treatment which must be borne from friends by a man who hitherto, on the ground of his upright blameless life, stood as a brave godly person in intimate, wellsped intercourse with God, when he prayed found a hearing, but now must hear God appealed to against himself, ver. 4 (although what is at this point a mournful memory soon becomes, after somewhat freer reflection, a happy assistance, since surely, if Job had formerly such successful and beneficial intercourse with God, he may still expect a similar result from an appeal to Him (xiii. 3—16). And inasmuch as Job looking upon the past of his life appears to himself to be as it were a historical character, the first person changes in his speech involuntarily into the third; with regard to שְׂחֹק, see § 150 *b*.—And this gloomy displeasure when once excited easily leads to the terrible consideration of the wrong state of things which is likewise found to prevail throughout the entire human world, vv. 5, 6. *To fatal misfortune* (פִּיד a word which is almost peculiar to this book, xxx. 24; xxxi. 29) *contempt* (as ver. 21, xxxi. 34)! expressed almost as an exclamation, contempt is due *according to the thoughts of him who lives without care* in secure prosperity, it must be allowed that is the way of the world; *it*, this contempt, *is prepared*, waits beforehand (as xv. 23; xviii. 12) *for those with tottering foot*, near to a complete fall, and who can prevent that? scarcely does any appear to stumble without any one to save him, when he is already generally overwhelmed with scorn. But, on the other hand, *peaceful dwellings* and in their conduct confident *security* have *devastators*, even the most desperate, who by word and deed defy *God Himself* and think to cause *Him to tremble*, as men are terrified; yea, even the most insolent, barbarous soldier, who acknowledges no right and no power beyond his own arm, so that he imagines that where his arm extends and rules thither God's power extends and rules and all must submit to it as to God, and who thus *brings* to people *God in his hand* (power); like Hab. i. 11, 16, and as the *contemptor Deûm* exclaims *dextra mihi Deus*, Virg. Æn. X. 773.

3. Vv. 7—12. But (thus Job, before it is too late, here makes an effort to escape from such gloomy considerations by a return to the thought with which he began), if it is desired to know how ordinary is that wisdom of the friends, let, in the first instance, vv. 7—10, only the living creatures of the

who of all these doth not know,
  that Jahvé's hand hath made *these* things?
10 He in whose hand is the soul of all living creatures,
  and the spirit of all bodies of men.

Doth not then the ear try words,
  and doth not the palate taste food for itself?
in old men is wisdom,
  and length of days equals understanding.

earth be asked: even of the irrational, dumb animals (מִי־ — בְּ—, ver. 9, as "Isa." l. 10) every one knows, experiences, and feels at least plainly enough the power of the Creator also when He sends (as in my case now) suffering, since, in fact, every living thing lives and enjoys its life only by the power of the Creator, knows therefore in so far that the *hand* (power) *of God has done this* which Job just now most feels, the infliction of profound suffering and pain, which the friends constantly describe as done by God as if he did not know that and could not learn it quite as well from every sensitive animal.[1] It is quite true that in a certain sense even the animals feel through their life or sufferings the omnipotence of the Creator, Ps. civ. 26—30, and the man that will deny this omnipotence may be pointed even to the feelings and experiences of animals to be taught by them. שִׂיחַ, ver. 8, cannot therefore in this connexion signify *shrub* as a noun, as the trees do not live in this sense like the animals. *Earth*, therefore, ver. 8, points only in contrast with heaven, ver. 7, to the small creeping things.—And, secondly, the same knowledge of the wonderful power of God may be easily, and certainly much more distinctly and particularly, learnt from the discourses of all experienced men; indeed, every man who is not wholly deaf and obtuse will know how to select and retain the best and truest things from such discourses which he has heard from the days of his youth, just as the palate distinguishes and retains the foot which suits it; for thus Job also always prized the wisdom of the aged men, and knows that to have lived long is generally equivalent to having much intelligence, vv. 11, 12. But at this point there fail manifestly two verses which ought to state that Job had himself by his own personal experience in his sufficiently long life learnt

---

[1] It might be thought that the short *this* was meant to point to all the visible universe, as *idam*, Manu i. 5, Bhagavad-Gîtâ iii. 38; and as the expression *all this* points in a suitable connexion to the whole world not only "Isa." lxvi. 2, comp. ver. 1, but also Jer. xiv. 22. But, first, the reference to suffering is here as everywhere most immediately present to Job's mind; and, secondly, it cannot very well be said that the animals *know* that God is the creator of the world, since such knowledge is beyond them: but they do know and feel by their sufferings that there is a higher power beyond them.

[*Thus to me also much of life was given,*
the number of years will already bow my head,
I saw many marvels of God's acts,
I heard the instructive word of the ancients.]

"He hath wisdom and might,
to Him belongeth counsel and understanding:
lo, He breaketh down—it will not be built up,
shutteth up the man—he will not get free again;
15 lo, He holdeth back waters—they dry up,
letteth them go—they lay waste the land.

the same lessons as he had heard by questioning older men: for this is presupposed xiii. 1 *a*, comp. xv. 10; xxx. 1, since the personal seeing of the wonders of God as they are enumerated vv. 13—25 cannot be referred, for instance, to what is said vv. 7—10; moreover, two verses are wanting to complete the strophe according to its proper structure, and the transition from ver. 12 to ver. 13 is at present too abrupt, particularly in a speech such as this. The general scope of the words is indicated in the translation of the text.

4. Vv. 13—25. Thus introduced, a very eloquent description of the divine power and wisdom begins to flow from the lips of the afflicted man, in four strophes, each of three verses, the last strophe being lengthened to four verses. However, he makes this description not in mere rivalry with the friends, but manifestly with far superior power and wealth of ideas; and if even his first essay of this kind, ix. 4—10, could rival those of the opponents, this far surpasses in point of wealth and copiousness his earlier description. Nor does he here repeat the fine illustrations which he had used in his previous speech, ch. ix., but applies with extreme skill the details of his description precisely to the present case, doing this without any express indication of it but yet quite perceptibly. For while he could have described the power of God and his wisdom, which according to the feeling of the ancients displayed itself more particularly in enigmas and marvels, in very various ways, dwelling very much upon most various things in which the ancient world felt the mysterious, hidden wisdom and power of God, he takes another course and designedly brings forward partly the great vicissitudes in human affairs, according to which God sends both weal and woe, prosperity and disaster, and partly the experience, that even the wisest of the earth may easily become fools before God and get into helpless perplexity. That first phenomenon the opponents will do well to give heed to, inasmuch as they see in the vicissitudes of Job's fortunes nothing but his guilt, since the cause may after all be another one hidden from men; the latter phenomenon let them apply to themselves, and at the same time remember, acc. ver. 22, that at last God can bring all hidden things into the light, the beginnings of them also, xiii. 10, and that the misled and the mis-

He hath strength as well as true weal,
to Him belongeth the misled and the misleader:
He who causeth counsellors to go barefoot,
and maketh judges fools,
fetters looseth from kings,
and fasteneth a bond on their loins;

He who maketh priests go barefoot,
and overturneth established things,
20 who taketh speech from the approved,
and withdraweth judgment from the old men;
He who poureth contempt upon nobles,
slackeneth the girdle of the mightiest;

leader, the oppressed and the prosperous oppressor, both alike really depend upon God, ver. 16 *b*, which two particulars do in fact introduce something of a more cheerful nature into this long description which is otherwise so mournful. Of the objects of nature which were more referred to ch. ix., there is here but little mention, and those which are mentioned are also by preference of a gloomy and injurious nature, ver. 15. Thus this description, which can scarcely come to an end, advances, after a double commencement of a more general nature at the head of the first two strophes, in such a way, that the strange infatuation, even of the wisest, is expressly touched upon in the second and third strophes, is brought more prominently forward in the last, and closes the speech with great emphasis. Ver. 14: *He shutteth up* עַל_ *over the man*, as usually a cistern closing at the top served as a prison, Gen. xxxvii. sq.; Ex. xii. 29; Jer. xxxvii., as Job here says with reference to xi. 10, but evidently in a figurative sense, and as he so often complains regarding himself that he is as it were shut up by his sufferings, without help or exit (see *ante* p. 4); therefore this instance manifestly occurs to him involuntarily at the very commencement of the long description. *Judges* and *priests* who must go barefoot into imprisonment, vv. 17, 19, are, according to an ancient mode of speaking, examples of the most powerful and honoured men of the earth and are thus placed by the side of counsellors kings and nobles, vv. 17, 18, 21; on an equality with all these the *proved experts*, who can always speak and advise, *e.g.*, the ancient prophets, are placed, ver. 20: but the course of events brings something so new and obscure that all prophets and wise men and ancients are put to silence or even misled and act unwisely. מוּסַר, ver. 18, must come from מוֹסֵר *fetter*, acc. § 213 *c*, on account of the antithesis alone: He unfetters and fetters kings, fastening on their loins again a close band, a chain; whilst reversely the *loosened girdle*, ver. 21, is, acc. Isa. v. 27, sign and symbol of failing courage. שִׁטַּח, ver. 23, used without an accusative and with לְ- of the indirect object exactly like יַפְתְּ, Gen. ix. 27; *led them away*, ver. 23, into

He who layeth bare deep things from the darkness,
and bringeth to the light black-gloom;
He who giveth growth to nations—and destroyeth them,
to the nations enlargement—and leadeth them away;
taketh away the mind of the chiefs of the nations of the earth
and causeth them to wander trackless in a wilderness,
without light they grope in darkness,
and He causeth them to wander like the drunken."

xiii. 2.

1 Lo, all hath mine eye seen,
mine ear heard and observed for itself:
as much as ye know I know also,
I do not fall below you.
But I will speak to the Highest,
and to argue my case with God I desire.—

imprisonment, which had already, vv. 17, 19, been mentioned. With the two last verses Job evidently intends to surpass the description of Eliphaz, v. 13, 14.

II. xiii. 1—22. With such superiority in the knowledge of divine things, Job has no need to be threatened by his opponents with the appearance of God: but, on the contrary, he can openly, and with all the force derived from a good conscience, himself appeal to God, representing to Him his good cause and expecting, indeed requiring, His judgment. If any one shall be threatened with this appearance, it is the friends, who in this difficult contention speak (as Job justly thinks, comp. xlii 7) against their better knowledge, whom therefore Job rather must most earnestly warn, if it is necessary that he should at last speak against them. Thus the direct and natural course of his thought soon conducts him to this second and still more resentful correction of the friends, vv. 1—12. But as he now, suddenly turning from them as victor, and yet aloud in their hearing, sets about directing his complaint to God and challenging the divine judgment with vehemence, by force putting down all doubts which were multiplying against this at the very last moment, his discourse, which had hitherto been on the whole collected on account of the superiority of his wisdom, becomes immediately more violently agitated again and driven hither and thither by the waves of an almost uncontrolled despair, vv. 13—22. To the haste which prevails through this very comprehensive speech, corresponds its arrangement in short strophes of three verses each; whilst in the middle, where occurs the sudden and complete turning away from the friends and the decided turning to God in spite of all remaining doubts, a solitary verse is introduced, ver. 13.

But ye are only lie-patchers,
  stitchers of nothingness are ye all.
5 O that ye would only keep silence,
  that it might be unto you as wisdom!
Hear ye then my reproof,
  and unto the rebukes of my lips give heed:

For God will ye speak—wrong,
  and for Him will ye speak—deceit?
will ye be partial for Him,
  or for God will ye contend?
is it seemly that He should search you through?
  or as men are deceived will ye deceive Him?

1. Vv. 1—12. The first strophe, vv. 1—3, is occupied with the transition: *seen* and *heard*, acc. xii. 11. 12 and what was remarked upon those verses: ver. 3*b* in this case in express difference from ix. 3.—But before he carries out the intention which he has just expressed of defending his just cause before God, he must still, as he thinks, speak a last word with the friends, vv. 3—12: precisely because they endeavoured to terrify him by that very thing which he has now determined to seize as his last resource—the appeal to God. Hence the most severely pointed word against them becomes now inevitable. For if he must of necessity speak of his guilt or innocence, as the friends have conceived it, the only course open to him is really to wholly forbid their interference, since they infatuatedly enough only allege vain, and indeed false, things concerning him, and would do better to wholly hold their peace; so that he himself must rather correct them, instead of their correcting him, vv. 4—6. טָפַל signifies properly to besmear, stick-together, join, hence like the related תָּפַר *to sew* (with עַל *over* a thing, *sew-up* xiv. 17); but is used here figuratively of the toilsome putting together and connecting of invented lies.—As he must therefore in self-defence begin to correct them, it is easy for him to throw at them the most righteous censure, vv. 7—9, and threat, vv. 10—12, in place of the unjust censure and threat with which they had persecuted him, and this just reproof they must necessarily now hear from him whether they will or not. For now, indeed, as long as God has not yet appeared, they may allege against better knowledge the most false things regarding Job's case and God's purposes with regard to him, only imputing guilt to the sufferer in order to flatter the Almighty: but will they then when He actually appears (as Job is now about to demand His appearance), dare to speak regarding Him as if He required their lying voices, just as an earthly magnate likes to find partiality *for* himself? do they wish to have the shame of being more narrowly examined and seen through and through by Him who cannot be deceived or endure partiality

10 **H**e will correct, correct you,
  if in secret ye are partial!
will not His majesty terrify you,
  His dread fall upon you?
your sayings become ashen-proverbs,
  shields of clay your shields' bosses.—

—**H**old your peace from me, that *I* may speak,
  let come upon me what may!—

Wherefore do I carry my body with my teeth,
  and risk my soul in my fist?

for Himself? vv. 7—9, comp. Prov. xxviii. 11; the ־לְ is *for*, *on behalf of*, both ver. 7 and ver. 8, comp. Judges vi. 31.—No, for the secret partiality against the sufferer He will chastise them (as Job now at last, vv. 10—12, adds with the confidence of the victor); and if He appears, his majesty, terrifying all the profane, will immediately confound them as sinners, so that all the fine memorial sayings and other arguments with which they now defend themselves dissolve at once into their native nothingness! Inasmuch as they appeal so gladly to ancient doctrines and wise proverbs, Job here ironically calls their glib words *memorial* sayings.

2. Ver. 13, vv. 14—22. With this sudden resolve, turning from the vanquished opponents with whom he is determined not to speak further, and collecting his thoughts alone for the arguing of his case with God, which had already been announced, ver. 3, he is, it is true, seized by a vague fear as to what will be the issue, as soon as he more closely considers the tremendous risk to which he exposes himself. For according to the ancient belief, a man had cause to fear immediate death if God by sudden appearance should approach too close to him, how much more if he challenges Him almost defiantly (Ex. xxxiii. 20; Judg. xiii. 22; Gen. xviii. 23 sq.): and such religious feelings and fears come upon Job all the more powerfully at this moment since he previously believed he was suffering under the divine wrath. But still more quickly does he cast them off with the brief, abrupt, and vehement exclamation ver. 13.—Indeed, when he reflects more calmly, sufficient reasons present themselves which can encourage him to run this risk, or at all events to a certain extent excuse him: of these there is particularly the desperate situation in which he finds himself. For in any case he already supposes that he cannot escape impending death: for what purpose therefore is vain labour and planning to save his life, in some such way as a wild beast carries off in his teeth with great toil his threatened prey (a sufficiently intelligible figure), or as one, already wholly lost, who seeks to fight a way of escape with his fist, at once perishes if the power of arm forsakes him (Judg. xii. 3; 1 Sam. xix. 5; xxviii. 21; Ps. cxix. 109)? in

15 He will nevertheless slay me! I have no hope;
only my ways will I maintain before Him!
that is also for my weal,
that no profane man cometh before Him.

Hear ye, hear attentively my words,
what I explain, [hear] with your ears!
behold now, I have ordered the case:
I know that *I* shall be in the right;
who is it that will contend with me?
for then would I hold my peace and expire!

such a case, is it not after all a consolation to be able freely to utter his most sacred conviction at least before his death? vv. 14, 15. With this, it is true, there overtakes him here too a feeling of the former despair (vii. 11, 16; ix. 21, 25, 35; x. 1), threatening wholly to overcome him. But as quickly he remembers, on the other hand, that his innocence must really in the end serve to promote his weal, inasmuch as no profane man may come before God, and he is not conscious of unholy inclinations, ver. 16: a thought which is expressed here much more reassuringly than vi. 10 *c* and far less vehemently than ix. 21.—Thus prepared and thus undaunted, just about to begin his case against God, he then, with lofty courage and as if already assured of victory, calls upon his opponents themselves to listen attentively to his accusation, addressing them once more: in the full consciousness of his innocence, he really trusts firmly that not even anyone will be able to appear (not God Himself even) as a decided opponent and counter-plaintiff, since in case such an one should appear and refute him, he would as a punishment prefer at once to hold his peace and die, vv. 17—19, comp. xxxi. 22.—But now in the immediate neighbourhood of God and at the last decisive moment overtaken afresh involuntarily by that vague fear, he ventures, already beginning to address God, first to make two requests to Him that he may be able calmly to present his case: the two requests being, that He do not so intensify his pains during his speech that he must sink under them (to remove His *hand* from him), and then, by His sudden appearance, for instance, not confound him by His terror (comp. ver. 11). These are the same two requests which he had already made as preliminaries of his open complaint in a similar connexion in the previous speech, ix. 34, only that here, where he prepares a plaintiff's charge with set purpose, he offers them much more distinctly: just as before human judges guarantees of unrestrained speech may be requested as preliminary to the trial. Under these conditions, therefore, let the contention begin, God Himself beginning by calling him to account, or Job beginning to speak, the latter of which, since God does not call upon him, he does on his own responsibility, vv. 20—22. Thus this entire section, vv. 11—22, which is in the highest degree agitated between hope and fear, shows what self-conquest and hard inward struggles

20 **O**nly two things do not with me,
then from Thy face will I not hide me:
the weight of Thy hand withdraw far from me,
and let not Thy fear terrify me!
then call, and *I* will answer,
or I speak, and answer Thou me!

3.

How many iniquities, misdeeds, have I?
my transgression and misdeed cause Thou me to know!

this step cost Job, precisely because he ventures upon it before he is sufficiently purified and prepared, since he does not yet possess the complete clearness and repose without which no man can see the Lord: how totally different is it subsequently, ch. xxix—xxxi.

III. xiii. 23—ch. xiv. The speech against God, thus introduced and proudly commenced in the presence of his opponents, begins like an actual plaintiff's accusation with the appropriate question, xiii. 23, 24, as only an unfortunate defendant can complain before a superior lord and judge whom he considers as also his prosecutor. But as God, although so distinctly appealed to, indeed, challenged, delays to appear, the speech is further continued, issues in other considerations, and thus once more becomes like the conclusions of the two previous speeches, ch. vii., x.; indeed at last, xiv. 13 sq., as the feeling of the uselessness of this effort also can no longer be overcome and gets the complete mastery, the speech comes back once more to despair of all present things. Inasmuch, therefore, as it becomes the third similar speech of this kind, although beginning quite differently, it gathers up in a firmer and more forcible form what had been twice before indicated and hastily uttered, giving equal prominence both to the moral aspects of the case, from which the complaint must start, and to the natural aspects of it, but carrying both to an extreme. If previously the moral aspects of the contention, vii. 17—21, were only just touched upon, but then x. 2—17, solely brought forward with passionate vehemence, here the question is at once proposed, how much then he has really sinned who is himself not conscious of any great transgression, and wherefore he suffers? and the natural aspects, which were forcibly enough referred to vii. 1—16, but scarcely at all ch. x., are here treated once more, as if for the last time, with great emphasis and agonising grief. But just because the plaintiff here gathers up all that he had hitherto felt of this kind and exhausts it with the utmost effort, there arises in him irresistibly at last the foreboding of the vanity of all such endeavours, and involuntarily the first dim outlook into a new world forces itself upon him: gradually the complaint becomes more collected, the speech quieter, more resigned in its melancholy, and thereby most dissimilar to its predecessors. First, the short, severe complaint of the wrong

Wherefore hidest Thou Thy face,
considerest me Thine enemy!

25 A driven leaf—that wilt Thou scare,
and the dry stubble still pursue,
that Thou prescribest for me bitter punishments
and causest me to inherit youthful sins,
puttest my feet in the block
and watchest all my paths,
of the soles of my feet makest Thyself sure?
although like a rotten thing he falleth away,
like a garment devoured by the moth!—

which he believes he endures although so weak and harmless, xiii. 23—28; then the reflection becomes of a more general nature, pervaded by profound melancholy, regarding the physical as well as moral weakness and imperfection of man in comparison with God, of man who when once he has died appears to have the most mournful lot, which is wholly out of proportion to his deserts, of never being permitted again to enjoy life, xiv. 1—12: O that a return into life were possible, that at least after his death his innocence might be recognised, since in the present life this seems, on account of the certainty of impending death, impossible to be attained (this is the new and logical but infinitely important inference by which Job returns to himself and his case)! xiv. 13—22. Thus this long speech, which deals with such a great number of thoughts, requires five long strophes to exhaust it, the first three having six, the last two five verses each.

1. xiii. 23—28. Vv. 23, 24 the complaint in the strict sense finds brief expression, in a different way from x. 2. *How many sins—?* it would seem from such severe punishments that I must have many: but I do not know of any, save that perhaps, ver. 26, Thou must desire so severely to charge upon me and not forgive the slight, pardonable transgressions of my youth, Ps. xxv. 7. But inasmuch as the natural consideration is here immediately brought into the moral one, he also asks bitterly, ver. 25 (as vii. 12): wilt Thou, the Almighty, scare, persecute a driven leaf or the dry stubble? me who am already become wholly weak and helpless, Thou with all Thy terrible power? that Thou on that account, as if I must not yield to every gust of wind even, *writest* (dictatest as judge) such bitter punishments for me, and as if I could escape holdest me so strictly and severely, as into the worst prison[1] settest

[1] The block, or log of wood, in which the feet were put, or which had to be dragged along on the foot, Lat. *codex*, Russ. *dybys*, Turk. طومرق *ṭumruq*, Acts xvi. 24, Abdias' *Hist. Apost.* iii. 2, Burckhardt's *Notes on the Bed.* p. 302; Aristoph. *Equit.* 367, 707, 1054, *Lysistr.* 679, *Plut.* 276, Journ. asiat. 1852, I. p. 373.

xiv.

1 Man born of woman
  is short-lived and full of restlessness;
like the flower he springeth up and—is withered,
  and fled as a shadow, never staying:
and upon such an one hast Thou fixed Thine eye,
  and me bringest Thou into judgment with Thee?
O that but a pure man might come from an impure,
  were it only one!

my feet and *watchest all my ways* (vii. 12; x. 14), yea, makest *thyself sure*[1] *of the soles of my feet*, where they may be and where they shall be forced to continue without any movement, just as certainly a strict guard must know how far he will grant freedom to them: although in reality this weak man Job already perishes like a rotten thing, and, inwardly ruined and wasted, will soon fall away like a moth-eaten garment. The conclusion, ver. 28, thus reverts in sense to what was already indicated ver. 25: but as Job both here and there looks upon himself more as suffering under the common lot of human weakness, this general reflection can now easily become,

2 and 3, xiv. 1—12, exclusively prevalent. But in this general reflection still more than the simple toil and moil of human life, which had previously been strongly dwelt upon, iii. 17, vii. 1—5, is the brief life of the frail son of woman brought forward, even much more emphatically than vii. 6—10: for it is precisely around this terrible thought, that man, and with him his innocence, must perish by death for ever, that in the end all the sorrow, complaint and despair gather, since Job can very easily let go his life but not his innocence. If with this natural, physical weakness of man there is strictly compared his spiritual, or moral, weakness, according to which no one (much as this were to be desired)[2] can really be quite pure before God, how unjust does it then appear that God should so strictly judge him and persecute him so incessantly with punishment and suffering (as had been previously said xiii. 26, 27), since surely

[1] This is the most probable signification of הִתְחַקָּה, ver. 27, formed from חָק, acc. § 121 *a*, like تحقّق with على *to certify oneself of a thing*, as similarly تحكّم على to make oneself arbitrarily judge concerning a matter, to dispose of it arbitrarily. The interpretation of the Vulg. and the Pesh., *vestigia pedum meorum considerasti*, may also be tolerably well combined with this, though it is too general and indefinite.

[2] The לֹא, ver. 4 *b*, must acc. § 358 *b* be equivalent to לוּ: and if this member contains properly an interjected wish, as it were a sigh, its unusual brevity is also explained.

5 If his days are determined,
the number of his moons with Thee,
bounds Thou hast set, not to be passed:
then look away from him that he may rest,
at least enjoy as a hireling his day!

For the tree even hath hope:
if it is hewn, it sprouteth again,
and its young shoot faileth not;
if in the earth its root wax old,
or in the dust its stock die,
—from the scent of water it bursteth forth again,
and maketh boughs like young plants:
10 but a man, he dieth—and is cut off,
and when men die—they are gone!
Flowed away is the water from the sea,
and the stream is parched away, dried up:
so when men have lain down, they never arise,
until the heavens vanish, they never awake,
they are not aroused from their sleep.—

even a man like Job can easily at some time sin although (as was indicated xiii. 25) it is only in smaller and pardonable matters, vv. 1—4. So that it must be thence inferred, if life is really so brief and it is determined on God's part that there shall be no possibility of prolonging it, surely God ought all the more to grant man rest in this brief space, in order that he may at least (עַד) endure the weariness of his life as the hireling willingly bears the toil of his in hope of the remunerative evening, vv. 5, 6, comp. vii. 19; x. 20: the hireling finds the present hard and weary, but it is brightened by hope for the future; the man who, with the vain wish to be permitted longer life, looks with terror into the future, and who is nevertheless in the present incessantly tortured, can have no enjoyment at all, neither in the present nor the future: thus the picture vii. 1 is here still darker.—For, alas, it is a mournful truth, that man has no hope of ever living again after death, vv. 7—12: so far even the tree seems better off than man, since if above the earth it is hewn down it has still hidden roots below, which are able to strike out afresh, ver. 7; or if from its own debility it is about to die in the dry ground, still as soon as it even from a distance scents the reviving water and feels it near, it is at once made young again, vv. 8, 9. In the case of the tree, therefore, the possibility of a new life is not excluded, but it is wholly different in the case of a deceased man: as the dried-up water leaves behind it no trace in the lake or stream

—Would that in the Underworld Thou didst hide me,
didst conceal me till Thy wrath turned,
didst set me a term—and rememberedst me!
If a man die, doth he live again?
all my service-time would I hope,
until my relief came;

and never returns (vii. 9), so man when dead returneth not until the heaven is no more, and that is eternal (Ps. lxxxix. 30, 38, 39; not as "Isa." li. 6), therefore cometh never again from his motionless sleep in Hades into this life in the Upper-world!

4 and 5, xiv. 13—22. But precisely that which is unsatisfactory and comfortless in this general belief of antiquity leads at last, when Job, reverting from it to himself and his innocence, is about to draw his conclusion, unexpectedly and yet logically to a new thought. That thought, which here first suddenly comes to light, takes its place in the imagination as merely a distant wish, there to be fully recognised and realised in the first place. In this its first conception in the imagination it does not attain to full certainty. The speaker who is surprised by it, at first simply considers how beautiful and glorious the case would be if it were a reality. But inasmuch as the thought contains a truth which has really its proper place here, it can never be lost again, but when more closely followed must become increasingly certain. Previously, on the consciousness that his innocence could not be for ever overlooked by God, Job in view of death cherished the profoundly painful, perfectly comfortless idea, that God would some day, when He would desire to acknowledge the justice of his cause and restore to him his due, seek in vain for him on the earth, in vain, therefore, desire to declare perceptibly to him his innocence, vii. 8, 21. But now, after the consciousness of his innocence has already in the course of the contention become much more distinct, suddenly an entirely different idea, full of comfort and opening up to him an infinite hope, forces itself upon his mind. It is the idea, whether his innocence may not possibly be acknowledged in a new life after death? And now he rapidly surveys with a clear glance both the presupposed conditions and the exceedingly glorious consequences of the truth of this idea. The heart of the man, who thinks he must despair as regards the present and was only just now feeling that he was wholly without outlook in his utter darkness, swells with the thoughts and prospects which thus crowd upon him: a bright light comes suddenly to divide by its flash this darkness. First, the desire to be hidden, it is true, in the Underworld, whither he must soon come, as in a dark place of refuge from the divine wrath which is determined to pursue him at present until death is passed, but to be hidden only for a set time, then to be judged! ver. 13. But if the last thing is to take place, a new life must be granted, since the judgment can be held over the living only: but is a new life possible? a previous question which had been almost forgotten in the fervour and suddenness of the wish,

15 Thou wouldest call, I answer Thee,
   Thou wouldest long for the work of Thy hands!—
For now Thou numberest my steps,
   passest not by my sin:
my transgression is sealed up in a bag,
   Thou hast sewed up my punishment.

ver. 14 *a*. If it were possible, O how would he patiently wait all his *time of forced labour*, *i.e.*, as long as his innocence shall be unrecognised and he shall thereby be most profoundly tortured and alarmed, on the earth and in the Underworld, until his *relief* from this hard forced-service *should come* by the divine appearing, quickening, and redemption! and how marvellously glorious would be the issue of this! how would *he* with expectation and joy answer the *call* of God (whilst God's call to him to the defence of his innocence, xiii. 22, is now in vain expected), and how would the Creator *long after his creature*, from whom He cannot surely for ever turn away, because His creature is a part of Himself, He who now overlooks the child which is profoundly longing after Him! ver. 15, more briefly reechoed from x. 8—12. *For now*, indeed (thus he falls back, vv. 16, 17, from the bright picture, which had suddenly come as from another world and suddenly vanished again, into the dark reality), he thinks that he can expect nothing else than a continuance of the wrong: now God seems *to count his steps*, *i.e.*, not to grant him the least liberty or rest, xiii. 27, and *not to overlook his transgression.*[1] On the contrary, the guilt of Job, in the sense of his condemnation to death, appears to be already unalterably determined, solemnly written down and sealed like a judicial sentence, yea, to lie preserved with other recorded resolutions in the carefully sewed-up *bag*, to be brought forth and carried out at the convenient time! This figure, which is worked out so completely, ver. 17, is often used by other poets and speakers of those centuries, Hos. xiii. 12; Deut. xxxii. 34; on טפל על, see *ante* on xiii. 4, and comp. also *Beiträge zur Geschichte der ältesten Auslegung des*

[1] In the text of the second as well as of the first edition Ewald followed the Mass. reading שָׁמַר עַל, translating *hast not regard to my transgression*, with the comment, "whether it deserves to be so severely punished as it actually is, or whether the contrary is not the case according to xiii. 23, 26; as an earthly ruler often punishes without himself paying much regard to the measure of the transgression, or even to the guilt or innocence." In a foot-note he said: "Although this meaning of שָׁמַר עַל is unusual, the reading of the LXX תַּעֲבֹר עָלֶיךָ, understood according to vii. 21 *b*, appears to be still less suitable in this connection." But in the *addenda et corrigenda* of the second edition, he partly adopted the reading of the LXX (which is substituted for that of the Mass. in this translation of the text) with the remark: "If, on the other hand, simply תַּעֲבֹר is adopted from the LXX, the reading really suits xiii. 23—26; xiv. 4; vii. 21 also so completely that we must after all prefer it." Tr.

But even a mountain falleth crumbling away,
  and a rock moveth from its place;
Stones are hollowed by water,
  its floods wash away the dust of the earth:
    —and the hope of man hast Thou destroyed!
20 Thou fallest upon him continually—he vanisheth away,
  with his face disfigured—Thou sendest him forth:
are his sons honoured—he knoweth it not,
  unhonoured—he heedeth it not:
only *his* own body giveth him pain,
  his soul grieveth him.

A. T., by Ewald and Dukes, Vol. I. p. 94.—But if Job has long borne the incessant attacks, calamities, and tortures of all kinds, he cannot surely stand against them for ever; even the most steadfast and strongest things succumb at last to the incessant, secret or open attack of hostile forces, no less mountains and rocks by internal dissolution than hard stones gradually worn away and hollowed out by perpetually dropping water, and as an extensive, heavy mass of earth is at last entirely washed away by floods: how much more must the body of weak man in the end succumb, yea, the hope of this man Job God has already destroyed! ver. 18; the ־וְ before the last member connects with inimitable brevity and point what has already been sufficiently proved as analogous, still more pointedly than v. 7, xii. 11. To the incessant attacks of the Almighty this man Job must yield and he yields already: yea, as the superior antagonist often does not let go the weaker opponent, who tries somewhat to defend himself, until after he has disfigured his face and put upon him a mark of his superiority, so He does not release Job before death, when all beauty of form has departed from him and simply the horrible image of death remains (ותשלחהו corresponds to ויהלך, משנה is a circumstantial clause to תתקפהו); there, in the Underworld, he then knows nothing more of the things of the earth, joyous or sorrowful, so his departure from the earth affects Job thus painfully because he must fear that his children (see *ante*, p. 73) may have after him a sad lot upon the earth without his being able to help them: for in the Underworld the dead man, without further knowledge of the Upperworld, without activity or movement, simply endures his own physical and mental pain in desolate retirement. Thus this speech also closes with the same dark outlook into the Underworld as all the former ones, since the cheering picture, vv. 13—15, which suddenly suggested itself, is too little fixed and certain to be able to remain: still, it has great emphasis and important consequences, that Job, after all, here also at last, vv. 19—22, just as xiii. 28, causes in this complaint the general human lot involuntarily to take precedence of his own feelings, inasmuch as his own personal case is so pure and so great that it can become that of mankind generally and in reality does become that more and more.

THIRD STAGE OF THE DRAMA:

UTMOST INTRICACY.

SECOND ADVANCE IN THE CONTENTION.

CH. XV—XXI.

The last speech of Job's and the failure of God to appear have altered the past position of the contending parties entirely. The friends, seeing not only their endeavours frustrated but also themselves so painfully attacked, are compelled to transfer the contention to another point, if they intend to continue it (and as at the commencement men of purely benevolent intentions, they desire this). As their first position has been rendered useless, indeed, has at last been stormed and taken by Job, they must take up a second and more decisive one. How can they continue to show consideration and kindness if Job spurns all their words with indignation and scorn; if while they supposed that they deserved a reward from him and from God, he threatens them with even divine punishment? How can they continue to intersperse comfort and hope, if he meets all their consolatory words with outbreaks of hopeless, indeed, wild despair? And (which was the chief thing in their attitude hitherto) how can they continue to endeavour to keep from unconsidered, profane words against God the man who at last dared, in a to them incomprehensible manner, to challenge God even on his own behalf and against them? Their first gentler weapon has thereby been now completely wrested from them. Forced by this turn of the contention, they seek a sharper one which shall pierce deeper; and they find it in the exposure of himself which Job had just plainly enough made precisely when he drove his opponents from their position. For whether he was misled to it by his opponents or not, Job's defiant challenge of God to appear, which has already been punished by its futility, being incontestably an act of grievous rashness, must serve in the view of his opponents as a plain proof, that the man who can now speak so perversely has serious past sin upon him. And this inference conducts them to the thought, that when Job appeals to God against them, he intends simply in his despair to shield himself from the mournful but unavoidable consequences of his previous sins, just as cunning criminals, whose guilt cannot be immediately plainly proved, audaciously pervert the accusation into a charge against the accusers, xv. 5*b*. But as they consider the prove of Job's guilt just mentioned as certain, they are determined not to be deceived by his daring cunning: they now direct their second main principle, which is here most appropriate, the principle of the inviolable universal divine righteousness, against the man who is about by openly speaking against God to intrench upon divine righteousness generally. They do this with great emphasis, and draw the longest, most terrible descriptions of the certain shocking destruction of the wicked, in order to place before their friend, as manifestly an offender, a mirror in which he may see his own present and future lot. That which Bildad, ch. viii., had in this respect begun in a distant way, is now carried to the greatest extreme: and the bitterness and indignation of the friends have already reached such a pitch, that an understanding or reconciliation becomes impossible, since they who desired to advise, help and comfort are unable sufficiently to express their unmeasured horror at Job's entire attitude and life. Still, a secret weakness and inability is already observable in the opponents. They permit the clue to the understanding of Job's case to be entirely snatched from them, and in the special matter from which the whole contention arose, they get more and more into confusion. They now seek to make their strong point really simply the horrible descriptions of the overthrow of the wicked, to which they are driven by the progress of the contention, without clearly knowing that the descriptions completely meet Job's case. So two of them—the second and the third—repeat in the main section of their speeches, with but little variation, the terrible pictures which Eliphaz first draws. But Bildad, notwithstanding his great indignation, is able to utter little more than most obvious generalities with regard to Job's case, xviii. 2—4, and Zophar speaks already simply because he supposes that his honour demands that he should speak against Job, xx. 2—3. Thus gradually the opponents already lose their strength, and a prolix expansion of their few thoughts must at last, at this height of the contention even, in their case conceal the want of an intrinsic progress. But although Eliphaz regards the sufferer especially as a crafty perverter, xv. 5*b*, and Bildad regards him as mad xviii. 4, while Zophar deems him personally insulting, xx. 3, all such untrue reproaches can have no other effect than to bring the contention into increasing confusion.

But it is not alone this extremely hostile attitude of the friends which now comes upon Job as the first evil consequence of his futile challenge of the divine judgment: a second, a more righteous, and far more severe punishment of that presumptuous rashness, follows the first immediately. The more boldly, in consequence of having perceived the unfaithfulness of the friends, he had referred his complaint to God and expected deliverance and victory from Him, ch. xiii., the more painfully does the disappointment of this last earthly hope affect him, around which his whole thought and endeavour had really at last gathered more cheeringly if spasmodically. It is now, therefore, that he first feels himself completely abandoned of everything on which his love and his confidence had previously depended, not merely of all men without exception, but of the God of the outward world Himself, as he had hitherto known and revered Him. And still more than by the unfaithfulness and want of feeling of the dearest human friends is he grieved and perplexed by the wholly unexpected indifference and withdrawal of the God who intentionally, as it seems, declines to attend to his most urgent petition and his clearest right: with the thought that God fails him all intelligible thinking ceases, and instead of it an infinite trouble, or illimitable confusion and boundless despair take possession of him.

Here therefore the climax of complication, the greatest intricacy, of the entire action begins; the suffering (pathos) attains a degree of intensity which cannot be surpassed, the language of the sufferer a measure of sadness which cannot be increased. If in the first stage of the contention each of his speeches issued in reflections which after all sought for the indispensable bases of the divine mercy, and secretly served to sustain, though with waning brightness, the fire of hope, thereby that the weak mortal believed he might perhaps be still able to obtain the divine compassion by the most yearning longing and the most touching complaint[1], he must now, having attained the certainty that God has nevertheless not appeared, nor will appear in answer to mortal effort of this kind, give up every glimmer of a like hope. As far as this mode of approaching Him is concerned, the God whom he has hitherto known is for ever lost to him, and the mortal who is thus bitterly disappointed can only bitterly complain over the disappointment of his hope, xvii. 15, 16; xix. 4, 5.

It is true, that it is precisely here that the immeasurable power of the good conscience and the invincible strength of innocence are most splendidly and surprisingly displayed. If everything on earth is lost and all present things are destroyed, if even the ancient God of the outward world appears to fail and must be given up, nevertheless innocence, with its clear conscience, can neither give up itself nor the eternal, necessary God. On the contrary, surveying all the future, it rises all the more boldly with unexpected

[1] As in Ps. xxxix., lxxxviii., see *ante* p. 9 sq.

might the more men seek to deprive it of the true possessions—its consciousness of being bound up with the eternally divine itself and its infinite assurance based thereon. Having been disappointed with regard to all past earthly hope, it recovers itself with all the greater intensity, purity, and clearness of conviction in the eternal hope; it gets all the more profoundly absorbed in the things which when all else has failed are eternally certain; and reveals with victorious power the most marvellous surmisings and truths in the midst of the most extreme calamity and distress. Thus in the most perilous hour, when he seems to be wholly lost, Job saves himself thereby that, by becoming clearly conscious for the first time of the immortality of the soul and of the indestructibility of innocence before God, he triumphs over death and life and all the vicissitudes of time in a pure intuition of the future. That which at the end of the first advance of the contention surprised him at first as a sudden, happy desire, xiv. 13, 14, now presses itself upon him with growing certainty as true and necessary, xvi. 18, 19; xvii. 3, 9; xix. 25—29. And this first pure gain of the contention and the sufferings must be attended by unending consequences, since the new truth, which has been brought out so powerfully, necessarily and logically, can never be wholly lost again. Indeed, the great, true, decisive turning-point of the entire contention as between these men, and, in fact, the favourable turning-point in the life and the cause of Job, is this, that while he in the present and in this life despairs of everything, even of the God who had hitherto been regarded as the true one, he nevertheless holds fast to the eternal, hidden God of the future, and with the assured faith in the immortality of his soul and of his cause marvellously rises just when, according to human conceptions, he seems to be about inevitably to perish.

Notwithstanding, as far as the present is concerned, with its terrors and constantly fresh trials, he is unable to discern immediately any fresh light beyond that frustrated hope. In elevated moments, it is true, he secures the truth of the divine righteousness by escaping into the future after his death, and thus by the aid of it maintains and refreshes himself against the attacks of the opponents; but precisely as regards the present, he does not see it realised. He considers that he is tormented to certain death, xvii. 1, 11—16; he goes unwillingly to die, because he beholds his innocence completely disbelieved on earth, xvii. 2, 4; and he specially regards God as all along hostile to him, and is unable to comprehend the reason why He does not appear and why He does not deliver him. All along therefore the most gloomy disconsolateness and melancholy prevails within him, through which at times only, particularly when reference to the foolish charges of his opponents urge him to it, the above-mentioned inspired glance into the future pierces. In this melancholy the danger is always present of charging God with witholding, at all events for the present, the right, of injustice therefore in this matter, xix. 7, xxi. 4. And since when he considers the world around under the light of this personal experience, he finds, with his dull eye for the present, confirmed in it simply what corresponds to his sad mood, he may in the end be easily misled to deny the general divine justice in the earth and to lose himself in confusion and perplexity as regards all human and divine concerns. Whilst therefore the opponents are constantly threatening with the divine righteousness and the hard lot of the wicked, Job is, on the other hand, from the first more inclined to doubt both in relation to the present and the existing world; and the unintelligent and weak resistance of his opponents more and more provokes him to develop with force and precision his dark thoughts, which are wholly onesided though, according to the assumptions of the opponents, they are correct. We have had this progress in the contention in the first advance on a smaller scale, ch. viii. and ch. ix. 21—35. The first two times when he must speak, he is, after the hard blow which he suffered at the ènd of the first advance, still too depressed and absorbed in himself, and must first get accustomed to his new situation, to be able at once to advance to the full attack of the opponents with their new weapons: he contents himself with representing his true, vastly miserable condition, and as against the terrors of his opponents, to threaten them with the hidden judge of his own future which reaches beyond death. Observing generally that there is here a superhuman enigma, a terribly dark fatality, which men vainly strive to illuminate, he speaks against men only under compulsion, mocking bitterly at their vain endeavours, xvi. 2—5; xvii. 10—16, once seeking, even in the climax of the complication, although in vain, as he soon observes, to excite the pity of his opponents, ch. xix., at last distinctly declaring that really he is only complaining against God, xxi. 2—5. Thus the first two times he really simply in self-defence wards off the blows of the opponents, a hero contending with the greatest conceivable pain, truly deserving of all pity and exciting the compassion of every noble breast, nevertheless strong and borne up, in spite of all persistent troubles and unintelligible problems, by inward strength and assurance, indeed, looking forth beyond death triumphantly into the future. But if ch. xvi., xvii. he finds it difficult at first to get accustomed to his new situation, putting an end to all previous thoughts and endeavours, he has attained ch. xix. the climax of the tragical pathos of his case. At this point is reached the profoundest melancholy on account of the awful abyss of life which is now first fully perceived; his pain outbids even his feeling of indignation and seeks to rouse the friends to pity; and yet at the same time the greatest strength of his good conscience is put forth, and marvellously assails the opponents! Truly, it is now or never that the opponents must have learnt wisdom and compassion. But as the third opponent nevertheless begins once more the same old story unsparingly against Job, at last the latter, as he now considers exclusively this second weapon of the opponents, namely, the general divine righteousness, enters almost against his will upon the offensive, and shows, that he is compelled to doubt the existence of that righteousness which his opponents are perpetually magnifying, ch. xxi. By this means he drives the opponents also from this position of theirs, but permits himself once more to be led astray by the want of clearness and the confusion, in which he still continues, but which he must himself reject on calmer reflection.

There accordingly hangs over this second advance the most oppressive sultriness of midday. The human combatants bring each other into the greatest confusion and perplexity, and the divine truth appears to be more and more lost in the darkness. The speeches become more agitated, more at variance, more forced and unwieldly, and therefore to some extent also shorter and more uniform. If in the first advance all the speeches of the friends conclude with hope, all Job's with personal reflections, now all those of the friends issue in terrible pictures, all Job's in a brief, pointed repulse of the friends. They had really at the end of the previous advance been finally repulsed by him, and by these recurring sharp repudiations, although he really desires to cease speaking altogether, he continues no less to show his own mental superiority and the hollowness of the opposition than to give fresh provocation and renew the contention. To the former offence against God Job adds now a second, in that he not only complains of His not coming to mediate, but also doubts His righteousness in the present history of the world generally. Yet while outwardly everything appears in confusion, beneath the surface the true possibility of the solution is germinating. Whilst Job is despairing of the ancient God, he is beginning all the more feelingly to embrace the true God of the future, and in the midst of the profoundest misery is borne up by a new immortal hope.

1. ELIPHAZ AND JOB.

a. ELIPHAZ. CH. XV.

Eliphaz by virtue of his reputation and of his experience and wisdom first prepares the way for the new position to be assumed against Job. Being prepared openly to censure Job's attitude and to infer the worst from it, he must at first, in order to obtain again with reference to Job the position of an admonisher, endeavour to put down and humiliate the reckless speaker who sought so proudly to magnify himself. This he accomplishes with great dexterity. Starting from just doubts of Job's wisdom, and, indeed, from proofs of his guilt which have now been made quite clear, he comes with scornful seriousness to place before him his false position. He represents to him that he has no reason whatever to proudly exalt himself, neither as an individual beyond other men—he of a recent generation, of little knowledge, agitated by passion,—nor as a member of the human race against God, before whom no man is righteous; and thus having come back to his favourite proposition (comp. iv. 17 sq.), on the basis of it he assumes again the position of a teacher of Job, as if urged by the greatness of the thought and the ancient truth. The wise sentiment itself which he has thus introduced consists, however, simply of a long, terrible exposition of the general truth, that the sinner, because by living merely for himself he despises God and man, will be tormented as long as he lives and all his possessions will be insecure. Whence Job may himself make the application to his own case! The discourse, therefore, falls into two equal halves; the first half consisting of the proof in three stages of increasing force, vv. 2—19, the second containing the calm, pregnant, sententious declaration of wisdom, vv. 20—35. The first simply shows that Eliphaz is entitled to deliver such a serious lecture upon the divine righteousness against the sinner; and thus this long, laboured discourse nevertheless falls perceptibly behind the former one of this opponent of Job's as regards substance, wealth and calm exposition.

xv. 1 Then answered Eliphaz the Tæmanite and said:

1.

Doth a wise man answer windy knowledge,
  and fill out with the blast his belly?
correcting with words—doth not serve,
  and with speeches—therewith he doeth no good!

And thou indeed annullest religion
  and lessenest devotion before God!
5 no, thine own mouth teacheth thy guilt,
  and thou choosest the language of the crafty;
thy mouth condemneth thee—not *I*,
  and thy lips witness against thee!

1. Vv. 2—19, answering to the rapid treatment, there are six short strophes of three verses each, the first, indeed, having but two; in the middle only, after Job has been corrected and Eliphaz comes back to his own previous speech, is there a somewhat longer pause, so that the third strophe is lengthened to four verses, while this part of the whole speech is divided into two halves of nine verses each.—The introduction, vv. 2—6, touches at once the main point: not only may just doubts be raised as to Job's wisdom, vv. 2, 3, since a truly wise man would not deliver speeches which are both windy, *i.e.*, empty, and still worse-stormy, *i.e.*, passionate, speeches which proceed from the belly, the seat of unruly passion, not even from the heart (viii. 10), and since generally in fact, correction by means of mere words is of no use without corresponding deeds; but also in the very deeds of Job there lie clear proofs of his guilt, vv. 4—6, since he utters even godless, shocking speeches, outraging and diminishing the religion (iv. 6) of others also (ver. 4 גרע to take something from a thing, therefore to lessen it); which he could not do unless he were already wholly depraved inwardly, so that this language itself betrays his guilt, as Eliphaz imagines himself also to be astute enough to perceive that Job by seeking to throw his own guilt upon others only uses the language of crafty thieves, who when accused seek to cast suspicion on their accusers.—How little reason Job has to do this, is shown him first, vv. 7—13, from the human aspect of the case, with cutting severity. He who will be wiser than all other men, does he perhaps occupy a place at the head of the whole human race (like the Logos), the first in point of age as well as of dignity and nearness to God?

Wast thou born as the first man?
and before the hills wast thou already in being?
hearest thou in God's secret council,
or dost thou suck in wisdom to thee in full draught?
What dost thou know—and we knew it not,
understandest thou—and we lacked it?
10 the hoary man also, the old man also is in our midst,
greater than thy father in years!

—Too poor for thee then are God's consolations,
the word which dealt mildly with thee?
Why doth thine heart carry thee away
and why roll thine eyes,
that thou turnest against God thy fury,
drawest words out of thy mouth!

What is man that he should be pure,
and that the son of a woman should be righteous!
15 lo, in His holy ones He putteth no trust,
and the heavens are not pure in His eyes:
how then the abominable one, he that hath turned sour,
the man who drinketh iniquity like water!

(comp. similar ideas Ezek. xxviii. 12 sq.; in reality the figures vv. 7, 8 appear to be almost borrowed from the subsequent Logos doctrine, so natural is this doctrine as regards its constituent elements). Or does he really know anything unknown to the friends, who have after all in their midst a man of years and experience, vv. 9, 10, whereby Eliphaz manifestly refers in modest, veiled language to himself, in order to refute what Job had said of his experience xii. 11, 12; xiii. 1, 2; the force of the two words *hoary man also* is repeated in the following *old man also* simply for the sake of the great emphasis which is conveyed by it.—And in order to get closer to the matter itself and to set upon him still more violently, it is forthwith, as Eliphaz himself and the meaning of his previous speech, therefore, have been insensibly approached, further asked, whether the divine consolations, which had at first been granted to him so gently and considerately (precisely by Eliphaz), iv. 12 sq.; v. 8—26, were too poor, that carried away by his passion he should direct his wild words even (not merely against his friends but) against God Himself? vv. 11—13; with רזם comp. رمز, the most emphatic word אֶל־אֵל in the 13th verse is referred back to by the second member of the verse. Having come thus to the consideration of divine relations, he presents the second, the divine, aspect of the case, according to

Let me instruct thee, hearken unto me,
  what I have experienced let me narrate!
the things which wise men declare,
  without concealment, from their fathers,
unto whom alone the land was given,
  and among whom no foreigner had entered:—

2.

20 As long as the wicked liveth is he tormented,
  however many years are granted to the tyrant:
alarms sound in his ears,
  in peace the devastator cometh upon him;
he believeth that he shall never escape the darkness,
  and he is only reserved for the sword,
he wandereth abroad after bread—where—?
  knoweth that the day of darkness is before him!
distress and anguish overwhelm him,
  it terrifieth him as a king prepared for the attack:

which Job can have no right to rebel against God, before whom no man is pure; and already he is in a position to repeat, with stronger assurance, his previous main principle, vv. 14—16, from iv. 17—v. 7, only that now the picture of the sinfulness of man is still more strongly drawn than before: he is said to be, ver. 16, one who is like disgusting food *to be abominated, gone sour,* wholly depraved within, since he commits iniquity as eagerly as a thirsty man drinks as much water as he can (Prov. xxvi. 6), as if sin were his natural element. And thus impressed by a superior displeasure and regret towards a sinner offending against this fundamental truth, he demands, vv. 17—19, an attentive hearing for the compassionate instruction which he is obliged to give him, and which he can give him with all the more confidence as it contains the certain, genuine wisdom of the fathers of old, to whom the freshest spring of true, uncontaminated wisdom flowed, inasmuch as they still dwelt unmixed with and unsubjugated by foreign peoples. Ver. 19 the feeling of the later contemporaries of the poet makes itself plainly perceptible; see *ante,* p. 75.

2. Vv. 20—35. The sinner is assailed his life long by the most terrible tortures, vv. 20—24, because as he wishes to live simply for himself he really rebels against God, vv. 25, 26: though therefore he may have destroyed the well-being of many men for the sake of the immoderate welfare of his own body, vv. 27, 28, all his earthly possessions, which he has amassed with such vast, unhappy pains, are nevertheless insecure and injurious, vv. 29—33: how foolish therefore is his whole life and endeavour when regarded from the horrible end! The description accordingly follows in two lengthy strophes of seven

25 because he stretched out against God his hand,
against the Almighty setteth himself,
runneth against Him with proud neck,
with the thick bosses of his shields.

Though he hath covered his face with fat,
filled up his loins with fatness,
and inhabiteth wholly wasted cities,
houses which are no more habitable,
which when rebuilt—became ruins:
still he groweth not rich, his treasure remaineth not,
and his power doth not extend into the earth;
30 still he will not get away from the darkness,
—his shoots heat drieth up—
—he will be put away in the breath of His mouth!

verses each, closing rapidly with a brief concluding word, vv. 34, 35. In general therefore we find here the usual course of a brave denunciation such as would then be delivered against a sinner who had become powerful and attained the position of a ruler, and in the form in which such speeches would perfectly suit the circumstances of the eighth or the seventh century; they suit Job's case here, because he had previously been powerful, like a small prince, yet thoughts such as ver. 28 must admit of another reference than Job's previously limited power; at all events the views of the author of the affairs of his own time make themselves felt. On צָפַן לְ־, as *to lay by*, ver. 20, comp. xxi. 10; xxiv. 1; xx. 26; the second member ver. 20 is only a further definition of the time: however long he may live, and in any case only a certain, often brief period is reserved for him, he will be always tortured; see xxi. 21. The detailed description, vv. 21—24, is very graphic: how the sinner, though in peace or outward tranquility, is nevertheless continually wasted, besieged, and stormed by a powerful enemy suddenly advancing, being all the time impressed by the true presentiment, that he will at last not escape the danger which is everywhere in ambush, the divine sword of vengeance; it is then as if, impelled by a ravenous hunger, he strayed wildly about (a figure which is further worked out xviii. 12, 13), this haste being then forcibly described in the broken, abrupt language (comp. ix. 19; it is accordingly not necessary to read with the LXX לְלֶחֶם אַיָּה, he fleeth, it is true, but simply *to the food of the vulture*, xxviii. 7, to be devoured by the vulture as carrion, which would be here too strong); צָפוּ, § 149 *g*, is watched = kept, reserved for אל the *sword*, namely, of God, as xix. 29, "Zech." xiii. 7 sq.; בְּיָדוֹ, ver. 23, at his hand, at his side, lying in secret ambush close by, as xviii. 12 *b* similarly; comp. i. 14; with 24 *b* comp. Prov. vi. 11. And he must be thus tormented, thus assailed, because the fool

Let him not trust vanity, the deceived man!
for vanity will be his exchange:
before his day it is passed,
his palm never becometh green,
his unripe grapes he casteth pitilessly like the vine,
flingeth them down, as the olive its blossom.

For the band of the profane is unfruitful,
fire devoureth the tents of bribery;

attacked God Himself, revolting so insolently against Him and His ordinances, vv. 25, 26 (comp. Ps. lxxv. 6; on ver. 26 *b* comp. § 293 *c*).—But although (the second strophe begins again, ver. 27, with somewhat increased emphasis, כִּי in the protasis acc. § 362 *b*), caring for himself alone, he may have tortured hosts of weaker men, depopulated populous, flourishing cities, in order to dwell in them alone, as if the fool could not find dwelling room enough for his body, and preferred to dwell alone in the midst of extended ruin rather than peacefully amongst happy multitudes (comp. Isa. v. 8; Hab. ii. 5, 12, 17; עשה is probably not be explained in the sense in which it is used of plants xiv. 9, but is used, in accordance with its primary signification, as equivalent to פִּסָּה, comp. the note on ix. 9, *ante* p. 136); although therefore he may by such cruelty have gained vast earthly possessions, they do not nevertheless remain, but come with himself to a mournful end. This pointed antithesis is conveyed by the very position of the words and thoughts, ver. 29. It is true he might seem entitled to expect from his pains and anxieties splendid fruit at last: but the tree of his labours is from the very beginning not less inwardly corrupt than outwardly imperilled, his roots do not go down deep into the earth, so that every external misfortune becomes to him extremely dangerous, and he casts off all his bloom and fruit unripe before the harvest, a mournful example of disappointed hope! This, as the most expressive figure, pervades the entire description vv. 29—33, mainly ver. 29 *b*, ver. 30 *b*, vv. 32, 33 (מִנְלֶה appears to signify *that which has been gained*, from נלה = ניל نال *to attain;* תְּמַלֵּא fem. as neut., it fulfils itself, goes by, comes to an end); the figure of an exchange is also by no means far-fetched, ver. 31: he believes, indeed, that in place of the scornfully rejected integrity he has made a splendid gain of possessions and enjoyments, but let him not trust the vain exchange! Along with these figures that of darkness occurs again from vv. 20—24, which he escapes from only to get into the breath of the mouth, or the hot wrath-blast, of God (iv. 9) ver. 30 *a. c.*—But a different end is in no way possible; because the native soil of the whole tribe of the profane is barren and unfruitful, upon which no lasting fruits can grow; the time of ripeness and harvest must be a manifestation of corruption and ruin, just as the woman that has conceived an abortive birth may long remain deceived, but must at last, at the birth, painfully perceive

conceiving sin, bearing vanity!
and their belly ripeneth—deceit!

the nature of the manifested vanity, as is added with great emphasis, vv. 34, 35; the treatment and the end correspond to the thought and the position of the case! comp. Ps. vii. 14—17; Isa. xxxiii. 11.

b. JOB. CH. XVI., XVII.

Job's answer is very far from coming at once to a definite refutation of this new manner of speaking on the part of the opponents. He is too profoundly depressed by the unexpected situation in which he finds himself, and must first of all most earnestly summon up all his energies to familiarise himself with it. For it is only now that he first discovers that all conceivable calamities are arrayed against him: and the complete change of the friends into cruel persecutors even now for the first time comes fully home to him as one of the last of the many evil consequences of the mysterious wrath of God, who appears to be implacably hostile to him even to death. When he compares this excessive measure of calamity with the consciousness of his innocence, which has now become so clear and strong, the incomprehensibility, indeed, the unreasonableness of the proportion, must fill him with infinite pain. But he is not less filled with indignation at the victory of the opponents which now seems to be complete, who are able to draw precisely from this unmerited, extreme suffering of which he complains the conclusion, that he is burdened with the greatest guilt. Against that conclusion his inmost knowledge and purpose convulsively revolt; with marvellously heightened energy he demands, beseeches, establishes the necessity of a complete acknowledgment, at least after his martyr's death, of his innocence by the God who is as yet hidden, and he wrestles with a hero's strength against the abyss of moral degradation and misrepresentation which is about to open before him, against the fear of the eternal destruction of the best part of his being which threatens to get possession of him. He has already, on calm reflection, completely renounced all earthly hope, and is on the point of making himself in thought quite familiar with the horror of death and the Underworld, resigned and patient even to the uttermost, xvi. 20; xvii. 1, 10—16: it is only the doubt lest his innocence, at his death unrecognised, should remain after death also for ever under a cloud (since among men the idea of the deceased so naturally remains in memory as it was when he departed from the earth), which causes him still profound disquiet and compels him, because he is least able to conceive precisely this most horrible thought at the point when he is called upon to conceive it, to rise up against it with all his powers of indignation and rebellion, and to contend with thoughts and reasons which can set forth the impossibility of the realisation of that which is impossible in God. To God, therefore, as the final judge of the dead and the living he must after all again turn, in spite of the terrible darkness of the present; indeed, there occurs again from ch. xiii. something approaching to an invocation of God, though certainly in a suppressed form and with the resignation of all earthly hope, xvi. 20, 21; xvii. 3, since he finds it so difficult to convince himself that God will on no account hear him. The first consciousness of the complete ruin of all his earthly hopes this side death, and the first indignant revolt from the thought of an eternal ruin of the soul also and of its treasure of innocence, as well as the first uplifting of the aspiring glance into the certainty of an eternal recompense beyond death,—these two tremendous antitheses form the heart of this highly pathetic speech. In some respects of style the speech is similar to the previous ones, but it prepares a way to a completely new outlook, hope, and assurance by means of the final efforts of the most tremendous despair, and bringing everything which had gone before to a conclusion, enters, still wrestling and in pain, a new and glorious territory not without secured results. It also confirms

Job in his new position, just as the first speech, ch. vi., vii., had in the first advance served this purpose. There is but little in the speech against the friends: nothing directly against their fearful representations of the ruin of sinners, although more closely considered the entire character of Job's speech refutes the application of these representations to him; there are a few words of bitter scorn at the beginning and in the review of the whole at the end against the useless and wrong speeches, in order to reply to the reproaches of Eliphaz on account of ingratitude, xv. 11, just enough not to fall into mere self-inspection, but to show to the opponent the speaker's spiritual superiority and to provoke him afresh. Thus after a short angrily scornful word of defence against the friends, xvi. 2—5, first the melancholy absorption in the consideration of the misery which had now reached its full measure—in spite of all his innocence, xvi. 6—17, till, in a sudden revulsion against it, the higher consciousness arouses itself with irresistible force, wrestling with all its reasons, xvi. 18—xvii. 9, and finally a word against the friends follows, lest they should suppose that he is afraid of them, while, on the contrary, it is only now that from the position of his higher inward experience he can take a full view of the perversity of their extolled speeches, xvii. 10—16. Four parts therefore, but so that the two middle ones are the most important and in antithesis to each other, the fourth although prepared for by the third refers back to the first in order to complete it. The first two bring gloomy despair to its extreme pitch, until at the opening of the third resolution and self-consciousness arise and continue in considerable strength to the end of the whole speech; in the middle these antitheses come into most direct collision.

xvi. 1 And Job answered and said:

1.

I have heard many such things,
  distressing comforters are ye all!
is there an end to the windy words?
  or what afflicteth thee that thou repliest?
I also should speak like you
  if my soul were in the place of yours;
should be a wiseacre concerning you—with words,
  and shake over you—my head,
5 I should strengthen you—with my mouth,
  the pity of the lips should put a check!—

2.

If I will speak,—no check is put to my grief,
  and if I will forbear—what goeth from me?—

1. xvi. 2—5. Brief repudiation of such useless speeches, which often passes from deep displeasure into scorn. It is true they propose to administer comfort, and Eliphaz has just resentfully reminded Job of this, xv. 11: but their perfectly common-place thoughts and arguments are in reality the vainest and most useless words, which instead of giving comfort cause trouble and pain, which had better at once cease, since nobody really desires such replies and Job does not at all know what offends Eliphaz particularly and led him to make such merciless speeches, vv. 2, 3. If the point were merely to console a sufferer on account of his helplessness with useless words and empty condolences instead of with acts and real sympathy, then he also could (as regards the possibility, though not as regards feeling) easily, if the relation of the persons concerned were reversed, speak just as they do, be mighty wise concerning them—with mere words, with no wisdom beneath them, and shake over them full of scornful pity—the head (Ps. xxii. 7, 8; Isa. xxxvii. 22), as if that could help at all, strengthen them—with the mouth merely, as if the thing required for strengthening were not acts, and mere lip-pity could *put a check* on calamity, as if this could in the least diminish the calamity! vv. 4, 5. הֶחְבִּיר, which occurs here only, ver. 4, is most probably, according to this context, equivalent to *to act shrewdly*, *wisely*, from خبر *to learn by experience*, *to know*, with which חֹבֵר *magician*, properly wise man, is connected.

2. xvi. 6—17. Reflection: Certainly, by loud speaking a healthy man can get rid of what oppresses him, as the friends appear to find pleasure in this way, whilst the vast pain of Job is not stayed by speaking, and it might therefore seem that he would do better to remain silent; yet even supposing he

Certainly, now He hath wearied me out!
—Thou hast laid waste my whole circle,
and as a witness calamity layeth hold on me,
sickness rising up against me witnesseth to my face!

Wrath from Him teareth maketh war upon me,
He gnasheth upon me with His teeth,
as mine adversary He whetteth the eyes against me:
10 they revile me with open mouth,
with insult smite my cheeks,
band themselves together against me:
to sinners God delivereth me over,
casteth me into the hands of the wicked!

were to hold his peace, *what* would *go from him* of his pain and calamity, what would be taken from him? nothing at all! accordingly, whether he speaks or not, his deep pain and illimitable woe remain the same! ver. 6. Thus on the point of speaking further, though with much inward conflict, he is compelled, when he reviews his calamities generally, to say this at least (אַךְ), that He (God) has *now* exhausted him, driven him to the utmost distress, so that he scarcely knows how to hold up in any way! ver. 7 *a*, comp. vi. 3. And now completely absorbed in the gloomy contemplation of all the calamities of his present situation, he sketches the terrible picture of them, how he succumbs to the most violent attack of all possible calamities, vv. 7 *b*—14, in the profoundest humiliation and grief, vv. 15, 16,—although quite innocent in deed and word before God! which said thus briefly at the end, after the long mournful description, is emphatic and produces the effect of surprise, ver. 17. The description of his sufferings is only completed in four short strophes of three verses each. First, that which is here the most immediate calamity, how God, in sending his calamities, has also brought upon him the new one of a complete desolation of his dwelling-place, which was visited formerly by so many happy sympathetic friends, but now beholds not a single true friend (further xix. 13—19), and here the discourse is almost broken off by pain, and agitated in the highest degree turns to God in direct address, whilst elsewhere He is always spoken of in the third person, vv. 7—17; how therefore outward misery and wasting sickness, these things which he has least deserved, thus come forward as witnesses of the divine wrath, both in order to deceive men who do not know him and also specially to seize upon him even openly and boldly as divine punishments against his better knowledge and to conduct him to death, ver. 8; accordingly הַיָּה *calamity* must be read instead of הָיָה, corresponding to כחשׁ, Ps. cix. 24, according to vi. 2; xxx. 13 also; the present reading would signify, *and Thou* (O God) *laidest hold on me—for a witness* this *became*, but it would be far less suitable, because it is here an outwardly visible thing, the

At ease was I—then He dashed me to shivers,
seizing me by the neck, dashed me to shatters,
set me up for His mark:
around me His arrows fall,
He cleaveth my reins without sparing,
poureth to the earth my gall;
breaketh me, breach upon breach,
runneth as a warrior against me!

15 Sackcloth I sewed upon my skin,
thrust my horn into the dust;
burning is my face from weeping,
upon my eyelids hangeth darkness:—
although wrong is not in my hands,
and my prayer also is pure.

calamity and the sickness themselves, which must be introduced as witnesses. When now he contemplates both, the hostility of men and his sufferings, as the consequence of the divine anger, it seems to him as if upon the terrible, angry attack of a great ravening beast of prey (comp. *ante* p. 4, Hos. xiii. 7, 8), now a multitude of smaller, shameless, but not less blood-thirsty beasts of prey band themselves against him (comp. מְלֹא Isa. xxxi. 4), the most cruel men, that is, who fall upon the man with mad outrage who has been given into their power by the great enemy (just as the smaller, cowardly, shameless animals collect in troops around the prey of a great and nobler beast of prey), vv. 9—11.—Second, the attack was the more terrible that Job was as innocent living quite without anxiety and had reason not to expect anything of a hostile nature, when an overpowering enemy, suddenly arriving, dashed him to pieces with an irresistible hand, and, as if it were not enough to hurl him down, even cruelly cast repeatedly his arrows at him as his mark, piercing him more and more deeply and mortally wounding him (comp. vi. 4; רַב is correctly explained by the ancient translators as *missiles*), indeed, as if he were a fortress, like a warrior storming him, slowly but surely breaks in the walls of his body, and must soon force his way completely into the shattered, desolated fortress (a figure further worked out xix. 12) vv. 12—14. Then the noble, dignified hero must surely succumb in shame and sorrow, fix a close, prickly mourning-garment of coarse hair upon his bare skin and thrust his horn, *i.e.*, his noble, honoured head, in humiliation in the dust (after ii. 8, 13), most painfully overwhelmed by sorrow and almost blinded by incessant weeping, vv. 13, 16, with which the description refers back to the commencement ver. 7 *a*.

3.

O earth, cover not my blood,
  and let there be no place for my cry!—
And now also, behold in heaven is my witness,
  and my testifier in the heights!
20 My friends are my scorners only:
  unto God mine eye sheddeth tears,
that He would accord justice to the man before God,
  and justify the man against his friend!—
For a few years will come,
  the path with no return I shall go;

3. xvi. 18—xvii. 9. Scarcely has he brought the truth of his innocence, ver. 17, into conjunction with the terrible picture of his sufferings, the further pursuance of which course of reflection must logically lead to the belief of the final denial of his innocence, when he starts back with horror from this thought: he is in the greatest alarm, but in the midst of his greatest distress is suddenly made conscious of a power within which he had hitherto not suspected; by an unlooked for inspiration he flees to the diametrically opposite thought; in the wildest pain he agonises to become conscious of the certainty and the bases of the impossibility of the true ruin of innocence in physical death; despairing of all earthly hopes, he gains all the more strength by means of the eternal God and the inward, ineradicable energy of his good conscience. At the beginning this sudden opposite thought comes into violent and direct collision with the previous despair, in that the new thought breaks forth with all the force of new life, vv. 18—21, until, precisely by the backward glance of despair at the brief period which is yet reserved for life and suffering, a moderation of the antithesis is commenced but is rendered vain by a glance at the friends, vv. 22—xvii. 2: so that in spite of all terrible reflections, a sad, supplicating glance of hope to God is all that remains, xxvii. 3—9. Thus this portion of the speech, which amid the wildest agitation seeks and with difficulty finds repose, falls into two strophes, of seven verses each.

xvi. 18—xvii. 2. If he must, as now seems inevitable, die for no fault of his own, he must also boldly exclaim, *Earth, cover not my* innocently shed *blood*, but let it openly lie there, unabsorbed and unremoved, as a witness *(martyrium)* of the innocent victim, just as according to the belief of antiquity no rain or dew which fell upon the blood-stains of a man who had been unjustly slain would wash them away or change the horrible appearance of the place by covering it with smiling verdure; *and let there be no place for my cry*, but being by nothing detained and weakened, let it sound through the whole world and rise aloud even to the furthest heavens, as the last cry for help of such an one is restrained at first by the distraction and diversion oc-

xvii.
1 my spirit is destroyed, my day extinct,
graves are mine:
would that mockery were not practised with me,
and that mine eye took not offence at their provocation!

O enter a pledge, be Thou surety for me with Thyself,
who is he that would pledge himself for my hand?—

casioned by the thirst for revenge. These are, it is true, phrases taken from the ancient sacred duty of blood vengeance (Gen. iv. 10, 11, comp. Isa. xxvi. 21; 2 Sam. i. 21); but the circumstances in which the desire not to die for ever unrevenged here occurs, are quite different from those which were previously common amongst men, since here one, who is not merely persecuted by men, but still more, as he believes, by God, maintains as he is evidently near to death his innocence against both God and men. But if he will still entertain hope beyond death, he must flee to the hidden God of the future and refer to Him as the only witness (although from unknown causes He does not at present show Himself); therefore already more calmly, ver. 19: *also now* still, when I am wholly betrayed by men and by the external, visible God (ver. 21), and lost, I say, there *in heaven* invisible *is my witness and testifier! My friends*, instead of being my true comforters and mediators, are only *my scorners:* from them there is nothing to hope, therefore *to God* I call *with weeping eyes*, that *He*, acc. ver. 18, at least after my death may appear and at the same time hold a two-fold judgment, first, *awarding justice to the man before God*, declaring, that is, that the weak and now deceased man Job was just before God though he was regarded as guilty, and, secondly, which then follows of itself, *judging the son of man Job against his* persecuting *friend;* accordingly the construction of וְיוֹכַח in the second verse-member is twice varied. This is actually fulfilled xlii. 7, even before death, whilst here Job is resolved to let life go but not the conviction of his innocence, ver. 20.—After such violent agitation, a certain measure of calmness is about to be recovered, even by means of the despairing glance at the present and the short space of life which seems still to remain to him. As one who is *inwardly* already completely *destroyed, belonging to the graves*, he must, although perhaps after *some years* (since the Elephantiasis is a slow disease), certainly and early enough resign the present life, and would gladly do it, having made up his mind to this last act of earthly resignation, *if* only *the deceptive mockery* (xiii. 9) of the friends did not surround him (אם לא, here used to express a desire, *if* only—*not*, acc. § 329 *b*) and if only his *eye were not offended at* their incessant cruel *provocation!* Thus these brief words, which are uttered as in broken sighs, are clear, vv. 22—xvii. 2; and הֵלֵן, ver. 2, can here be most correctly understood in the sense of *to rebel against*, as its construction with בְּ־ in this sense is not impossible.

xvii. 3—9. Therefore, since he cannot bear to think of dying in this terrible

Their heart hast Thou hidden from understanding:
therefore there is no improvement!
5 to the lot even friends are betrayed,
whilst the eyes of his sons fail;
and I am set as a byword of the people,
an open abomination must I become,

uncertainty, and of having his innocence for ever unrecognised, indeed, as it seems to be a divine concern that such things should not happen, he is after all once more impelled to turn with mournful supplication to God. He asks, since there is absolutely no one amongst men who will take his part in his last moments, as a friend and guarantor giving a promise and deposing a pledge with regard to his innocence to be revenged after his death, that God Himself instead of men may become a surety for him, give him the pledge with the hand *(Handschlag)* and depose a pledge, were it merely one single clear word from heaven, a small and easily given sign, which could the more easily be given by Him as in this case the surety and the persecutor of the sufferer are one and the same person, He would, therefore, only have to declare, that though He continued the calamities and the wrath to the utmost destruction, yet in the future, after Job's death, He would certainly vindicate his innocence! vv. 3[1]). Thus the contemplation, getting again absorbed in the troubles of the present, endeavours to become fully convinced of that which the inspired glance upwards had just before, xvi. 18, 19, demanded as necessary in its agonising desire. Yet in that this entirely new outlook and higher demand does not as yet remain sufficiently steadfast, particularly as soon as the glance is again turned to the terrors and the whole confusion of the present, that inspiration also tends more and more to decline, and the previous despair, xvi. 7—17, almost threatens completely to return when he once more brings the behaviour of his friends into close comparison with all his sufferings. At first, ver. 4, he continues, more in the previous melancholy tone, to explain how he is compelled to utter that wish to God, because God has in fact *so completely darkened* the mind of his friends and deprived them of perception (xvi. 9—11), that no *improvement*[2]) and no success in his matter is to be expected from them. But then a general review of his hard lot forces itself upon him, primarily with reference to his friends: *to the lot*, that the lot may be cast over them as over prisoners, *one* tells of or *betrays* (the third pers. sing., vv. 5, 6, like xv. 3,

---

[1] Comp. *Antiquities of Israel* p. 184 (p. 211).

[2] תְּרוֹמֵם from Hithpael, formed acc. § 161 *c*, and after the sense of the figure Hos. xi. 7. This is at all events the most probable explanation: the supposition is also possible, that the word is thus vocalised, acc. § 81 *a*, for תְּרוֹמְמֵם *therefore wilt Thou not cause them to triumph;* but Job by no means foresees in this connection the defeat of his friends so distinctly.

so that for grief mine eye is quenched,
  and my limbs are all like a shadow.
The upright are amazed at this,
  the pure rouseth himself against the profane:
yet the righteous holdeth fast his way,
  he of pure hands will only wax stronger!

4.

10 **B**ut all of you may return! come now,
  and I do not find among you one wise man!

used indefinitely acc. § 294 *b*, although from the underlying meaning the real persons intended, but intentionally left unnamed, are plain enough, namely ver. 5 men, ver. 6 God) *friends* who are persecuted by cruel power, instead of granting protection to them in their misery betraying them to their persecutor, and without any further compassion, whilst the children, still minors, of the persecuted and betrayed man languish and perish without the unhappy father: thus Job now, together with his children that have not yet grown up, over whose lot he had previously lamented, xiv. 21, seems to himself to have been faithlessly misunderstood and betrayed by the friends, as he had previously vi. 27 foreseen that it would come to this; and because in the end he means himself by the faithlessly betrayed friends, the plur. רֵעִים then insensibly changes in the following member in the case of בָּנָיו into the sing.; ועיני etc. is a circumstantial clause, § 341 *a*. The further calamity is God's matter, who alone can make him by such immense sufferings an object of the mockery of people generally, in that now far and wide in the earth his history and his name become an evil proverb, and many do not scruple to express their disgust openly and actively to his face, as is further explained xxx. 9 sq.; as also the ultimate consequence of all that is for him a complete exhaustion of all the energies of his body, ver. 7.—But terrible as all this may be, particularly as an evil example for the small number of the faithful, who are amazed, or even made violently indignant, at such endless punishments of an innocent man, after all the truly innocent will by all such hindrances and terrors find his inward strength only intensified and increased, because a latent infinite capacity within him has thereby been aroused and called into activity! Thus Job here, vv. 8, 9, shakes himself free in time from complete despair, just when it threatened again to overpower him: the great pregnant utterance, ver. 9, is itself the fruit of that outburst of inspiration xvi. 19; we get a profound glance into this great soul with its conflicts and possible victories, and feel that it is hardly possible that it should wholly perish after it has been made conscious of its own infinite strength! In ver. 8, however, there is a clear reflection of the prevailing tone of feeling of the author's contemporaries, see *ante* p. 75.

4. xvii. 10—16. Thus having become more collected and calmer even under the worst circumstances, he might close the speech. But still feels at

My days have gone by,
my plans are broken off,
they the bands of my heart:
nevertheless night they make into day,
light is nearer than the plain darkness!
If I hope for the Underworld as my house,
if in the darkness I spread out my couch,
if to corruption I exclaim "my father thou",
"mother, sister" to putrefaction:
15 then, where is my hope?
and my hope—who will behold it?

the close strong enough to make this speech the answer to an entirely new position of his antagonists; and precisely from this newly gained higher calm and perception of the complete hopelessness of earthly life, he reviews the absolute perversity of all the earlier and later speeches of the friends under a brighter light than ever before, since under certain requirements they desired to hold out to him hopes where so far as men could can see the direct opposite might be easily discerned, v. 8—27; viii. 21, 22; xi. 15—20, and as Eliphaz had at last, xv. 11, reproached him with having neglected such words of hope, and had based further and worse reproaches upon this one, he is here at the end unable, without intending to deal with the latter, to leave the first reproach upon which the later ones are based without somewhat closer consideration. If he is compelled in this respect to give prominence to the complete destruction of all his earthly hopes, this addition to his speech changes involuntarily into a severe word of censure against the friends, who are about to base new and worse reproaches upon a groundless one; and this closing word of righteous displeasure with such friends, spoken with the higher courage which has been gathered in the course of the speech, serves to supply what was wanting in the word of displeasure which was too briefly uttered at the beginning, xvi. 2—5; only that thus at last, as the picture of this hopelessness is dwelt upon, once more a touch of dark despair is introduced, and this speech also closes with the same dark outlook beyond death like all the earlier ones, as if Job felt urged thus to confirm once more all his earlier speeches. Like the whole speech, this conclusion is also in the highest degree agitated. First, lest he should seem to be flagging in opposition to the friends, since in the main portions of this speech he has really pursued his own reflections only, the stinging challenge to speak as foolishly again in the future if they like, he will only afresh behold their ignorance! ver. 10. The proof of this more briefly vv. 11, 12: whilst his life is already as good as past, his dearest plans and schemes with regard to it, to which his heart was formerly so firmly attached, have been violently broken off by death, so surely close at hand, they reverse everything and promise happy prospects, as if they meant to change the plainest darkness, in which

—into the bars of the Underworld it goeth down,
if also upon the dust there is rest!

he already finds himself, in to bright, joyous day![1] And further the same proof, vv. 13—16: if he reposes all his hope as yet simply—upon the Underworld as the ultimate resting-place after such long tormenting sufferings, and, difficult as that may have been to him, seeks to make himself quite at home and familiar with the things of the Underworld (with ver. 14 comp. Prov. vii. 4), where in that case is his earthly hope of which these friends have so much to say? (the וְ— before אַיֵּה is illative, § 353 *a*) and what wise man will perceive it even in the distance?—No, into the bars of the Underworld (for it has gates) will my hope go down to remain shut up there for ever—if at the same time as this descent Job himself at last finds rest in the grave! for on the earth he remains without it. This is the last melancholy ending of this kind, but it is at the same time only as a final most painful conclusion, as it were a sigh convulsively brought to a close.

2. BILDAD AND JOB.

a. BILDAD. CH. XVIII.

Almost without intending it, Job has just now, in the first speech of the second advance (as above in the first speech of the first advance, ch. vi., vii.), spoken severely against the friends, comparing them, in the spasms of the pain which they more and more aggravate, with the profane and fools, xvi. 10, 11; xvii. 4, 5, 10—16; for too much of the violence against the friends, which first broke out ch. xii., xiii., was reechoed here from the end of the previous advance. By this Bildad accordingly is deeply offended, and he finds in the terrible rashness and agonising despair of Job, which he fails to understand, the madness of a bad conscience, which while it turns in frantic rage against everything in the world after all only reacts to its own destruction. After a brief, bitter introduction, vv. 2—4, he passes, therefore, at once to the general truth, that

[1] מוֹרָשׁ, ver. 11 *c*, is in this connection, since it is required to complete the figure of breaking-off, plainly equivalent to מוֹתָר, or more briefly יֶתֶר *a bond*, nasmuch as יָרַשׁ and יָתַר are originally related roots. With זִמּוֹת comp. מְזִמּוֹת, xxi. 27, and מְזִמָּה xlii. 2: זִמָּה has everywhere (xxxi. 11 also) a bad meaning in the sing. only.

the wicked man, however much he may resist, goes down in an exceedingly horrible, endless destruction, without any hope of a happy future even in the case of his descendants; which is here intentionally insisted upon vv. 5—21, as Job in his speech pointed to the future. But eloquently as he seeks to expound this thought and correctly as it is here, apart from its application, worked out with telling effect, the commencing helplessness of Job's opponents is betrayed by the simple fact, that Bildad is able to do scarcely anything more than bring forward this general truth.

xviii. 1 Then answered Bildad the Shuite and said:

How long yet will ye give chase—after words?
have but understanding, and afterwards let us speak!
Wherefore are we counted as cattle,
are impure even in your eyes?—
Thou that teareth himself in his anger:
for thy sake then shall the earth be forsaken,
and a rock move from its place?

Vv. 2—4. The word קִנְצֵי, ver. 2, which occurs here only, is as regards its more definite force somewhat obscure, but most probably signifies, as derived from قنص (*Wâqid. Aeg.* p. 9. 6 and elsewhere) *instruments of the chase; as venari, aucupari verba.* The commencement therefore is like viii. 2: just as it may generally be remarked, that the poet likes to make the same persons appear with some uniformity in different speeches, as far as the connection permits. Inasmuch as it seems to Bildad as if in his extreme despair, Job was simply hunting for words in order to find something to say, he requires, previous to any further discourse, understanding on the part of the opponent, who quite incomprehensibly so far forgets himself, that he can speak of him and his friends as base, impure men (he the impure thus describe them the pure![1]): in connection wherewith Bildad on his part cannot sufficiently express his contempt, as if he were determined at first not even to address Job individually at all, but only him and the like of him, the company of the impure (xv. 34):

---

[1] There is no reason whatever to give to נִטְמִינוּ the merely conjectural signification, *we are shut up, stupid, foolish,* which would here be much too weak and generally inappropriate.

5 Nevertheless the light of the wicked will go out,
and the brightness of his fire will not shine;
the light is darkened in his tent,
his lamp over him goeth out!
his strong steps are straitened,
so that his own counsel casteth him down:
for into the net his feet urge him,
and over network he walketh,
a snare seizeth fast the heel,
nooses seize hold upon him,
10 in the ground his toil is hidden,
his trap upon the way;
round about mortal terrors confound him,
and scare him wherever he goeth.

as then in reality the contention with Job tends gradually to assume a more general character and to become the struggle between two sections of the whole human race.—Yet (to bring the attack closer home to Job), does this madman who complained xvi. 9 that God's wrath tore him, but who, on the contrary, sufficiently betrays his own bad conscience by tearing himself in his anger, then really demand that on his account, *i.e.*, however, that his will may be done and he may be justified though he is absolutely wrong, the earth may be desolated (since really if God Himself should, according to the desire of this madman, pervert justice, order, and peace, accordingly the blessings of the happy occupation of the earth could not subsist), and also that which is firmest, the divine order of the world, should be removed from its place (xiv. 18)? O, the fool, who simply from his own perversity and confused ideas rebels against the everlasting order of the universe!

Vv. 5—21. But however much he may rebel against it, nevertheless (גַּם as Ps. cxxix. 2, see § 354 *a*) the eternal divine order with regard to the destruction of every sinner will remain unchanged, as Bildad now, like Eliphaz xv. 20—35, describes it in two long strophes of seven verses each, with half a one as the conclusion. The light of the wicked goes out as suddenly and as horribly as when the lamp which is fastened at the top of the tent of the traveller suddenly goes out at midnight in the midst of the horrible wilderness, xxix. 3: so that he with all his belongings comes into the darkness of death, no more relieved by a ray of divine mercy! Upon the basis of this thought and figure, vv. 5, 6, there is first, vv. 7—11, the manner in which the sudden overthrow of such a sinner of itself takes place further expanded, how the powerful sinner, who was just before advancing with such strong proud strides, finds himself suddenly as straitened and everywhere as insecure as if he walked

Famished his strength then becometh,
  calamity standeth always at his side;
he devoureth the members of his skin,
  devoureth his members, he the firstborn of death!
from his tent confidence is torn from him,
  and to the king of terrors it marcheth him.—
15 that which is no more his dwelleth in his tent,
  upon his pasture brimstone is scattered;
beneath his roots dry up,
  and above his branch withereth:
his remembrance hath perished from the earth,
  and there is no name to him in the wide field,
he is hunted from light into darkness,
  and from the round earth he is chased.

upon innumerable secret nets and traps of all kinds, inasmuch as the destructive counsel of his own heart must thus cast him down and everywhere lead him to his death. The construction ver. 8 *a* is exactly like Judg. v. 15, comp. below xxx. 12; the עַל with החזיק, ver. 9, expresses the overwhelming nature of the grasp, from which he cannot defend himself; הֵפִיץ as Hab. iii. 14, לרגליו, ver. 11, also as Hab. iii. 5; "Isa." xli. 2.—The second strophe in the first instance, vv. 12—14, resumes this description in order to finish it with still more powerful figures, namely, how he is at last driven by this terror and helplessness to such great madness and rage, that like a famished vagabond he devours his own arm (Isa. ix. 19 [A. V. 20]), he *the first-born of death*, who before all others belongs to death and deserves it (formed after the simpler phrase 1 Sam. xx. 31), and who precisely at the time of danger is so far from finding protection and confidence in his own house (tent) that it casteth him out as a stranger and, just as a criminal is solemnly led to the place of execution, it causeth him to march to the dark king of terrors (*i.e.*, to Abaddon, Rev. ix. 11, or the Hindoo Jamas) and not to the celestial king; as regards the fem. תצעידר see § 174 *d*. But it is further, vv. 15—18, equally important that after this his terrible overthrow his family also perishes for ever, branded by divine retribution, desolate and forsaken, a horribly warning example for all the world, as Sodom once was (to which the word *brimstone*, ver. 15, alludes, after Gen. xix. 24; Ps. xi. 6): so that he becomes like a tree which is wholly dried up from root to branch, ver. 16, comp. viii. 16—18; Amos ii. 9, and his name, once so honoured, finds nowhere any more respect, but wherever he seeks to come into the light again he is immediately chased away into his deserved darkness, vv. 17, 18. תִּשְׁכּוֹן, ver. 15, belongs probably as neut. to מִבְּלִי לוֹ which has the force of the subject of the clause, acc. § 294 *a*.—The short closing strophe once more, ver. 19, insists on what had been so emphatically said at the end

Offspring and offshoot he lacketh among his people,
  no fugitive is in his hamlets.
20 At his day they of the west are amazed,
  them of the east horror seizeth.—
Only this are the dwellings of the sinner,
  this the place of him that knoweth not God!

of the second strophe, in order by a backward reference, ver. 20, once more to pourtray with a new figure the terrible character of the *day*, *i.e.*, the day of punishment which is becoming notorious, of such a man, as it had been described at greater length vv. 11—14, and thus to close the whole speech by a reference to the beginning, ver. 21. *Offspring* and *offshoot*, ver. 19, are approximate renderings of the assonance of נִין and נֶכֶד, *i.e.*, descendants of all kinds, after an old proverb; it need hardly be remarked that *those from West and East*, ver. 20, comp. vv. 17, 18, means the inhabitants of the whole earth.

b. JOB. CH. XIX.

If the last speech of Job's was pervaded by a repressed prayer for at least a pledge of the future acknowledgment of his innocence, xvii. 3, he now sees by its uselessness even this last atom of earthly hope and this most modest desire frustrated. It is now, therefore, that for the first time he feels himself totally deceived with regard to all his past ideas and hopes of God and divine righteousness. The God of the present, as he had hitherto with the rest of the world regarded Him as the true one, has been for him destroyed beyond recovery, and thereby he finds himself cast into an abyss of despair and helplessness which could not be deeper, so that the profoundest lamentation which was commenced xvi. 7—16, here vv. 7—20, reaches the most extreme point possible in the contention. But all the time he sees the attacks of the friends most unsparingly continued, indeed, carried to a pitch of rage which can hardly be worse; and this precisely with regard to the question of the divine righteousness. But on this question, according to his present opinion, they as well as himself and the rest of the world have been so greatly mistaken, only that he alone, but not they, is in a position by his most personal and irrefutable experiences in the first instance to perceive and to confess this error, indeed, is compelled even by the past results of the discussion of his case to do this. He now stands therefore between two fires, either of which burns him more severely than the other if he comes nearer to it: injustice, the most cruel and worst conceivable, he meets with from his friends, and he believes that he likewise, and in the same highest matter, the matter of his innocence and his life, meets with it from God. It is here that he first finds the last conceivable extremity of suffering and an inexpressible torture, which could not in this life be worse for a good man and more likely to lead him into temptation.

As the suffering is at this stage the most extreme conceivable and the torture the most full of temptation, we cannot be surprised that the wildest storm of diametrically opposite feelings, temptations, and resolutions now sweeps over the struggling hero, lashing him from one extreme to the other, and causing him to attempt most impossible things, to wish and think what had never been wished or thought, to behold and hope for what had never been beheld or hoped for. Placed between two angry mortal enemies, to whom shall he turn in this hour, whom shall he supplicate, as one already seized by the angel of death, for compassion? Here confronts him a strange Being, whom he had hitherto looked upon as the true, just God, and revered above everything, and who has now so completely disappointed all his hopes; there confront him men who were once his best friends. O he himself is also a man, and ought not man to take pity on man? and does not the deepest misery urge even the open enemy to plead for protection? or does the enemy who is thus supplicated by his humbled enemy reject his last most agonising pleas for life? Thus after some desponding words of displeasure at the want of feeling of the friends, vv. 2, 3, the thought flashes through his tortured soul, whether in his profoundest grief on account of God's dealings with him he may not be able to excite the human pity of his enemies to sympathise with him in a lot darker and more cruel than ever man had borne? And, see, he is at this moment prepared to attempt this, overcomes his natural indignation at the past conduct of the friends, and prays for their compassion. He accordingly confesses to them without reserve the error in which he had hitherto been regarding God, places before them his bitterest complaint against Him openly with the most agonising pain, and closes, like one persecuted to death, with the most heart-rending plea for pity and protection against his persecutor, vv. 4—22. Indeed, the grievous inequality of the relations subsisting between himself and God, appears to be a calamity which concerns all mankind, and Job is brought by it in the greatest depth of his troubles simply back to the same complaint with which he formerly began, ch. iii.

But in vain does he attempt this also under most violent emotion; in vain does he humble himself before men to supplicate help from them: they are too immovable and blinded to comprehend this despairing agony of innocence and to take pity on the pains of this most miserable of men. Accordingly in the end there remains nothing for him but to resign even this last attempt to get comfort and help, and once more to seek salvation alone from the future and the eternal God. Slowly, like one feeling for the right way, he turns from the most unhelpful of men to the highest God, until at last the full certainty dawns upon his soul, that it is the eternal, true God who is also the one deliverer of innocence, and that the indestructible spirit will after the death of the body behold the divine revelation in infinite joy, whereby he finds unexpectedly the proper weapons against the terrible threats of the friends who have wholly lost all compassion, vv. 23—29. So that he who appeared at the beginning of the speech wholly lost and in despair, yea, humiliated himself so far as to make humble entreaties to mean and remorseless enemies, is at the end for the first time filled with the enthusiasm of the most assured and happy hope; while he holds fast simply to this hope he is able to rise against his enemies with the most triumphant courage and the most righteous threat; and whilst in the first advance he deferred the necessary attack upon them until the last speech, in this case he inflicts a mortal wound upon them as early as the close of the second, though this was not at all his intention when he began it.

Thus this profoundly pathetic speech combines the lowest human humiliation and the highest divine exaltation, the utmost despair and the most enthusiastic hope and most enraptured certainty. It occupies not only the highest central point of the contention and of the action of the whole drama, but it also effects the first real and decisive change in favour of Job: because it is in it that the two most pointed issues of all Job's thoughts and aims—the unbelief which springs from the old superstition and the genuine, higher faith which has to be produced—come into such sharp and effective contact that this higher faith is called forth from non-existence with irresistible might, and is afterwards, although without reconciliation with its antithesis, maintained, gradually gains greater victories, and finally remains alone triumphant. At this point Job would either have to perish wholly, or the pure truth must at last rise brightly and powerfully before him in the sharpest conflict with its opposites. But it is only in a soul like that of Job's, which remains in such pure innocence faithful to the uttermost, that the fire of truth at last springs forth with overwhelming force and far-shining brightness from the strongest friction of all past principles and counter-principles. For the sparks of the eternal hope that is raised above all time and vicissitudes of time, which at first faintly glimmered, ch. xiv., then sprang forth more brightly, ch. xvi., xvii., here burst into a clear fire, warming and sustaining the man who would otherwise have now perished in the ancient superstition and in the dark abyss of unbelief. Accordingly this speech consists of two parts only, the beginning and end of which are diametrically opposed, as if at the beginning in the violent storm Job had not fully known whither he should turn the helm at the end, until an unexpected wind, which nevertheless came at the right moment as already prepared for, drives him into the right haven. Moreover, these two parts (and this is the first time that an answer of Job's consists of merely two parts) are externally quite unequal: for the marvellous weight of the thought of the second part far outweighs any outward size.

xix. 1 And Job answered and said:

1.

How long will ye grieve my soul,
  and crush me completely with words?
ten times already ye make me ashamed,
  ye are without blushing unfeeling towards me!

1. Vv. 2—22. The extreme agitation which prevails in the first part, is also reflected clearly in the rapid variations and great inequality of the strophes. At first, in the somewhat difficult and as it were tentative beginning, two strophes, quite short, of two verses each; then the complaint, growing somewhat calmer, is poured forth in two longer strophes of seven verses each, until a third, which has only just been begun, is rapidly finished in one verse, as if interrupted by uncontrollable sobs, and in greatest agitation the discourse returns with a similarly short strophe of two verses to the two strophes at the beginning.—The first word, vv. 2, 3, is in this case already somewhat more subdued, as if the speaker did not yet realise his latent intense agitation. *Ashamed*, ver. 3, by the most painful reproaches, which a man must blush to answer; הכר is most probably, according to this context, equivalent to impudent, unfeeling, to be compared therefore with حكر, nor can the word be otherwise understood Isa. iii. 9.[1]—The transition is formed by vv. 4, 5. What does it avail to attack the friends, inasmuch as he has himself in his former faith in the divine righteousness and in God's appearance for judgment been fundamentally in error, and the rage of the friends has after all some excuse in this very failure of God to appear; they may really believe that God will not appear because of Job's sins. Would it not therefore be possible if, now that he is completely disappointed as regards God, he should declare his whole situation to the friends and how in reality his complaint was not against them but against

[1] Comp. *Ewald und Duke's Beiträge etc.* I. p. 99.

And truly too I have erred,
well known to me is my error!
5 Or—will ye then really disdain me,
and reproach me—with my disgrace?

Know then that God hath wronged me,
and cast over me His net round about!
Lo, of wrong I cry out—without being heard,
cry for help—there is no judgment!
My path He hath hedged up—impassably,
placeth darkness upon my footways;
of my glory hath He stripped me,
taken away the crown of my head,
10 He pulleth me down round about—and I depart,
plucketh up like a tree my hope,

God, that they might then show compassion instead of such severity to the innocent sufferer? This reflection is implied in ver. 4; and based upon this honest confession, that he had hitherto been in error as to his hope of righteousness and judgment on God's part, he immediately adds in a friendly confidential tone, ver. 5, *or* (אם) *will ye really* (as has hitherto been the case, yet he would like to think not deliberately) *act grandly against me*, as dishonourable, base men treat me scornfully simply because I suffer severely from an irresistible persecutor, *and reproach me with my shame* which I must, although innocent, endure from this cruel persecutor, as if I had deserved it? Perhaps they do not know *who* is intended by this cruel persecutor, against whom he will now, as a supplicating client of antiquity, entreat their help, bowing down before them, embracing their knees in supplication? If they do not know, then he will tell them: it is God Himself!—Therewith the complaint against God begins, how He has *twisted* him, *i.e.*, treated him wrongly and unjustly, and cast *His net* over him round about, so that he cannot escape from the calamities and wrongs which he has to endure (iii. 23; xiii. 27), and how, though repeatedly entreated by the persecuted man to grant him justice, He has nevertheless refused to grant it, vv. 6, 7. From this commencement the complaint is now continued further, in order, in the first instance as far as the end of the first strophe, to describe his innumerable sufferings generally with a few great telling strokes, vv. 8—12: namely, the oppressive feeling of darkness and hindrances on all hands, in that he sees neither way nor light that he may escape from the vortex in which he is now caught, ver. 8 after the figure which was commenced ver. 6 *b*; then, vv. 9, 10, how he feels his outward dignity (xvi. 15; xxix. 8; Gen. xxiii. 6) as well as all his earthly hope (xiv. 20) completely destroyed, as if a great, splendid tree were totally shattered; yea, how, to indicate

and causeth His wrath to burn against me,
  counteth me like His true enemies:
altogether His troops come,
  and cast up their way against me,
    encamp round about my tent.

My brethren hath He removed far from me,
  and mine acquaintances—they are only strangers to me,
my kinsfolk fail,
  familiar friends have forgotten me;
15 dependents in my house and maids deem me a stranger,
  an alien am I in their eyes,
to my man-servant I call—without getting an answer,
  with mine own mouth must I entreat him:

the worst with one figure, as it were a whole army of pains and calamities, aroused and conducted by the divine wrath, charge against him to take his fortress, vv. 11, 12, comp. vii. 20; x. 17; xiii. 24; xvi. 9—14.—Still, amongst all the innumerable pains and woes which beset him, there is one especially which he feels most deeply precisely at this time, and describes therefore with greatest sadness in the course of the whole of the second strophe: namely, the woe of having to bear the unfaithfulness, the contempt, and the reviling of all men, from his relatives, ver. 13 *a*, ver. 14 *a*, as well as from the dearest acquaintances, ver. 13 *b*, ver. 14 *b*, who were formerly in the habit of visiting him with affection and respect (xlii. 11, מֵעַל, inasmuch as עַל can be used of the person who is about anyone with affection and kindly services); then vv. 15, 16, from the more subordinate people, dependant clients, maids, and man-servants, who formerly attended to every sign of their lord, but now flee from him and even refuse to answer him as he entreats them mournfully on account of a physical necessity; lastly, even from his wife and the children of his body, who flee from his stinking breath, ver. 17, just as also all the other children ridicule him, *e.g.*, when he tries to rise but is not strong enough to do so, and precisely his dearest and most familiar friends also have now all the more turned against him, vv. 18, 19.[1]—Yet when Job comes now, thirdly, ver. 20,

---

[1] חנותי, ver. 17 *b*, must be compared with خنّ, وخن, which again are ultimately the same as خمّ and وخم, and signify a corrupt, bad smell, originally probably the corruption, or wasting away, itself, so that خان *to deceive* (lit. to withdraw, take away, comp. כחש) is connected with these roots. עֲוִילִים, ver. 18, is not from עֲוִיל, xvi. 11, but from a עֲוִיל = עוּל, xxi. 11.

my breath is loathsome to my wife,
  I stink to the sons of my body,
children even despise me,
  if I will rise—*they* revile me:
all my close friends abhor me,
  those whom I loved are turned against me.

20 To skin and flesh cleaveth my bone,
  so that I hardly escaped with the flesh of my teeth . . . .

O have pity, have pity on me, ye my friends!
  for God's hand—it hath touched me;
wherefore persecute ye me as God,
  and are never satisfied with my flesh?

to describe the inexpressibly sad state of his body, suddenly his language fails him in the midst of the new beginning, fatigued and exhausted from infinite pain; so that he only says that *his bone cleaves to his skin and flesh*, from the lack of all humours in his completely emaciated body, Ps. xxii. 16, 18; cii. 6; and *he has* barely *saved himself with his tooth-flesh*, gums, it is only the meager flesh of the gums which he feels as not already consumed by the fatal corruption, as the elephantiasis in reality attacks last of all the tongue and gums and thereby makes speech even impossible.—And scarcely can he find strength for the cry which he meant from the beginning to raise and simply to justify by this speech of complaint, the cry to the friends for human mercy and help against the persecutor; and if like clings more closely to like precisely in danger, it might be supposed that all men must now take the part of one who is persecuted with such incomprehensible severity, in order to protect human rights generally, if from no other motive, ver. 21; imperceptibly, however, ver. 22, there is introduced, as if it could not be wholly repressed, a censure of the friends in the question, wherefore they desired then to persecute him as inexorably as God, incessantly devouring, as in ravenous rage, his flesh, not indeed by physical mistreatment, but (which wounds and kills none the less) by injurious, cutting and slanderous words (Dan. iii. 8).

2. Vv. 23—29. Pause: the friends are silent and remain unmoved. With that the entire position of the action is changed: this last earthly hope also, which it is true Job could have conceived only in a final, convulsive moment of deepest despair, is absolutely destroyed; he knows at last as certainly as possible that neither the friends or any men, nor the God of the present, will listen to his complaints or his protestations; and accordingly he must at this point wholly perish if help did not come to him just at this pause. At this moment a glance is opened to his spirit, which is all along conscious of its innocence and unable to rest and be silent, into the distant future after death—

2.

O that then my words were written down,
  in the book—O that they were imprinted;
with iron graver and with lead
  that they were for ever hewn in rock!—

a future as yet open to it alone. This glance surprises him in his condition, by its own necessity, truth, and righteousness, it at once raises him marvellously higher and higher from stage to stage, and opens for him an outlook by which he is able for the first time in this deepest despair nevertheless to hold his ground, indeed, to find the most wonderful, divine courage hitherto unknown to him. As by an inward necessity he is conducted to this new point of view: imperceptibly at first and with profound modesty the wish arises, that after all his speeches and the solemn protestations of his innocence, as they have now been heard but have died away without effect, might at least be preserved for future times, written down in a book, or rather (for it is only the most distant future which he can now be thinking of) engraved in stone with an iron graver and with lead (which is poured into the fissures cut by the graver), for an eternal memorial! vv. 23, 24, comp. Isa. viii. 1; xxx. 8; Ex. xxxi. 18; Deut. xxvii. 8; Josh. viii. 32; Layard's *Nineveh* II. p. 188. As a fact this wish is on Job's part nothing exorbitant: for we now know quite well that in those countries people endeavoured not only to immortalise in rock and stone inscriptions, short laws, but also somewhat longer historical memorials, public desires, prayers, etc.; and if such costly works could be executed only by princes and kings, it must be remembered that Job was also a great man in his time who might very well express such a desire. Nevertheless, another moment of brief reflection must convince this most miserable of men how useless it was for him to express this desire with the view of testifying the certainty of his innocence at all events for the time after his death, and of seeing it perhaps acknowledged by future generations: he sees no one who would be prepared to execute this wish, or even so much as to listen willingly to it.—Thus then this wish only serves to conduct the glance of the sufferer, which is now directed with the most intense energy to the future alone, towards that one thing which can come to him thence with strength and assurance. But as soon as that one needful truth rises once more before him, which had twice previously forced itself upon him in the last two speeches, but had been again lost sight of, it then fills his longing heart, which can be revived again by it alone, immediately with that marvellous, blessed certainty which is always its peculiar gift when it finds the prepared heart. And thus spring forth, vv. 25—27, as from a purer, celestial air, borne by the spirit, those few but infinitely weighty, sublime words which constitute the crown of the whole contention, words of the purest splendour of divine truth, without anything to dim them, which suddenly make the speaker an inspired prophet, so that he here at once

25 But I know it, my redeemer liveth,
a successor will arise upon the dust;
after my skin, which they hack off, this, [skin]
and free from the body shall I behold—God:

begins quite unexpectedly with higher certainty. *But* (to what purpose further thoughts?) *I know, my Redeemer liveth,* although I die unredeemed, misunderstood, persecuted, he does not die and will become my Redeemer after my death; *and a successor,* a survivor who lives and remains after me, a successor in my just cause and its advocacy, *will arise upon the dust,* the grave (xvii. 16; xx. 11; xxi. 26), as in purely human relations the surviving *afterman* and successor in all the rights and duties of the deceased, redeeming (גאל) all his rights and having particularly the duty of revenging the innocently murdered, visiting the grave of the slain man and rising from it with courage and strength against the slayer[1], comp. xvi. 18. But although this utterance is borrowed from the ancient sacred duty of avenging blood, as this duty had at least originated in the thought of an unchanging righteousness and necessary retribution, everything here appears at the same time in quite new relations, because it is not a man but God alone who can be thought as the revenger, or restorer, of the innocence of the man who dies from no sin of his own, comp. xvi. 19. But it would hardly be a partial restoration if merely men of a later generation but not the spirit of the innocent victim himself had knowledge of it, the spirit which is here the central interest. If this thought is more closely followed up, it becomes clear that the spirit of the deceased must behold its own justification even after the destruction of the body. And when thus the idea of the indestructibility of the pure spirit comes clearly out, the words are added in completion of the whole thought: *and after my skin,* after my skin, or according to xviii. 13 my body, is no more, yet as this is expressed too briefly it is added, *which they* (who is here unimportant) *have hewn off,* as when a tree is lopped and thereby pitilessly destroyed according to the figure xiv. 7, comp. Isa. x. 34[2], *this* very skin which ye here see already in such a pitiable condition, as is further remarked with great sadness, *and without my flesh* (on מִן see § 217 *b,* without having this, which words together with the previous verse-member therefore complete the sentence, "after I shall have lost skin and flesh, my whole body as far as it is sensitive and mortal, this body which has been so much tortured", *I shall* nevertheless *behold—God,* shall then still feel the joy of the appearance and immediate presence of God also as the judge and defender of my innocence, which I cannot enjoy before the death of the body! and then, as follows of itself, with spiritual eyes, not with my present ones, and yet as certainly and as clearly and sensibly as possible. Whoever beholds God becomes conscious of the pure light, the clear truth, and the eternal life,

---

1 *Exoriare aliquis nostris ex ossibus ultor.*

2 Comp. ፈገፈ, used of leaves and trees Enoch iii. 1.

Him whom *I* shall behold for *myself*,
shall have seen by *mine* own eyes and no one else's!
—my reins are consumed in my bosom!

feeling no separation and no disagreement at all between himself and God, accordingly no alarm, no fear nor punishment: of being able to do this in this bodily life Job has long ago completely despaired, but he now knows that he can and certainly will do it spiritually after physical death. Full of joyful exultation, here at last his heart leaps at the surprisingly clear picture of this awful future moment which is now so certain to him, and as if foretasting this long-desired highest joy, and the more the present will deprive him of this hope and depress him with the terrors of the divine wrath, the more boldly and exultingly he exclaims here in conclusion: *Him whom I shall behold for myself*, for *my* joy, because He will acknowledge *my* right, *my* innocence, and *my eyes will* then *have seen Him* (רָאוּ in this connection *perf. fut.*), *not a stranger*, another than myself, no without doubt *I myself*, so deeply does he feel this joy as already by anticipation his, as if, wholly absorbed in himself and with the outward world forgotten, he could not sufficiently satiate himself with it, nor sufficiently convince himself that precisely he himself will enjoy it, so that at last as if fainting in the highest rapture he exclaims *O, I die* almost from joyous agitation and highest longing! Ps. lxxxiv. 3; cxix. 81.

If the opponents could still be in uncertainty at the first sentence of this utterance, ver. 25, which came upon them as unexpectedly as spirit-words, as to whom Job really meant by the avenger who was to rise upon his grave, and whether he might not, in what seems to them his madness, really mean a man, they must be in the highest degree surprised when, after a few further slow solemn words, he names at the end, ver. 26, God Himself as such an avenger. But for the sufferer himself, who had shortly before in vain humbled himself to them, there has now, particularly after the last words, ver. 27 *c*, of a passionate tendency again, and with reference to the beginning and course of the whole speech, a transition been prepared for to a most emphatic, overwhelming application of this highest certainty to these opponents, who instead of threatening him with the terrors of a divine judgment have themselves need to fear it when it comes, as it most surely will! Thus the end of the speech is quite different from what was expected from the beginning, and Job's castigating words were never more keen and penetrating than in this short but agitated conclusion, vv. 28, 29. *When ye say* (xxi. 28), or think, *how will we gladly persecute him* the wholly helpless being! (comp. vv. 5, 22), *and the foundation* (the root) *of the matter*, the ultimate and true cause of the matter of this action, of the sufferings, *is found in me* (accordingly in *b*, acc. § 328, indirect narration interchanging with direct in *a*, just as xxii. 17, so that there is no necessity to read בוֹ, with many MSS. and the ancient versions, instead of בִּי), when ye thus make both perfidious and wholly false speeches, as ye have hitherto done, *then be ye afraid for yourselves of the sword*, fear ye its threatening strokes, and the sword which is emphatically so called is that great, eternal punishment of the

—If ye think "how will we persecute him!"
and the root of the matter is found in me:
then fear ye the sword
for burning are the sword's punishments:
—in order that ye may know the Almighty! [1]

divine judgment, xv. 22; xxvii. 14; "Zech." xi. 17; xiii. 7: *for glowing heat*, nothing but glowing heat (§ 296 *b*) *are* this *sword's punishments*, devouring at once everyone whom they in the burning of the divine wrath overtake, with which therefore there may be no playing; but they must, if ye continue, overtake you *in order that ye may come to the knowledge of* the truth, that your blindness and obduracy may cease were it only by your death. The only difficulty here is the word שדין, which the Massôra with the Targ. (Pesh. Vulg.) explains as אֲשֶׁר דִּין, or דּוּן Q'ri, *in order that ye may know that* there is *judgment!* This meaning would not be unsuitable: but ש abbreviated from אשר is not found in the Book of Job, and the weight of this objection follows from § 181 *b*; further, the root דין, in all the forms derived therefrom, is equally foreign to the vocabulary of the original Book of Job, while it occurs frequently in Elihu's speeches, xxxv. 14; xxxvi. 17 twice, 31. If it is determined not to restore שַׁדַּי, which is so frequent in our book, it might be conjectured from the surprising translation of the LXX ποῦ ἔστιν αὐτῶν ἡ ὕλη (or ἰσχύς Cod. Alex.), that the text has been somewhat corrupted here at the end, perhaps אֵי שָׁדְּכֶם that ye *may know how*, of what nature, *your violence*, or cruelty, *is*. In any case the meaning of the important passage as a whole does not in the least depend on this last clause.

As was said above, pp. 16, 56, we have vv. 25—27 the undoubted utterance of the truth of the higher hope which looks joyfully beyond physical death into the immortality of the soul. It is true that this hope is as yet without any of the luxuriant developments of it which were often carried beyond all proportion in later times: we see it here quite in its first fresh germination, as a new and certain view just as it springs forth from an inward necessity. Later readers, particularly of Christian times, did not distinguish the stages of the growth of the hope with sufficient precision, and transferred many of the conceptions which arose later into this passage. But the view of perhaps nearly all modern scholars, that Job expresses here an earthly hope and does not at all speak of the time after death, is much worse, and, indeed, totally false. This view is opposed to the words themselves, it is opposed to the connection of the thoughts, it sins against the meaning of the whole book and against the plain advance from xiv. 13—15 to xvi. 18 sq., and finally to this passage. Neither is one justified in saying that the poet must then have kept back the thought of immortality for the end of the book: on the contrary, we have here the climax of the contention, which can only be triumphantly conducted by means of the certainty of the immortality of the soul, whilst at the end of the book it is not

[1] Or according to another reading, *that ye may know what your cruelty is!*

this but wholly different truths which must be added to the one here declared. To which considerations we must add, that this idea did not come to the poet as one which was current, but as completely new, which he ventured to introduce and to expound only briefly and in relation to its first but most inward necessity. If the truth was to the poet more like a germinating surmise and anticipation, he was compelled to put it into Job's mouth as such, and this is precisely the most suitable place where we have the vortex of the greatest despair.[1]

3. ZOPHAR AND JOB.

a. ZOPHAR. CH. XX.

The following speech shows plainly enough how right Job was in feeling towards the end of his speech, that that last effort in favour of peace with his opponents would be in vain. For of these most profound words of Job's, which must, if anything could do so, excite the pity of the opponents, the third friend has really understood nothing but the forcible threats at the end, which appear to him to be the scornful mockery of perfect madness, the sneering defiance of sin, and which vex him the more as he, the youngest of the combatants, has from the beginning taken the most passionate view of the question concerning Job. As regards the matter itself, he really does not know anything fresh to say: but his personal feeling has been too much mortified to permit him to remain quite silent. Accordingly he attempts to do the best he can. After a brief opening, in which he declares that his profoundly offended, greatly agitated, spirit will not permit him to hold his peace, vv. 2, 3, he begins to preach the truth, that the exultation of the wicked lasts but for a little while, and though he ascend ever so high and lift himself ever so proudly, or however much pleasure he may have in the enjoyment of his evil works, he will nevertheless be cast down to the greatest depth and be

---

[1] As early as 1843, after the first edition of this work (1836), I defended more definitely and at length this view in the *Tübinger theologische Jahrbücher*, 1843, pp. 718 sq., against the most recent interpreters who sought again to deny the truth in this important question.

compelled to resign his sweetest enjoyment, because he cannot with impunity have violated human and divine law, vv. 4—29. For the third time, therefore, the same denunciation occurs, and here at greatest length, everything that can be brought into it being handled with utmost effort: at the same time with this advance, that whilst Eliphaz had drawn only in general frightful descriptions of the overthrow of the sinner, and while Bildad had already said more definitely that he would perish in spite of his desperate resistance, this time, because Job had at last so unsparingly appealed to the future, Zophar insists upon even the near end of the mad exultation.

xx. 1. Then answered Zophar the Naamathite and said:

Therefore my wild thought replieth to me,
  and thence cometh mine inward eagerness:
correction which insulteth me I hear,
  and the spirit answereth me according to my understanding:
Knowest thou how *this* is from of old,
  since man was placed upon earth,

Vv. 2, 3 can hardly be properly understood unless it is remembered that בַּעֲבוּר corresponds in every respect to לָכֵן, and is left without any complement simply because this can be easily supplied from the כֵּן in לָכֵן, comp. the second כְּעַל Isa. lix. 18, بَعْدُ as adv. without complement *Gramm. Arab.* I. p. 345, further לְמַעַן even for *because* Neh. vi. 13 (strangely Chald. מְטוּל Targ. Ps. xi. 3). Thus the two similar members of the highly agitated words ver. 2 refer to ver. 3 *a* as the moving cause, and ver. 3 *b* then returns more calmly to the commencement: *therefore* he feels a reply, which otherwise he would prefer to wholly omit, proclaimed to him by his agitated thoughts, and *thence* his inward violent eagerness, which gives him no rest (חוּשִׁי בִּי like יתרם בם, iv. 21 and עזרתי בי vi. 13), because he hears an insulting, deeply wounding correction of himself from Job, not to reply to which is contrary to his inmost nature, so that the spirit which is so profoundly insulted and excited compels him to make the following answer according to his best understanding and wisdom. This answer now follows first briefly, vv. 4, 5: dost thou know (from thy present behaviour it could not be believed), that *this* has been so as long as men have been

5 That the loud rejoicing of the wicked is but short,
and the joy of the impure but for a moment?
Although to heaven his excellency ascendeth,
his head reacheth to the clouds:
just as he is great, he perisheth for ever,
they who saw him say, where is he?
as a dream he fleeth away, no more to be found,
and is chased away as a night-vision,
eyes beheld him—they do so no more,
no longer doth his place look upon him;
10 his fists smote down the low:
his hands restore the power,
his bones were filled with his youthful vigour:
but with him upon the dust they lie down!

placed on the earth (lit. since the placing (one placed) man, § 304 *a*), namely, that the exultation of the wicked is shortlived, not extending far into either the past or the future? The construction of ver. 4 *a* is as concisely contracted as the Lat. construction *hoccine scis aeternum esse?* All the rest from ver. 6 to the end is but the elaboration of this sentence: it begins with the certainty of the overthrow itself, vv. 6—18, and it then proceeds to the causes of it, vv. 19—28; but the whole, from ver. 5 (ver. 4 forms the transition) is divided into three somewhat long strophes of seven verses each, until at last a shorter one closes the speech in great agitation.—That certainty holds in spite of all appearances to the contrary and of all resistance: for though the wicked man exalt himself to heaven in power or pride, yet his overthrow is certain, vv. 6—11, and how terrible an overthrow, mocking all human pride! *according to his greatness* he perishes, so that his destruction is the greater in proportion as he himself is great (this appears to be the meaning of כגללו, perhaps to be pointed פִּגְלָלוֹ; the Massora, with Vulg. Targ., *like his dung*, probably too coarse a figure, and here also, since a clearing away, or a trampling, is not spoken of, one that is not very suitable; ver. 18 *b* is rather to be compared); and this is a sudden and yet eternal ruin, so that his existence in the great world, when the matter is looked at from its end, appears as fleeting as that of a dream or a spectre; accordingly the fool must by this very overthrow surrender all the power which he cruelly robbed from the helpless, whilst his sons are still suffering from the injustice of their father, and then he lies there in the grave in spite of all the well preserved vigour of youth! This antithesis appears to run through vv. 10, 11, יְרַצּוּ is in that case acc. § 121 *a* from רָצָה = רָצַץ, as the phrase is plainly connected with that which recurs ver. 19 *a*; with the sense of ver. 10 comp. vv. 19, 22 *b* and v. 5, Job also appears to allude below xxi. 19 precisely to these words; between the two members of ver. 10 there is thus no

Though wickedness taste sweet in his mouth,
though he hide it under his tongue,
spareth it and letteth it not go,
keepeth it back in the midst of his palate:
nevertheless his bread hath been changed in his bowels,
venom of snakes is within him,
15 power he swallowed—vomiteth it again,
from his belly God expelleth it,
poison of snakes he sucketh,
the tongue of the adder slayeth him;
he may not enjoy the brooks
streams floods of honey and milk,
he who restoreth earnings, swalloweth not,
however great his gain, yet he rejoiceth not!—

For he forsook the weak crushed,
robbed houses and buildeth them not;
20 surely he knew not quietness in his body:
and his dearest things he will not save,

connection, and it cannot be denied that זְרֹעָיו, xxii. 8; xxxviii. 15, or חָפְנָיו, instead of בָּנָיו, would contribute a very suitable addition to this connection. It is true he seeks further, vv. 12—18, to enjoy as long as possible his wickedly gained possessions; like dainties he holds them hidden as long as possible by the tongue and fast to the palate, in order to feast on them: but as soon as ever the sweet dainty of sin has entered more deeply into the system, it reacts as a destructive poison, all enjoyment is frustrated with unexpected rapidity (hence the *perf.* נהפך, ver. 14), indeed, really he may not enjoy at all his immense treasures—the fool who the more he has gained the more and the more painfully must he give back everything without any quiet enjoyment! Ver. 17 acc. § 289 *c* and Ex. iii. 8, 17; ver. 18 כחיל תמורתו must be connected with ולא יעלס, משיב יגע is a collateral adverbial clause to the whole sentence; תְּמוּרָה *exchange*, xxviii. 17, can probably denote also *gain*, or entire possession itself, as people exchange what is their own only for what is better (apparently, xv. 31, or really better).—Thus far the causes of such a terrible overthrow have not been intentionally dwelt upon, the third strophe of this description, vv. 19—25 starts from them particularly, in order to return with greater emphasis to the beginning. And now the two previous thoughts vv. 6 sq., 12 sq. are more concisely reiterated: because he let the helpless lie crushed by proud power and contempt, without concerning himself about them (the copula is intentionally omitted between עזב and רצץ, § 285 *b*), and because he was insatiable greed and

there hath nothing escaped his greed:
  therefore his best good endureth not,
in his richest abundance it is strait to him,
  every hand of the suffering overtaketh him,
in order to fill his belly, must God
  send into him the heat of His anger,
    rain upon him what can satisfy him!
If he avoideth the armour of iron,
  yet the bow of metal rusheth after him:
25 he draweth it out and—it cometh forth from the back,
  and a gleam goeth out of his gall,
    over him terrors!

love of pleasure itself, so that no victim escaped this passion, ver. 20 *a*, ver. 21 *a*, therefore will he with his dearest possession, to which his whole soul is attached, not escape with his perishable material treasures (מִלֵּט without an object, as פִּלֵּט xxiii. 7 [1]), ver. 20 *b*, ver. 21 *b*, therefore will all people who have been wronged by him at last make him feel their revenge at a most unexpected moment, ver. 22; yea, may God, in order to satisfy for ever the man's greed for material pleasures, send down upon him His burning materials, fire-rain and lightnings, as his food, in order that he may be satiated with it for ever! ver. 23, comp. xviii. 15. This divine punishment he will not escape, vv. 24, 25, for it is as various and endless as it is sharp and deeply penetrating, as when one flees from heavy armour and is from behind unexpectedly overtaken by the distant bow, and drawing out the arrow, in order to try again to save himself, finds the sharpest and most gleaming iron has entered into the very centre of his body, surprised at that moment by the terrors of death—a very graphic description!—Then at last, vv. 26—28, with everything lost, all kinds of darkness, all calamity must be stored up for his stored treasures, in order to destroy his many vainly well-preserved treasures, and to frustrate their enjoyment, comp. ver. 28 *a*, a play upon the word and the thought; no ordinary fire, such as is blown by men, but a divine, irresistible fire, must feed away him and all his belongings! Isa. xxxiii. 11—14. And thus at last (quite contrary to Job's hope xvi. 19, 20; xix. 25) Heaven and earth must turn with overwhelming power against the insufferable man whose guilt Heaven itself thus reveals; on the day of the divine punishment all the heaped-up wealth of his house, apparently so firmly founded, must flow away, having now become as liquid and unsteady as water when running away, comp. with the last figure xi. 16; 2 Sam. xiv. 14; instead of יִגַּל *to be compelled to go into exile*, which does not harmonise well

[1] The translation "sein Liebstes wird er nicht erretten", which Ewald has given above, appears inconsistent with this construction. Tr.

Let darkness only be stored up for his stores;
let a fire devour him, not blown,
let it feed off the rest in his tent!
May the heavens uncover his guilt,
whilst the earth riseth against him!
let the produce of his house stream away,
waters running away on the day of His punishment!—
This the lot of the wicked man from God,
and the heritage appointed him from the Highest.

with the figure of the verse, יִגַּל, Amos v. 24, must be read.— —After the great agitation at the beginning, which then gradually increases towards the end of this speech, it is not to be wondered at that in the description the language here and there makes corresponding changes and demands punishment, indeed, that at the end this demand prevails, vv. 17, 23, 26—28; the forms תְּאָכְלֵהוּ *t'oklêhu* from תֹּאכַל, and יֵרַע from רעה *to feed off*, ver. 26, may accordingly be explained as shortened Jussiv forms. Comp. xv. 31. יְהִי, ver. 23, strangely placed before an abrupt anticipatory clause, as in the instances § 344 *b*; on the other hand, יְהִי xviii. 12, xxiv. 14 must be understood acc. § 224 *c*.

It may be further observed that these descriptions of the fate of the wicked may start from the idea of an indefinite number of sinners, xviii. 5 *a*; xx. 5 *a* and return to that idea again, xv. 34, 35: but in the course of the delineation itself, inasmuch as after all everything is intended to refer to Job, the sing. is so predominant that the plur. appears but twice in an unimportant suff. xv. 29 *b*, xx. 23, in the last passage, as well as in the similar one xxvii. 23, somewhat less certainly acc. xxii. 2 and § 247 *d*. On the other hand, in the corresponding general descriptions of Job's, the plur. predominates, ch. xxi. it is only in a new sentence that the sing. once, ver. 10, is used, ch. xxiv. somewhat more frequently, at first in a collateral clause, ver. 5 *c*, then more frequently varying with several verses, or even verse-members, vv. 16—24.

b. JOB. CH. XXI.

In vain has Job accordingly made a last venture in order to warn the friends against further contention of this kind: they simply make their strong descriptions still more frightful, with the almost unveiled object of holding up a mirror in which Job may see himself. And equally in vain has he endeavoured to withdraw his gaze from the absolute confusion of the present times and circumstances and direct it to the bright future and to eternity, as well as to raise the thought of his friends even to the same height. They do not in the least comprehend this elevation, and are always dragging the contention down again into the abyss, not to sink into which has hitherto required the exercise of Job's utmost efforts. They do not observe that by thus attempting to drag Job per force into the abyss, they at the same time give him the power to precipitate themselves. For while they hold before him perpetually the divine righteousness against sinners, and desire to judge him according to the general standard which they have derived from these sinners, they compel him at last, partly from weariness and partly into order to defend himself against their unsparing attacks, to look more closely into this thought. But when he examines it more narrowly, he must from his stand-point deny the matter as the opponents represent it, and destroy the entire basis of this position of the friends. For, indeed, he would gladly accept the principle of the friends; because if it were as they conceive it and as he himself had hitherto believed, then the deliverance of all the innocent, particularly of himself, must at once follow, inasmuch as he knows so clearly that he is innocent. But he does not feel himself merely just now injured, persecuted, destroyed by a dark, incomprehensible lot, but, when called upon to direct his glance to the world around, he observes in the wide world, in the broad daylight of human society, similar monstrous wrong and confusion, the wicked prosperous and innocence suffering. The outward appearance, on which the opponents are wholly dependent, really teaches this reverse side of their view and experience, inasmuch as the innocent is by no means always outwardly prosperous, the guilty is not always outwardly unprosperous. If some men, like the friends, insist merely upon one aspect of experience, other people, equally or still more experienced, declare the exact contrary, vv. 29 sq. For the man, therefore, who desires to examine this question more closely, simple fairness and strictness of judgment demand that he shall look equally at all manifestations and expressions of the divine activity in the world, and not permit merely one aspect of it to hold good, as if one claimed to know better than God Himself, ver. 22. And whoever once gets above the customary opinion, easily discovers its weak points, how it is untrue and cruel towards so many unfortunate sufferers, how it is unable to maintain its position by means of the assertion, that at least the descendants of the prosperous sinner are punished, inasmuch as a punishment which does not fall upon the really guilty person would be both unworthy and to no purpose, vv. 19—21. Whoever, now, is compelled so forcibly to look for the first time at the reverse side and its truth, may not he, losing his balance, eagerly follow up so exclusively the picture of this reverse side, so fascinated by its painful and yet certain truth, that he grows incapable in the moment of his grief of seeing anything else? Job is in this state now. The third opponent had set upon him, and exhausted all the strength by which he had endeavoured to preserve a certain degree of self-control; he had been compelled to study the general righteousness of God which had been extolled; and now, straitened on all hands, he is compelled openly to declare, that he cannot anywhere find that righteousness as the friends represent it. The earlier, incidental, interrupted, suppressed, and, indeed, once (ch. xiii) with difficulty combated doubts of the divine righteousness, and the mournful glances into the perverse condition of things prevailing in the wide world also, ix. 23, 24; xii. 6, reach here at last perfect clearness and supremacy, and are exclusively put forward. The joyful thought of the future which had just before been obtained, disappears again, because the present, into the abyss of which he is again drawn down, had all along remained perfectly dark, and as yet no bridge from the dark present to the bright future can be discovered.

Accordingly, straitened by the most painful despondency, Job falls, at the end of an advance of the contention for the second time into the fault of speaking of God as he ought not to speak, and as he would not speak on calmer consideration, inasmuch as to call in question the divine righteousness is when strictly considered folly. The speech to which he is here driven, is when taken by itself inexcusable, because it is as onesided as those of the friends, and is at the same time more dangerous than those of the latter; and it will appear below plainly, how he must suffer for having uttered it. During the course of his speech, he himself perceives that it may well do harm, and must add an incidental observation, lest it should be thought, that he describes with personal satisfaction and sympathy the insane thoughts of the prosperous sinner, ver. 16. Nevertheless there is perceptible here a deeper, hidden calm, in that being already fully convinced that a superhuman enigma, a universal, unexplained human lot under which he suffers, is here in operation, he simply brings the dark problem, although horrified at it, honestly and fully into broad daylight, himself most intensely desiring that it may be explained, and yet compelled to acknowledge it. By this means the thick, unbroken gloom which oppresses him becomes for the first time less dense and more likely to be dispersed, as if it were about to break up through a higher prophetic longing and the feeling of its own insufficiency. If the error is still too firmly rooted to give way at once, it is nevertheless an advantage that it becomes at least clear to itself and beholds fully its own misery, honestly bringing forth all its doubts: of this we have here the beginning. Therefore this speech is not simply a disputation, although it serves to completely refute the friends, inasmuch as it thus presents exactly the true antithesis to their principle. Under the feeling that there is here a superhuman enigma, which the friends least of all can solve, this speech, although bitter as following upon such a severe provocation, begins with unexpected repose, as if Job were not at all complaining of men, but of a dark, tormenting enigma, far above men, which must indeed carry him away to impatience and fill everyone with gloomy amazement who honestly considers it, as it shall now be expounded, vv. 2—5. Thus the calm, self-possessed exposition of the dreadful enigma of the world, to deny which is so frivolous, is begun in the main part of the speech, vv. 6—26, until at the end, since in consequence of the increasing warmth of the speech the remembrance of the intentional denial by the friends of the broad universal fact, and of their cruel treatment of the sufferer based on that denial, has grown vivid, the speech without any constraint changes by the natural progress of the thought to a severe castigation of the opponents, vv. 27—34.

xxi. 1. And Job answered and said:

1.

O hear ye carefully, hear ye my speech,
  in order that *these* may be your consolations!
bear with me that *I* may speak:
  after my speaking thou mayst mock!
I—is then of man my complaint?
  or how should I *not* be impatient?
5 O look upon me and—be astonished,
  and lay the hand upon the mouth!

1. Vv. 2—5. The request for a patient hearing, vv. 2, 3, strengthened by the fact that it is not of men that he complains, but of something with regard to which he must be impatient (vi. 11), at which his hearers themselves must be dumb with amazement (v. 16) if they would candidly hear and consider (vi. 28) the speaker, the victim of the mysterious enigma, as he now calls upon them to do, vv. 4, 5. But into that request for a hearing there is introduced an element of almost insuppressible bitterness, which though at first kept back at the end vents itself more freely, vv. 27 sq.: it is observable after the mild words ver. 2 *a* (like xiii. 17) and ver. 3 *a* as a bitter addition, ver. 2 *b* and ver. 3 *b*: instead of the consolations, which they came to administer but certainly did anything but administer, they might at least comfort him by a patient hearing, comp. ver. 34; and if Zophar desires again to mock him as if he were an incorrigible sinner, let him at least wait till after the enigma now to be expounded has been well considered and see whether he has then still the heart to mock at the man who has no other fault than that he suffers under the most terrible enigma! Thus the wholly unusual address in the second person

2.

If I think thereon, I am greatly terrified,
violent trembling layeth hold of my body:
Wherefore do the wicked live then,
have grown old, strong even in power?
lastingly is their seed before—, with them,
their offspring under their eyes,
their houses prosperous, without fear,
the rod of God cometh not upon them;
their bull also gendereth without loathing,
their cow calveth easily, slippeth not.

of the last speaker alone in the bitter word 3 *b* is also explained: it is at the same time evident that it is from pity that Job has hitherto everywhere spoken against the friends collectively only, without pointing to one in particular; when he here for the first time does the opposite, his word is all the more severe upon this individual, indeed, so severe that the opponent thus addressed does not answer again at all in the next advance; at the right place Job treats Bildad similarly, xxvi. 2—4; against Eliphaz, on the contrary, he is unwilling to proceed thus, ch. xxiii., xxiv.

2. Vv. 6—26. Job is, indeed, himself seized by indescribable terror when he reflects more closely upon this enigma, ver. 6. Wherefore, thus must he inquire, do sinners (whilst the godly suffer from no fault of their own) live in all material prosperity without any divine punishment, though they cherish the most shocking and criminal thoughts of God? vv. 7—16, and how defective are all the arguments which are produced for the contrary? vv. 17—21; is it not rather, in view of such palpable outward proofs, truly insane to deny from a partial view of the case the real state of the matter as regards the lot awarded to men on the earth, as if one claimed to know better than God? vv. 22—26. Thus this statement of the enigma, which began so calmly, has already become more agitated and indignant towards the end, in proportion as it comes into collision with the opposite views, although it is still without any direct address to the opponents. This part of the whole speech falls into four somewhat long strophes of five verses each, whilst exactly in the middle, after the first ten verses, a sudden and unusually vehement thought comes in abruptly, ver. 16, and by that means introduces at the proper place a somewhat greater break: exactly as in the following great speech, xxiv. 13, something in every respect very similar occurs, and as essentially the same thing occurred above also, ch. vii., ix., xiii., xv., comp. ch. xix.—The description of the wicked mentions first the general prosperity of their house, particularly how they can lastingly enjoy their children (Job's lost!), vv. 8, 9, then the good condition of their cattle, ver. 10, where for once in the new sentence the sing. is used instead of the generic plur. which is elsewhere adhered to, comp. Ps. cxliv. 13, 14, finally,

They send forth their little ones like flocks,
and their children leap merrily,
they sing aloud with timbrel, cithern,
rejoice to the sound of the pipe,
they waste in ease all their days,
and in a moment they sink down to the Underworld:—
yet saying to God: "depart from us!
Thy ways we desire not to know;
15 what is the Almighty, that we should serve Him,
and what profiteth it us to pray to Him?"

—Ha, not in their hand is their real good;
let the counsel of the wicked be far from me!—

How often then doth the lamp of the wicked go out,
doth then the proper calamity come upon them,
doth He distribute lots in His wrath,

how joyously they in general with their numerous children consume their life as a possession (בִּלָּה *K'thîb*, comp. "Isa." lxv. 22), still further favoured with a quick death, vv. 11—13 (יחתו, ver. 13 *b* is in any case *to go down*, from נָחַת, § 139 *c*, or from חַת as equivalent in meaning, whether or not the Massora may by their pointing have explained it as "to be terrified", here an unsuitable meaning). Instead of תְּפַלֵּט, ver. 10, it probably better to read תְּפַלַּח, acc. xxxix. 3, since פלח may like שָׁבַר be very well said of the breaking forth of the fruit of the womb. It is true, that the latter passage might seem to require emendation in conformity with the first, because מִלֵּט, "Isa." xxxiv. 15, appears to have a kindred signification: but in reality the latter verb is not used of quadrupeds. The utterance *depart from us*, vv. 14, xxii. 17, with the words connected with it, supplies the best explanation of the expression used above, *to bid God farewell*, ch. i., ii., as further it becomes here quite plain, that Job even in the most questionable passages never permits himself to be so far carried away as the Satan had maliciously suggested ii. 5, but becomes on the contrary more and more firmly convinced of the opposite. Indeed, after quoting the words of the ungodly, which it nevertheless seems they use secretly or openly with impunity, vv. 14, 15, Job feels himself at once, as compelled by his deepest personal revulsion, ver. 16, to declare his own inmost abhorence of them, how he himself is wholly unable to believe that they thus really possess their best weal (טוב as xx. 21, very different from טוֹבָה, see on xxii. 21), and how he does not in the least justify such language, comp. xxii. 18 *b*.—The inferences from the general weal of the wicked serve in the first instance, vv. 17—21, to refute some of the pleasing assertions made by the holders of

do they become like stubble before the wind,
  like the chaff, stolen by the storm?
"God layeth up his punishment for his sons!"
  let Him repay to him that he may feel it,
20 that *his* eyes may see his fall,
  from the hot-anger of the Almighty let him drink!
for what careth he about his future house,
  if the number of the moons is allotted him?—

Unto God even will one teach knowledge,
  while He judgeth the Highest ones?
One dieth in his perfection itself,
  wholly at ease and in peace,

the popular view: if it has been said that the light of the wicked goes out, xviii. 5, 6, that their (deserved) calamity overtakes them, xviii. 12, that He (God) apportions to them in anger lots, or portions in life, xx. 28, 29 (comp. Ps. xvi. 6), Job is, on the contrary, compelled in view of the above facts of experience to ask, *how often* (כַּמָּה as Ps. lxxviii. 40, not *how long* vii. 19) then all these hard lots befell the wicked so that they were dispersed like chaff before the wind (xxvii. 20; Ps. i. 4)? since the reverse, surely, is met with, and they are so long and so frequently in the possession of all material prosperity; and if it is said, for the sons of the wicked at all events God lays up calamity (אָוֶן, not אוֹן = הוֹן, as xviii. 7, 12; xx. 10) and punishment, xviii. 10; v. 5, what is really required is, that the sinner should himself experience the divine retribution and punishment by his own personal suffering (ידע Hos. ix. 7), that he should see his own overthrow and drink from the divine wrath-cup (ver. 17 *c*, Ps. xi. 6 *b*, Jer. xxv. 15, 16), inasmuch as he, precisely as a frivolous sinner, would not concern himself should his family meet with calamity after his death, if only his own moons which he has to live through are definitely allotted and fixed, as the opponents themselves had said xv. 20 *b*, so that he can at least enjoy undisturbed his personal good fortune in the portion of life assigned to him; ver. 21 *b* is a circumstantial clause § 341 *b*; one might conjecture חֹרָצוּ, after xiv. 5, instead of חֻצָּצוּ, yet the latter is explained by חצץ = خط, as I remarked long ago in connection with Prov. xxx. 27 and other passages.—Accordingly whoever looks at this from all sides must, in opposition to those who dwell simply upon some one accidental aspect of God's work, rather ask, whether one is insane and reckless enough to think he understands the matter better than God Himself, who, as the friends themselves think, judges even the exalted celestial spirits (iv. 18; xv. 15), and will therefore punish miserable men who judge Him hastily for their intentional misconception of His truth; וְהוּא 22 *b* is again a circumstantial clause. The restoration of the true relation of the phenomena is rather as follows: that one man dies in the full en-

his pans full of milk,
the marrow of his bones well moistened;
25 but *another* dieth with a troubled soul,
not having enjoyed good:
alike they lay themselves down upon the dust,
and corruption covereth them both.

3.

See, I know your thoughts,
what cruel devices ye plot against me!
Say ye, "Where is the house of the tyrant,
and where the tent of the dwellings of the wicked?"
have ye then not asked the wayfarers,
and their signs do ye not know?

joyment of external prosperity, another in the deepest grief, but nevertheless, as appears from what has been said above, the first may be a sinner and the latter an innocent man (*e.g.*, Job himself), the difference therefore between the two must be something else than their outward lot and common death, vv. 23—26. עטין, ver. 24, acc. LXX, Vulg. Pesh. *bowels*, in which case חֵלֶב *fat* would have to be read, comp. عضا *member* of the body, for the ן— might be an addition: still, although the second verse-member would in that case more closely accord with the first, the verb *to be full* would with difficulty suit such a meaning: it is better therefore to take the word, after the Chaldee, in the sense of *vessel* for preserving a store, comp. חֲסִינָא, which appears to be derived from the same root; thus there is an appropriate allusion to xx. 17. Ver. 25 *a* after iii. 20, *b* after ix. 25.

3. Vv. 27—34. What therefore can the object of the friends be in thus deliberately putting out of sight one aspect of human life? nothing, one must believe, but to deceive the unfortunate sufferer by false threats of the divine judgment and wrath, in order that he may take error for truth and do that which is unworthy! But he now knows, as they perceive, these their thoughts and cruel plots against him (the plots *in which* ye are cruel = which ye cruelly cherish, תחמסו, relative clause, § 332 *a*) ver. 27; and is determined himself now to place clearly before them their deception and injustice. Have they then, as they are constantly holding up to him the certain overthrow of the tyrants (נָדִיב as *ruler* in the bad sense, Isa. xii. 2), not at any time heard the well-known words of the experienced travellers who have seen the world, how they testify the exact contrary, basing their statements on *signs* or proofs known to everybody? These travellers speak, it is true, of great judgments inflicted upon whole countries, of days when the outbursts of wrath (עברות xl. 11; Ps. vii. 7) arrive as in overwhelming floods (comp. xxii. 11; Isa. viii.

30 that "upon the day of calamity the wicked is spared,
upon the day when wrath-outbursts come up."

Who declareth to Him in His face His way?
He hath done it: who will repay *Him?*
—"But *that* man will be brought to the burying-place,
and upon the grave-stone he keepeth watch;
sweet seem to him the clods of the valley,
and after him follow all people,
and before him are countless numbers."—
And how can ye comfort me so vainly!
the remainder of your answers is—treachery!

7, 8), but they do not find that the guilty man is always overtaken by them. Who, moreover, can rise up against God, even when incomprehensible things happen? ver. 31 (it is clear from ix. 19; xxiii. 13; xxiv. 22, 23 and the whole thought and connection itself, that both in this speech and elsewhere this somewhat timid form of expression, in which the name of God does not openly occur, is nevertheless meant to refer to Him). But while thus no single man can resist the divine decrees, one sees the sinner in death still having honours heaped upon him, attended by men to his burying-place, and in his lofty monument as it were proudly keeping watch over his grave, that no one may come irreverently near (גדיש comp. جَدَثٌ *Ham.* p. 409, ver. 3, مسنم, Koseg. Chrest. p. 54, and Abel Rémusat's Nouv. Mél. Asiat. I. p. 241); indeed, apparently sleeping quite softly and sweetly under the ground, as if the word *sit ei terra levis* were true of him; and, moreover, still admired in innumerable successors and imitators, just as, indeed, there were before him sinners in countless numbers (Ecc. iv. 15, 16)! vv. 32, 33. Accordingly if all these truths are subtracted from the talk of the friends who wish to administer comfort, there remains from their consoling answers nothing but—deception! the intention to deceive the sufferer and to precipitate him still lower!—Thus the third part of this speech takes the form of two strophes of four verses each, as if the first part, which was too short with its strophe of the same length, should thereby be completed. It may be further remarked, that it is implied in the meaning of the speech itself, that the words of the travellers who have seen the world, to which Job appeals, must be extended to ver. 30 and vv. 32, 33, because these verses describe the experience of the world which is referred to; whilst ver. 31 at the beginning of the second strophe shows by the form of it that it is spoken directly by Job.

FOURTH STAGE OF THE DRAMA.

COMMENCEMENT OF A SETTLEMENT.

THIRD AND LAST ADVANCE OF THE CONTENTION.

CH. XXII—XXVIII.

However shocking and insufferable the representation of the injustice of the world was which Job at last made in his gloomy melancholy, and however hard the complaint based upon it which he directed against the friends, the accused are nevertheless able neither to refute the representation, nor to weaken the complaint on the ground of such a refutation. For plainly they had really expected, that Job would be compelled to hold his peace upon their threatening descriptions and would not think of adhering so tenaciously to the logical outcome of his case as to maintain the general injustice of the world under which he suffered rather than confess his own guilt. But as Job is nevertheless so unexpectedly reckless and so incomprehensibly immovable and stubborn, they are the more surprised and amazed in proportion as they find themselves in reality unable easily to deny at the same time the existence of the unhappy enigma which Job had insisted upon. They cannot make this enigma their own or really enter into it, because they have not themselves passed through such mental trials as Job, while they prefer, in the limited range of their opinions, to pass over, or to interpret in a onesided manner, the particular external phenomena which in reality contradict their view. Moreover, these hostile phenomena have really been too emphatically and too generally insisted upon by Job as the last speaker, to encourage them to venture further into this slippery territory. Their most weighty argument against Job has so simply melted away under their hands from the fact that the accused sufferer had confronted them with the harsh and dangerous, yet no less real, reverse of their opinion; and for a second time the spectacle recurs, that an unfortunate sufferer just when he seemed wholly lost and was most violently attacked, rises in a wholly unexpected turn of the contention to the position of the victorious assailant by his marvellous daring. Now, therefore, when the contention is about to enter upon its third phase, their ranks are in reality from the commencement weakened and pierced: the bold assurance with which they entered upon the second advance has irretrievably vanished, for their two first and sharpest weapons, which they were able with a good conscience to use against Job—their general warnings not to speak against God nor against the divine righteousness—have been used up and turned against themselves; their third argument only remains, but it is the bluntest and most insulting of all. If they will venture to make one more attempt of importance, they must at last express quite baldly and undisguisedly what they had hitherto been in reality ashamed to utter at length and so wholly without circumlocution: they must reproach him with certain definite and particular sins of great magnitude, which (according to their opinion) he committed before his calamities, as they in accordance with their presupposition assume as certain but can never prove, were one disposed to interpret strictly the words of helpless confusion which were spoken in the last heat of an expiring struggle. To this depth, therefore, does the conflict, which has already become quite unequal, bring them, that they are about to descend from the elevation of a contention for principles to personal considerations. It is true that according to their way of looking at things, the last speech of Job had entitled them to do this, in which he had as openly called in question the divine justice as if he were himself a sinner, and to that extent Job himself compels them to this extreme step. But they thus suffer themselves to be misled to make assertions which bring them into complete confusion, and which must, if they are not proved, prepare for them very soon the most ignominious defeat. Still, these men are, on the other hand, in accordance with ancient manners, too dignified to permit the conflict thus to issue at last merely in personal recriminations and reckless altercation (to which Job too would have been indisposed). They prefer, making a last effort, to give the contention at the same time a more conciliatory tone and to recur to the commencement of it, and they choose rather to hold their peace in helplessness than either to sanction Job's speeches against God and divine righteousness, which in their consciences they cannot do, or to speak in any other other respect unworthily. They very soon get exhausted accordingly in the third advance, being at the same time simply reduced to silence by the great enigma and the vehemence of Job, not conceding to him his position nor making terms with him.

The attitude which Job has to assume, is, on the other hand, easier to foresee. For he is now on the way to complete victory, and advancing on that road must gain both in confidence and self-possession, while the opponents sink down exhausted and gradually lose courage and clearness of judgment. With regard to the few new things which can be further urged against him, especially the open accusations which Eliphaz attempts to make, he has the less need to answer at once, as it would now have been foolish to attach so much importance to the last, desperate effort of the opponent. As if he deemed it beneath him at once to answer definitely to these charges, lest it should seem as if it were necessary to be in haste with his self-defence, and, on the other hand, still profoundly weighed down by the burden of that terrible enigma, he prefers to continue in gloomy soliloquy the general consideration of all the enigmatical and in God incomprehensible things, and to present them in their most pointed form. Thereby he makes, without expressing it directly, a challenge to the opponents, if they propose to add anything further to the purpose, to first of all scatter this lamentable darkness and thereby to refute him, since really all further contention is useless until the preliminary questions have been answered, ch. xxiii., xxiv. As now nothing follows from Bildad after this check but an extremely weak, meager speech, which without adding anything new reveals only too plainly the complete inability of the friends to produce anything further of a sound and helpful nature, ch. xxv., he considers it worth his while with a brief, sharp attack, as already conscious of his superiority, to break off if possible the contention now that it had become useless, ch. xxvi. And at last, since the last friend is really unable to speak any more, Job, after some rest and reflection, comes forward for the last time instead of him, with the intention of entirely concluding the contention which had been so violently broken off. This conclusion he makes by gathering up the results of it, both those which are clear and those which are still obscure, with the firm voice of a conqueror and the lucidity of a teacher, and so far as the enigma is concerned, which must candidly be acknowledged, submitting himself with calm self-possession to the highest Wispom, ch. xxvii., xxviii.

1. ELIPHAZ AND JOB.

a. ELIPHAZ. CH. XXII.

Eliphaz, it is true, undertakes for the third time, relying upon his reputation and his profound wisdom, to take up a new position against Job, bringing forward the last further principle which remains to the assailants. No less deeply shocked by the last speech of Job's, and fully strengthened in his suspicion that Job who thus strangely describes the injustice of the world must himself be inwardly wrong, than compelled by the whole course of the contention, he declares without any circumlocution that Job has committed great sins, as if he desired to put into his mouth the confession of sin which he has hitherto always repudiated. At the same time he is unable to do more than infer these severe incriminations as the subjective explanation of Job's present condition and as the not unnatural result of Job's previous position of exposure to temptation: he cannot establish them by producing human witnesses, but can only base them upon the probabilities derived from Job's situation: he simply attempts to prove that Job *must* have thus sinned, because otherwise his present condition could not be understood. It is at this point, therefore, that we get in the briefest and concisest form the whole view which the friends take of Job's sufferings, as regards its inmost reasons and most cogent proof. That which is deepest and most hidden in every respect compels Job by contradiction to seek to be as plain as possible.—But as if in the vague feeling that the incrimination established in such a way would after all produce alone but little effect, and at the same time wearied from the heat of the contention, Eliphaz summons up his last remaining strength and resources in the endeavour at the same time to prepare the way for an honourable cessation of the conflict. This he attempts in the first instance by connecting with the unveiled incrimination a serious warning against ungodly thoughts, such as Job cherishes, and against the further following of the conduct of the sinners of evil repute in ancient history; next, by calling upon him in a friendly tone to amend his ways, and by closing with the brightest pictures of a noble future calculated to excite hope. But the warning is simply repeated in a weaker form almost unaltered from the second advance of the contention; the excitement of the hope of a better life after repentance simply recurs from the first advance. Accordingly when Eliphaz here makes a last attempt, using his last resources and bringing forward his last new thought, he at the same time calls up afresh all the previous thoughts and resources and renews the attack for the last time by comprehensively stating all that can be said. He thus recurs by degrees to the beginning and thereby reveals that the friends have exhausted their resources and must desire to rest. This speech accordingly falls into three equal parts, of which the first only expounds a new thought, the other two gradually go back to the thoughts of the earlier advances: (1) the open incrimination, in the form in which Eliphaz is able to establish it, vv. 2—11; (2) the serious warning, vv. 12—20; (3) the exhortation to hope, vv. 21—30.

xxii. 1 Then answered Eliphaz the Tæmanite and said:

1.

Doth then man bring profit to God?
  no, to *himself* only the thoughtful bringeth profit!
is it a concern to the Almighty that thou art righteous,
  or an advantage that thou conductest thyself blamelessly!

1. Vv. 2—11. Eliphaz is unable (apart from mere conjectures based on Job's past history which was full of temptations) to bring any other proof of the statement from which he does not now shrink, that Job *must* be guilty of definite grievous sins, than what he derives from the present condition of Job, which serves him as an external proof, inasmuch as he compares his ideas and truths regarding God with this condition. As he attempts to produce the strictest proof with perfect calmness, he starts accordingly from the highest truth, that God as absolutely perfect and blessed in reality stands in no need whatever of human duties and virtues, but in His exaltation above them would lose none of His blessedness did they not exist: let no man anywhere ever forget, that when he fulfils the divine will he only secures his own weal, fulfils a personal necessity of his own and attains his own true destination, and let him never imagine that God would not be blessed without him and his good works! Were it otherwise, it could certainly be then thought, that, in order to increase His own blessedness, God inflicted, from motives of necessity or advantage, sufferings without any just cause, *i.e.*, without any guilt in the sufferer, simply in order that men, being thus humbled and tormented, might the more fear Him, just as when a human lord, who thinks it necessary to make himself feared, arbitrarily torments his subjects. But what an unworthy thought of God! Therefore if God sends punishments, man must have deserved them; God does not punish on His own account, still less on account of man's piety, but on account of man's sin and thus for the profit of man himself, because the human race could not exist without the reaction of sin in the form of the punishment of the sinner, punishment is also a warning for living men. Now, Job's sufferings are such punishments: therefore he must, according to these proofs and evi-

on account of thy religion will He correct thee,
  will He enter with thee into judgment?
5 is then thy wickedness not great,
  no limit to thy misdeeds?

For from thy brethren thou takest pledges for nought,
  and strippest off the clothes of the naked;
water thou givest not to the weary,
  and from the famished withholdest bread,
the man of arm—his is the earth,
  and he that is in honour dwelleth therein!
widows thou hast sent away unhelped,
  the arms of the orphans have been crushed!

dences, have grievously sinned! This series of inferences is pointed, connected, and in itself clear. But at last comes unobserved a tremendous fallacy, occasioned by the fundamental error, that sufferings are as such punishments. If one starts from this erroneous principle, one is landed in the alternative, vv. 4, 5, that sufferings are sent either on account of piety (which is impious to suppose) or on account of the sins of the sufferer, and then arrives accordingly at the conclusion, that every sufferer has been a sinner. Yet Eliphaz is so little able to escape from this error that it is here precisely most clearly brought out. As to מוֹ—, ver. 2, which is here plainly sing., see § 247 *d.* חֵפֶץ, ver. 3, as xxi. 21, is *studium*, desire and zeal, then solicitude and care about a matter, a *concern*, business; whence, ver. 3 *b*, an *advantage*, *profit*, can correspond to it. יִרְאָה, ver. 4, as iv. 6, xv. 4: a favourite word with Eliphaz, as the poet generally gives to each speaker certain favourite words and modes of expression; the opposite of יראה is רעה, ver. 5.—After thus, vv. 2—5, the proof has been supplied (with perfect calmness and stringency, only at last with a little more agitation, when the inference is drawn as to the necessity of Job's guilt), that Job must have grievously sinned, Eliphaz then enumerates to him, by way of more definite incrimination, certain great vices, vv. 6—9, and then reverts to the beginning, observing that precisely on their account the present great dangers (snares, xviii. 8—10) and unexpected terrors came upon Job; or does he still mean not to heed and avoid the fatal destruction (darkness, floods of water, both figurative) which is so near and certain? vv. 10, 11, with which question, ver. 11, Eliphaz passes to the warning, vv. 12 sq., and it also appears therefrom that in reality it is only at the dangers and sufferings of Job that the friends are horrified. The question arises, from what source Eliphaz obtained his knowledge of the particular sins with which he here charges Job; did he really overtake him in their commission, and can he produce men even as witnesses of them? Impossible: not only is this contradicted by the entire book, but neither does God Himself afterwards refute Job's subsequent protestations, ch. xxxi. Therefore

10 Therefore are snares round about thee,
sudden terror confoundeth thee:
or the darkness seest thou not,
and water-floods covering thee?

2.

Is not then God high as heaven?
see, how high the summit of the stars!
and yet thou thinkest: "what doth God then know?
behind dense fogs will He judge?
clouds hide Him so that He seeth not,
and the circle of the heaven He walketh through!"

simply because Eliphaz has firmly persuaded himself that Job must have sinned in some such manner, as so many others of his rank and power have done, and as a great man may so easily sin, does he charge Job with these sins. Moreover, the instances themselves are really only those of sins which were at that time very generally laid at the door of the potentates of that time, with no proof whatever that Job was personally guilty of them. This was the case with unmerciful taking of pledges, particularly as the most necessary articles of clothing were taken as pledges by the powerful, Ex. xxii. 25, 26; Deut. xxiv. 6—10; cruelty towards necessitous suppliants of all kinds, ver. 7, "Isa." lviii. 10, only in order that the powerful man may flourish alone in the desolate, devastated land! Ver. 8 comp. xv. 28; Isa. v. 8; finally, ver. 9, the very general cruelty against the unprotected members of weaker houses.

2. Vv. 12—20. The serious warning, introduced by ver. 11, once more mentions first, after the favourite manner of Eliphaz, ver. 12, the greatness of God as compared with men, which is as great, or higher than the heaven and the highest stars, xv. 15 (on גבה see xi. 8): how can Job therefore, in view of this sublime exaltation, nevertheless think that God, as hidden behind clouds and merely walking through the arch of heaven ("Isa." xl. 22; Prov. viii. 27), does not concern Himself about the earth and does not judge it! (which Job, indeed, has never said or thought in this sense, as if God had *not the power* to judge: but the serious doubts about the divine judgment on the earth, ch. xxi., cause Eliphaz, with his other false opinions, to suppose that Job means really that God is determined to know nothing about the earth). Whoever cherishes such thoughts of God must be inclined to sin and on the road to the same vast destruction which in the primæval world overtook the sinners as a perpetual warning to those who come after them, Gen. vi. 1—12; xviii., xix.: wilt thou follow the ancient example of these people, who, seized upon before the time by the omnipotence of the God of punishment, perished without resistance (xvi. 8), in that the entire ground and foundation on which they rested becoming a stream sank beneath them and became like water? (there being an

15 The way of olden time wilt thou then keep,
which once sinful people went?
who were seized upon before the time;
as a stream their firm basis was poured away!
they who say of God: "depart from us!"
and the Almighty will do nothing to them,
although *He* filled their houses with good,
—but may the counsel of the wicked be far from me!—
The godly will see it and rejoice,
the blameless will mock at them:
20 "verily, our adversaries are cut off,
their remnant the fire hath devoured!"

3.

Rely, now, on his covenant, and be at peace!
thereby good will befall thee;
receive now from His mouth instruction,
and put His words in thine heart!

allusion particularly to Gen. xix), vv. 15, 16. As to the orthography יוּצַּק instead of יֻצַּק, see § 15 *b*, note 2, it is Pual acc. § 131 *b*, with accusat. acc. § 281 *e*.—And this way of the primæval sinners continues still to be the way of those people who are determined to know nothing of God, although He has made them rich and powerful (ver. 18 *b* is a circumstantial clause, § 341 *a*): but if Job has said of these people that they are prosperous, expressing at the same time his abomination of them, xxi. 14—16, Eliphaz likewise protests his abomination of them, ver. 18 *b*, knowing, however, also that in the future the righteous will witness with rejoicing their complete overthrow, vv. 19, 20, quite unlike Job's expression xvii. 8, 9. Thus Eliphaz simply reverses what appears to him unsafe in Job's speech, without refuting it! and how carefully he adopts the expression of repudiation, xxi. 16 *b*, as if by taking it out of Job's mouth he would intimate that Job has no right to use it! ver. 18 *a* appears also to allude intentionally to xxi. 16 *a*.

3. Vv. 21—30. The exhortation to a return to God, passing gradually into charming pictures of the happy consequences of a restored relation of friendship with God: at first the exhortation predominating, vv. 21, 22, then both in equal proportions, vv. 23—25, lastly, in a second strophe, the description alone prevailing, vv. 26—30. In vv. 21, 22 the description of the happy consequences is found only in the centre, from וְשִׁלַּם, § 347 *a*, to the end of ver. 21 *b*; תבואתך is according to the connection most appropriately a verb §§ 191 *c*, 249 *c*, not a substantive = תְּבוּאָתְךָ; for טוֹבָה is manifestly intended to allude to the

If thou returnest to God humbling thyself,
  puttest iniquity far from thy tents:
(and cast away upon the dust the finest gold,
  and into the stones of the streams Ophir's treasure,
25 in order that the Almighty may be thy treasure,
  and silver of greatest brightness unto thee!):

Surely then in the Almighty thou delightest thyself,
  and raisest unto God thy face,
thou prayest unto Him and He heareth thee,
  what thou hast vowed thou wilt pay;
if thou wilt determine a thing, it standeth before thee,
  upon thy ways shineth light;
if they go downwards, thou sayest, "elevation!"
  downcast looks He helpeth;

same word xxi. 25, comp. ix. 25, and תְּבוּאָה might according to xxxi. 12 even denote simply material gain and possessions, with which again טוֹב *good*, adj., would not agree; and a sentence such as, *thereby is thy gain* which thou wouldst then have *prosperity*, would not be sufficiently simple and natural. Ver. 23 also, in which the transition is made from inward weal to outward prosperity, the consequence would[1] be indicated only by the last word of the first member, with *b* comp. xi. 14: but vv. 24, 25 the exhortation and the consequences are perfectly parallel, the picture of outward good being presented: cast away thy pieces of gold (בצרים), even the precious *Ophir*, *i.e.*, gold of Ophir (xxviii. 16: just as مَنْدَل a city in India signifies also the commodity coming therefrom) as useless things, upon the dust or into the pebbles of the streams, the gain of the true prosperity will make up for all that (Ecc. xi. 1); on תועפות, see my note on Ps. xcv. 4, only that the word is here not used in the local sense. Like this antithesis the entire following description of the prosperity is very admirable, vv. 26—30, beginning appropriately with the prospect, that then instead of fear and estrangement a no less brightly contented than confident relation of friendship with God will follow, ver. 26, adjusting gradually all that is still involved in darkness and fulfilling all pure desires, vv. 27, 28, so that if even sometime the ways of life go downwards, he praying with a humble look and having been saved can soon notwithstanding let the cry of triumph again be heard—"elevation"! ver. 29, yea, so that he himself, having become a saint, will be able to pray to God with efficacy for those who are not wholly blameless (אי, see § 215*b*), as Gen. xviii. 23 sq., xx. 7. This conclusion, ver. 30, is

[1] if the Mass. reading were followed, see below. Tr.

30 He will deliver the not-blameless,
delivered by the cleanness of thy hands!

particularly in the mouth of Eliphaz extremely appropriate: it contains the gentle reproach that Job has not from the beginning accepted the offered mediation of Eliphaz, v. 8, and therefore at the same time the silent intimation that Job, although not wholly innocent, may yet thus be saved, yea, may have in future the happiness of thus saving others. In a similar, and yet after all entirely different manner, is the sequel decided, xlii. 8, 9.—If תִּבָּנֶה, ver. 23, is the correct reading[1], it must signify acc. xii. 14; xx. 19, *then thou wilt be* again *restored:* yet in that case the apodosis would be here so very short and merely parenthetical. But if the reading of the LXX תֵּעָנֶה is followed, so that vv. 24, 25 form simply a parenthesis, we get here the same extended form of sentence which occurs with a similar meaning xi. 13—15, comp. viii. 5, 6. It is true, נענה does not occur elsewhere in this poem, but this objection cannot alone weigh much against the very suitable meaning it here supplies.

b. JOB. CH. XXIII., XXIV.

Nothing can move Job here at once expressly to answer the open incrimination, as strictly the only new thing in the last speech: he has hitherto never hastened at the beginning of a new advance of the contention to make his defence, but has always first translated himself into the new situation and signified his right as against the attack. Much more can he do this in the present instance, inasmuch as Eliphaz in simply recapitulating what had been said before alleges nothing fresh save what is wholly false, which needs no proper refutation at all on Job's part, in the consciousness of his innocence and as against assailants who have now become wholly perplexed. If, however, the reference to personal guilt, which Eliphaz has so painfully made, stirs in Job here at the beginning of the new advance one thought and wish, it must especially be, that it may be granted to him to establish his innocence before God Himself, since he is as firmly convinced on the one hand of his innocence as on the other of the im-

[1] Which the author adopted in the first edition. Tr.

possibility that the friends should ever properly understand his case. This turn of the contention is in reality a very important one: though Job had already despaired of obtaining in this life justice from God, he is nevertheless again drawn by the force of the contention to look to the true source of salvation even in this life, and is surprised by a wish which he had quite let go in the highest confusion of the conflict. Thus, with or without Job's will, the necessity makes itself more and more felt, that the true salvation and the solution of the enigma must come from some other source than the men who have hitherto existed; Job shows this involuntarily here by the desire for a divine decision, which repeatedly grows out of the force of the circumstances.—Still Job feels himself at present, from a multitude of causes, too perplexed and too depressed to pursue this passing desire. Reviewing the whole of his situation to the present time and the vicissitudes of the contention, as yet profoundly oppressed particularly by that terrible enigma of life, he sees nothing but what is obstructive, perplexing, and incomprehensible, both as regards the question of the appearance of God to settle the one matter in hand, and as regards the question of the general divine righteousness on the earth, all the doubts as to which the last speech of Job's, ch. xxi., had only commenced to bring forward. These dark things Job here feels compelled, no less by the matter itself and his own grief than by the unwise behaviour of the friends, to call forth in all their extent and in their true connection, and to state them, although with profound pain, fully and candidly. The attitude of the friends is so unintelligent that they are determined merely to suppress and obliterate by empty reproaches and unsatisfactory representations and not to solve the enigmas which are really plain to all who will see them. But Job is now at last gaining the victory over his opponents, precisely because, having correctly grasped the enigma in one aspect of it, he presses it under their notice, and cannot permit himself to be hindered by vain accusations and weak consolations from following up both the matter itself and his victory. Accordingly this long gloomy speech, which may more properly be termed a soliloquy, becomes the sharpest weapon against the opponents simply from the fact that it pursues the enigmas which have been started, particularly the last one, to their extreme consequences, and by implication merely, without any direct address to them, calls upon the opponents first to penetrate the darkness of the matter before continuing the personal contention: thus their whole attack is checked without any direct and formal counter charge, and Job's matter is continued in the same manner as hitherto with the greatest perseverance to its extreme point. The speech falls, in accordance with this twofold division of the subject-matter, into two parts of growing length and weight: (1) the renewed desire for a divine judgment, which is, however, immediately checked by the terrible thought that God will not appear in this matter, ch. xxiii., as, indeed, (2) there are many and strong reasons for generally denying the existence of the divine justice on the earth, ch. xxiv. The first part is in many of its reflections almost a short re-echo of one of the earliest speeches of Job's, ch. ix., only that the reflections here do not any more bear the character of stormy vehemence of the earlier ones, but as already moderated pass over like distant tempests, as if the speaker, urged by an inward voice, intentionally restrained their storm; the second part completes what had been commenced ch. xxi.

xxiii. 1 And Job answered and said:

1.

To-day also of His hand I complain,
His hand is heavy upon my sighs.

1. Ch. xxiii., in strophes of greater calmness, each of four verses, the second and to a certain extent the last also being somewhat more agitated. ידי, ver. 2, *my hand* would have to signify, acc. i. 15, xix. 21, the blow (hand) of God which I must endure, weighs down my sighing, so that I am not able

O that, having known, I might find Him,
  might come unto His judgment-seat,
might order before Him the cause,
  fill my mouth with proofs,
might know what answer He would give me,
  observe what He said to me!

With mighty power shall He contend with me?
  no, only let Him give heed to me!
then would an upright man litigate with him,
  in order that I might get free for ever from my judge!—
Behold, I go forwards—He is not there,
  backwards—I perceive Him not;
if He turneth aside to the left—I behold Him not,
  if He inclineth to the right—I see Him not!

even freely to give vent to my sighs and so obtain a little relief. But the word *hand* would then be far from clear, and מרי in the first verse-member is neither very intelligible nor found elsewhere in this poet: but if we read in the second member יָדוֹ with the LXX and in the first מִיָּדוֹ, where the LXX still read at all events מִיָּדִי, this commencement corresponds admirably to that of the previous speech, xxi. 4, and a repetition of the same weighty word in both members of the verse is very common with our poet. With such difficulty, though immediately getting enraptured as it comes to be dwelt upon, does the wish find expression, that he might only, having already learnt what means are necessary for the purpose, having become wise and capable (as regards the parenthetical perf. ידעתי, ver. 3, and similarly בחנני, ver. 10, see the note on iv. 2) find Him, the author of these pains and calamities, sitting upon His judgment seat, that he might boldly lay before Him all his well-arranged proofs of his case (comp. xiii. 18, xxxi. 35) and might then await the answer, which, surely, unless everything deceives him, cannot possibly give a decision against his innocence! vv. 3—5. Certainly, in this enraptured consideration the fear finds a place, that he will be hindered in his speaking and self-defence by the overwhelming power of God, and the question irresistibly suggests itself: *shall He with mighty force* (xxx. 18) *contend with me?* as had been previously feared ix. 19, 34; xiii. 21; and he answers, *no!* that I do not wish, *only let Him pay heed to me!* (iv. 20, vi. 28), I can wish nothing further than that He may be a judge that will listen, not a ruler displaying his irresistible strength! *then*, if it were so, *will an upright* man *be at law with Him*, *in order that I might escape for ever from my Judge*, as completely acquitted by Him and never again accused, as really my case is such that the just judge must favourably decide it for ever with one sentence.—With ver. 8 sudden, abrupt reflection; revulsion of feeling. But, alas, with all my pains, I know not where to find

10 For He knoweth my accustomed way:
if He trieth me, as gold I go forth;
to His track my foot held close,
His way I kept, not declining,
the commandment of His lips— I forsook it not,
more than my claim I treasured His word:
but He is as none else[1]: who stoppeth Him?
His soul hath desired it—He doeth it!

Surely, He will accomplish my appointment:
and to such things is He greatly accustomed.

Him, vv. 8, 9, because incontestably He is determined not to examine my good case (for some mysterious reasons), having resolved upon my death, vv. 10—14: therefore precisely the feeling of horror and dismay at the thought of such an incomprehensible act on the part of God! vv. 15—17. The fact that he can find God nowhere, he explains to himself by reflecting, that God has the power to make Himself everywhere invisible, as is parenthetically said ver. 9: if he could not find Him in the East (in the front) or the West, so that He might perhaps be in the North (on the left) or South, He would easily make Himself invisible in any other quarter to which He might by a sudden turn incline; עשׂה must signify here, as used for עטה, *to incline* (comp. *History of Israel* IV. 74 (III. 537), so that it is almost equivalent to the following עטף; for this root עטף, which does not occur elsewhere in the Book of Job, must here, as nowhere else, bear the meaning of the Arab. عطف.—As a reason, Job is unable to conceive any other than one which is again itself dark and terrible, that God having (for unknown reasons) without doubt resolved upon his death, is determined not now to examine him, knowing that the examination of his case must bring after it his acquittal: but, however greatly Job has reason to rejoice in his own innocence, who can do anything against the omnipotence of the incomparable One? This is, vv. 10—14, so explained, that with peculiarly deep satisfaction the strong consciousness of innocence is declared and described as never before; as, indeed, this consciousness generally, with its joy, insensibly grows, and thereby at the same time unintentionally the best refutation of the opponents is uttered; ver. 14 first expounds the final cause after vv. 10—13. Ver. 12: the commandment of His lips—with regard to it, *I never departed*, see iv. 6; more than my own claim, what was due to me, what I as an influential, wealthy man could have claimed in accordance with my circumstances and rights with relation to other men, have I held sacred the words of His mouth, His clear revelations; on באחד, ver. 13, see

[1] Germ. *Er ist einzig;* Grammar § 217*f*, *Er ist ein einziger;* Gesenius' *Thesaurus*, p. 62, *unicus in suo genere, incomparabilis.* Tr.

15 Therefore before Him am I sorely alarmed,
I consider it—and tremble at Him;
and God maketh my heart fearful,
and the Almighty greatly alarmeth me:
for at darkness I am not struck dumb,
nor at *myself*, covered by Him with darkness.

xxiv. 2.

1 Wherefore hath God not treasured up times,
and His friends behold not His days?—
Boundaries are removed,
herds are stolen and fed,

§§ 217 *f*, 299 *b*; ver. 13 *b* like ix. 12. It is said at the end, vv. 15—17, with great truth and force, that the more deeply he reflects by himself upon such incomprehensible things in God (comp. xxi. 6, 7), the more is he terrified and alarmed, and that this is the true reason for his present state of fear, but not the darkness or the calamity itself, nor even his own person, which bears this calamity filling all the world with horror, acc. xix. 13 sq., whilst his opponents are dismayed only at this external misery and its object, indeed, endeavoured to make Job also fear on account of it, xxi. 11. Moreover, ix. 35 is similar, as here generally there is much reechoed from ch. ix.

2. Ch. xxiv. Already xxiii. 14 *b* the transition to the universal absence of justice, under which Job also feels himself now a sufferer, was on the point of being made; but this aspect of the matter was not then pursued, in order that the picture of Job's personal condition might be first completed. Now, however, that aspect is again taken up to be completely worked out. After the difficult question, ver. 1, as a gloomy continuation of the doubts xxi. 7, wherefore the times and days of God, or the times of the revealed, triumphant divine righteousness, promised to the godly, did not come [1], examples of all kinds of the shocking injustice, as endless as lamentable, which prevails on the earth, are multiplied in the most striking colours, vv. 2—24, with the short conclusion, who can deny all this? ver. 25. In order to make this terrible picture complete, not only is the material prosperity of the wicked described, as ch. xxi., but, what is still more painful, the sad, shameful condition of so many sufferers whose afflictions come solely from the unpunished cruelties of the wicked, and the insolent impunity of so many kinds of profligates, are depicted. We are here brought into the very midst of all the barbarities and disorders of the age of the poet, the connected picture of which is really so terrible that it might

[1] The characteristics of the speech are here, xxiv. 1, quite those of the great prophets of the 9th and 8th century, who spoke so much of the great coming *day of God*.

the ass of the orphans is driven away,
  the ox of the widow is taken for a pledge,
the poor are thrust from the way,
  altogether the oppressed of the earth lie in hiding.

5 Lo, as wild asses, they go forth into deserts
  with their work, seeking for victuals:
    the steppe is their bread for the children,
in the field they harvest his fodder,
  they glean the vineyard of the sinner;
naked they pass the night, unclothed
  and with no covering in the cold,
get soaked from the downpour of the mountains,
  having embraced the rocks without shelter.

well give rise to the most perilous despair of many of the thoughtful people of the time. Yet while thus the numerous shocking illustrations of the crimes committed by men in the very midst of civilised society are produced in succession, the poet avoids representing Job as taking any secret pleasure in such delineations. On the contrary, in the midst of the fearful description he must be seized by a violent feeling of horror, and at the same time clearly show, that he, if the point were simply to make pleasing but untrue, sentimental pictures of the opposite, can do this equally as well or better than the friends, since he himself most devoutly desires to see the opposite realised in life, if he were not compelled in loyalty to truth candidly to acknowledge the actual experiences of life. So he presents first cruelties against the unprotected, vv. 2—4, then over against them the lamentable condition of the unfortunate of all classes, where at last his shocked feeling breaks out, vv. 5—12, next some more of the worst disgraceful deeds of the most hardened sinners, vv. 14—17, at last the false and the true description of the end of the sinner, vv. 18—24. Thus arise four groups of pictures so arranged that the second and fourth form in each case the counter-sketch to the previous ones: cruel tyrants—tormented sufferers and unprotected people; most abominable wickedness—the happy end of those who commit it. Accordingly the long description is unfolded in six strophes of four verses each, but so that it still falls into two equal halves, as evidently we have here again in ver. 13, as in the exactly similar case xxi. 16, a point at which the two halves are separated by a pause.—(1) Vv. 2—13. On the one hand, vv. 2—4, acts of violence of all kinds against the helpless, comp. with ver. 2 Hos. v. 10; Deut. xix. 14; xxvii. 17; with ver. 4 Judg. v. 6; Isa. xxxiii. 8. On the other hand, vv. 5—12, undeserved sufferings of all kinds endured by the unprotected from human violence: both by those who are not in direct dependence, vv. 5—8, and by those who under civil government live in complete dependence on their lords, vv. 9—12. The former are most probably

The orphan is stolen from the breast,
  and upon the suffering this pledge is laid;
10 they creep along naked, unclothed,
  and famishing they carry sheaves,
between the walls of those they press oil,
  they tread the wine-presses—and thirst;
from out cities groan the dying,
  aloud the soul of the wounded crieth:
    yet God doeth not heed the offence!

—*Those* are amongst the bitter enemies of the light,
  who have never acknowledged His ways,
    and have never dwelt upon His paths!—

the remnants of the subjugated aborigines further described xxx. 1 sq., who pushed back into deserts and caves dragged along the most wretched existence, like wild asses roaming through the deserts for themselves and their children and contented if they can get together some sustenance, even from the cattle-fodder or from the vintage-gleaning of the powerful sinner (the sing. suff. in בלילו refers to the רשה who is immediately more definitely mentioned), moreover, without clothing or shelter abandoned to all forms of misery, which the rich man scarcely knows by hearsay. However, still more sad is the lot of those who are bound in social bonds, slaves, corvees, villains, or dependants in other forms; who groan under the burden of debts to such an extent that the infant is torn from the mother as a pledge by the debtor, ver. 9; who while they work for the superabundance of others are themselves famishing, vv. 10, 11; yea, who from the midst of the vast slavery of society, under the tortures of which they suffer, groan in vain to God for help as they die! ver. 12 (מְתִים would have to be connected with מעיר: *from the city of people*, *i.e.*, from the thickly peopled city, yet the addition of the word would then be superfluous; and מֵתִים, as some MSS. and the Pesh. read, suits the second member better). To the godly this cry for help from the sufferer, which is not heeded by God even when it comes from the dying, is a true offence and *skandalon* (i. 22), particularly when the entirely different end of the wicked is compared with it, which is described at the close of the second half, vv. 22—24: Job also in conclusion, ver. 13, shocked to madness, cries out, in order to testify his horror: *they*, the tyrants who have from the first been here described openly vv. 2—4, then plainly enough included also in the description of all the following verses, vv. 5—10, but not the sufferers like Job, are the people who intentionally rebel against the light in thought and deed, who love confusion and sin only!—(2) Vv. 14—24. Again, one sees on the one hand, vv. 14—17, still worse sinners of another kind, men who do not shun simply the celestial light, like those previously named, but even the light of earth and seek the darkness with its terrors, in order that they may the more undisturbed prosecute their villany; *e.g.*, the

Towards daylight the murderer riseth,
killeth the sufferer and needy,
and at night doeth like the thief;
15 the eye of the adulterer waiteth for the twilight
thinking "not an eye will spy me!"
and a covering he putteth about the face;
in the darkness they break into houses—
who by day shut themselves up,
do not know the light:
because to them morning is at once darkness,
because the terrors of darkness are familiar.

—"Swift is he in his *course* on the water's face,
—a *curse* overtaketh his lot on the earth—
he turneth not towards happy fields:

notable high-wayman, who quite early in the morning slays the people who are alone and then further uses the night like a thief, ver. 14, comp. ver. 15; the adulterer who pays heed to the twilight that he may use it, and with it puts on as it were a covering for his face, a mask, by which he becomes unrecognisable (Prov. vii. 9), ver. 15; violent men in the darkness break into houses (*e.g.*, in times of civil commotions when houses are searched), but in the day, as genuine enemies of the light in every sense, closely shutting up themselves (and their houses), in order that they may not be recognised and punished, since they, knowing well the district which is favourable to them, and defying every light, always surround themselves with horrible night, make the morning for themselves at once into the darkest night, vv. 16, 17, comp. xxxi. 33, 34. But what, on the other hand, vv. 18—24, is the end of these men? When one hears the opponents, one would suppose that they must all in the briefest space of time vanish with all that belongs to them overtaken by the divine punishment; and Job too is master of such speeches and can present this view probably still more forcibly than his opponents (as, indeed, he also formerly believed that this was the state of the case) vv. 18—21: but the case is wholly different when the actual facts are honestly looked at! vv. 22—24. Accordingly vv. 18—21 contain a representation of the same view as the friends had asserted which is meant to vie with their efforts, just as Job likes to give such rival pictures when they are appropriate; only that in this instance the imitation, with which the speaker enters so thoroughly into the view of his opponents that it is as if he meant to adopt it, suddenly changes by the direct counter presentation of the truth of the matter into the scornful exposure of the opposite opinion (becoming a parody of it); it is plain also that the words contain an intentional exaggeration of the representations used by the opponents, which of itself conveys an element of ridicule; and probably they were words

drought, heat also carry forth snow-waters:
  the Underworld them that thus sinned;
20 the womb forgetteth him, his sweet drink is corruption,
  never again will he be mentioned,
    so that as a tree wickedness is broken;
he who devoureth the barren childless woman,
  and to the widow doeth not good!"

—Yet He sustaineth mighty ones by His power,
  they rise up, though despairing of life:
He letteth them rest—and they confide,
  and His eyes are upon their ways:
they rise high: a little while—they are gone,
  they fall low: like all others they depart
    and wither like the tops of ears!—

of a poem then well-known which our poet thought it proper to pour some ridicule upon. The tone of ch. ix. was similar, though not so bitter. The passage cannot be taken as a serious utterance of what *ought* to be but is not, inasmuch as the language shows nothing of the character of a demand and requirement. *Swift*, fleeting *is he* in his *course upon the face of the water*, as something swimming on the surface of water is rapidly carried away beyond recovery, with equal rapidity he vanishes (xx. 28; Hos. x. 7; Ecc. xi. 1), in that when he disappears, his inheritance, his fine landed property in the earth is *cursed* (paronomasia[1]) by those beholding his just ruin, comp. xviii. 20, xx. 27; so he turneth his steps no more towards *vineyards*, *i.e.*, smiling, fruitful fields, such as his extensive landed possessions were: but into the dark, desolate underworld sinners are as rapidly and completely carried away as snow-waters soon vanish without a trace on sudden drought or even heat (dry or even hot wind) (vi. 16, 17, חטאו relative, acc. § 332*a*): thus gone down into the underworld and drinking in corruption only like his sweet milk (xxi. 33), he will be wholly forgotten on earth even by his nearest friends, by the womb which bore him, and the root of all the wickedness even appears, as by the uprooting of a great tree, to be destroyed with him who was as a devouring fire to all the unprotected, to both the woman that has been cast off and the widow (xx. 26). Certainly, all that is very fine!—*and yet*, notwithstanding these great utterances and fine pictures, *after all* He (God, who for awe is scarcely indicated) sustains by His power the tyrants, even when at some time they already des-

[1] Ewald reproduces the paronomasia between קל and תקלל by "Auf Wassers Fläche er *verfliegt*, *verflucht* sein Loos". In English another reproduction of it has had to be attempted. Tr.

25 If not—well then who will prove me a liar,
and to nothing make my speech?

pair of life, causeth them to be secure (לבטח) and calm, taking their ways under His protection (x. 3 *c*); and moreover their death is enviable, inasmuch as they depart from their elevation in a short period without long suffering (xxi. 13 *b*), but if they are cast down from their elevation, they really only gather together their feet like all other men, *i.e.*, die, Gen. xlix. 33[1], and that moreover only according to the course of nature at the time of ripeness (in contradiction of v. 26)! The antithesis cannot be more pointed, or the refutation (even if only certain instances are in Job's favour, others in favour of the opponents) more complete. ומשך, ver. 22, can equally as well as ואמרתָּ, xxii. 13, and other instances of the kind, § 345 *a*, signify, *and yet He sustaineth.*

2. BILDAD AND JOB.

CH. XXV., XXVI.

As therefore Job has now himself most emphatically put before the friends, who had reproached him with some atrocious deed which they had discovered, a much more serious stumbling-block and occasion of offence of an exactly opposite character, to which they, as has already been brought out, are in reality unable to produce any satisfactory reply, and as he, moreover, declines to answer their personal incriminations further than by an appeal to God, it is evident that the opponents have come to the end of their materials, as they had long ago become exhausted in insight and force. Bildad, whose turn it is now to speak, can neither continue the useless personal attack, which had been fruitless even when made by Eliphaz whose dignity could command respect, nor can he again begin with the atrocious deed, inasmuch as he would have in that case to first to refute the counter position which Job has been placing before them. Bildad feels therefore that the contention is coming to a stand-still, and can in fact, inasmuch as

[1] נקפץ cannot in any case signify in this connection anything which does not take place until *after* death, such as burial, cannot therefore be brought into connection with נקבץ, Ezek. xxix. 5; it can only express, like the corresponding *withering* in *c*, an ordinary decease.

he would still like to speak, only bring forward one thing, or rather call something to remembrance once more. He desires, namely, to say, that notwithstanding the immense darkness of the enigma, which now forcibly descends upon the friends and makes them dumb, they must nevertheless hold fast the true feeling that Job has gone too far and ought not to speak as he is now speaking, because his words really offend against the divine majesty, and whatever the issue of the contention may be, they are attended by great danger and can never be completely satisfactory. This, which is all that now remains for the friends to call attention to, Bildad here ventures, with timidity and uncertainty, to bring forward in a few feeble words, in order as far as possible to stop Job from the prosecution of his exceedingly perilous course, and he thus reverts to the general truth with which Eliphaz had started at first, to the truth of the great distance between God and man, and that this weak creature may never consider himself righteous before that mighty One, iv. 17 sq., xv. 15; which are remarks without any new distinctive meaning or force.

But if this truth, put in this vague general way, was even at the commencement of the contention, when his opponents had the advantage, rejected by Job as long ago known and of no use to him in this form, how can he now allow it to pass as a satisfactory answer on the part of the opponents, when it only returns as a weak echo from the earlier speeches of Eliphaz, when at this point and in view of the immense enigma, to which Job now directs attention, it is wholly inappropriate, when as it appears in this form it sufficiently proclaims the complete perplexity of the exhausted opponents? As if seized by displeasure at the contradiction of men as it has now shown itself to be useless, he resolves to conclude as far as possible, by a short, sharp answer to the weak speech, the contention as between men, having long ago perceived that really men generally will be unable to give in his peculiar case either comfort or enlightenment. Whilst in the previous advances he had always kept back his attack until the third friend had spoken, in this case the evident fatigue of the opponents provokes him to make a merciless attack after the speech of the second; and while previously he had never answered merely personally, he is able here, as the opponent produces absolutely nothing new, at once briefly to give a personal reply to his speech. Yet, in order at the same time somewhat further to evince in all calmness his superiority in productive effort, after the brief word of scornful rebuff, xxvi. 2—4, he begins, as Bildad had tried to describe the greatness of God, in rivalry with him, but with far superior power, a much more magnificent, complete, and richer description of this greatness, which is at the same time more profoundly modest, xxvi. 5—14, whence follows plainly enough, without any application, how unprofitable the opponent's speech had been to him who knows everything touched upon in it incomparably better and can describe it not only more eloquently but also with deeper human modesty; comp. similar rivalry ix. 4—11, xii. 13—25, xxiv. 18—21.

xxv. 1 Then answered Bildad the Shuhite and said:

Dominion and terror is with Him,
  who maketh peace in His heights!
have His armies a number?
  but whom doth not His light surpass?
and how should man be righteous before God,
  and how should one born of woman be pure!

I. xxv. 2—6: a twofold comparison of God in His infinite power and His transcendent splendour with man in his inferiority, in consequence of which man may particularly never contend with God with respect to justice and injustice; the first comparison is the most exhaustive, vv. 2—4, the second proceeds to insist further more on the transcendent divine splendour, vv. 5—6. In the background lies the idea, which prevails elsewhere in the book, of the celestial powers and spirits, visibly represented by the innumerable host of stars, which may, indeed, at some time come into disagreement and conflict, but are always reduced to order and peace again by the superior Power, which shine illustriously but are nevertheless outshone by the highest radiance of Him that is

5 Behold, even the moon—it shineth not,
and the stars are not bright before Him:
how then mortal man, corruption,
and the son of man, the worm!

xxvi. 1 And Job answered and said:

1.

How hast thou helped him who hath no strength,
supported the arm of him who hath no power!
how hast thou counselled him who hath no wisdom,
and abundantly made known sure insight!
whom hast thou taught words,
and whose breath went from thee?

2.

5 **T**here the shades are made to sorely tremble
underneath the sea and its inhabitants;

invisible to the earth, so that before Him moon and stars do not shine (the sun is not mentioned, just as Ps. viii.). In conformity with the general sense of the passage and the connection of the particular words, יאהיל, ver. 5, is undoubtedly equivalent to יָהֵל, as some MSS. read and ancient versions explain it, whether this was the original reading, or whether אהל is to be regarded as = הלל or not; the meaning *to tent*, Gen. xiii. 12, 18, is foreign to the passage. The ו of ולא יאהיל as iv. 6, acc. § 348 *a*.

II. xxvi. 2—4. An extremely scornful finishing off of the opponent. True, most likely it is so, and I am myself conscious of it, that I am a man without power or intelligence; but then what kind of help, what kind of abundant wisdom hast thou lent to the man without either power or wisdom! (thou with thy feeble, meager words of little wisdom!) Or, to speak a little more seriously, to whom hast thou then really spoken instructive words? (to me, dost thou imagine?) and whose mightily inspiring breath went forth from thee? (the spirit of God from thee, who hast merely repeated the words and spirit of Eliphaz?)

xxvi. 5—14. This description of the power and greatness of God is in various respects superior to that of Bildad: first, in wealth and brilliancy of material, although Job repeats nothing from the similar pictures which he had previously made: whilst Bildad only refurbishes the words of Eliphaz in feeble outlines. Second, that he takes his illustrations not merely from the heavens, as Bildad does, although they supply most opportunity for a description of greatness and splendour, but also from the Underworld and the earth, so that he now starts very suitably, exactly contrary to Bildad, from the Underworld,

naked is the Underworld before Him,
and no covering hath Destruction!
He who stretched the north over emptiness,
hung the earth over nothing!

He who shut the waters within His clouds,
so that the cloud-mass is never rent under them,
who enclosed the face of His throne,
spreading round about it His cloud-masses;

vv. 5, 6, then ascends to the earth, ver. 7, lingering longest certainly over the wonders of the heavens, vv. 8—13. But, thirdly, the noblest proof of his superiority is this, that at the end, ver. 14, he confesses with great modesty that he is able to do no more than describe the very barest and most distant outlines of the divine wonders; which is, again, one of the many proofs, that Job is now continually striving after higher knowledge with resignation and diffidence; for that which is here for the first time, ver. 14, so briefly thrown out, namely, that in God there remains so much that is incomprehensible, is subsequently, ch. xxviii, further worked out with the same modest sincerity, and forms there the sublime conclusion and the result of the whole contention as waged between men. So easy would it have been for Job to bring forward thus early the thoughts which are further discussed ch. xxvii., xxviii!—The details are arranged in three small strophes of three verses each, which are then followed by a brief, powerful conclusion, ver. 14. The lowest Underworld even, far beneath the sea and its inhabitants (for the Underworld (Sheol) begins at the confines of the deepest ocean streams (see my note on Ps. xviii. 5), must feel the power of God, in that, *e.g.*, an earthquake so rends the firmest surface of the earth that the black Underworld for once lies open before God and His light and the Shades, which are at other times quite motionless (iii. 17—19; x. 21, 22; xiv. 21, 22), being suddenly convulsed become agitated and terrified; אבדון *Destruction* = Death, the Underworld here and xxviii. 22; xxxi. 12; Prov. xv. 11; thence quoted later Ps. lxxxviii. 12. Of the earth is here immediately, ver. 7, mentioned only the one but the greatest wonder, that although as a very heavy disk it rests upon nothing, suspended unattached over the dark atmosphere of the Underworld, as if stretched over vacuity and hanging over nothing, and yet remaining firm and not sinking into the abyss (the Underworld); that the *North* is here first and especially mentioned is probably owing to the fact, that the North was regarded by the ancients as the highest and firmest (and next to the East the most sacred) quarter, just as the South was the lowest and nearest to the Underworld (comp. Sâvitri-upâkhjânam, v. 8 sq.; "Isa." xiv. 13), and here precisely the wonderfully strong and firm position of the heavy earth over nothing is intended to be emphasized: the high mountains especially in the north, which are elsewhere called the pillars of the earth, constitute the deepest foundation for this disk.—Of the heavens and their relation to the earth there is first, vv. 8, 9, mentioned the wonder of

10 set bounds around upon the face of the sea,
  most perfectly, of light as of darkness.

The pillars of heaven are struck with trembling,
  and become amazed at His threat;
with His strength He stirreth up the sea:
  by His understanding smote Rahab;
His breath maketh the heaven bright
  His hand pierced the fleeing Dragon!

the formation of the clouds, which although they contain such heavy masses of water do not burst and open themselves at the wrong time, which as reaching into the highest heaven enclose at the divine command like a veiling ornament the outer side of the divine throne, as it is elsewhere said that God builds for Himself His higher cloud-dwelling Amos ix. 6; Ps. civ. 3, 13. Then, ver. 10, the wonder of the heavens as a light-giving dome, which, carrying the sun to the ends of the earth, where the ocean has its circuit, is so stretched out that everything which lies on this side of the round confines is perfectly light, everything on the other side is perfectly dark, just as subsequently, as late as into the Middle Ages, the Atlantic Ocean, as lying beyond these limits of the course of the sun and the celestial dome, was considered to be perfectly dark and was called *the dark* sea simply[1]; חג comp. חוג, xxii. 14, אור belongs remotely to חק, acc. § 289 *c*, עד־תכלית adverbial as xxviii. 3.—Yet the most magnificent scene is presented, vv. 11—13, by the heavens, as in their most violent commotion affecting the earth, when at the mighty threat of the angry Creator their pillars, the highest mountains, which seem also to support the heavens, are struck with trembling and the sea rises in violent agitation: whilst nevertheless a single breath from His elevation is sufficient to make the most stormy heavens calm and bright again, all tempests being chased away, and whilst the constellations which then appear, formerly raging monsters but now captured and fastened by Him to the sky, as Rahab (ix. 13) and the fleeing Dragon (Isa. xxvii. 1, Virg. Georg. i. 244, Sil. iii. 192), sufficiently attest that He has also intelligence in abundance to restore the order of the world in the midst of the greatest confusion! see on ix. 13. שפרה is a substantive: *by His breath*, as soon as He breathes and commands, *is the heaven brightness*, although it had just been dark. חללה from חלל *to pierce*, but חולל, ver. 5, from חול. *The ends of His ways*, ver. 14, the extreme points, the more easily perceptible outward aspects of his marvellous activity: and even this limited outward aspect we really discern

[1] Comp. Enoch xvii. 6, xviii. 14, xxi. 1, 2, xxxiii. 2, Abdias's *Hist. Apost.* viii. 1, *Jahrbb. der Bibl. Wiss.* III. p. 112, *Zeitschr. für die Kunde des Morgenl.* vii. p. 334; as according to the Greeks, Atlas sustains not only the heaven but also the earth, see Gerhard's *Archemoros und die Hesperiden*, Berlin, 1838.

Behold, these are the ends of His ways,
 and how gentle is the word we hear!
  but the thunder of His powers—who understandeth?

only by the low, gentle (iv. 12) voice of God, which speaks within and permits itself to be heard there, or by the divine spirit within us (שמע here construed with ב, as the verbs of *attending* to, *understanding;* שמץ is in the const. st. to דבר: and what a low, soft word is that which we hear!); more powerfully and loftily God seems to speak in the thunder to the whole world and to proclaim his secrets (Rev. x. 3, 4), yet what mortal understands this language? In which words there is in fact nothing other expressed than the consciousness, as it was then found amongst the enlightened spirits of the people, that man as he now is does not yet understand many of the awful truths and secrets with regard to God, and must prostrate himself before His terrible revelation, which is of force not merely for the small heart but also for the whole, wide world, if once it vibrates through the world as in thunder-language!

3. JOB ALONE, AS CONQUEROR.

CH. XXVII., XXVIII.

After such a crushing rejoinder, in which Job deals scornfully with his opponent and shows his own superiority, the third friend can the less venture a further word, as the entire view of the opponents has now been shaken and upset to its deepest foundation. At this point therefore the contention comes outwardly also to a stand-still, as already with the last change of speakers no progress was made in the matter itself; the friends hold their peace from perplexity and helplessness, without having arrived at any clearer insight and conviction. However, this forced cessation of the long contention with its many vicissitudes is too severe and abrupt not to make him who in the first instance provoked it, Job himself, feel in the midst of his incontestable victory the necessity of relieving the abruptness of the ending as far as he is able. In reality, under the last convulsions of the dying contention a misplacement of its foundations has taken place as regards Job, a misplacement which he must, on the first opportunity of calmer reflection, consider himself bound to rectify. He has permitted himself to be led away to the description of the prosperity of the wicked, greatly as this shocked the friends and strengthened their suspicion against him, as if he took a secret pleasure in this prosperity: and undoubtedly, as long as the opponents, in order to fill him with terror, held up to him in the strongest light the destruction of the wicked, he was compelled to put before them absolutely hostile propositions and to give up the solution of the hard enigma involved in the opposite of their assertion. But now that he has overcome them with this sharp sword, a little reflection suffices to enable him to avoid everything that can appear ambiguous, and to take a position upon a much higher elevation. For, first, Job has after all urged those doubts against his own better consciousness, inasmuch as he has through his whole life acted under the conviction, that sin involves its own punishment and destruction, xxxi. 2, 3, comp. here xxvii. 12 sq.: where there is such a firm conviction of an entire fruitful life, doubts may for a moment take possession of the purest man, particularly in the painful circumstances which oppressed Job, but it is impossible that they should become perpetual and get the upperhand. Secondly, it is just now in the development of the dark lot of Job that the time has come when doubts of this kind, after they have been honestly brought out and made clear in all their strength, must decidedly begin to work their own cure. For it is precisely at this moment when he looks back calmly upon the whole contention, that he feels more strongly than ever before, what an infinite blessing lies in his integrity, since it is, surely, simply through it that he was saved in the utmost peril and now stands with the great gain of a grand experience and inward strength as conqueror on the threshold of a new time. This newly gained certainty, moreover, so reacts upon his view of the regions of life which are still dark that he must perceive, however much both in the world and in God may still be incomprehensible, and although the sinner often appears outwardly prosperous and the godly suffers though innocent, that nevertheless in the eternal development of things innocence cannot remain without its fruits nor wickedness for ever go unpunished. By these reflections those doubts are not, indeed, as yet removed, but as less dark and more harmless they retreat into the background. Finally, Job now for the first time places himself towards the friends fully in the position of a conqueror, thereby that he now clearly utters what he had really all along prophetically felt in his heart and freely declares his highest, purest truths. For he surrenders nothing whatever of his fundamental opinion, since as regards the matter about which the whole contention had been raised, reverting to the point at which he commenced, he maintains firm as a rock his innocence against all the contrary asseverations and opinions of the friends, and a brief, powerful word on this point from him as conqueror suffices, as a simple inference from all that has been said hitherto, which then becomes at the same time unintentionally the most dignified answer to the last endeavours of the opponents, xxii. 5—11. On the other hand, he gains much, in fact, the last thing which is still possible to be won from the vanquished opponents, in order completely to shame them. For in that he now voluntarily appropriates that part of their views which was true when taken generally, but became perpetually false in its application to Job, namely, the certainty that the sinner cannot enjoy true prosperity (which he can appropriate inasmuch as in reality he had always even in the midst of the storm of assailing doubt [1], believed it but has now afresh experienced it so powerfully in his own case), he wrests from them every pretext even for such bad suspicions, and shows to them their inability to establish anything substantial with their own truths, since in fact, their own words even, as far as they are true, speak for Job, who,

[1] Precisely in this respect do such words of Job's as those above which are as if incidentally inserted, xvii. 9, xxi. 16, xxiv. 13, become doubly important now, because he here really only takes up more definitely and pursues deliberately what he had above all along meant in his heart.

as experience had already shown and as prophetic anticipation encourages him further to hope, has not been like a sinner forsaken in his need of true hope and strength. Accordingly everything combines to bring about this last phase of the contention as between men, everything urges Job to make this last possible step of progress, and the first fruit of his victory is that here, after a little reflection, he, coming forward without contradiction instead of the third opponent, who without a word leaves him in possession of the field, concludes earnestly and benignantly the contention. Emphatically maintaining all the clear results of this contention, in view of the still remaining obscurities submitting in humility to a higher Wisdom, he here utters the sublimest words, which must no less surprise the opponents than exhibit him as not only the powerful but also as the marvellously thoughtful and modest conqueror. It is first at this point that he bears off the crown of the true triumph by striving after higher clearness of view, as he overcomes himself in the moment of his victory over others. It is here at the close that he expounds to his astonished fellow men the purest conceptions of his inmost soul, that in view of the still unsolved enigmas he is prepared to submit alone to the divine wisdom, and thus turns from men in devout awe to the eternal source of knowledge and salvation. The brilliant conclusion of the contention as between men, which gathers up with a firm hand its results, prepares at the same time the transition to the final development of Job's cause in quite another sphere.—As therefore Job, starting from the incontestable certainty of his innocence, here declares before his opponents really the state of his soul in conformity with that certainty, or the deepest convictions of his heart answering to it, the speech falls into three parts of increasing length and importance: (1) the emphatic assertion of his inalienable innocence, because he knows what an incalculably precious possession this is, xxvii. 2—10; so that (2) he also not less than the friends, but without the false application which they constantly infer from it, and therefore much more absolutely and correctly than they, maintains the outward misery of the godless as really desired by God and as always possible through God's omnipotence, xxvii. 11—23; inasmuch as (3) he well knows, notwithstanding many enigmas which still remain to him, that the wisdom of man is never under any circumstances to let go the true fear of God, ch. xxviii., the most characteristic and brilliant portion of this speech.

xxvii. 1 And Job took up further his utterance and said:

1.

As God liveth, who hath taken from me my right,
the Almighty, who hath grieved my soul:
—for wholly is my life-breath still within me
and God's breath in my nostrils—
certainly, my lips do not speak iniquity,
and my tongue—it meditateth not deceit!

1. xxvii. 2—10, an address, full of bold strong feeling, yet calm in the consciousness of victory, in three strophes each of three verses. The most solemn oath (and it is the first which Job permits himself) by Him who, as Job harshly but truly as far as the opponents are concerned (reverting as conqueror to ch. iii) maintains, in spite of the assertion of the contrary by the friends, has taken from him as an innocent man (according to the view of the world at that time) his right, or the just acknowledgment of his innocence, and has thus grieved him, is explained as regards the matter sworn, ver. 4; but first there is inserted parenthetically, ver. 3, the grounds of such bold language: he still feels within him all divine energy of life and the irresistible impulses of the spirit; instead of finding life and inspiration expiring within, as was to be expected after his vast sufferings and as the opponents imagine, he feels himself, on the contrary, wonderfully strengthened and still vigorous enough to say the boldest things even swearing by God; as to כל, see § 289 *a*. It is true the strong oath declares in general that Job does not in the least speak untruly, which would be opposed to the law of his whole life: but this still refers primarily to the great instance with which the contention was started, or to the question of the innocence of Job which the opponents had denied and he himself had all along either expressly or incidentally asserted: hence in the more detailed explanation, vv. 5—7, he protests with the most solemn earnestness that he is determined steadfastly to maintain his innocence to his death; so that the reproach of hostility, cruelty and guilt returns, on the contrary, upon his opponents, who unsparingly per-

5 **F**ar be it from me to grant that you are right:
till I depart, will
I not let my innocence be taken from me!
to my right I hold fast and let it not go,
my heart upbraideth me not as long as I live:
let mine enemy appear guilty,
mine adversary as a sinner!

For what is a sinner's hope, when cutteth off,
when God draweth out his soul?
his lamentable cry will God hear,
when distress cometh upon him?
10 or in the Almighty hath he his pleasure,
doth he call upon God at all times?

2.

Let me teach you concerning the hand of God,
what is in the Almighty's power not conceal;

secute the innocent man with false charges. יֶחֱרַף, ver. 6, must as intransitive signify *to blame oneself*, or rather to be torn by inward reproaches, to waver on account of the upbraiding of the conscience, to be in uncertainty.—For how could he belong to those who are justly deemed sinners? He has the most immediate and vivid inward consciousness that a sinner cannot have this immoveable hope and serenity in God, such as he has now strongly felt even in the most extreme dangers, in the nearness of death, ch. xvi., xvii., xix., and such as must equally pervade the whole life of the godly, as Job knows from his own experience. There thus shines through the fine description, vv. 8—10, the elevating feeling of a newly gained experience of a true inward treasure and happiness: the serene height is observable to which he who has always been a true man of God has now risen with new intensity of feeling, with the gain of purer and larger truth; and if he no longer, as ch. xvi., xix., feels the distress of death so near at hand, but already the hope for the present life gets firmer the more the darkness of his case is relieved, he could nevertheless not lay hold of this more immediate hope if he had not previously passed through that trying school of the absolute resignation of all earthly things: already at this point the fruits of that brave struggle in extremities show themselves. With the figure of the cutting off, or drawing out, of the soul from the body, ver. 8, comp. vi. 9; xxxiv. 14; Ps. civ. 29; Ecc. xii. 6, 7; Dan. vii. 15, and the manner in which Jamas is described in the Sâvitri epic of the Mahâbhârata.

2. But if Job now feels with such wholly new delight and certainty the eternal, inward misery of the godless, it requires but one more step to enable

ye have, surely, yourselves all beheld it,
and why then are ye so wholly vain?
This is the lot of the wicked man with God,
the heritage the tyrants receive from the Almighty:

If his sons are multiplied—for the sword!
his offspring have not enough bread,
15 death burieth the remnants of his house,
his widows weep not;

him to feel with equal certainty, that this inward misery must surely in the end be followed by corresponding outward misery; and that God has the power to bring this about he has, moreover, never doubted. Accordingly it comes upon him as a flash of lightning, that he is so far from being able, or from desiring, to deny the outward uncertainty and misery of the godless as a simple matter which the divine omnipotence may bring about, that, on the contrary, he can and must maintain it still more strongly and certainly than the opponents; indeed, that he can speak to them with regard to it as their teacher, since he has really all along intended it, but now feels more clearly than ever before that precisely if this misery is such as the opponents also maintain, then the ultimate lot of the godless cannot overtake him, as they had all along falsely maintained. Thus he reverses this weapon also, being now in the midst of victory, wresting it from them and using it against themselves, as if he already anticipates that God also on His part will not treat him, even as regards external misery, in the same way as the sinner; and the noble displeasure at the perversity of the opponents, who although knowing and frequently describing the sad fate of the godless, yet nevertheless make such a false application of it to Job, as if he belonged to them, urges him now to come forward as their teacher, so long as the question is simply the divine possibility, desirability, and ultimate necessity of the matter, xxvii. 11—13.—And thus is commenced, vv. 14—23, a description of the end of the sinner, which Job makes in rivalry with the friends and in which much that they had said reappears in a stronger form: only in such a way, that what the friends used to condemn Job with must now avail for him against them, in that the hope becomes strong in him that he will not meet with such a fate, and that when Job alleges this, he does not thereby deny that sinners may nevertheless often be outwardly prosperous for a long time and that the godly may sometimes be in grievous calamity, as his own history, in fact, is now so plainly teaching. When correctly understood, this description accords completely with the present feeling of Job, as he is on the way to anticipate the certainty of his own deliverance, or, which is the same thing, the impossibility that he can perish like the wicked. But the particular illustrations, which are spoken in rivalry with the opponents, must not be too slavishly applied, but taken only as representing the eternal reprobation of sinners before God and the necessity, which is involved therein, that they cannot after

if he heap silver like dust,
  and procure clothing like clay:
he procureth—but the righteous clotheth himself,
  and the silver the blameless divideth;
he hath like the moth built his house,
  as the booth which the watchman maketh.

He lieth down rich and—he doeth it not again,
  openeth his eyes—he is no more.
20 swift terror overtaketh him like floods,
  at night the tempest hath stolen him:
the east taketh him up so that he disappeareth,
  carrieth him in storm from his place,
casteth upon him without sparing,
  from whose hand he can only *flee*;

all be even externally truly and permanently prosperous, but, even when they appear to be so, their overthrow is to be expected from the divine omnipotence even in the visible world. The introduction, ver. 13, is intentionally like xx. 29, xv. 20. Without permanence is the house of the sinner, vv. 14, 15, is his great wealth, vv. 16—18, but particularly his own life, vv. 19—23; therefore two strophes of considerable length, of five verses each. After his death his house feels the full calamity which he brought upon it, and instead of being able to lament and bewail him, the members of it will be at once buried by death, so that death and burial are one, because no friend, or relative, appears to show them this last respect, Isa. xiv. 19; Amos vi. 9, 10. His wealth, silver, *e.g.*, and clothing (Gen. xlv. 22), may be as endless as the grains of dust or clay (ver. 16 *a* recurs in exactly the same way Zech. ix. 3), yet it will at last pass into the hands of the final conquerors (see subsequently Matt. v. 5), as he has built his whole house from the foundation rotten and frail, as frail as a moth, iv. 19, or as a miserable watchman's booth in a garden, built merely for the summer, Isa. i. 8; Mic. i. 6. Indeed, a single night is enough to destroy him and all his wealth, so that, when he has at the last moment of terror and destruction just opened his eyes heavy with sleep, he is carried off, as if he might be allowed only once more to wake for a moment that he might see his destruction; accordingly יֹאסִף must be read with some MSS. instead of יֵאָסֵף, as xx. 9; xl. 5. The most terrible is the description, thus introduced ver. 19, of the overthrow of the sinner himself, vv. 20—23: sudden mortal terror (xviii. 14) overtaketh him like an overwhelming flood (Isa. viii. 7, 8; Nah. i. 8), or rather a swift tempest from the east (i. 19) taketh him up and carrieth him away with irresistible force, so that before it, as before the missiles of a strong, armed warrior, he can do nothing else than flee, for in this storm the divine power is hidden Ps. xxxv. 5, 6; so he flees accordingly still pursued by the

men clap their hands over him,
hiss him forth from his place!

xxviii. 3.

1 **F**or there is to silver a source,
a place to the gold which has to be refined,

scorn and ridicule of his own place, which ought to protect him! comp. viii. 18; Nah. iii. 19; Lam. ii. 15. ישפק and ישרק, ver. 23, have an indefinite subject, so that the suff. in כפימו as plur. can be referred to the implied plur.: but the מוֹ— in עלימו must be regarded as in the case xx. 23, *ante* p. 208.

3. Ch. xxviii. This being so, the extreme sufferings of a godly man like Job are certainly all the more incomprehensible: yet this is not the place to pursue further this dark aspect of the case, but Job hastens to close with the best that he has to say in the capacity of a teacher of the friends. Just now his deepest feeling is, as it has never been before, that the godly man may not, notwithstanding such enigmas as still remain unsolved, let God go, and this feeling he must declare before the friends didactically with higher confidence. Accordingly his mind remains here in this loftier mood, and from the midst of it he begins to expound the last and highest thought that he has yet to speak before men, and which serves at the same time to further explain the unexpected boldness of the previous words of this speech. *For*, although many things may still be dark in the divine allotments, *e.g.*, the sufferings of the godly, the truly godly man does not nevertheless permit himself to be made thereby unstable in his faithfulness and constancy, since he is certain of the general truth that man, as incapable of finding the highest, purest truth anywhere all at once, is, on the contrary, from the creation called to permit the wisdom which has been granted to him as his own to show itself in the acknowledgment of the highest divine wisdom, or in the fear of God. This brilliant passage contains in a veiled form the exposition of the highest principle, according to which Job always lived, of which, however, he has now in his calamities become still more clearly conscious after severe conflicts: that is, never on account of any single dark and mysterious things in life and of new enigmas in God to give up religion and faith, since if they remain faithful and operative they present the one possibility of entering into the secrets of God, xvii. 9, xix. 25. It is only because Job has been led, by the force of the contention and the victory, himself to come forward as the teacher of the friends, that he here presents the lofty truth not as his feeling but in its more general form of universal validity, and seeks to establish it with greatest calmness and reflection as of itself necessary. And in reality this principle which is here proved is not merely amongst the Hebrews one of the highest views to which they attained, but it is also perfectly correct independently of them. For if it is in the first instance true that wisdom is the most precious treasure which man can gain (Prov. iii. 14, 15, comp. here with ver. 18 *b*), then surely wisdom in the highest and

iron is taken from the dust,
and stones are melted into copper:
an end men have made to darkness,
and most perfectly men seach out
the stones of darkness and of gloom;
opened up gangways, far from the sojourner,

purest sense, or the wisdom which embraces and permeates everything, must be for man an infinite, highest possession, which can neither be found anywhere like a material possession, nor gained with any amount of toil or with the greatest visible treasures, nor compared with any external possessions, nor can ever be exhausted by individuals. It is, on the contrary, a purely divine possession, hidden in God and come forth from him and operative since the creation, a possession which therefore man, as he follows the traces of wisdom as it becomes manifest, can find only in God. So that for man the fear of God, or the bringing of all his thought and action into relation with God, is the true wisdom, because being again truly taken possession of by God, he finds in Him the wisdom of the things of the world. And again, this truth is, on the one hand, elevating and inspiring, inasmuch as according to it an endless progress in human wisdom in accordance with the infinity of God can be conceived, while, on the other hand, it exerts a moderating and educating influence, inasmuch as in accordance with it man is always conducted to that which is primary and of universal necessity—to devotion to God and faithfulness towards Him—as the true means of being able in the new, hard enigmas of life, when the divine wisdom is hidden in the particular case, still to continue in the frame of mind and with the ability really to attain at the favourable moment that divine wisdom if it presents itself for human apprehension. The connection at this point as well as the past course of the contention requires that the principle should be here conceived from the latter point of view: the pointed contrast between divine and human wisdom, between the false and the true way for man to find wisdom, must here be brought forward, and that which is wrong is first described at length in order that the one simple true thing may be at last uttered with the greater brevity and more overwhelming effect: it is the few words of tremendous force ver. 28 to which the whole speech tends from the beginning. Accordingly it falls, it is true, into three parts: (1) man has undoubtedly a wonderful power of bringing the most hidden tangible things from their deepest abysses and finds the toil and pains he employs for this purpose at last rewarded by rich gain, vv. 1—11; but (2) wisdom, no tangible and visible thing, confined to a particular locality, cannot thus be found by the expenditure of any amount of trouble, or gained by any external treasures, vv. 12—22, because (3) God alone possesses it, who has appointed for man religion as his wisdom, vv. 23—28. But the last of these three parts, into which the highest truths are compressed, is with emphasis the shortest, the most solemn in its calmness and abruptness, because the thought finds scarcely

have they who have been forgotten of the foot
  and in the depth stray far from men;
5 the earth—*from* it springeth forth bread,
  yet *under* it men ravage like fire!
the place of its most brilliant stones,
  nuggets of gold become man's,
that path which the eagle never knew,
  which the vulture's eye hath never pierced,
proud animals have never trodden,
  to which the lion hath never penetrated;
on the pebble man hath laid his hand,
  overturned from the roots mountains,

any corresponding words, losing itself in its immeasurable elevation, and opening an infinite field for further meditation.—(1) Vv. 1—11. Mining operations, particularly inasmuch as they were then still uncommon and probably the Hebrews were occupied with them only quite in the north on the Phœnician borders, or in the south on the Idumean and Egyptian borders [1], are here very suitably mentioned as an example of the way in which man understands how to bring even the most hidden things to light, when they are only capable of being laid hold of, and how nobly his pains are rewarded. How deep and how firm lie the treasures of the earth, and how dangerous and daring are the labours of mining: yet nevertheless man has the joy and the gain of bringing all these most secret treasures into the light of day to use them as he will! Accordingly (*a*) it is quite possible to call forth as by magic the deepest treasures of the earth for use, vv. 1, 2: silver has a source from which it can be drawn forth, the gold which has to be refined (יזקו is relative clause, *which men refine*, in contrast with gold found in rivers and sand) has a place where it can be found, like metal-ore and iron. יָצוּק third per. sing. from צוק, with indefinite subject *one*, *men*, hence the plur. appears in subordinate clauses, ver. 4 *b*, *c*, § 319 *a*, although the sing. is in such cases as this, acc. § 294 *b*, *β*, more frequent. (*b*) By what means? by the most daring, vv. 3—5, thereby that men most minutely search through the darkest things, as if an end had already been put to all darkness and no more fear was felt of its horrors, ver. 3; thereby further that men have broken open dripping gangways (channels, shafts, as יאר, ver. 10, and נהר, ver. 11) through rocks, far from the traveller, who walks carelessly over this mountain and treads above the heads of the miners,

[1] See *Hist. of Israel* IV. 192 (III. 695, 848); as regards the mines near Phænon in Idumea, see the Onomasticon in Jerome, Opp. II. p. 442.—[see later note in the *History* above. Tr.]—I do not find in this description any trace of perpendicular mines.

10 hath hewn passages in the rocks
—and all splendour his eye seeth:
he hath stayed the gangways from weeping
—and hidden things he bringeth into light.

But wisdom—whence can it be found?
and where is the place of understanding?
no man knoweth its value,
it is not to be found in the land of life;
the abyss also saith: "I have it not!"
and the sea saith: "it is not with me!"
15 fine gold is not given for it,
silver is not weighed down as its price,

whilst those who are swaying too and fro in the dangerous depths below know nothing of what is going on above their heads! ver. 4[1] (*by the foot* which walks over the mountain); lastly, by a merciless turning up of the bowels of mother earth, whose bright, sunny surface gives bread to the ungrateful men who destroy her inwardly as with fire! ver. 5. (*c*) But the gain of such toils is certain! vv. 6—11: the place both of the noblest metals and the most precious stones (of the brilliant one of the stones, *i.e.*, the most brilliant stone, § 313 *c*), that path which neither the longest sighted birds of prey, which best see everything that is in the lowest depths, nor the proud beasts of prey, which force their way through everything, have ever known and trodden,—all these wonderful regions become the possession of man! vv. 6—8; and, once more briefly to sum up everything, after he has put his bold hand upon the hard pebble, turned up mountains from the bottom, hewn passages in the rocks, and purified and made passable the latter by the collection and diversion of the water which is wept (cönstantly drips) from them, his eye beholds enraptured all splendour and he brings the most hidden things to light! vv. 9—11. This appears to be the most reliable sense of this passage, which is important as regards the history of ancient mining.—(2) Vv. 12—22. But can wisdom also be thus discovered? impossible, it is nothing palpable, material, confined to a certain place, is neither to be found in the light of the upper-world, nor in the darkness of Sheol and the sea; accordingly neither can it be balanced and purchased by all visible, material treasures, it has a supernatural value, is quite invaluable and incomparable. In order to express this its incomparable and transcendent character, all the precious treasures of antiquity are enumerated and compared with it, vv. 15—19, in such an order that the noblest metals are taken first, vv. 15—16 *a*,

---

[1] A literal rendering of this verse would be, *one hath broken open a gangway removed from a sojourner, they who had been forgotten of a foot, hung far from men, were suspended.* Tr.

it is not balanced by Ophir's treasure,
onyx, most precious, and sapphire,
gold and glass doth not equal it,
nor as its exchange the most splendid vessels;
crystal is not to be mentioned and coral:
the possession of wisdom is before pearls,
topaz also of Cush doth not equal it;
by the purest gold it is not balanced.—
20 And wisdom—from where cometh it?
where is the place of understanding?
wisdom—hidden from the eye of all life
is it, and concealed from the birds of heaven;
Destruction and Death always said:
"by the ear only did we hear of it!"

God understandeth the way to it,
and *He* knoweth its place:

and then returned to again, ver. 19 *b*, whilst in the middle it is more particularly other chief valuables which are mentioned in large numbers; by the turn ver. 18 *a*, that coral and crystal are not even worthy of mention in comparison with it (לא יזכר acc. § 136 *e*), a certain amount of variety is brought into the long series. סְגוֹר, ver. 15, is a new form derived from זָהָב סָגוּר, 1 Kings vi. 20, x. 21, acc. § 153 *a*, *refined gold* (comp. 2 Chron. iii. 4), from سجر to *distend* (whence סגריר the name of a *rain*), *to seethe, boil.* פטדה the same word as τοπάζιον, with transposition of the first two letters; Ephræm Syr. is probably too free when he substitutes for it *pearls*, Hahn et Sieffert *Chrest. Syr.* p. 21. The other names have been rendered according to the suppositions which seem at present to have most in their favour. Inasmuch as the fundamental thought has been somewhat too much put into the background by this long enumeration, in order to hasten to the plain conclusion, the whole beginning, ver. 12, is repeated ver. 20: but since this question recurs not for the sake of interrogation, or of doubt, but answers itself in the negative, the thought is immediately further pursued, ver. 21, by the vav conseq., § 348 *a*: so far is wisdom from being at some place visibly discoverable, and to be fetched thence, that, on the contrary, no creature endowed only with the senses has ever seen it, either on the earth, or above in the air (acc. ver. 7, to which this verse corresponds), or in the underworld.—(3) Vv. 23—28. The description of the relation of wisdom to God is now at last made as far as possible by the aid of the same illustrations, although with a pointed antithesis in the thoughts. First, vv. 23—25, on the one hand the proposition cannot be shaken, that God only and not man knows,

for *He* looketh to the ends of the earth,
seeth under the whole heaven,
25 to give to the wind weight,
and that He might weigh the sea by measure.
When He gave to the rain a law,
a way for the thunder-flash:
then He saw it, explained it,
understood it, examined it also,

to speak after the manner of men, the place of this wisdom, beholds it as it were in its complete, firm outline and figure, because He has always used it, as it were, as His servant and artist (Prov. viii)[1], in His supervision and government of the whole world (which would be impossible without the highest wisdom), in order, amongst other things, to give to the terrible wind its measure, that it may not be weaker and yet not more destructive, and similarly to reduce the water upon the earth (ver. 25 *b* corresponding to ver. 24 *a* and *vice versa*) within its limits (xxxviii. 8—11), which continues from the creation of the earth in such order (hence ver. 25 *b* changes into the past). But, on the other hand, vv. 26—28, it is surely also a divine necessity that He should not for ever shut up within Himself this wisdom, which is at first His peculiar possession and in Him: because it is as Creator that He first becomes fully God, and in the creation wisdom, as forming and preserving, must appear and reveal itself, in order that it may be prophetically longed for and sought in the fear of God particularly by the image of God. So that it may be said that with the creation God Himself expounded and offered to view wisdom in the works of the creation, that He also immediately, not earlier, ceased as it were from creating, when as the true master of the work He had Himself examined and acknowledged as correct His work and accordingly the wisdom which shone forth from it (Gen. i. 31), and thus as a wisdom to be beheld in the creation He finally at once then expounded, narrated and revealed it with His other truths also to man (as His image), to the extent to which man can behold and attain, or rather strive after it; and from that time man has preserved a primitive remembrance of wisdom, or a tradition of it. Accordingly: *when He* gave to the rain a law, that it should come neither too scantily nor too destructively, and prepared a way through the clouds for the thunder-flash (xxxviii. 34, 35; Zech. x. 1), that is at the creation, to which the transition was made ver. 25 *b*, when the present creation arose by means of wisdom, *then* He saw and understood, examined also as the work-master that wisdom which was by no one else understood, tested, and approved, with regard to its works in detail, and, narrating (ex-

[1] Comp. now *Gott und die Bibel*, III. p. 75 sq., where the author treats Prov. viii. as presenting a further stage than our passage in the development of the doctrine of *Wisdom*. Tr.

and said then unto man:
"behold, fear of the Lord is wisdom,
and to depart from evil—understanding!"

plaining them in order) them to man, He spoke to him the great eternal truth, that for him wisdom is to be found in the fear of God only! Wonderfully great thoughts thrown out in the fewest words; one of the finest passages of the whole book, and the most admirable close both of this chief part of the book as well as of the entire contention as conducted between men. Finally, instead of הכינה, ver. 27, הבינה must be read with many MSS., comp. ver. 23: for the preparation, or creation, of wisdom is appropriate in such passages as Prov. viii. 22—32, where even the preexistence of it before the world is described, but not here, where nothing whatever is yet said of a creation of wisdom *before* the creation of the world.

FIFTH STAGE OF THE DRAMA.

THE SOLUTION.

1. JOB'S DEEPEST REFLECTION AND CRY TO GOD.

CH. XXIX—XXXI.

The contention as waged between men has now been brought to silence, without the solution of the enigma about which it had been raised. A higher revelation must shed its light upon this darkness, if it is to be dispelled. And already both parties in the contention, having in this respect become equal, long with more or less clear consciousness after divine revelation, the friends in silence as vanquished and wholly perplexed, Job holding his ground as conqueror and courageous enough to speak further, but yet already prostrating himself before God as the only one who is able to scatter this darkness as well as so many other mysteries in human life. And thus precisely the fact, that both human parties to the contest have clearly perceived their inability from their existing knowledge to solve the enigma, becomes the first step towards its actual solution. For incontestably as long as man in a partial onesided view of a matter, whether that view be superstitious or unbelieving, shuts himself off from all other views in a self-satisfied spirit, or defiantly adheres to his imperfect notion, no single ray of a new light can reach his closed and blinded sight: the thick, hard film of infatuation must be removed before the light can find its way into the dark recesses of his mind. In Job, however, this perception that there is here a divine enigma before which all human conceit must come to shame, has become much more clear, strong, and influential than in the friends.

It is by him therefore that the first step of progress towards the solution of the difficult question of his life is taken. On the one hand, he has learnt by the course of the contention, to submit himself, without stubborn trust in his righteousness and without complaining of the general injustice prevailing in the earth, to the divine wisdom alone. On the other hand, he has at the same time become so vividly conscious of his freedom from guilt, the alleged cause of his calamities, that by this consciousness alone he has overcome all outward and inward dangers of the struggle, and now feels himself placed with higher energy and hope upon the threshold of a new development of the case. Accordingly the whole result of the contention to this point urges him to pass beyond that dumb, modest acknowledgment of a higher understanding, ch. xxviii.: he must precisely after this acknowledgment and from the basis of the higher position which he has now won, make an utmost venture to get from God the final solution of the trying enigma. For it is only the man that summons all the powers of his nature, with all awe and fear, in order to question the secret mind of God, only the man who does not totter and fall when he comes to the last steps leading to the door of the possible but still concealed sanctuary, that will reap the fruit of his struggles, receiving the reward of a divine answer which scatters the darkness to the question that has been correctly and unweariedly put. And Job now stands precisely at that point where he is necessarily urged by the lessons and the result of his past struggle, no less than by the unexhausted treasure of his spiritual powers and hopes, to make the last decisive effort.

Thus beginning afresh after a short pause, quite turned away from the friends and directing his glance exclusively to the question and to God with great intensity, Job gathers up everything that he can still say in God's sight with regard to the unsolved enigma under which he suffers. This he does with warm and holy fervour, in the most intense struggle for salvation from his dark, inexplicable sufferings and for the full and happy enlightenment of his views of God, with an honest exposition of the reasons why he cannot yet find rest, at all events before God and in his thought and feeling towards Him. At the same time he does this with the most thoughtful moderation and reserve, which, whenever feeling threatens to become passionate and stormy, immediately seizes again the reins of thought and speech, and from the commencement to the end keeps the command with such steadiness, that neither the former defiant appeal to his own right, nor the former vague complaint at the prevalence of wrong in the earth, ever appears again, as indeed, Job must have already attained to the view that if only his own enigma were solved, then all the other kindred phenomena on the earth would easily have sufficient light thrown upon them. Hence Job takes here the calmest view both of all the periods and vicissitudes of his past life and of his true spiritual condition, and presents here for the first time the most complete and truest picture of himself, bringing into open day, with the greatest detail as well as with the most unreserved sincerity, his entire inner man, just as he was before his calamities, as he now is, and as he desires to be, spreading out before God the inmost recesses of his heart, calmly declaring with perfect candour before God all his highest experiences and views, desires and pains, what he has upon his conscience and what he has not, and in a manner worthy of himself exhausting all that can be said in the greatest effort of which he is capable.

In this frame of mind he turns to the enigma. He compares the past and the present, the justly gained great prosperity of the former, to which he once more (with no longer any weariness of life from unreasonable despair) looks back with intense longing, and the wholly undeserved, most bitter, apparently utmost possible calamities of the latter: he compares what he might reasonably expect when he considers his relation to God and what he has received instead in the way of wholly unexpected and dark calamities. As he makes this comparison, he is quite unable to discover the divine connection between things apparently so incompatible, and closes with nothing else than the strongest protestations of his innocence together with the greatest longing for a judgment and sentence. Thereby he reaches the real point which he must urge in this last effort. For the speech thus brings together all his longings, his griefs and pains, his sincere and purifying confessions, and although it incites and stimulates a divine decision, it does not call for it defiantly or by an arbitrary claim: but the speech calls for it simply thereby, that after he has exhausted every human resource, with longing desire, with wrestling, holy fervour, as a man he seeks the divine decision and excites the divine compassion. On that account this is not only the longest and most exhaustive, but it is also the crown of all Job's speeches. It is here that he first shines in his full brightness, inasmuch as it appears quite clearly at the same time how his greatness comes forth in still greater purity from the withstood trial than it could possess before it. And while he never deemed it necessary to defend his innocence at length before the friends, there shines forth from this speech, without the intention of the speaker, the picture of such an exceedingly noble life that it is of itself in the highest degree pleasing and edifying and at the same time supplies the full explanation of all that had gone before, and it also excites the expectation that such a man as Job must necessarily be in some way delivered. It falls, in conformity with what has been said, into three parts: (1) a longing backward glance at the past, beginning quite calmly, ch. xxix.; (2) a description of the mournful present, in which thoughtful reflection has to put forth its utmost efforts to command the revolting and disturbed feelings, ch. xxx.; (3) the holiest, most agonizing protestations of innocence with the most intense longing for a hearing and acquittal, ch. xxxi.

xxix. 1 And Job took up further his utterance and said:

1.

O that I had moons like the former ones,
like that time when God kept me!

1. Ch. xxix. The happiness of former years, to which Job looks longingly back, consists when generally regarded, it is true, in the clear and strong feeling of the divine nearness and friendship, which has not yet completely recovered from all the wounds it has received. But when regarded in detail, or with reference to the special human circumstances, he now misses less the outward superabundance of those times, ver. 6, than the high respect and esteem in which he then stood with all men, particularly in public life, in the council and court of justice, where his word and his dignity obtained the noblest victories, and where again he felt himself so strong and happy as the welcome and beneficent advocate, spiritual prince and comforter of his fellow citizens who were often in distress and despair, vv. 7—10, 21—25; whilst he is also quite well aware of the grounds of such esteem, inasmuch as all his labours were employed simply in the promotion of justice and the alleviation of others' sufferings, so that he might therefore not unreasonably expect to lead the most undisturbed and longest life in such strength and honour, vv. 11—20. But he would not give such special mention to these details, if the results of the conflict just finished did not naturally lead the man, who had so long been despised by the friends that had come to comfort him, and who had been so cruelly reproached, now at last to recall with all the deeper longing the opposite of this contempt and accusation in his own earlier life. From the midst of the sad present he dwells with deepest pleasure on the recollection precisely of this aspect of his former life, and mentions with noble emphasis the mutual relation, of which he had always been conscious, between esteem, prosperity, and happy hope on the one hand and self-sacrificing, active labour for others' weal, on the other. But inasmuch as the recollection of the high esteem, which he formerly always enjoyed as a public man in the midst of his fellow-citizens, must most painfully affect him, and of which he has just bitterly experienced the mournful opposite, the whole course of the speech accordingly divides itself into two and a half long strophes[1]: after the general longing for the former

---

[1] Vv. 2—10; 11—20; 21—25. In the clause of the LXX, οἱ δ' ἀκούσαντες ἐμακάρισάν με, instead of ver. 10 *a*, there is probably, since these words cannot have been taken from ver. 11, a trace of the verse which is wanting in the first strophe and could be restored ver. 10 thus:

the voice of the nobles was hidden,
and all listened with awe to my counsel,
those who heard pronounced me happy,
and their tongue etc.

when His lamp shone over my head,
by His light I walked through darkness,
as I was in the days of my summer,
when God's counsel was over my tent,
5 when the Almighty was still with me,
round about me my children;
when my goings were bathed in cream,
and a rock poured streams of oil near me;
when I still went out early up to the city,
in the market placed my seat:

life has passed at the very commencement into this cheering picture, vv. 2—10, then the virtue which begets such esteem and answers to it, as well as the hope of lasting happiness built upon this noble manner of life, has been described, vv. 11—20, at last that bright scene of the past, that glorious recollection of the times of untroubled, exuberant hope, is once more reverted to, as if the imagination found it difficult to let it go, vv. 21—25. And shall he then not actually soon taste all this happiness once more? and does he then not already here feel as it were the maternal joy of this approaching birth?

(1) xxix. 2—10. Most gentle, collected commencement, the general happiness of the divine friendship and the prosperity founded on it being described in the fairest colours of joyful recollection, vv. 2—5, then more briefly, ver. 6, the outward blessing, and more at length the high honour in the gladly visited assembly of the people, vv. 7—10. He who stands to God in the relation of one protected by Him, ver. 2, is both himself enlightened in all dangers by His bright, near light, ver. 3, and also sees the blessing of the divine confidence and friendship coming down upon his entire circle, vv. 4 *b*, 5 *a*, so that all such days are those of a gentle, cheerful autumn, חֹרֶף, ver. 4 *a*. Thus the description passes gradually from inward to outward, from general to particular matters. With regard to בְּהִלּוֹ it is a question whether the Massora intend it should be regarded as *Qal*, in which case we should expect according to analogy, § 238 *b*, בְּהַלּוֹ, but see § 255 *a*, or for *Hiph'îl*, as the Targ. explains it: *when He caused to shine;* the first form would meet the requirements of the sense, but the construction explained § 309 *c* is not found elsewhere in this poet; and since the reference to a divine act really suits the figure and the thought much better, it is possible to punctuate בָּהִלּוֹ, *Hiph'îl* contracted from בְּהַהִלּוֹ, acc. § 71 *c*. With ver. 6 comp. xx. 17: only the figure is here carried out more perfectly, the steps of the prosperous man being bathed in cream with which his path overflows, and a hard rock by his side pouring streams of oil along his way, he is everywhere therefore attended by all possible abundance. Still his favourite way was that which led to the assembly of the citizens, ver. 7, since we must think of Job as a wealthy, independent resident in the country at a distance from the city, who took an active share in the affairs of the

young men saw me—and hid themselves,
  and old men having risen remained standing,
princes even refrained from speaking
  and laid the hand upon their mouth,
10 the nobles' voice was hidden,
  and their tongue clave to their palate.

For when an ear heard it pronounced me happy,
  and when an eye saw it bore witness to me:
that I delivered the sufferer calling for help,
  the orphan who had no helper.

nearest city and had his appointed seat in the assembly, as Abraham is generally described in a very similar way Gen. xxiii. שער might be strictly construed with צאתי in the sense, *when I left the gate*, namely my own, *for the city*, in order to go to the city: but in that case we should expect שְׁעָרַי, or rather בֵּיתִי, whilst שער appears, on the contrary, plainly to correspond to רחוב, comp. v. 4, xxxi. 21, 34; accordingly it would have to be only loosely connected with צאתי, *when I went out* of my house *towards the gate*, *i.e.*, the market, going *up to the city*, as the towns usually lay higher than the surrounding country. Still the reading of the LXX שַׁחַר is much easier. When he arrived, the younger men then evinced their respect by their reverent retirement, the older men by their readiness to wait upon him, and when he spoke even the noblest honoured his voice by their respectful silence, as enchained during his speaking by conviction, v. 16, xxi. 5. With regard to the construction קול—נחבאו, see § 317 *c*.

(2) xxix. 11—21. How could it be otherwise, inasmuch as all who had only heard of Job by report pronounced him happy before they saw him, and all who really saw him, how he acted and spoke, convinced by what they saw, gave him again the best attestation as regards his constant readiness to help the unfortunate, inasmuch, therefore, as the good reputation which always preceded him was confirmed in all cases afresh by experience, ver. 11, comp. xxviii. 22, xlii. 5; with the last word ver. 11, however, ver. 12 must be closely connected as its explanation. On the other hand, he received also the glad blessing of the unfortunate, because he devoted his whole life in society to the noblest objects, vv. 13—17, considering righteousness as the best ornament and armour, and being in return adorned and strengthened by it as by the noblest array, ver. 14, comp. Isa. xi. 5, and thus he sought to supply every want of those who were suffering in any way, but particularly to save the unfortunate, even if they were personally unknown to him, when they came into the court of justice, and to rescue from the sinner who was pursuing them the prey which he had already seized, vv. 15—17 (as to רב לא ידעתי *the cause* of him whom *I did not know*, see § 333 *b*; what is said vv. 12, 13 refers also especially to the important defence in the court of justice, where ולא as well as משוע are

The blessing of him that was perishing came upon me,
  and the heart of the widow I made joyful:
I adorned myself with justice—it adorned me,
  as a robe and diadem my virtue;
15 to the blind I was eyes
  and feet to the lame I,
a father I to the needy,
  the cause of him whom I knew not—I examined it,
I broke the fangs of the sinner
  and wrested from his teeth the prey:
and I said: "near my nest will I die,
  and like the phœnix live many days:
my root is open towards water,
  and dew abideth upon my branch;
20 my honour is always new with me,
  my bow keepeth green in my hand!"

circumstantial clauses acc. § 341 *b*). After all that, he might therefore justly expect to become permanently happy and prosperous, like the phœnix after a long life to die like it by his nest, ver. 18, since he saw his trunk as well protected on all sides, on the part of the earth and of God, as a tree well-watered from above and from below (xviii. 16), and his honour and strength (bow) always being afresh rejuvenated just as a well-watered tree is always putting on fresh verdure (xiv. 7), vv. 19, 20. According to this connection, חול, which is in certain MSS. pointed חוֹל in accordance with early tradition, cannot be understood of the *sand*, inasmuch as the countlessness of the sand might be a figure of the multitude of creatures or even of the extent of knowledge (1 Kings v. 9 [A.V. iv. 29], but hardly of days or time, particularly in such a short description, and inasmuch as the completion of the figure of the *nest* requires the myth of the phœnix. According to a myth which originated precisely in the more distant part of Asia, the phœnix bird after the longest life dies on its nest to live again rejuvenated [1].

---

[1] The Arabs call it Samandel, confound it also with the griffin عنقا and with the Kerkes كركس; Pers. *sîmurg*, see Bochart's *Hierozoikon*, p. 809 sq., of the early ed.; d'Herbelot s. v. *Samander;* Dalberg in *Fundgruben des Orients* I. p. 199—208; Izzeddins *Vögel und Blumen*, p. 110—113; Arab. Qirq Vezir p. 175, par. 4; Tac. Ann. vi. 28; Clem. Epist. I. ad Cor. ch. xxv; Const. Apost. v. 7; Tert. de resurr. car., ch. xiii. See also Wilkinson's Manners and Customs of Anc. Egypt., pl. xxx A; Lepsius' Chron. der Egypter, p. 170 sq.; Raoul Rochette in the Mémoires de l'Acad. XVII. 2, p. 311—23. As the bird, which

Unto me they hearkened, waited,
  and kept silence at my counsel:
after my word they spoke not again,
  and upon them fell my speech in drops,
they waited for me as for rain,
  opened their mouth wide for plentiful rain;
I smiled upon them if they despaired,
  and the light of my countenance they never dimmed;
25 gladly I took their way, and sat as head
  and dwelt as a king in the troop,
    as one that comforteth mourners!

(3) xxix. 21—25. As the *honour* of Job has been again mentioned, ver. 20, this suffices to lead him to further work out and complete the description he had begun vv. 7—10, because this aspect of his recollections is really that which is most attractive to him and from which he finds it difficult to part. Accordingly he describes afresh the bright picture, how that in the assembly, when everybody was in despair, his word was often waited for as for the most refreshing rain and no one desired to oppose his speech when finished and his counsel, vv. 21—23, how that, with a cheerful countenance and never without successful advice, he always smiled helpfully upon the despairing, never depressed by their despondency and infected by their despair, ver. 24 (לא יאמינו is an abbreviated circumstantial clause without וְ, since without לא the *part.* might be used in such a dependent clause, as Ps. lxix. 4, comp. § 341 *b*: as האמין used alone can signify *to believe* Ps. cxvi. 10, so לא האמין when used alone may mean *to despair;* with *b* comp. Gen. iv. 5; Prov. xvi. 15; Ps. civ. 15), and how that in the assembly (אבחר דרכם reverts to ver. 7), which he always gladly frequented, he was enthroned as voluntarily acknowledged chief, as proud as any king can be in the midst of the company of his warriors, or rather obtaining such happy victories as he who comforts mourners and is acknowledged by them as their moral lord and benefactor. The last comparison is, contrary to his intention, a pointed arrow against the friends, who had so

according to the myth was very rare and only returned in certain periods of time, was a symbol of the rejuvenation of changing time, it might very well take its name חול from the idea of changing, turning, although it has in Egyptian also a similar name (Zeitschrift der Deutsch. Morgenl. Ges. III. p. 64). The ὡς στέλεχος φοίνικος of the LXX is perhaps a later alteration of the translation, by some one who understood φοῖνιξ of the palm and further confounded קני with קָנֶה; there is no etymological reason for the signification *palm*, and if the palm can also serve as a symbol of long life, it does not accord with the figure of a *nest* and is in appearance only supported by ver. 19.

xxx. 2.

1 But now laugh at me
they that are younger than I in days,
whose fathers I had despised
to set beside the dogs of my flock.
the strength of their hands also—what could it profit me?
to them prime of life hath perished:

miserably comforted the man who as administering true consolation to others was highly honoured by them. And thus at the same time the easy transition is made to the lamentation that follows.

2. Ch. xxx. Although may things have to be complained of, this lamentation starts with that calamity which, considering Job's former life as above described, must be the most unexpected and painful—the contempt of all men, vv. 1—10; it then passes to the more distant causes—the countless afflictions sent by God—which must weigh him down, with regard to which he complains in vain, vv. 11—22, although he is compelled by the excessive pains and alarms to make complaint, vv. 23—31. According to the construction of these verses, they fall into four strophes of eight verses each; and the first three begin the complaint each time afresh with the sad words *but now* . . . .

(1) xxx. 1—8. It is not of the three friends that Job complains here: for to provoke them further would not be fair; neither of members of his household, of whom sufficient was said ch. xix.; but of a class of people whose contempt is undoubtedly of the coarsest and most extreme character, and to whom there was an obscure reference xvii. 6. Whilst Job sits alone and helpless in the open air [1], abandoned of his friends and members of his household, there come forth, as one must conceive the situation according to the poet's intention, from their hiding places the basest and coarsest men, in order to heap at their will scorn and cruelty of all kinds upon the sufferer; even the most despicable men make him feel their satisfaction at his humiliation, and he must complain of the worst form of persecution which a man who has already so much to bear can meet with! But this sad lot, as it is here described in detail, is, however, of too peculiar a nature to have been without some historical basis; and if the entire description is looked at, we may with probability conceive that basis as follows. The men of whom Job here complains are the aborigines of those countries, who had long before been subjugated by the tribe to which Job's family belonged, and as completely debased degenerated into this miserable condition, so that those who refused to submit to slavery fled into the hiding places of the land, led there the most miserable life, and were again hunted forth by society, if they ever came near it in quest of assistance, with loathing, as weak, despicable creatures. A relation of this kind appears to have existed between Seirites and

[1] See p. 95.

through want and famine wholly dry,
  they gnaw the desert,
    what was long ago wild and waste,
they who pluck marsh-mallows by bushes,
  whose bread is genista-root;
5 from the midst they are driven,
  as if it were thieves, the hue and cry is after them:
they must dwell in the most dismal valleys,
  in caves of the ground and the rocks,

Idumeans, Gen. xxxvi.: but this is the plainest description of them in the whole of the O. T. Previously, xxiv. 5—8, the poet has put a description of them into Job's mouth: but in that passage Job described their lot with compassion and indignation at their oppressors, as in any case we must suppose that this their condition had existed long before Job's time, and that he was personally not responsible for it. But miserable as the condition of such men is and deserving as it is of the pity of every feeling heart, if at any time a calamity befalls the family of their ancient oppressors, the old jealousy immediately revives again, breaking out into base insults and low contempt; a sufferer like Job, who as he sits helpless in the open air is exposed to all attacks, they cause to feel most bitterly their delight at his humiliation, and the one innocent descendant of stern conquerors must endure the entire assault of a wild, accumulated vengeance! A hero, an independent prince, a man of spotless fame, must endure the worst from the weakest, basest, and utterly infamous men; yea, though he had as a man pitied their wretched lot! These pointed antitheses are here so plainly brought out that we obtain a vivid glance into the extremely unhappy and disturbed condition of those times and nationalities, and learn to understand the pain of those who innocently suffered in consequence. Comp. also *History of Israel* I. 227 (I. 304 sq.). First, the painful contrast is briefly stated, ver. 1, then both sides are more calmly described, the contemptible character of those people, vv. 2—8, and the scorn which he has to endure from them, vv. 9, 10. The insufferable feature of this scorn is, acc. ver. 1, that it comes from people who are not only younger than Job, but also the weakest and most miserable wretches conceivable, who on account of their frail bodies cannot even live long, with whom no one would enter into a judicial contest, whose fathers even (xv. 10) Job declined to as much as associate with his sheep-dogs, because they are less strong and useful than the dogs! They are the weakest, vv. 2—4, and universally most hated people, vv. 5—8: the weakest, inasmuch as, if one attempted to deal with them, they could not do even manual labour, every moment subject to death and never reaching the prime of life, ver. 2 (עלימו is more than לחם the so-called *dativus incommodi*), in that as completely dried up from want of all kinds (גלמוד really a substantive *a dryness*, but also as predicate iii. 7, xv. 34) they are compelled to

among bushes they roar,
  under nettles they gather from around,
sons of godless also of nameless people,
  who have been whipped out of the land!

But now I am become their song,
  and I became a by-word to them;
10 they abhor me, avoid me,
  spare not my face with spittle.
For with bared bow He afflicted me,
  a bridle men hung from my head:

seek the most miserable means of subsistence in the most barren deserts which had long ago (אמש like תמול, Mic. ii. 8; Isa. xxx. 33) been abandoned by all other people, vv. 3, 4, comp. xxiv. 5; the most hated, because as sprung from a heathen, insignificant race they have from the earliest times been thrust out of the land, and if at any time they show themselves again they are most carefully chased forth once more, so that they are obliged to dwell in hiding places and collect with a wild cry like animals without any fixed house or covering under the first bush that offers, ver. 8 contains in conclusion the last historical explanation to the description which it closes, vv. 5—7; on ערוץ as st. constr. comp. § 313 *c*; on לשכן, which suffices without לחם in such a connection, § 237 *c*.

(2) and (3) xxx. 9—23. Yet such a particular calamity must necessarily come, since, sent from God generally, the mightiest host of outward calamities assailed him, spreading mortal terror, vv. 11—15, so that his inward condition has become distressing in the extreme, vv. 16—19, in which state he now complains, but in vain, or, indeed, to the increase of his pain, vv. 20—23. This middle double member of the complaint is therefore really its chief part, the ultimate causes of his sufferings as well as their profoundest dangers and terrors being therein explained, and God being again spoken of with the greatest tension of feeling that is still possible: although even the worst that is said here and that which seems most violent, is uttered after all with much greater moderation and reserve than in earlier passages of the same kind, as if a hard word with regard to God escaped the speaker only now and then against his will. In the first place, the numerous calamities which come from without, from which the description here must start, as from the ultimate cause of his present condition, vv. 11—15, seem to him (as xvi. 9, 12—14; xix. 10—12) like an irresistible host of wantonly destructive besiegers, vv. 12—14, set on by God, ver. 11, and only too well accomplishing their object, spreading mortal terrors and chasing away all welfare, ver. 15, as the wind the clouds, vii. 9; "Isa." lxiv. 6. As soon as He (God) had subdued and put him in fetters, the individual and smaller enemies (*i.e.* his calamities) came in troops, rising out of

on the right riseth a growing band,
  they throw out their flying feet,
    prepare against me their calamitous paths;
they break up my way,
  assist only to my overthrow,
    none helpeth against them;
they come as through a wide breach,
  roll up under crashing:
15 against me mortal terrors are turned,
  they hunt like winds my nobility,
    and like clouds my welfare is gone!

the ground to seize him like a growing evil brood, or mob: hence the perf. ver. 11 interchanges with the imperf. vv. 12—14, the perfects amongst the imperfects vv. 12—14 receive their proper force from the latter and relate to them. And inasmuch as the figure of war predominates in the description of the attack of his sufferings, it is brought in at the very commencement: *His string* on His bow, accordingly His bow He *opened*, bared (Isa. xxii. 6; Hab. iii. 9, comp. Ezek. xxi. 33; A.V. ver. 28) or took into His hand *and prostrated me* hitting me with sharp arrows, vi. 4; then merely a similar figure: *a bridle from my face they let down*, I was bound, fettered so that I could not defend myself, Isa. xxx. 28; xxxvii. 29, the sense like xiii. 27.[1] Thus the *K'thibh* יִתְרִי; the *Q'rî* would be, *my cord*, my vigour, He *relaxed*, but the passage iv. 21 is totally different. The host of various assailants we see rising first *on the right*, as accusers at the same time, xvi. 8; Zech. iii. 1; Ps. cix. 6, then rapidly put their feet in motion for a charge (comp. substantially the same phrase xviii. 8; that is, the reading רַגְלֵיהֶם, which the LXX has, is the more probable), getting nearer and nearer to their object, they prepare irresistibly a way to the walls of this fortress, simply destroying and profitting for an overthrow, at last break through the walls and as if with a wide breach therein rolling up amid the crash of the ruins, whilst no one helps the assailed against them! The לָמוֹ, ver. 13 *c*, can in this connection hardly refer to anything else than the assailants; the לְ־ therefore expresses only a general relation (as in the similar instance Ps. lxviii. 21), notwithstanding the fact that in this phrase it could have a much closer relation, comp. xxix. 12. Finally, the words βέλεσιν αὐτοῦ

[1] It might be supposed that the words ver. 11 *b*, with the meaning *the bridle is thrown off before me*, was still referring to the shamelessness of the men who had been described as far as ver. 10, as خليع الرسن and also خليع alone can have this force. However, this neither suits the whole connection, nor could מִפָּנַי then signify *before me*.

But now my soul is poured out unto me,
  days of affliction take hold upon me:
night eateth away my wasting bones,
  my gnawers sleep not;
great power disfigureth my garment,
  it girdeth me round as the shirt-collar;
He hath cast me into the mire,
  so that I am become like dust and ashes.
20 I complain aloud unto Thee—Thou hearest me not;
  I stand still—Thou settest Thyself against me,
turnest Thyself into a cruel enemy unto me,
  with the strength of Thine hand waylayest me,
liftest me up, causest me to ride into the wind
  and causest me to melt into the thunder-crash!

κατηκόντισέ με instead of ver. 13 *c* and other things in the LXX point to the fact that an entire verse has been lost before ver. 14, which probably described something like the shooting before the walls.—In consequence of such an attack of calamities from without, his soul, to which the transition was made ver. 15, is full of all conceivable distress, vv. 16—19: despair under incessant affliction, ver. 16; pains which the night also keeps up (comp. vii. 4; the night is an active agent, as iii. 3; מעלי signifies, as ver. 30, a change of the outward form to such an extent that something disappears from the person which had hitherto been *upon* it, visibly clothed it) and by which the whole body, succumbing to the irresistible power (xxiii. 6), *i.e.* God, so shrinks up that the wide upper-garment לבוש wholly concealing itself around the middle of the body docs nothing more than gird or inclose him around as at other times the shirt, or undergarment, quite at the top about the neck, or as the *mouth*, *i.e.*, the border of the shirt which is very closely drawn together at the neck (comp. the last song but one in the 228th Night of the *Arabian Nights*, bk. iii. p. 238, 7 sq. of Habicht's Arab. ed.; כפי is therefore here not *in proportion to*, as xxxiii. 6, Zech. ii. 4, but פי expresses, inasmuch as a garment is spoken of, the uppermost part, or the border round the neck, Ps. cxxxiii. 2), vv. 17, 18; lastly the total collapse and exhaustion, ver. 19 (comp. xvi. 15, only that here a new thought is added). The complaint which naturally arises in such a condition; but in vain, indeed increasing the pains by persistence therein! vv. 20—23; here his feeling almost gets the mastery of the speaker, so that it is only with difficulty that he can restrain himself; the speaking of God changes into a direct address to Him. If after the first vain complaint he remains standing, without getting calmer, if he waits therefore, then God resents it (*animadvertis in me*, in a bad sense), yea, becomes a cruel pursuing enemy, causes him when he has been lifted up by violence to ride away and perish in wind and storm, as

For I know to death Thou wilt bring me,
  to the gathering-house for all life.—

At least—in the overthrow is not the hand stretched out?
  if in ruins—is there not therefore complaint?
25 or did I not weep for the man in misfortune,
  did not my soul grieve for the needy?
For good indeed I hoped—and evil came,
  I waited for light—and darkness came:
my bowels are boiling without rest,
  a time of affliction hath come upon me;
I creep along black, but not with sun's heat,
  I stand up in the assembly complaining aloud,
I am become a brother of jackals,
  and a friend of the ostriches;

if death had already seized him to carry him away, ix. 17, 18; instead of תְּשֻׁוָּה *Q'ri* תְּשֻׁוָּה *K'thîbh* must be read = תְּשֻׁאָה, xxxvi. 29; Prov. i. 27, so that it is an accusative of motion and simply stronger than רוח. Instead of תחבנן, the meaning of which has been conjectured only, it is probably better to read with two MSS. תחכנן, which acc. Ps. lix. 4 would suit the context much better, describing how at the least sign of Job's resistance immediately follows a worse resistance from the opposite side.

(4) xxx. 24—31. Reflection: according to human calculation therefore Job must naturally despair of life, as he had just said, ver. 23: yet (אך as xvi. 7) is it surprising in the sufferer that in the overthrow, in the very midst of the ruins, he stretches out his hand (Hab. iii. 10) calling for help? and is not this a law with all living creatures? ver. 24, or has not Job himself always shown pity in all cases of misfortune, as was said ch. xxix., so that when himself in distress he has a right to complain and to expect sympathy? ver. 25. Indeed, all Job's grief is concentrated in the thought, that while he can, according to ch. xxix. and xxxi., hope for prosperity and blessing from the future, he is visited by the deepest calamity and finds himself in the most extreme misery, vv. 26—31. Thus here also there comes in again at last the recollection of all the greatness and glory of the past, by which the speech both reverts to its commencement, ch. xxix., and also at the same time prepares the way to the oaths concerning his past life which soon follow, ch. xxxi.: but the reflection and collected feeling is overborne by new billows of most bitter grief. In the difficult ver. 24 עי *overthrow*, *ruin* and פיד *destruction* plainly correspond, לָהֵן *on that account*, Ruth i. 13; the sentence is of a general nature, but interrogative: *only does not a man in an overthrow*, if he is brought to ruin, *stretch out the hand? if he* (this man as a general example) is *in his utmost danger*, is there not

30 my skin wasteth from me black,
and my bone burneth from heat,
so that my harp turned to mourning,
my pipe to loud weeping.

xxxi. 3.

1 A covenant I made with mine eyes,
and "how could I look upon a maid"

on that account a cry for help? The force of the negation is perpetuated in the second member, § 351 *a*. The extreme misery is at last once more described with most emphatic brevity as the most violent inward commotion under afflictions, ver. 27, as the condition of one who is vainly bitterly complaining and howling in the profoundest mourning for the wrong he suffers, vv. 28, 29 (*black* in mourning, xvi. 15, not burnt by the sun but by his afflictions, in that his afflictions by blackening his skin, ver. 30, have put on him a natural, bodily mourning garment; thus he stands *in the assembly*, *i.e.*, before the tribunal, seeking a judge amid complaints, xi. 10), as the wasting away of his body consumed by an inward heat, so that his former joy and happiness, ch. xxix., is turned into the most mournful contrary, vv. 30, 31.[1] Accordingly ver. 26 and ver. 31, or the first and last words of the last description, glance back to ch. xxix.

3. Ch. xxxi. As now Job is unable to discover any connection between these deepest afflictions and that well-founded hope of his earlier life, save the supposition of his personal sin, a superstition from which he is fast getting entirely free, there is nothing left for him, in his present intensified longing for deliverance, than at the close to protest most solemnly his innocence, invoking upon himself the heaviest penalties if he has not been precisely as free from blame as he has protested. Thereby the above want of connection remains in reality as great as ever, and is made still worse in that the attempt to lessen it by any use of Job's guilt has been most emphatically forbidden. These most solemn protestations of his own innocence under the most terrible imprecations are, it is true, so many challenges of God as the judge: for who but God can actually carry out the fearful punishments which the speaker evokes against himself if he lies, and of whom as witness and judge can Job be in the end thinking but Him? But warned by his previous experience, he adopts language of great diffidence and moderation with reference to God, without any of the previous

[1] The *weeping* which is not mentioned here only, xxx. 31, where it occurs in a more figurative sense, but frequently elsewhere in Job's case, is produced by physical causes also exactly in the disease of Elephantiasis, see Danielssen et W. Bœck, traité de la Spedalskhed ou Eléphantiasis des Grecs. Paris 1848, p. 201.

and "what is the lot of God from above,
the heritage of the Almighty from the heights?

defiance or the vehemently excited challenge. He is content to let the simple facts themselves speak and to express his most solemn convictions, so that the challenge of the higher judge becomes greatly moderated and is barely directly uttered, and contains no infringement of the divine majesty. It is only parenthetically that the direct wish is expressed for a divine judgment, at first briefly, ver. 6, then more energetically towards the end, after the speech has generally grown more violently agitated, vv. 35—37. With all the greater freedom and emphasis, on the contrary, does the speech proceed in that field which is quite open to it, in the protestation of perfect innocence. In order to show that this protestation is made with greatest seriousness and after full consideration, he enters first very minutely into the various sins which might be suspected in the case of a man in Job's position, and seeks to bring them all forward with exhaustive completeness; whereby he does not forget in subordinate sentences the fact, that it is not enough merely to avoid crimes, but that the opposite virtues must also be practised, vv. 18, 30—32. Then, however, he observes that it is not enough simply to protest that he is not guilty of such sins and to challenge the heaviest punishments if that is not the case. If it is to appear of itself by a moral necessity that he cannot have been guilty of such sins, the inmost motives of his thought and desire must be brought forward. Accordingly he also declares incidentally in short, emphatic words the entire state and character of his inner nature, his clear perception of the wrongness, indeed, the atrocity of the various sins, the steadfast resolve which he made from the very first to avoid them, and his continually strong consciousness of the necessity of the severest punishments, vv. 1—4; 11, 12; 14, 15; 23; 28. There is thus introduced into these imprecations a beautiful variety and life, by means of the no less sincere than clear, calm description of his inward man: one observes that the man who thus undertakes to bring into the light of day the holiest within him, as it now is and always was, cannot speak thoughtlessly. Finally, the kind of punishment which he calls down upon himself corresponds to the various sins that he repudiates: yet it is not needful that the imprecation should immediately follow each protestation, which if very often repeated would become monotonous; but gradually the protestations accumulate in greater numbers, as the stream of the discourse is swollen by the warmth of his feeling, and a single horrible imprecation has more emphasis when uttered at the end after all these various protestations. For these reasons, and further because a suitable progression in the picture of the sins must also be observed, this most impressive and exhaustive working out of this part of the speech falls into three parts, beginning with the source of all the various evil deeds—the evil desires—vv. 1—12, considering then the great power of a magnate with regard to others, vv. 13—23, and finally returning to a number of secret, hidden sins, vv. 24—40: yet, with the growing haste observed in bringing together all the various things that have to be said in these last words, a

is it not then calamity to the sinner,
  and severe punishment to evil-doers?
doth *He* not see my ways
  and count all my steps?"
5 If I have walked with wickedness,
  so that my foot hastened unto deceit:
—let Him weigh me in just balances,
  and let God acknowledge my innocence!—

division into a number of somewhat long, though not too long, strophes is most suitable, namely into strophes of from 7 to 6 verses each.[1] Accordingly neither in respect of evil desire, nor in respect of brutal force, nor in respect of dishonourable conduct, will Job admit that he has offended, and indeed as regards either God or man: thus his brief survey of all possible human transgressions is completed. It must be further remarked, that the correct understanding of the whole depends on the constant recollection of the fact, that the simple form of protestation can alone prevail throughout, that all the rest can only be subsidiary addition, needful setting, or slight digression; the imprecations always stand quite plainly as invocations, the protestations of the innocence of his former life always beginning with *if*, either in the *perf.*, which is the most natural, or in the *imperf. præteriti*, when the duration of the matter in the past is insisted upon, ver. 7*a*, 13, 16, 17, 18*b*, 19, 20*b*, 25, 26, 29.

(1) and (2) xxxi. 1—12. Starting from evil desire as the ultimate source of all sin, the speaker will touch upon the sins which most directly spring from it: this therefore is the most suitable place at once to explain the prevailing principles and sentiments of the life of the speaker, in conformity with which he was wholly incapable of these and other sins, vv. 1—4, whereby the transition from xxx. 25 to the following protestations is at the same time made easier; then the first protestation asserting that he has never in the affairs of life generally thus given way to evil desire, vv. 5—8, and the second protestation with the special asservation that he has never been misled by it to attempt one act of unchastity, vv. 9—12; each of the two protestations is accompanied in this case by its corresponding imprecation. The introductory declaration, vv. 1—4, is particularly fine, in which the nobility and purity of the view of things which prevailed in the whole of Job's life, and the practical law of life which he based thereon, are sketched most graphically with greatest brevity; and as

[1] It is only after ver. 23 that in that case a verse has probably been lost, and another probably after ver. 27; of the latter we have perhaps some fragments in the unintelligible words of the LXX ver. 26.—We might also be inclined to adopt five great strophes of eight verses each: in that case a verse would be wanting after ver. 15. Still the above strophic division appears to me on the whole most suitable.

If my step swerved from the way,
  and after mine eyes went my heart,
    and to my hands cleaved a blot:
then I will sow—and another shall eat,
  and my offspring shall be uprooted!
If my heart was enticed on account of a woman,
  and at a neighbour's threshold I lay in wait:
10 then let another dishonour also my wife,
  and let others abuse her!
for that is a crime,
  and that is sin for the judges;

afterwards of the many sins which spring immediately from evil desires it is particularly unchastity which is mentioned, so here likewise in the description of the general principle of his whole life, ver. 1: *a covenant I* as lord of my senses *made for mine eyes*, that they should obey my mind, not mislead and subdue it, since evil desire is excited by the senses, particularly by the eye, ver. 7 *b*; and in the case of such a man as Job there must necessarily be early some understanding come to with his senses, some deliberate law of life with regard to them, and in his case the understanding had long since been arrived at, amongst the resolutions of which this law was imposed on his will, that least of all should his eyes be misused for purposes of unchastity, expressed here with repudiation: *and how should I look upon a maid!* With this turn ver. 1 *b* he begins therefore to state the thoughts which occupied his mind when he made the covenant, which he presents as vividly as they were at first and still are in his mind, vv. 2—4, and how could I come to any other resolution? more strictly considered, what then is the eternally enduring lot from above but calamity and severe punishment in every form for evil-doers? can man really withdraw himself from God and His eye, from Him before whom all the necessary consequences of sin are manifest beforehand? To this clearly conceived and adopted rule of life he cannot have become unfaithful; and if he had, he would have to pronounce his own sentence, invoke upon himself the worst punishments! if he ever practised deceit (and he knows what he is saying when he appeals to God as judge! ver. 6), or committed a shameful act at the seduction of evil desire, then the whole work of his life on the earth shall be in vain! vv. 5—8; if he attempted unchaste acts, he will pay the most painful penalty by the most dishonouring treatment of his own wife, inasmuch as he quite well knows the criminal, and, indeed, the terrible nature of such a wickedness which brings with it the worst destruction! vv. 9—12; hence at the end, ver. 12 *b*, the discourse, which had become calmer, reverts to imprecation. תִּטְחַן *let my wife grind, i.e.*, become the basest slave, Ex. xi. 5; Judg. xvi. 21; "Isa." xlvii. 2, would here be too far from clear and also too feeble, since ver. 10 the words manifestly cannot be chosen sufficiently strong and terrible: accordingly it is

truly it is a fire, which consumeth unto hell,
and all my wealth shall it uproot!

If I rejected the right of my manservant and maidservant,
when they had a contention with me,
—and what should I do when God arose,
when He visited, what should I answer?
15 hath not He who formed me in the belly formed him,
and hath not One created us in the womb?—;
if I withheld his need from the poor,
caused the widow's eyes to fail,
and ate my morsel alone,
without the fatherless also eating thereof,
—no, from my youth he grew up to me as a father,
as long as I have been alive, I guided her!—;

If I saw one perishing without clothing,
and no covering with the poor,
20 if his loins did not bless me,
he did not warm himself from the fleece of my lambs;
if I swung my hand against orphans,
because I saw my help in the gate:

either used intransitively, or, if this usage cannot be established, must be taken passively תְּשָׁחֵן. Ver. 11 there is no reason for altering עֲוֹן פְלִילִים, acc. ver. 28, into עָוֹן פ׳ with the *Q'rî*.

(3) and (4) xxxi. 13—23. As forms of the misuse of power by a magnate are brought forward, first, the deliberate withholding of the right of servants in household quarrels, ver. 13, in connection with which Job again, as vv. 1—4, finds a suitable occasion to state how he could not by any means have done this according to his conception of things, remembering that he could not at all defend himself with regard to such a wickedness before God the Creator of all men, before whom all are equal, if once his judgment really came! vv. 14, 15 (אחד is both when taken alone and from the sense of the first verse-member, to be referred to God); second, cruelty towards the unprotected, whom a magnate can send away by his power simply, whilst Job, on the contrary, always, as far back as he can remember, even as a youth, was as a father and son to orphans and widows and plentifully clothed the poor, vv. 16—20, comp. xxii. 6, 7, 9, xxix. 12 sq. (as regards גְּדֵלַנִי see § 315 *b*); third, violence towards the unprotected before the tribunal, inasmuch as the magnate can easily corrupt or terrify even the court of justice, ver. 21. To all these forms of the abuse of

then let my shoulder fall from its side,
  and my arm break from its socket!
for a terror God's punishment appeareth unto me,
  and for His majesty I am powerless.

If I made gold my hope,
  and to the treasure said, thou art my trust,
25 if I rejoiced that my power was great,
  that my hand had obtained much;
if I saw the light how it shone,
  the moon walking in splendour,
and then my heart was secretly enticed,
  and my hand kissed my mouth,
—that also is a judicial sin,
  because I denied the God above—;

power the punishment corresponds completely, ver. 22, which Job's wishes to be so terrible with deliberation, not from thoughtlessness, but really trembling at the divine punishment and knowing that all human power shrinks to nothing before the divine majesty, ver. 23.

(5—7) xxxi. 24—40. There are really only four more hidden and cowardly sins which are here enumerated: first of all covetousness and blind worship of power, vv. 24, 25; second, an inclination, although but clandestine, to heathenism, allowing his senses to be dazzled by the splendour of the stars, as well as by that of gold, and so to be carried away to clandestinely worship them, a form of superstition which may appear insignificant, though it is really in the highest degree criminal as a conscious denial of the invisible spiritual deity and as a relapse into more materialistic tendencies in the case of one who has once acknowledged the true God, vv. 26—28. This passage on the clandestine worship of the *light*, *i.e.* of the sun (Hab. iii. 4) and of the moon by means of kisses flung to them is at the same time historically of great importance, and refers probably to the spread of the Zarathustric doctrine at the beginning of the seventh century, Deut. iv. 19; xvii. 3; Ezek. viii. 16. Third, hatred and pleasure in the calamities of others, from which Job is conscious of being so free that he never allowed himself, even in clandestine, half-uttered words, to throw out an imprecation against his enemy, and that on the contrary his house always stood open with noblest hospitality to all men without distinction, in that at his command his people everywhere carefully sought up men who had not yet been satiated from his rich table (hence meat, *flesh*, alone is here mentioned, Isa. xxii. 13), vv. 29—32; with ver. 31 it appears therefore that Gen. xviii. 1—8; xix. 1—3 must be compared, so that נשבע is part. *Niph.*; it is true that the *Niph.* of שׂבע does not occur elsewhere, comp. however נמלא as well

If I rejoiced at the overthrow of my enemy,
  and I exulted because evil had befallen him.
30 —neither did I permit my palate to sin,
  by an oath to require his soul—,
if the people of my tent did not say
  "would that there were one not satisfied from his flesh!"
—in the street no stranger tarried,
  to the caravan I opened the door—;
if I concealed after the way of the world my guilt,
  to hide in my bosom my sin,
because I dreaded the great multitude,
  and the contempt of the families terrified me,
    so that I was silent without going out:

as מלא with a somewhat different meaning; at all events the phrase xix. 22 can by no possibility suit this passage.[1] Fourth, a cowardly concealment of his guilt, so that from fear of public accusation and contempt he preferred to keep at home in hiding and not to visit the public assembly, nor ventured to speak in it, vv. 33, 34, comp. xxiv. 16; xxix. 7 sq.; Ex. xxiii. 2 and *History of Israel* II. p. 446 (II. p. 315 sq.) (אדם common people, the *world*, Ps. xvii. 4, 14). But here at the end of so many protestations and imprecations, particularly just after the mention of the sin of hypocrisy, which would also cast suspicion upon his present contention if he had committed it, his vehement longing for judgment cannot be longer repressed, but breaks forth all the more violently and forcibly, although in this outbreak it is still moderated. Conscious of no cowardly hypocrisy, prepared, indeed, vehemently longing to hear an answer and judgment with regard to his present complaint from the one Being who can now bring him justice as well as help and deliverance, he exclaims with intense agitation, vv. 35—37: *O that I had* one (who can be no other than God, only he does not venture to challenge Him directly) *who would hearken unto me* and my complaint! *there is my cross, i.e.*, my signature to the document containing my complaint, the last word attesting all that has before been said, therefore *let the Almighty answer me*, since I have said everything! and would that I had *the book which my opponent has written, i.e.*, the document of accusation, handed in by my opponent, in order that I might at least know with what I am really charged and wherefore I suffer. The figures are therefore taken entirely from the ordinary legal proceedure, according to which the opponent had to present his written accusation to the opposite party, and then

---

[1] Neither does the suggestion that the meaning is, as is said in common life, "we should like to eat him" (*i.e.* how sweet and dear he is!), suit the context.

35 —**O** that I had one who would hear me!
lo, there is my sign: let the Almighty answer me!
and that I had my Opponent's book:
surely, upon my shoulder would I take it,
I would bind it as a crown for me;
I would declare unto Him the number of my steps,
I would as a prince approach Him!—;
if over me my field crieth,
and altogether its furrows weep,
if I ate its strength without reward,
and blew out the soul of its possessor:
40 then let thorns spring instead of wheat,
and instead of barley poisonous weeds!
[Job's words are ended.]

the judgment was given. The third member of ver. 35 is still dependent on מי יתן לי, the second is parenthetical. Job is so little afraid of the accusation that, on the contrary, if it came, he would receive it with the greatest delight as his most precious treasure, take it upon his shoulder, take it upon his head and wear it as an ornament[1], and publicly show it to every one, and his accuser, who would be at the same time the highest judge, he would not meet timidly and tardily, but give Him an account of the very smallest things, approach Him with a confident step like a prince, not like a humbled sufferer! קָרֵב, like הִלֵּךְ, § 120 *a*, *to come near slowly*, in this case with a firm, unwavering step. Still this intense desire, which is expressed very appropriately at the end, vv. 35—37, is after all a parenthesis, as ver. 6[2]: the protestations which have been begun are still left without a conclusion, and in order to resume them and close them with the greatest emphasis, the first of the protestations—that referring to covetousness, vv. 24, 25,—is repeated in a more forcible illustration, vv. 38, 39, and put in such a way that it really includes the chief sin of a powerful magnate, since he can from covetousness torment to death the men who are dependent on him in the cultivation of the land, so that his wide fields, treated by him in such a cruel way and full of the traces of his sanguinary tortures of the smaller owners, cry against him as it were to heaven for

[1] These are well-known ways of honouring a thing in the sight of everybody in those parts of the world, comp. *Wellsted's Travels in Arabia* I. p. 362, *Fletcher's* Narrative of a Residence in Koordistan, II. p. 15, *Harivansa*, ed. Langlois, tom. I. p. VI., and the custom still observed there of kissing a written command or decision and laying it upon the head.

[2] It follows of itself from the above exposition that these words vv. 35—37, as well as all the rest in this chapter, are quite in their proper place.

vengeance, xvi. 18; the last imprecation, ver. 40, referring to this has again great similarity with the first, ver. 8.

The closing note appears to have been added after the speeches of Elihu had been inserted in the book, and Job appeared not to speak any more at such an unusual length. There is no reason whatever for ascribing them to the poet himself.

2. THE APPEARANCE OF JAHVÉ.

CH. XXXVIII. 1—XL. 14, XLII. 1—6.

As Job has at last exhausted all mortal powers in order to prevail upon God without defiance and without murmuring, and to behold the solution of the dark enigma, He who has so long been desired and entreated cannot longer withhold His appearance. He now appears at the right time, since an earlier appearance would either have been perilous to the man who was still insufficiently prepared for it, because it would then necessarily have been an angry and destructive response to the defiant or murmuring challenge of man, or else have been incompatible with the proper majesty of God, supposing it had been mercifully condescending and conciliatory, as if man in his ignorance could force such a gracious appearance by rebellion. But now, after the sufferer has at last tried every human means of prevailing upon God in the proper manner, and already, as conqueror over himself, endeavours without passionate feeling to obtain a higher revelation and final deliverance, this is granted to him at the right moment. It thus appears as if Jahvé had so long delayed simply because He had from the beginning anticipated and known that such a brave sufferer as Job would not wholly lose himself even in the utmost temptation and danger, but would triumphantly go forth from it with higher power and capacity, so as to be able to experience the awful moment of the revelation of a truth and glory such as had been previously never thought of. He who had appeared to men hidden and unapproachable, who had so long been a silent and hidden spectator of the contention as conducted by men, as if He had determined to take no part in human affairs, whilst He really, as at least the readers know from ch. i., ii., from the first conducts and follows everything with active interest,—He now comes forth from the darkness in order to give that light after which the earth is longing and to supply that which men in this new, great enigma of the world vainly sought to obtain by means of the resources hitherto in their possession. After earth has risen in the sacred contention near Heaven, Heaven also stoops to the earth, in order that by this conjunction a new divine truth may be established in the heart of humanity.

A revelation coming in this manner must, it is true, be for Job a friendly and gracious one. For God cannot charge him with guilt previous to his sufferings in the strict sense and chastise him for it, as the brave contender has justly always maintained amid all the darknesses of his life, even if the reader did not know this from the very beginning of the piece. On the contrary, God is prepared to deliver the man who triumphantly seeks after Him from the midst of his trial, and is resolved to permit him to glance into His glory as He supplies the final solution of the enigma by the act of deliverance. But just as little as the revelation can be purely unfriendly and ungracious, can its immediate effect be one of outward deliverance. For the deliverance from outward evil can with advantage only follow the inward deliverance from all false ideas, and as yet Job is not free from that false notion which is the ground of his suffering in the truest sense, inasmuch as if he were free from it his outward sufferings would be easily borne. He still, as from the first, cherishes the error, that God does him as an innocent man a wrong: and inasmuch as man can never regard God as unjust and incomprehensible simply with reference to himself and his own case, Job still stands in danger of letting go God's truth and righteousness in the whole world also. Inasmuch as the source of the false notion, namely, the supposition that God does him a wrong by sending his calamities as punishments, is not stopped, in spite of all the progress which he has made, he cannot attain the due knowledge without which a full deliverance is impossible. It is true, he might at last as taught by experience seek as far as possible to avoid, as is the case ch. xxvii—xxxi., the two dangers and transgressions which resulted from this error, namely, his vague ideas generally of God and the divine justice and his special discontent and complaining as to his own supposed unjust lot, in conjunction with his defiant attitude at not experiencing the divine appearance and deliverance: he might dimly surmise that the enigma must be solved in another way. Still as yet he has not arrived either at a repentant acknowledgment of his twofold precipitancy and sin, committed in the tumult of the contention, or at an elevating joyous perception of the truth. He has as yet not clearly enough perceived, nor yet acted upon the perception, that by defiance and complaint, however much they may be moderated and repressed, as long as they have not yielded to the most modest and joyful acknowledgment of the glory and inviolable righteousness of God, he closes the way to his own deliverance. In such a case how can the outward deliverance immediately come? But if he arrives at the happy perception, that the divine law, holiness, and justice have remained perfectly unviolated in his case as in all others, and will remain eternally so, he must, with the complete certainty of the innocence of his previous life, also get rid of the last erroneous idea, that his afflictions are the sign of the divine anger, and when the old terrible darkness has thus been pierced the light of the divine mercy can then pour its rays upon him. The first step in the solution of the enigma was reached as soon as man put forth all his energies to subdue those two errors—the defiance and the complaint—which tended to confuse the pure truth, and to make himself worthy to receive the divine revelation, ch. xxix—xxxi.: the second step which must now be taken is, that the complete, joyous perception of the perversity of these errors shall take the place of them as merely suppressed; and this higher step man must now attain by means of the divine appearance, which must precede all further outward deliverance and redemption.

As now every error regarding God and divine righteousness, as soon as it passes into action, though this may be as in Job's case action in words only, constitutes actual human guilt such as, while it is not cancelled, prevents the full experience of the divine mercy, majesty, and glory, and, indeed, does not permit man to glance into the pure light of God as He reveals Himself, in this case though God appears to Job at the right time He is still at first wrapped in clouds and speaks in a terrible voice from the storm. Thus in this case Jahvé presents at first His terrible aspect, behind which the milder one is hidden. Glancing not only at the last speech, but also, as the case required, at all the former speeches of Job, reviewing and gathering up the entire human contention, in order at last to settle everything as judge, He becomes as He now appears forthwith the stern interrogator and judge of Job, who when at last He appears, as Job had so long desired, shows Himself really infinitely more exalted and divine than Job had ever anticipated before this awful moment, and who intends before everything else to overcome the human folly which yet remains and to bring about the acknowledgment of the pure truth. It is true that even in this highest region no compulsion or blind force proceeds from Him whom Job had often previously thought of as his despotic lord: on the contrary, Job shall prepare for his self-defence, and every opportunity of doing this is freely presented to him; and lest he should have the most remote cause to complain of compulsion, the exalted speaker deigns, where necessary, to give him also complete explanation of the divine meaning and intention. But it is equally unbecoming that Jahvé should, like a man, or even a human judge, enter into any kind of doubtful examination, contention, or litigation with Job, as if He were not the being who knows and decides everything, who even by every slightest utterance of His true mind teaches infallibly and expresses perfectly the truth: but every one of his words must contain the most immediate and undoubted certainty and spiritual necessity, uttered from a region totally unlike that from which all the former speeches came, producing with marvellous magic the greatest effect by the most direct means, so that quickly the most willing and joyful conviction on the part of man must follow so much purest and brightest light as here breaks forth as if unexpectedly and so much overwhelming and yet beneficent power as here wonderfully makes itself felt.

Will Job really doubt or even deny that the Creator graciously sustains, both in the general universe as well as in the smaller human world and the special affairs of an individual godly man, the divine order—God who needs merely to speak in order to show how marvellously He sustains it and has always sustained it, who will also sustain it in this most special case, as may be inferred from most general considerations, and as He permits it plainly to appear what is in this matter His ultimate intention, only that as yet He cannot on man's account effect immediate deliverance in the way in which man desires it? Everything is here included in this double question: but as soon as the divine comes to confront in its purity the human, a disproportionate relation is thereby created, which, when the divine graciously stoops to the human, can be relieved only by means of sportive seriousness and bitter raillery. Accordingly the most suitable manner for these divine speeches is that of irony, which combines with concealed severity and calm superiority the effective and benevolent incisiveness of a higher insight, which is used as in bright sportiveness, a manner of speech which shows, without wounding or annihilating, clearly and tellingly the disproportion of the human in its onesidedness to the truly divine, of the clouded human understanding to the clear, complete wisdom, of powerless human defiance to true power. If the perfectly divine reveals itself in opposition to the limited and human, it is always like an involuntary irony in relation to the latter, even when it punishes and destroys: but in this case there is also a condescension which is really in its inmost nature of the most gracious character. The essence of the words of Jahvé lies therefore in the thought which may be expressed thus: did Job, the weak man, with his limited, confused knowledge, really mean, or does he now really mean, to defy and to charge with general unrighteousness Him who here reveals Himself as the Being that He is eternally, as not only the strict Judge but also as the wise Arranger of the Universe, as the marvellous Restorer of right, as the gracious Revealer of His Glory? So that the refutation, as supplied without any effort or much search, is incidentally interspersed and concealed in the speech itself.

If then Jahvé, although still veiled and speaking only from the storm, permits with such strict earnestness, and yet really at the same time with kindness and mercy, man so clearly and closely to glance into His inner sanctuary, how can Job in that case longer resist? The same Job that previously held his peace before no one, now, when enlightened by the higher wisdom, hardly ventures to express a few words of profound reverence of that which he has now clearly perceived and of deep regret at his previous blindness: at the same time his present timid, quiet word is not less eloquent than the full stream of his language before the divine appearance; and his acknowledgment and reverence now, after he has obtained higher knowledge, are not less sincere than formerly his indignation and displeasure at the misconception of the divine things. Job remains here precisely the same in point of human dignity and glory, only that he makes a rapid advance in knowledge of infinite value. Man ought everywhere to be prepared to be warned and taught by higher wisdom wherever it reveals itself to him in his struggles, and he also who already occupies a lofty height gladly submits to its correction, inasmuch as when it finally approaches as the prize of the struggle, it then again reacts by its light in instruction and correction. Thus the hero who is invincible in conflict with men, as he boldly seeks to come into the secret of God and contends with Him, who can be subdued by nothing in the world save God, here at last carries off, before his outward deliverance and beatification, some few remaining deep scars showing the divine superiority and correction, and suffers himself before it is too late to be admonished and led by the pure wisdom which he has bravely won.

Yet it is impossible, even for the greatest power of divine eloquence, to comprehend the entire matter within the compass of one single discourse, inasmuch as the two errors which have to be corrected in Job are of too dissimilar a nature to be recognised both at once. It is true there easily springs from the defiance, which failing to perceive the divine way imagines it may contend with God and challenge His appearance, the second transgression of murmuring at supposed injustice in the personal affairs of the sufferer himself as well as in the whole world: nevertheless before this special error can be destroyed, the previous more general and injurious one must be got rid of. Thus two speeches are here required from Jahvé:

a. JAHVÉ AND JOB THE FIRST TIME.

CH. XXXVIII. 1—XL. 5.

Will Job defy God, as he has already so long called for His appearance? Well then, He who has so long been missed is now at hand, in order to contend with Job according to his desire! But if he will really, as he imagined he could do, dispute with Him, that is know and do more than God, then let him show his power to do so! let him show that eternity, that power, and that wisdom, which God possesses, and into which He now here grants man a glance in order to show him how little he possesses them, he the creature, who is surrounded by limitations and knows so little!—Accordingly in the chief section of the speech, xxxviii. 4—xxxix. 30, everything of the most wonderful kind is briefly produced, amid the most ironical questions and references taken from creation,—from the present inanimate world and from the animal world,—that can not only reveal to man his limitation and compel him to look beyond himself and acknowledge in his astonishment many other powers and worlds which another being than himself must sustain, but also fills him with admiration of the order and wisdom which prevail there as everywhere; while at the same time it is admirably remarked incidentally, how by the divine order of creation human wrong is always cancelled, xxxviii. 13—15, 23.

We have here the first endeavours to take a general survey of creation and nature in detail, both as regards its extent and inward laws: and if here not a few things appear as wonderful which come before us already in a fuller light, it must not be forgotten that the element of miracle only retreats from the nearer spheres to baffle all enquiry in the more distant ones. The poet's century was one of the earliest in which such questions were put to the world of nature and general descriptions of nature were attempted; above in the contention between the mortal disputants similar series of pictures have been made, ch. v., ix., xii., xxv., xxvi.: yet the description which has been reserved for this place surpasses in point of affluence, vividness and surprising effect all former ones to the extent to be expected when it is the Lord of the world Himself who speaks. And inasmuch as the important point here is, that Job shall for the first time come to the complete knowledge of God and the acknowledgment of his own guilt, this first speech is made of almost disproportionate length, as, in fact, there is scarcely any end of the various matters which can here be brought forward: yet if the description of the world is intentionally presented in such a full stream that the commencement of the speech is almost forgotten in its progress, the speech at last naturally gathers itself up once more in a more brief and powerful close, xl. 2.

xxxviii. 1 Then answered Jahvé Job speaking from the storm and said:

> Who is this that darkeneth counsel
>   with words without knowledge?
> Gird now as a hero thy loins, that I may ask thee!
>   and declare thou unto me!
>
> Where wast thou when I laid the foundation of the earth?
>   make it known, if thou knowest to be wise!

xxxviii. 1: *from the tempest*, in which he approached, in a terrible form though veiled, nearer the earth, as from afar thundering, quite audible to the ear and visible to the eye in His terribly bright covering, yet still all the time veiled and not appearing in a bodily shape. This addition is wanting in the short second remark of resumption xl. 1, but properly recurs again before the second speech xl. 6.

1. xxxviii. 2, 3. The very first words with which this Speaker announces Himself, pierce with decisive severity all the previous speeches of Job: as in anger seeking the unclear speaker, He enquires as He approaches: *Who is this that darkeneth counsel by foolish words?* it is therefore intimated that in the entire affair of Job, it is not accident, but the well-considered, clear counsel, or plan, of God which prevails, namely, as we know from ch. i—ii., the plan to test Job's faithfulness, a plan which Job is so far from having discovered and brought to light that he has more and more darkened it by thoughts and words which are in this respect quite wrong. Still, he shall not be condemned unheard; now the desired time is come to contend with God and to defy Him: let him get ready to answer the questions to be proposed!

2. xxxviii. 4—xxxix. 30. This magnificent portion of the speech is worked out in six very long strophes of twelve verses each [1], in such a way that the first half is confined to the creation and apparently inanimate world, while the second passes to the wonders of the animal world. The questions begin

(1) xxxviii. 4—15 with the creation itself, accordingly primarily once more with the most magnificent and marvellous things in the creation of the earth,

---

[1] The fact that of the six strophes, according to the present text, there are wanting in the third and the fourth one verse each, and in the fifth two verses, proves nothing against the original law of the structure, since from xxxviii. 28 onwards the crowded thoughts are presented in such a detached manner that one or another verse might easily be very early omitted, *e.g.*, before ver. 30.

5 Who set its measures, that thou shouldest know?
or who stretched over it the line?
whereupon were sunk its foundations?
or who cast its corner-stone,
when the morning-stars rejoiced together,
all Sons of God shouted for joy;
and then shut in the sea with doors?
when from the mother's womb it came bursting forth,
when I gave it clouds as its garment,
thick-fog as its swaddling-clothes;
10 and brake for it my bound,
set bars and doors,
said: "hitherto comest thou—and no further!
here be stayed the pride of thy waves!"—

vv. 4—11, which is here described with that freedom which every poet, and particularly one of older times, may claim. Where was Job, the man of yesterday, in that primæval time of the foundation of the earth? ver. 4. Was *he* perhaps engaged in its foundation, or God, that he should know everything by personal experience? and upon what basis and space (xxvi. 7) was then the immense edifice of the earth, which itself bears all human edifices, from the very first assigned its dimensions and built—when as yet not ordinary mortals could rejoice (Zech. iv. 7) over its foundation and the commencement (usually in the morning) of the new erection, but the Morning-stars and the Angels, which answer to these bright bodies (i. 6, xxv. 5), jubilated in their innumerable ranks? vv. 5—7; or was it *he* who took the next step in creation—separated the mighty, restless sea from the Chaos and directed it within its established boundaries, Gen. i. 9, 10,—at that time when it was just born (יצא continuation of בגיחו, acc. § 346 *b*), was surrounded with clouds which still encircle it, like a newborn child with swaddling clothes, and when it received its established, unsurpassable boundaries, so that it can never bring back again the old Chaos, as also in human affairs such firm eternal limitations have been fixed which pride and defiance can never break through! vv. 8—11. *Broken bounds*, ver. 10, on account of the rent, broken, rugged shores of the sea, ῥηγμίν; שית ב, ver. 11, might seem to signify *to put a stay to*, and פא would then be used again as a subject: *here* = *this place*, the shore, § 294 *a*. If this construction appears too hard, we might read with the LXX, comp. ver. 15, יִשָּׁבֵר גְּא *here shall be broken the pride of thy waves*, or perhaps still better יִשְׁתֹּק *shall be hushed*, comp. *Jahrbb. der Bibl. Wiss.* IV. p. 64.—As now the first morning of creation had just been spoken of, vv. 5—7, when the rosy light of dawn for the first time illuminated the earth, the transition to the long survey of the present world is suitably made thereby that mention is now first

Hast thou, as long as thou hast lived, ordered the morning,
  appointed its place to the dayspring,
that it should seize the tips of the earth,
  and the wicked flee from it alarmed?
the earth is changed like seal-clay,
  its tips become light as a garment:
15 and from the wicked their light is kept back,
  the proud arm is broken.

Camest thou unto the torrents of the sea,
  walkedst thou in the bottom of the deep?
stood the gates of death open to thee,
  and the gates of darkness seest thou?

made of the wonderful nature of the perpetual return of the new morning, vv. 12—15. Of the dawn there are two things to be said: first, it returns everyday from eternity always in its appointed place: now has perhaps Job, the short-lived man, since his days, as long as he has lived (and how short is this moment of time!) commanded it to that place, just as God during His eternity? Second, it chases away the wicked, like every light, always every day afresh, so that they must hide themselves or be discovered, and is thus a symbol of the eternal flight and destruction of dark, unrighteous men before God; and how rapidly and marvellously this transformation takes place! on higher command the dawning light seizes in a moment the outspread wings of the earth, the mountains in the west and east; the earth changes its entire form as rapidly and easily as the seal-clay changes the forms which are impressed upon it (comp. Layard's *Discoveries* pp. 608 sq.), whilst its wings, or skirts, become shining like a garment[1]: and in a moment the wicked are aghast, inasmuch as *their* light, the darkness (xxiv. 14—17), is taken from them by a higher power!

(2) and (3). The infinitely varied objects of the world are taken up in turn, and in the first instance objects from the inanimate world: and of this class of objects it is, on the one hand, secret places and ways, xxxviii. 16—27, and on the other, vv. 28—38, unusual transformations and variations, in which their wonderful nature, pointing man to a divine wisdom above him, is specially revealed. And inasmuch as the speech had risen from the creation of the earth to the description of the sublime dawn, now, in order to continue to connect

[1] Instead of יתיצבו which would have to be understood according to i. 6, ii. 1, יתיבצו must be read, or rather must be so understood (since it does not occur again in the poetical part of the book of Job, except in the later pieces xxxiii. 5, xli. 2) from وبض = בוק, but رصف also is probably originally the same.

didst thou overlook the breadths of the earth?
declare it, if thou knowest it all!—
Which is the way where light dwelleth,
darkness—where is its place?
20 that thou shouldst take it to its boundary,
that thou shouldst know the paths of its house!
thou knowest! for then thou wast born,
the number of thy days is many!—
Camest thou to the storehouses of the snow,
and seest thou the chambers of the hail?
which I have reserved for time of distress,
for the day of battle and war.—
Which is the way where light parteth itself,
storm bursteth from the east over the earth?
25 who hath cleft a path for the waterspout,
a way for the thunderflash?

together the greatest contrasts, it descends first to the wonderful depths of the sea, vv. 16, 17, ascends thence again to the wonderfully extensive surface of the earth, ver. 18, in order then to dwell longer upon the wonderful ways and localities of the heavens, vv. 19—27. With vv. 16, 17 comp. xxvi. 5, 6. נבכי might be explained as *torrents*, from נבך == בוך *to be entangled, confused:* but there is greater probability, acc. Gen. vii. 11, viii. 2, for the πηγαὶ of the LXX, from נבך == נבע. In the case of the numerous celestial marvels, vv. 19—27, as in the case of vv. 12—15, light is again made the commencement, which seems to have its place in the infinite spaces *beyond* the arch of heaven and to come thence like the mysterious darkness by secret ways over the earth, vv. 19—21: knoweth Job perhaps the way where (see § 332*a*) it dwelleth, where it can be got at, that he could take it at his pleasure to its boundary (לקח אל Gen. xlviii. 9) and retain it in its proper sphere or carry it further off? certainly he knows it; for he is undoubtedly as old as the light, which streams over the earth ever since the creation! comp. ver. 12. There above the celestial arch appear to be also the hidden store-houses of snow and hail, these strange weapons of heaven for the destruction of the evil on the earth, vv. 22, 23, comp. Jos. x. 11; Ps. xviii. 13, 14; lxviii. 14, 15. Then that which comes to the earth making its way *through* the celestial arch is dwelt upon, vv. 24—27: light, storm, rain, lightning when they descend must divide the firmament, but does Job know where they break through it? who, he or God, has cleft the way for these wonderful heavenly objects—in order that not merely proud man and what belongs to him, but also the most desolate districts of the earth may enjoy the blessing from above? It is a chief point in the teaching of this speech, by which human pride is to be bowed, that the bene-

to bring rain upon uninhabited land,
the wilderness, where are no men,
to satisfy wasteness and desolation,
and to cause to spring forth the germ of green shoots.

Hath the rain a father,
or who hath begotten dew-drops?
from whose womb sprung the ice,
hoar-frost of heaven—who hath brought it forth?
30 having become like a stone, water is hidden,
and the face of the deep cleaveth firmly together.—
Bindest thou the fetters of the Pleiades,
or loosest thou the bands of Orion?
dost thou bring forth the Crown of the North in time,
guidest thou the Bear with its sons?

factions of the creation are not alone for man, and that he must everywhere discover traces of a Creator whose care extends far beyond him, comp. how ancient Arabic Poets of the Desert insist on similar truths, Hamâsa pp. 785—87.—But the last-named celestial objects naturally conduct further to the mention of numerous equally wise and wonderful transformations and variations in the lower inanimate world, vv. 28—38. Have rain, dew, ice and hoar-frost, so suddenly appearing as if by secret transformations, perhaps a human originator or father, that a man like Job could produce them at his pleasure—those marvels which unborn come into existence in a moment, that (particularly in Palestine) strange phenomenon, according to which flowing water becoming by frost firm as a stone entirely hides itself or loses itself by becoming indistinguishable. *In* and *under* the vault of heaven, finally, appear stars, further clouds and fiery phenomena, all moving marvellously and yet in order in obedience to a superhuman will, vv. 31—38.—The names of the four stars which are here mentioned by preeminence, three of which were previously, ix. 9, more briefly referred to, are in part obscure; most plain is ver. 31: *bindest thou* the bands of the Seven Stars, a compact group of stars, as it were bound together, so that this constellation always appears exactly thus? *or loosest thou Orion's fetters*, so that this foolish giant of the Underworld, bound to the heaven, at times comes nearer in the firmament, as if he had been unloosed? comp. on Orion C. O. Müller in the *Rheinisches Museum für Philol.*, vol. II. Ver. 32 מזרות is more difficult. The Targ. and many modern interpreters explain the word as a corruption of מזלות *the signs of the Zodiac*, 2 Kings xxiii. 5: however, the change of ל into ר in the poet of this book is difficult to accept, and here only a single constellation appears to be more suitable in conjunction with the other individual ones; it is better probably

dost thou know the ordinances of heaven,
  or settest thou its rule in the earth?—
Liftest thou to the cloud thy voice,
  that floods of water cover thee?
35 thou sendest forth lightnings and they go,
  they say to thee: "behold here we are!"
who put wisdom in celestial appearances?
  or who gave understanding to heavenly phenomena?
who numbereth the clouds with wisdom?
  causeth the pitchers of heaven to empty themselves?
when the dust poureth itself into molten-work,
  clods cleave to one another.

therefore to understand the stars of the Northern and those of the Southern Crown, from נֵזֶר *crown*, see Eichhorn's *Bibl. Biblioth.*, vol. VII. p. 415; Notices et Extr. t. XII. pp. 249, 268; Transact. Asiat. Soc. of Lond. vol. II. pp. 381, 391. עיש, as may with certainty be assumed, is only the fuller, original form of עש ix. 9: the latter has recently, according to Michælis *Supplementa*, p. 1901, been generally regarded as standing for the Great Bear, inasmuch as Niebuhr heard this name amongst the Arabs: however, it is still uncertain whether he did not mistake *âsch* for *nâsch* نعش; according to our passage, where the guiding of the ʿ*aisch* together with its young ones is spoken of, *capella* and the guide of the goat with the young ones (Eichhorn's *Bibl. Biblioth.* vol. VII. p. 429; *Transact. of the Asiat. Soc. of Lond.* vol. II. p. 382, comp. p. 379) might perhaps be thought of, so that ʿ*aisch* is merely a dialectical form of עֵז: it is probably, however, the most easy thing to think here of the *Lion*, so that its cubs are the خراتان (see Eichhorn's *Bibl. Biblioth.* VII. p. 464) for عايث or عيوث is the lion, and the Pesh. has probably in ܥܝܘܬܐ the same word. Still this would only be another name for the Great Bear: for that this most resplendent star is intended, cannot well be doubted. It may be gathered from the context that ver. 36 still refers to the things of the heavens; and if שכוי, formed acc. § 173*f*, can undoubtedly signify a *phenomenon*, טחות must be derived, with a kindred meaning, from טח = צח, ܨܚ, ضح, صوح, which roots express the brightest radiance or ray: whilst from the signification of shining, appearance, it can also denote the imagination, *i.e.*, thought, Ps. li. 8.—In that the phenomena, lightning and others, execute the divine will, as was just before said vv. 34, 35, they seem themselves to be endowed with wisdom and understanding, no less than living creatures; whence, in fact, the mythology of many other nations regards them as divine beings. But in the case of the Hebrews, there is always a Higher One above them, who acc. vv. 37, 38 with wisdom, in order that too much rain may never destroy the

Huntest thou prey for the lioness,
fillest the appetite of the young lions?
40 when they couch in dens,
sit in the thicket in ambush.
Who provideth the raven its prey,
when its young cry unto God,
xxxix. wander without food?—
1 Knowest thou when rock-chamois bring forth,
the giving birth of the hinds, dost thou observe it?
countest thou the moons they fill,
knowest thus when they bring forth?
bowing themselves, they bring forth easily their young,
get rid of their pains:
their children are strong, growing in the field,
go forth—and never return again.—
5 Who hath set the wild ass free,
his bands—who hath loosed them?
him whose house I made the desert,
steppes his dwellings:
he scorneth the noise of the city,
heareth not the shouting of the driver;

earth, Gen. viii. 22, counts the pitchers of heaven, the clouds, even when the rain is the strongest, when the dust becomes fluid and again firm, in some such way as molten-work changes its form,

(4—6) xxxviii. 39—xxxix. 30. Of the animals by preference wild ones only are chiefly distinguished, inasmuch as their life, preservation and peculiar nature most of all remind man of the fact that beside himself there are many, strange, and marvellous beings at work. Thus first the lion and raven, which also receive their food without any assistance from man, xxxviii. 39—41; as likewise chamois and hinds, xxxix. 1—4, bring forth their young without man caring for them as he does for the domesticated animals, and yet they bear very easily, and yet their young grow up most vigorously, quickly establishing new families! If these animals show that they do not need the help and care of man, the three following, xxxix. 5—19, prove that man, as he is at present, is unable even to subjugate all the animals and conduct them at his pleasure, inasmuch as some have a marvellous dislike of human society and servitude. The wild ass, called פרא or ערוד, has an extraordinary love of freedom, in the most desolate places of the earth, implanted in him by the Creator, so that he despises the noise of the city and of the drivers of the tame asses, content with

exploreth mountains, his pasture,
  searcheth after every green thing.

Will the wild buffalo consent to serve thee,
  or lodge the night in thy stall?
10 bindest thou him by the rope in the furrow,
  or will he harrow valleys following thee?
trustest thou to him, because his strength is great,
  committest thy toil to him?
believest thou him, that he will bring thy seed,
  gather-in thy threshing-floor?—
The wing of those she-ostriches, beating joyfully,
  is it a kind pinion and feather?

the scantiest nourishment (instead of יְתוּר, ver. 8, "*the surplus* of the mountains is his pasture", it is better on account of the context and the verb ידרוש to read יָתוּר, LXX κατασκέψεται), comp. Robert Ker Porter's *Travels in Georgia Persia* etc., part. I. p. 550, Germ. Trans.; Layard's *Nineveh* I. p. 324 sq., II. p. 429 f., *Discoveries* p. 270.—In the next strophe, xxxix. 9—18, two marvels from the animal world only, more exalted and wonderful things being successively brought forward, are treated of. The wild animal, called *Reém*, externally so similar to the ox, in spite of his similarity with the domesticated ox, and notwithstanding that his immense strength would make him suitable for it, will never consent to serve man, nor will man make the attempt to use in agriculture such an untamable, dangerous animal, for which purpose he can use only tame, reliable creatures! (Ver. 10*a bindest thou him in the furrow of his rope*, in the furrow which he shall make by following his rope). The wild buffalo, which is now called جاموس *G'âmûs*, is probably not meant thereby, which John Wilson (*Lands of the Bible*, II. 167 sq.) supposes that he found by the Lake el Hule in a too weak and tame condition, but a strong species of antilope, similar in appearance to the ox, the *Oryx* of the Greeks, to which also the name *Reém* points.[1]

In the case of the next still more wonderful animal, the ostrich, or rather the ostrich hen, the description almost loses sight of its commencement, vv. 13—18: so profoundly does the speaker apparently, and with him still more the hearer, become absorbed in the wide, inexhaustible subject. How marvellously

[1] To what extent the μονοκέρως of the LXX has now actually been found in Africa, or even in Asia, is notwithstanding all the assurances even of Fresnel still matter of uncertainty: see *Comptes rendus de l'acad. des Sciences*, 1848, p. 281; *Ausland*, 1849, pp. 639 sq., 1853, p. 742; *Allg. Zeit.*, 1853, p. 4684; also *Catalog. cdd. aeth. Mus. Brit.*, p. 56.

that she leaveth her eggs to the earth,
  upon the dust maketh them warm:
15 and forgetteth that the foot trampleth them,
  wild beasts crush them,
hard against her children, as if not her own,
  frustrating her toil, without fear!
because God hath caused her to forget wisdom,
  hath not imparted to her understanding.
When she once lifteth herself on high,
  she scorneth the horse and his rider.

Givest thou to the horse strength,
  clothest thou his neck with trembling?
20 makest thou him rattle like locusts?
  the splendour of his snorting how terrible!

does the mother ostrich appear, contrary to the feeling of all other animals and of men, to act towards her eggs, which, in an unkindly and also foolish way, as if they were not her fruit which she had brought forth with toil, she carelessly leaves to the earth and to be trampled on by the foot of man and beast! (comp. *Hamâsa*, p. 374, ver. 1, with the *scholia*) certainly man, if it had been his work to create the ostrich, would not have created it with this peculiarity which seems so hard to explain: therefore, let men understand the divine work, the truth that in addition to man there exists much that is wonderful reminding him of a higher rule! ver. 17. Inasmuch as the wing is the strongest weapon of the ostrich, with which it violently smites everything that assails it, and with the help of which it flies, ver. 18, the description begins thus: the wing of the ostrich, which is moved joyfully, is it then, is it perhaps (אם as interrogative particle, § 324 *c*), a kind pinion and feather? as the storch, so careful for its young, is called emphatically the kind one, חסידה, Ps. civ. 17, which is here alluded to; and inasmuch as the fem. is used throughout, it is better to read הַקְשִׁיחַ, inf. abs., acc. § 280 *a*, instead of הִקְשִׁיחַ, ver. 16. Yet a second marvellous thing is, that this great cumbrous creature, if it once lifts itself up, tries to fly, gets away with the greatest rapidity, mocking both horse and rider that pursue it, ver. 18 (כָּעֵת *at the time* Judg. xx. 22, relatively used *then when* ἐπειδή, Num. xxiii. 23, § 337 *c*).—Thus ver. 18 makes the transition to the horse, as the horse and the ostrich can really in a certain respect be compared with each other as similar: but much more powerful than the picture of the ostrich is that of the horse, vv. 19—25, of the war-horse, namely, a rare animal in the hills of Palestine, which Arabic poets also describe in rivalry with each other, and call the *opus artis* صنعة of the Almighty (Koseg. *Chrest. Arab.* p. 81; comp. Virg. *Georg.* iii. 73—90; Layard's *Discoveries* p. 330):

men spy forth in the valley, he rejoiceth at his strength,
advanceth to meet the arms,
mocketh at fear and trembleth not,
turneth not back before the sword;
above him rattle arrows,
flaming spears and lances;
rattling, rushing he drinketh up the ground,
standeth not when the trumpet soundeth;
25 as often as it soundeth, "hui!" he crieth,
and from afar scenteth he war,
the thunder of princes and battle-cry.—
According to thy understanding soareth the hawk,
spreadeth his wings out toward the south?
according to thy word mounteth the eagle,
building also his nest on high?
rocks he occupieth, and lodgeth
upon the peak of rock and the castle:
from thence he descrieth food,
far off pierce his eyes;
30 and his young suck up blood,
and wherever the slain are, there is he.

wonderfully magnificent is his strength, his mane, the roar and rattle of his gallop, resembling the roar made by locusts' as they leap (Joel ii. 4), his snorting, vv. 19, 20 (ver. 20*b* is like an exclamation of astonishment); still the most marvellous thing is that he has even still greater courage in battle than man, whilst the warriors still in the valley of the battle are delaying and taking observations, he is then already unable to await the moment of attack, running in the midst of deadly missiles or spears in the most daring haste, as if he drank and tore up the ground (نهب الارض *rapit terram*, Koseg. *Chrest.* p. 80, penult.), and as often as ever the trumpet sounds and the battle can be scented from afar, he is always afresh equally as eager!

After this description has thus occupied the largest portion of the entire last strophe, the strophe gently approaches its close, and vv. 26—30 it is only a few kinds of great birds of prey which form the conclusion. In these birds the wonderful thing is partly their instinct in certain seasons of the year to migrate to the South, partly their daring habit of making their nests on the highest crags and the barest mountain-peaks, from whence again nevertheless they peer through the lowest plains with piercing eye, and wherever any prey is, there they suddenly assemble with their young that drink up blood greedily! The xl. 1. And Jahvé answered Job and said:

Contend with the Almighty will he, the upbraider?
he that called God to account, let him answer!

And Job answered Jahvé and said:

Insignificant am I: what shall I answer Thee?
my hand I have laid upon my mouth.
Once I spoke—and do it not again;
and twice even—yet not another time!

כי in וכי, ver. 27 *b*, depends on על פיך: *and* is it at thy command, *that he* builds his nest on high? עֲלַלּ acc. § 118 *a* shortened from עלעל, root عل *to drink*, a formation which frequently occurs in Aramaic.

3. xl. 1—2. The last picture of the birds of prey is still very wonderful, but not so surprising as the previous ones. By it the description of the wonders of the world has gradually been brought to a certain repose. Still precisely through the multitude of these wonders and through the necessity here for the first time of representing emphatically and exhaustively the divine Being who is at work in them, the speech has almost lost sight of the point from which it started, and almost put Job's case out of view; so generally might these questions and this line of proof concern all men, and so naturally must man become wholly absorbed in hearing the divine discourse whenever it becomes audible. Therefore Jahvé reverts, as if beginning afresh, to Job, ver. 1, and closes with severe brevity, ver. 2: *contend with the Almighty*, as thus described and thus to be known, *will the upbraider?* will the disputatious reprover really deliberately, and after he has been warned and the true relation has been pointed out to him, continue further the contention which was at first begun in haste? let him declare himself on this point! *he* who previously *called God to account, let him answer it*, why he is now asked, whether he intends really to contend and show defiance? רֹב after § 328 *a*.

The answer of Job's, xl. 4, 5, as might be expected, is in the negative, under the influence of the new knowledge which he has gained: he will and must be silent as a man before the God whom he has now more clearly known; and if formerly he dared once, yea, carried away by his confusion and perplexity, even twice and oftener (Ps. lxii. 12) to speak against God, he will now take care not to do so again! This answer is no less brief, and by brevity eloquent, than completely adequate precisely at this point, since he is as yet not at all called upon nor entitled to answer more.

b. JAHVÉ AND JOB THE SECOND TIME.

CH. XL. 6—14, XLII. 1—6.

If Job had not thus placed himself once more with full consciousness in the true relation to God as regards the world generally, every further explanation with regard to a particular question would be impossible in his case: but now after the first of the two errors from which he suffered, see pp. 59 sq., as the most general and therefore universally injurious has been overcome, the second also may be the more easily removed, which concerns most closely and directly the matter itself which forms the central point of this entire contention. Jahvé can by continuing His speech approach more closely to the matter itself. Job had failed to perceive the righteousness of God in the whole world as well as most immediately and most undeniably in his own case: the whole of his calamity properly centres in this question. When he expressed, now loudly then faintly, despair of the manifestation of this righteousness, he put himself in opposition to it: he did not live under its laws and influence, but was always in danger of not only himself straying ever further from it, but also of leading others astray by his speeches. For it is only the man that seeks to make an ever closer acquaintance with the divine righteousness and to keep it more and more firmly, who will in return be kept by it; whilst the man that resists it, condemns God in order that he may be deemed righteous according to his own idea. Accordingly Job, for the second time summoned to the conflict, is here asked, whether he will really resist it, disannul it? And in this case the speech of Jahvé may dispense instruction in the fewest words: to what end proofs from beyond the sphere immediately concerned—the world of men and history,—inasmuch as the entire case of Job's turns upon this axis, and inasmuch as soon there can be given, in Job himself, the most illustrious example of divine justification! The brief, ironical challenge is here the most telling: let Job, then, if he is serious with his speeches against the divine righteousness, himself as judge rule the world with the power which is required, destroying for ever everything evil and—help himself by his own power!—just as, when the matter is looked at more closely, God ever destroys what is evil, on the other hand, is always ready to help all the faithful, amongst whom it is to be hoped Job is to be found.

The answer of Job cannot be doubtful: pervaded most deeply by the feeling of the folly of the human endeavour to oppose God and His righteousness, enlightened as well as quivering from the brightness of God who has now appeared, he declares the deepest, sincerest repentance, solemnly revoking everything that he had spoken in haste and folly in his previous condition of perplexity and darkness.

xl. 6 Then answered Jahvé Job speaking from the storm and said:

Gird up now as a hero thy loins!
  I will question thee; declare thou to Me:
Wilt thou also break My justice,
  condemn Me, that thou mayst be righteous?
Or hast thou an arm like God,
  wilt thou thunder as loud as He?—
10 Deck thyself now with majesty, exaltation,
  and in splendour and glory clothe thyself!
scatter forth the inflictions of thy wrath,
  behold everyone that is proud and humble him!

xlviii. 8: whoever fails to find, or even goes so far as to deny, the divine righteousness, and accordingly invites and invokes the opposite of it, he does not promote and establish it, but seems to seek to *break* it, to annul it, putting his own folly and unrighteousness in its place; and if Job has not in his previous life sinned, still he permitted himself in his sufferings to be carried away by an actual transgression precisely through this doubt of the divine righteousness, the danger of which transgression is here destroyed at the commencement for his advantage. Or has perhaps Job, if he will oppose God's righteousness, the means of executing his own imagined righteousness? Well, then, let him assume the full prerogatives of God when He reveals Himself as judge, ver. 10,

behold everyone that is proud, abase him!
cast down the wicked to the ground,
hide them in the dust together,
make fast their face in darkness:
then will *I* also praise thee,
that thy right hand helpeth thee!

xlii. 1 And Job answered Jahvé and said:

I know that Thou art all-powerful,
to Thee no thought is impossible.—
"Who is he that darkeneth counsel without knowledge?"
therefore I gave utterance—yet without understanding,
things too wonderful for me—without knowledge!

scatter abroad over the earth his punishments, and behold all that are proud and wicked upon the broad earth, that he may so cast the unrighteous (to whom Job may belong, if he continues in his present course) into the dust and into the Underworld, that they never venture again to lift up their faces?

xlii. 2—6. If Job makes the prefatory remark, ver. 2, that nothing is impossible to God, but that everything that He thinks becomes at the same time act, he cannot mean thereby, that what is contrary to the divine nature is also possible to Him; but simply, that whatever is in God conceivable and possible, that when thought by Him is at the same time done. To this, however, belongs also the punishment of the wicked as well as the redemption of the righteous; and in that Job thus expresses the general truth that in God exists the only true power, he thereby indicates that precisely He alone possesses that power spoken of, to destroy constantly unrighteousness in human affairs and to reestablish the right (to remove Job's calamities also), since, indeed, generally the omnipotence of God in relation to the confusion of human relations in the present world is limited by His righteousness, and neither of them can be conceived without the other. Therefore the brief utterance ver. 2 in reality contains the complete, appropriate answer to the address of God, xl. 9—14, in which perfect righteousness had just been thus connected with omnipotence; and vv. 3—6 there follows strictly nothing but the declaration of repentance for all that had been previously unwisely uttered. But this is not a cold, still less a forced declaration: on the contrary, because the divine revelation and appearance has most profoundly affected his inmost being and kindled in the most influential manner a purer light and established in him a new spiritual life, on this account he is urged by everything to repentance. Accordingly he declares briefly how indelibly and with what great consequences the mighty words of Jahvé make themselves felt: Jahvé designated him from the beginning as without true knowledge, xxxviii. 2; and in reality he has now

"Come, hear Me, and I will speak;
  I will question thee, declare thou to Me!"
5 As the ear heareth, I had knowledge of Thee;
  but now hath mine eye seen Thee:
therefore I revoke and repent
  in dust and ashes!

recognised himself as such an one, and does not shrink from the confession that he previously spoke foolishly regarding the enigma which was too difficult and wonderful for him, ver. 3; Jahvé challenged him to defend himself before His presence, xxxviii. 3, xl. 7: but after he has now with his own eyes seen God close at hand, of whom he had before only heard from a distance, and has perceived His true majesty and glory, ver. 5, there remains for him nothing but the most profound repentance. The antithesis of *hearing* and *seeing*, ver. 5, is frequent, xxviii. 22; xxix. 11; Ps. xlviii. 9; xviii. 45: *according to the hearing of the ear*, as the ear hears from a distance, without closer knowledge and personal conviction, thus *had I heard Thee*, heard Thy report, or the report of Thy truth and Thy words. Thus only have most men heard of Him, got some knowledge of Him only from a distance and dimly, have not beheld Him eye to eye and obtained immediate certainty from Him Himself.

3. JOB'S DELIVERANCE AND EXALTATION.

CH. XLII. 7—17.

Job has arrived at the happy knowledge and the voluntary confession, that the divine holiness and righteousness has remained unviolated and will eternally remain so, not only everywhere else but also in his own case. Thus those two errors, which had darkened the pure, true knowledge, have been removed, and with them finally the fundamental error, that sufferings are as such consequences and signs of the divine wrath; and there remains nothing further than the eternal love and mercy on the part of God, on the part of man free access opened to it as to deliverance from his sufferings. Now, in such a case as that of Job's, where previous sins have not to be first punished, the salvation which is inwardly possible can even at once become an outward deliverance from all calamities, since for the sufferer who has arrived at this higher perception, suffering is no longer regarded as wrath and punishment, and has accordingly lost its dark, terrible power. Thus, therefore, Jahvé is here at last prepared immediately to deliver the brave sufferer from all outward sufferings, and thereby to seal the truth on earth, that the innocent man may indeed suffer, but must also certainly triumph, if he is neither provoked to defiance nor to rebellious discontent but only becomes stronger and more conscious of his true self by his sufferings. Yet before this deliverance is carried out, judgment must first be passed upon the three friends. This judgment can be brief. Against their better knowledge, they proceeded on the supposition of Job's previous sin, relying upon this supposition they assailed Job and even cruelly treated him: therefore they, who previously desired to present intercession for Job, shall now on the contrary appeal to Job for his intercession on their behalf: wherewith Jahvé both gives to the friends the deserved humiliation and to Job the opportunity to take his revenge on them in the noblest manner. After that Job has thus by such forgiveness and intercession for the enemy given the first finest proof of his higher life, and thus appears before men and God as wholly pure and blameless, his deliverance immediately follows. But not this only, but also at the same time his exaltation. For whoever goes forth out of his sufferings as conqueror in such a way, can go forth from them only with higher gain, as having become twice as powerful and prosperous; as this is here described in detail, corresponding with the former description. And since thus, after the great, weighty truth and teaching of the piece has been clearly unfolded from all points of view, everything hastens to the necessary end, there appears here again as at the commencement a piece of simple narrative.

xlii. 7 And it came to pass after Jahvé had spoken these words
to Job, that Jahvé spake to Eliphaz the Temanite: "my anger
is enkindled against thee and against thy two friends, because
ye have not spoken of me sincerely like my servant Job;
8 so then taking to you seven bullocks and seven rams, go ye
to my servant Job and present an offering for yourselves,
and Job my servant shall pray for you: only to him will I
have respect, not to deal with you according to your folly,
that ye spoke not of me sincerely like my servant Job."
9 Then went Eliphaz the Temanite, Bildad the Shuhite, and
Zophar the Naamathite, and did as Jahvé had spoken to
10 them; and Jahvé had respect to Job.—But Jahvé restored Job
whilst he prayed for his friends; and Jahvé added to all the
11 possessions of Job twofold. And there came to him all his
brethren and all his sisters with all his former acquaintances,
and ate with him bread in his house, and condoled with him
and comforted him over all the evil which Jahvé had brought

Vv. 7—10. Eliphaz appears, with propriety, altogether as the representative of the other friends; since he had first spoken against Job, he must also be the first to humble himself. *Sincerely*, namely as regards the chief point upon which everything here depends: whether Job is innocent or not on account of his calamities; if they had not yielded to outward appearances and fear, if they had made pure sincerity to prevail, they would have been obliged to say with Job, that calamity comes from God in cases where there is no guilt, comp. ch. xiii.: and thus they committed a נבלה, ii. 10, *folly*, by denying calmly and deliberately the divine truth, and this ought to be punished as intentional sin before God; yet He will have regard to Job's intercession, *not to execute on them folly*, *i.s.*, the punishment which would answer to such folly, as עון and many words for sin denote also the punishment which is connected with the sin. As to כי אם see § 356.—If שבית in the phrase ver. 10 really signified *captivity*, as if God had turned this from Job, the figure might be chosen and appear tolerably appropriate after vii. 12, xii. 14, xiii. 27, as overwhelming sufferings hold a man as in prison. However, the entire phrase has another meaning, which is here also more appropriate, according to the discussion in the *Jahrbb. der Bibl. Wiss.* V. p. 217; and here it is only the restoration of Job's health which is primarily intended by it.[1] Yet before the restoration and the twofold increase

[1] If the elephantiasis has not as yet been developed to its worst stage, a recovery is at all events not impossible, see the work quoted *ante* p. 282, p. 344 sq.

upon him; and each one gave him a heavy coin and a gold-
12 ring.—But Jahvé blessed Job's latter life more than his early
life, and he received fourteen thousand sheep, six thousand
camels, a thousand yoke of oxen and a thousand she-asses.
13 And he received a line of seven sons, and three daughters;
14 and the name of the one was called "Dove", of the second
15 "Cassia", of the third "Pigment-box", as there were not found
women so fair as Job's daughters in the whole land; and their
father gave them an inheritance in their brethren's midst.—
16 And Job lived after this a hundred and forty years and saw his
17 sons and grandsons through four generations: then Job died
old and satisfied with life.

of Job's former prosperity, which can only gradually take place through a number of years, is further described, as begun ver. 10, the description, ver. 11, is inserted, how quickly and eagerly now all relatives and acquaintances, of whose absence Job had so painfully complained above, xix. 13—19, once more come to him, honouring him by word and deed, according to ancient custom also appearing with gifts before the higher magnate whose favour they now more zealously seek than before his calamities; comp. *Mahâbhâr.* II. cl. 1216 sq., 1297 sq. (vol. I. p. 352, 355); *Bhagavata Pur.* I. xii. 34, xv. 8. קשיטה, translated above only approximately by the general term *heavy coin*, is chosen as an allusion to the time of the patriarchs: the explanation belongs to Gen. xxxiii. 19.—Ver. 12 resumption of ver. 10. Though the number of the children cannot well, like that of the cattle (i. 3), be doubled, on the other hand, his domestic prosperity is the greater in that his daughters are not merely the fairest, so that the most beautiful names are accordingly given to them (ימימה is probably *the pure one,* washed, then the name of a species of dove), but also live in rarest harmony with his sons, so that their father, which seldom happened, assigned to them with the sons a special inheritance, in order that the brothers and sisters might never be separated as far as it depended on their will, comp. Num. xxvii. 8 sq., ch. xxxvi., and the *Antiquities* p. 179 (240).—Vv. 16, 17 after Gen. l. 23, xxv. 8.

It is not until it is viewed from this end that the highest thought of the book can be fully taken in, and the last words of it are still highly significant in completing the whole work. It is now first that the enigma on earth is satisfactorily solved on all sides, and a series of most important inferences and truths are presented on a backward glance at the whole from this ending. If such a blameless hero as Job suffered though innocent, how shall not other weaker men suffer more than they expected from the human point of view? and if he in early antiquity, before the beginning of a clearer revelation, was delivered only after these dangerous conflicts, because he had still to contend sorely with superstition and unbelief, ought not men of later times to avoid those rocks as they behold this example and the divine revelation which it contains, rocks on which a stronger hero than they almost suffered shipwreck? May every one in his darkness and suffering carry off by a lasting victory Job's noble reward! That reward is now easier than it was then, since Job's perilous, yet finally successful, conflict has pointed out the way to it. For if evil was able to effect so little against him even, upon whom it turned its whole force and resources, in spite of the great actual danger and the evil suspicion to which he was exposed, that God is able to rejoice over His faithful servant at the end as at the beginning, why should it necessarily overcome and destroy the man who has hardly in any case so much to suffer at one time as Job, who beholds in Job's example the purer light already revealed, and has no need, if he will only be wise, to contend so sorely as that hero! These as well as other fruitful inferences follow naturally here at the end: and what was above said of the lot of the world generally, becomes of itself plain from the clear pattern of the single case of Job.

The end therefore reverts to the beginning: the circle of ideas is completed. It cannot properly be said, that for the perfect closing of this circle of ideas the meeting of the deceived Satan and Jahvé in a celestial scene *must* follow; since in such a scene really nothing could be represented which the intelligent reader does not infer of himself from a backward glance at the whole drama. On the contrary, as in the first main section the preparation is effected principally by the purely divine suggestion and predetermination on the celestial stage, and as in the second main section the painful, weary entanglement of the question can be effected simply by a purely human contention, during the complete silence of the divine voice and apparent withdrawment of the celestial operation, so in the third the solution and reconciliation must be brought about by the meeting of God and man upon the earth, without requiring a fresh celestial scene.

One great advantage of a thorough interpretation of the book as a whole is further, that those pieces which do not belong to the original work naturally separate themselves. And in reality this is the first distinctive mark of the two pieces which have been inserted in the Book of Job, that they have no proper place and connection whatever in the structure of the constituent parts of the work, neither in the position which they now occupy, nor in any other that is conceivable. We should sooner be compelled wholly to give up the attempt to discover an interpretation than to look upon these two pieces as genuine portions of the original poem. As regards the thought and plan of the poem, according to the idea of the early poet, they are not only completely superfluous and of themselves naturally drop out of the poem, but they interfere in essential respects with its thought. And this argument from the inner meaning of the poem is supported by the more outward evidence of the language and style of these pieces. Though the language in the case of some words reminds us of that of the Book of Job, inasmuch as undoubtedly such later poets had repeatedly read the work of the earlier master, and had made certain passages particularly quite their own, yet, on the other hand, the language is elsewhere very different, full of words and phrases which are either new or foreign to the earlier work, and is already strongly tinged with Aramaisms; as is observed occasionally in passing in this volume, and might be easily shown at greater length. The style of the work has none of the elasticity, compression, combined with transparency, of the earlier work. It is, on the contrary, looser and weaker, more difficult and more prolix, and after all does not so fully express the thought in difficult passages: hence in spite of its prevailing amplitude, it is sometimes somewhat more obscure. But let it be remembered that these detractions are all relative. The remaining peculiarities follow from the special designs of these later pieces; and the piece which now stands first of the two is so long and important that the later author of it must have had a significant reason for making this interpolation. We prefer, however, to take the second piece first, because it appears, from many indications, to be of somewhat earlier date and by another author.[1]

DESCRIPTION OF THE HIPPOPOTAMUS AND OF THE CROCODILE. CH. xl. 15—xli. 26.

This piece, which forms one closely connected whole as regards matter, language, and style, has been assigned a place which is quite contrary to the meaning of the original poem. For a description of the power of God in the creation exclusive of man has its place in the speech ch. xxxviii., xxxix., but not here, since in the second speech of Jahvé's it is solely the human relation in the question of the divine righteousness which is treated of, so that it cannot be the inanimate and animal creation, or the power of God in general, which is further spoken of. Moreover, the object of the second speech of Jahvé's is attained with xl. 6—14, its close marked and clear; it is manifestly intended to be shorter than the first speech, as here there is neither the appropriate space for a

[1] I have further discussed and defended the true view of these pieces in the *Tübinger theol. Jahrbb.* 1843, pp. 740 sq. against the most recent scholars who seek again to ascribe both interpolations, particularly that which is above first explained, to the original poet.

[The most recent elaborate attempt of independent criticism to vindicate the genuineness of the Speeches of Elihu is that of Lic. Carl Budde, in his work *Beiträge zur Kritik des Buches Hiob*, Bonn, 1876. Tr.]

lengthy exposition, nor are there any plans made for supplying it. Neither is this piece connected internally by even the loosest and most slender thread with xl. 6—14; even outwardly every form of easy transition from the one piece to the other is wanting. Similarly, after the tremendous digression, which the piece would introduce at this point, we seek in vain for any such resumption of the discourse as we have xl. 1, 2.—Accordingly it might be supposed that the piece has simply been displaced, and ought properly to follow ch. xxxix. However, when it is more closely examined, it appears plainly that the piece cannot by its very nature be by our ancient poet at all, so that its externally unsuitable position in the poem is at the same time evidence of its later authorship. The rapidity, delicacy, and lightness of touch which mark the earlier descriptions of animals, ch. xxxix., are in vain looked for here: the prolixity of these two lengthy pictures, which vainly endeavour after precision and compression, is very different too even from pictures which are drawn upon the largest and most elaborate scale in ch. xxxix. Similarly, there is wanting here the sudden irony, the surprising elevation and boldness of the pictures ch. xxxviii., xxxix. Jahvé is almost wholly lost sight of here; He is felt only from afar, suddenly sending the flash of His word and the majesty of His presence: for the passages xl. 15*a*, 19*b*, xli. 2, 3, are as compared with the bright, pervading fire of ch. xxxviii., xxxix., but very weak examples of the overwhelming thunder of a divine discourse. Thus the whole piece, when compared with those earlier models, bears upon its surface the plain marks of later imitation. We find here also, when we come to details, a language which is considerably different from that of the earlier poem; and certain words and formations which this piece has in common with the earlier work (כרה על xl. 30, vi. 27; בני שחץ xxviii. 8, xli. 26; מוצק xi. 15, comp. יצוק xli. 15, 16; הִתְלַכֵּד xli. 9, xxxviii. 30; צפוּ as *part. pass.* xv. 22, comp. עָשׂוּ xli. 25, § 149 *g*) cannot be regarded as proof of the contrary, since the fact of an imitation of the earlier piece would sufficiently explain a good deal of this nature.

It might accordingly at first sight appear as if this piece had been inserted by the same later poet who likewise introduced Elihu's speeches not at the most appropriate place, as they would at all events have fitted into the poem after ch. xxviii. better than after ch. xxxi. There are in fact some things in both pieces which they have in common distinguishing them from the earlier poem, as the form of the long interrogative sentence without the interrogative part. ־הֲ, xl. 25, xxxvii. 18 (for the passage ii. 9 is from popular language). However, other things are different both as regards the details of language and the general style, which is here far colder, calmer, and more uniform than in Elihu's speeches. Moreover, a division into strophes, which cannot be discovered in those speeches (see below), is here discernible: namely, the whole piece falls into four long strophes of ten verses each [1], with a brief close. And if we are to judge from the general impression which the two pieces make upon us as regards their age, we should regard this piece describing the animal world as the earlier, which was probably added in the 7th or the beginning of the 6th century.[2]

We thus learn historically from these two pieces simply that the earlier work soon found those who admired, imitated, and enlarged it. Each of these two augmenters placed his addition to the work simply and without much art at the first place that seemed appropriate, without seeking to veil the inter-

[1] Only the second and the third would have eleven verses, which is probably of no great importance when the regularity of the piece in other respects is considered.

[2] There is probably a special proof of the somewhat earlier date of this piece in the fact that it describes xl. 25 sq. (A.V. xli. 1 sq.) the crocodile as impossible to be captured, whilst Herodotus, ii. 70, comp. Ezek. xxix. 4, xxxii. 3, observed just the contrary in Egypt.—Further, comp. regarding these two animals Ibn-Batuta in the *Journ. Asiat.* 1843, I. p. 222 sq., Rüppell's *Reisen in Nubien* (1829), p. 50—56, Wilkinson's *Manners and Customs of the Ancient Egyptians,* III. p. 68 sq.

polations by a number of smaller changes in other parts of the book. As the hippopotamus and crocodile are here very accurately described, and ch. xxxiii—xxxvii. so much is said of dethroned kings, we may most naturally suppose that both authors had been personally in Egypt, and the later of them was a descendant of the Judeans who fled with Jeremiah into Egypt, and who did not write until after the Persian rule had extended over Egypt, towards the end of the 6th century.

xl. 15 **B**ehold now Behemoth, which I created as well as thee,
which eateth grass like oxen:
behold now his strength in his loins,
his force in the sinews of his body,
he boweth his tail as if it were a cedar,
the thews of his loins are woven together,
his bones are brazen tubes,
his limb-bones like a bar of iron;
he is the first of God's works,
yet his Maker blunteth his sword:
20 for fruit the mountains present to him,
the beasts of the field all play there,
under the lotus-trees he lieth down,
in the covert of reed and fen,
the lotuses form his shady bower,
the willows of the brook surround him.
Though the river cometh with force, he trembleth not,
is careless, when the Jordan rolleth into his mouth.
Before his eyes he is captured,
with lines his nose is pierced.

1. xl. 15—24. *Behémoth* appears to be the Hebrew form of the Egyptian name for the hippopotamus, an apparently very dangerous and really almost harmless, herbivorous animal: after therefore his outward appearance, with his short tail, which is however as stiff as a cedar-branch, has been described, vv. 16—18, the point is again referred to, that his Creator has made the sword, *i.e.*, the devouring mouth, of this most wonderful animal harmless, with his well-known terrible tusks, has as it were so blunted it (נגש, comp. with نكس, نقص, ነቀሰ, which all signify the weakening and diminishing of something)

25 **D**rawest thou the Leviathan by a fish-hook,
and with a cord squeezest down his tongue?
puttest thou rushes into his nose,
borest his cheek through with a hook?
will he make much supplication to thee,
or will he speak soft words to thee?
will he make a covenant with thee,
wilt thou take him for a servant forever?
wilt thou play with him as with little birds,
and bind him even for thy maidens?
30 will partners trade about him,
will he be divided among Canaanites?
wilt thou fill with points his skin,
with a whirring harpoon his head?
put now on him thy hand,
and—think not again of war!

that it cannot do any harm, vv. 19—22; then further his power of endurance in a stream (Jordan), ver. 23, and the ease with which he can be captured, ver. 24. The words ver. 24 admit of no other meaning. It is true that recent travellers remark that this animal is very difficult to take in the water; but as the words are intended rather to describe its capture by artifice upon land, we should have first to enquire whether it was not actually caught in this way in Egypt.

2. xl. 25—xli. 26. Quite otherwise the *Livjathan*, which ancient name in this passage, unlike its usage in the earlier poet iii. 8, must denote an actual animal, namely, the crocodile: man may not imagine that he can take, tame, or sell him like a fish, xl. 25—30 [1] (*companions*, partners ver. 30 [2], that is of a trading company, *Canaanites* for Phœnicians, merchants generally): or if some one will really catch him like a fish, he shall not repeat the attempt, as even the mere sight of the monster casts him down; and how should man, who cannot even rouse this creature, lay with impunity a violating hand upon the Creator? xl. 31—xli. 3 (זְכֹר is infin., § 285 *c*, 328 *c* [3]; הקדים hostilely, as Amos ix. 10).—

---

[1] With regard to the absence of the הֲ before תמשך, ver. 25, Ewald suggests in a note to § 324 *a* of his Gramm., that it might be left out in order to make a paronomasia between this verb and the Egyptian name for the crocodile, *tmsôh* (Arab. تمساح), more evident. Tr.

[2] As Luke v. 7, 10 likewise of fishermen; comp. also *Corp. Inscr. Græc.* 4616 sq.

[3] In the later editions of his Hebrew Grammar, the author appears to treat זְכֹר as imper. conseq. § 347 *b*, comp. Dillmann's Commentary *in loco*. Tr.

xli. 1 —Behold, his hope is deceived!
is one even at the sight of him hurled down?
no daring one is there, that he should rouse him:
and *who* is he, who would plant himself before Me?
who surpriseth Me? then I will repay him:
under the whole heaven is he Mine!

His limbs will I not pass over,
the nature of his powers and manner of his structure.
5 Who uncovereth the outside of his garment,
his double jaw—who entereth?
the door of his face who openeth?
round about his teeth is terror!
Splendid are the tubes of the shields.
shut fast with a close seal,
one is joined to the other,
not a breath cometh between them,
cleaving fast one to the other,
taking hold of one another without separation!
10 His neesings make a light shine,
his eyes are like the eyelids of the dawn;
from his mouth torches go forth,
sparks of fire shoot forth;
from his nostrils proceedeth smoke
as if it were a pot blown hot with rushes,
his breath maketh red live coals,
and flame goeth forth from his mouth.

But as yet nothing has been said regarding the special characteristics of this creature, characteristics which the speaker cannot pass over in silence, ver. 4[1]: accordingly his front aspect is first described, his terrible jaws which no one likes to examine, the marvellously firm and thick scales which cover his whole body up to the mouth like a garment, his sneezing throwing out flames and his terrible breathing, so that it can be said that there is sublime power on his neck while dismay danceth before him, vv. 5—14; then his firm flesh in the

---

[1] חִין cannot stand simply as another form of חֵן, nor the latter signify any form of *beauty*, nor has *beauty* any place at all in this description: the word here answers to the previous דְּבַר and may as related to הִין *measure* denote, only somewhat more generally, the *manner* or *relation*.

Upon his neck dwelleth majesty,
 and before him danceth dismay.

15 The flaps of his flesh cleave firmly together,
 it is molten upon him, not to be moved;
his heart is molten like stone,
 molten like a nether millstone:
at his loftiness heroes are afraid,
 from wounds lost in terror;
if any one getteth to him, no sword will stand,
 nor spear, missile and coat of mail,
iron is considered as straw,
 metal as rotten wood;
20 the son of the bow doth not make him flee,
 into chaff to him slingstones are turned,
as chaff clubs are considered—
 and he laugheth at the whirring of the spear.
Beneath him are sharpest potsherds,
 he spreadeth pointed threshing-sledges upon the mire.
He maketh the deep to boil like a pot,
 the sea he maketh like an ointment-pot:
after him he causeth the path to shine,
 the deep is taken to be grey hair.

25 Nothing upon the dust can rule him,
 he which is created not to fear:

middle of his body, whilst an equally firm heart, as of cast metal, inhabits it, at the courage of which all heroes and weapons come to shame, vv. 15—21 (התחטא, ver. 17, is properly *to lose oneself*, to lose one's senses in sudden dismay); lastly, that he has underneath the most pointed, prickly skin, and lies on the ground like a pointed threshing-sledge (Isa. xxviii. 27), ver. 22, and that when he is looked at as he swims away the whole sea seems to be illuminated and agitated with bright foam, as if he used the sea as a man uses his ointment-pot, so that the sea appears to be coloured like grey hair (while the Mediterranean near Palestine and the Nile have usually a dark colour, comp. *mare canum*) vv. 23, 24. Then follows the general conclusion, vv. 25, 26.—סגור, ver. 7 *b* refers to *a*: *shut fast*, the tubes of the shields which one hath, or which have been, shut fast *with a close seal*, acc. § 294 *b*. And as the כְּ before אַגְמוֹן, ver. 12, can signify *with*, the remarks which I have made on

every high thing he seeth,
he the king over all proud beasts!

Ps. lvii. 10 in the *Jahrbb. der Bibl. Wiss.* V. p. 172 can be compared with this illustration.

These two marvellous animals have often been interpreted symbolically, and the strangest things have been imported into the description. As early as the Book of Enoch, lx. 1—10, 24, 25, this allegorical interpretation commenced, but only in the later piece of that book, which belongs really to the Noah-Book; comp. Dillmann's translation of the Book of Enoch and his commentary, and my remarks thereon in my *Abhandlung über das Buch Henokh.*

ELIHU'S SPEECHES. Ch. xxxii—xxxvii.

The consideration of the real meaning of these speeches conducts to the following view of their origin. A poet, some century or two centuries later than our author, observed in the book that many questionable, dangerous, and offensive thoughts had been uttered by Job with great force and without any hesitation, thoughts which when taken by themselves might seem really to border on blasphemy and to grievously offend every calm and sound mind. It is true that these misleading speeches of Job are completely refuted and retracted after ch. xxvii., partly by himself and partly by Jahvé's appearance, and the entire work, when viewed from its conclusion, leaves according to the intention of the ancient poet not the slightest doubt as regards the reprehensible mistake both of all unbelieving and all superstitious views of human suffering. Nevertheless undoubtedly many a reader might consider a far more deliberate, obvious, and outspoken refutation of the mistaken utterances of Job was desirable or necessary, particularly in that later age when people were generally becoming more anxiously scrupulous with regard to utterances on divine things and also began to entertain dread and fear of merely apparently dangerous expressions. Starting from this feeling the later poet sought to supply what appeared to him to be wanting in the work which in other respects was so highly admired by him; and there is no reason to doubt that he thereby rendered the marvellous work of the great poet, which was perhaps almost too lofty for the common mind, in the first instance more accessible and acceptable to his declining time. The means by which this end was to be attained could not be doubtful to him. He must introduce a fresh speaker, who, as a much wiser and closer thinker than Job and his friends, comes on the scene at the point where neither Job nor the friends know what can be further said, and who then charges the friends with their weakness and still more Job with all his errors and profane speeches: he makes the new speaker correct both the weakness of the former and the errors of the latter, and then at the same prepares as it were the way for Jahvé who appears immediately, and elaborately proves what Jahvé deems it sufficient more briefly to complete. He must ascribe to this new speaker, as the true prolocutor and interpreter of Jahvé, more than merely the highest human wisdom: he must also ascribe to him such an insurpassable ability and such overwhelming confidence in oratory, that Job, although he is not hindered by external pressure from answering, and is at first called upon several times to do so (if he can), is unable to make any reply at all, and this speaker hastens undisturbed from one victorious speech to another, delaying scarcely a few seconds before making a fresh commencement. The author could most easily introduce him as a young man, wholly unspoiled, who, although long indignant at the course the contention had taken and hardly able to contain his inspiration, had yet from youthful diffidence kept in the background, but now at length is unable any longer to keep silence.

Thus Elihu begins in his first speech, ch. xxxii., xxxiii., after the needful introduction, the proof of the truth, that man may never deem himself pure and righteous before God; in the second speech, ch. xxxiv., he proceeds to expound the truth, that notwithstanding the daring, criminal doubts of man God is always righteous and cannot be conceived of as without righteousness; and shows more briefly in his third speech, ch. xxxv., the folly of the delusive notion, that the fear of God does not bring greater profit than the contrary of it. But when the false ideas of the speeches have been in this way censured, in a fourth speech, ch. xxxvi., xxxvii., the speaker finally presents the truth in its undisturbed purity in contrast with the error, in that, thinking almost exclusively of God, and proclaiming His praise both from history and nature, he calls upon Job to acknowledge God in a like manner.

It is impossible not to see in this order of the thought a certain advance from what is close at hand and more obvious to that which is further removed, although in respect of the style of exposition and literary art, quite a different poet here presents himself. And it scarcely need be remarked, that the thoughts which are here expounded are in themselves pure and true; indeed, there are many things in this piece which have been more profoundly conceived and more strikingly presented by the later poet than in the earlier book, inasmuch as he enjoyed the help which was rendered, precisely in these reflections on divine things, by the more advanced time in which he lived: although here not a single wholly new thought occurs which cannot be found in the earlier book. The piece when taken alone on its own merits is beautiful and good: but every careful, critical attempt to regard it as included in the design of the earlier poet and as an integral portion of his work, fails in the process. It is of no use to try to find a way out of the difficulties—how it could be possible in harmony with the earlier work to make a man refute Job, since really he can be taught and humbled by Jahvé alone,—how this could be intended here precisely after ch. xxxi., where in reality it would be least of all in place and where Job cannot hold his peace with regard to such charges, because for the most part he does not deserve them in this form particularly at this place,—how it is that Elihu does not appear anywhere else in the book, since he surely could not be unmentioned at least in xlii. 7—17. On close and strict reflection we come upon nothing but insoluble difficulties; in which then precisely a warning lies not to regard this piece as belonging to the original work and not to require from it what it is not intended to be or to supply. The piece, when its external features only are looked at, really forms so little a part of the older work that it can be wholly removed from it without leaving any observable trace of its removal, still less of the least mutilation of the older book. Least of all do *those* modern readers understand either the remaining pieces of the present book or this particular piece, who suppose that the poet intentionally made the departures from the style and language of the older book in the speeches of Elihu simply on account of the change of the person speaking. While we find in the speeches of Job, Jahvé, and the friends, notwithstanding certain well chosen and firmly adhered to differences, after all the mind of one and the same poet in clear features, it is here equally clear that the poet himself is in every respect so totally different that fresh proofs of this may be discovered on every new examination of the piece.[1]

1. CH. xxxii., xxxiii.

xxxii. 1 And these three men ceased to answer Job, because he
2 appeared to himself to be righteous. Then was kindled the
wrath of Elihu the son of Barakhel, the Buzite of the kindred

xxxii. 1—6. The manner in which Elihu's descent is particularly described, ver. 2, differs from those of the friends in the earlier book. The author took it without doubt from genealogical tables of ancient families, of whom, however, we now know nothing further than that Buz was a small people and

[1] Many differences presented by this poet are more particularly referred to incidentally in the interpretation of the text below. Neither can a division of the long speeches into strophes be discovered, according to my repeated examinations. And even the text is here as regards single words less pure in comparison, because it was manifestly less pure from the very beginning, comp. xxxii. 5, xxxiii. 17, 24, xxxv. 14, 15, xxxvi. 18, xxxvii. 16.

of Ram: against Job was his wrath kindled, because he re-
3 garded himself as more righteous than God; and against his
three friends was his wrath kindled, because they did not
4 find answer and yet considered Job guilty. But Elihu had
already waited for Job with words, because they were older
5 than he in days: as now Elihu saw that there was no an-
swer in the mouth of the three men, then his wrath was
6 kindled; and

Elihu the son of Barakhel the Buzite answered and said:

Young am I in days, and ye grey:
therefore I held back and feared
to tell to you my knowledge;
I thought, let days speak,
and many years reveal wisdom.
But it is the spirit in man,
the breath of the Almighty, which giveth them understanding;
not the older are wise,
not the aged understand justice:
10 therefore I say, hearken ye to me!
I also will tell my knowledge!—

country east of Palestine, Gen. xxii. 21; Jer. xxv. 23. A family *Râm* from the land *Bûz* is otherwise unknown to us: yet this name, which was easily interchanged with Aram, according to Ruth iv. 19; 1 Chron. ii. 25 sq. compared with Matt. i. 4; Luke iii. 33, occurs again, Gen. xxii. 21, at least as a considerable family of another and younger branch of the Nahorites.—The reason of the silence of the friends is somewhat briefly given, ver. 1, to the effect that they had nothing more to say in reply because Job considered himself as in all respects justified. According to ver. 4 he had long had words against Job in readiness, but had waited to utter them from youthful modesty: but now this reason is no longer of force, inasmuch as the older opponents of Job have no more that they can say.

1. xxxii. 6—xxxiii. 7 the long introduction to this speech as the first. And first, xxxii. 6—10, an apology to all the former speakers that he the youngest now begins to speak: he has learnt that it is not really advanced years, but ultimately only the impulse of the divine spirit which gives understanding and ability; yet it does not suit the connection that he should at the end, ver. 10, call upon Job to hearken, so that instead of שִׁמְעָה we must read, after the LXX, שִׁמְעוּ, comp. xxxiv. 2, 10. דֵּעַ, which is formed afresh, acc. § 153 *b*,

Behold, I have waited for your words,
I give ear unto your reasons,
until ye would examine the speeches,
and unto you I paid attention:
but behold, no one of you decideth right against Job,
answereth his words;
ye might easily say: "we found wisdom;
God may put him down, but not a man!"
while he hath not prepared a word against me,
and not like you will I answer him.—
15 They are terrified, making no further answer,
the speeches have departed from them:
and should I wait, because they speak no more,
because coming to a stop they do not answer further?
I also answer my part,
I also tell my knowledge!
for I am full of words,
the spirit within me hath straitened me:
my inward-part is like wine which hath no vent,
like new skin-bottles it will burst;
20 I will speak that I may breathe freely,
open my lips and answer!

from בְּעַת, זחל, ver. 6, literally *to creep*, *to slink away abashed*, are new words; neither is אכן *but* found in the genuine book of Job.—But before the speech passes to Job, with whom it will then remain, it turns, and indeed for the first and last time (with the exception of the incidental addition xxxv. 4) to the three friends; and it gives freer vent to the indignation, which had been so long pent up, at their weakness, in a bold address to the three friends, vv. 11—14, inasmuch as he determines to speak, first, after he has vainly waited so long, that they might properly answer Job's speeches after they had been wisely examined, vv. 11, 12, and, secondly, that they may not suppose that they have found wisdom in what Job has said, and that God only can refute him, vv. 13, 14.—But when he has turned from them and calmly considers the matter by himself, he is brought back to the same necessity, vv. 15—20: shall he, as the friends are totally silent, on that account continue further to wait, *because* they do not speak? (והוחלתי acc. § 342 *c perf. cons.* and interrog.) how unreasonable! no, he must speak for the simple reason that his inward part is too full of spirit and straitened, as new, well pent-up wine, in fresh leathern bottles ferments most strongly and often even bursts this integument

But I may not consider any man,
  and a mortal will I not flatter:
for I do not know how to flatter;
xxxiii. easily might otherwise my Creator put me away!—
1 But O hear, Job, my speeches,
  to all my words give ear:
behold now, I have opened my mouth,
  my tongue speaketh already in my palate;
the uprightness of my heart are my words,
  what my lips know they speak purely:
the spirit of God hath made me,
  the breath of the Almighty given me life;
5 if thou canst, answer me,
  prepare thyself against me! take thy stand!
behold, I am of thy measure as regards God,
  from clay am *I* also cut:
behold, my terror shall not confound thee,
  and my burden shall not oppress thee!—
Only thou spakest, surely, in my hearing,
  and loud words I hear:
"pure am I, without transgression,
  clean am I, and have no guilt;
10 behold, He findeth quarrels against me,
  considereth me for an enemy to Him,

if it does not get vent in time (Matt. ix. 17). And this very impulse of the spirit, comp. ver. 8, xxxiii. 3, 4, briefly reminds him at last, vv. 21, 22, that though he begins to take part in the dispute, he may not seek honour and applause from men, which, indeed, he is unable to do, since precisely as impelled by the spirit he knows too well that he is not lord of his body, and if he should purposely not speak for the honour of God alone, his Creator would in a moment *carry him away*, *i.e.*, snatch him from life, demanding an account. עמד, ver. 16, *to come to a stop*, as xxxvii. 14; the construction of ידעתי, ver. 22, with the imperf. instead of the infin. is more Arabic than Hebrew, § 285 *c*.— But really intending to speak to Job, he calls upon him to listen to him attentively, xxxiii. 1, 2, since he intends to speak candidly in the consciousness of his own spiritual importance and mission (namely, that of speaking in the place of God) and yet not with hardness and compulsion, in case Job may be able to defend himself, as knowing well that he as a weak man confronts Job in relation to God only as an equal, like to like, that he is a piece of the same

setteth my feet in the stocks,
  watcheth all my paths!"
behold, in this thou art not right, I answer thee:
  for God is greater than a man.

Why hast thou contended against Him?
  since He doth not reply to all His words;
for once God speaketh,
  a second time He looketh not back thereon.
15 In a dream, a vision of the night,
  when deep sleep falleth upon men,
    in slumbers upon the bed:
then He openeth the ear of men,
  and putteth a seal upon their correction,
that He may withdraw man from the deed,
  and pride may remove far from the man,
may keep back his soul from destruction,
  his life from rushing upon the weapon:

mother-earth (כפי, see note on xxx. 18), vv. 3—7; only Job has uttered aloud thoughts such as too seriously violate the majesty of God, and which he must now reply to, vv. 8—12.

2. The chief subject of this speech, namely, the refutation of some of the utterances and thoughts of Job; to which the speech passes xxxiii. 8. From Job's speeches his opinion that he was innocent, is specially mentioned, that without cause God treated him as an enemy: ver. 10 *b* and ver. 11 are taken verbally from xiii. 24 *b*, 27, but otherwise much is freely altered, as also it is only here that the words חף, תנואות occur; אכף *burden* also is intentionally substituted, ver. 7, for כף xiii. 21, and קרץ, ver. 6, is new with this meaning, comp. the Aram. קְרַץ *a piece*. The refutation, vv. 13—30, proceeds therefrom, that man acts foolishly when he opposes the divine declarations, which when once they have gone forth from God are never altered, since, not like a man, who is responsible to others, He never reverts again to utterances which He has once made, so as perhaps to amend them (שור, ver. 14, as xxxv. 13), vv. 13, 14. Accordingly He does not withdraw the correction which He has inflicted upon men, and man must regard suffering as a chastisement unalterably determined upon and audibly announced by God: but if the sufferer will be admonished and made better under his sufferings by the revelations (*e.g.*, in dreams, ver. 15 elaborated after iv. 13, comp. Gen. xx.), which come to him during and through them, he may then still be delivered in a glorious manner, since God designs by such chastisement and revelation simply to draw man from further destruction. This line of thought is followed in a condensed manner, vv. 15—18; but

he is chastened in pain upon his bed
with the still vigorous multitude of his limbs,
20 and his desire of life maketh him loath bread,
his soul the desired food;
—already his flesh wasted away from comeliness,
and the leanness of his limbs scarcely suffers them to be seen,
and near to destruction is his soul,
his life to the angels of death—:
if there is then for him an angel,
a mediator, one of the thousand
to declare to man his uprightness,
and He hath compassion on him and saith:
"deliver him from going down into destruction!
I have found a ransom:"
25 then his flesh becometh fresher than in boyhood,
he returneth to the days of his youth,

then the wonderful aspects of this deliverance are further particularly described, on the one hand, the worst and immediate destruction which is already possible, on the other, the rapid, surprising recovery effected by the deliverance, vv. 19—28; and all this is again briefly summed up in conclusion, vv. 29, 30. Chief points therefore are ver. 16: *He openeth their ear*, that those who have long been hardened and deaf to the truth receive once more open ears, *and sealeth* (חתם with ב again xxxvii. 7) precisely thereby *their chastisement*, so that they clearly perceive their suffering is meant to improve them as correction from God, comp. ver. 19, xxxvi. 10; also *to pass into the missile* for to rush into open, present mortal peril, ver. 18, is expressed peculiarly xxxvi. 12, comp. ver. 24 *b*, ver. 28 *a*. If the reading ver. 17 *a* is correct, we must interpret the clause, *in order that man may remove* מַעֲשֶׂה in the bad sense (like *facinus*) *evil deed;* but here it is the action of God which is intended to be described, as what follows likewise shows: therefore a better reading is מַעֲשֵׂה, or better still מִמַּעֲשֵׂה, comp. ver. 30. As now the further description of this chastisement, vv. 19—22, is really already connected with vv. 16—18, the continuation is made with *vav conseq.* והוכח, so that this passage becomes at the same time the protasis to vv. 25—28, § 357 *a*. after a second conditional sentence has been parenthetically inserted, vv. 23, 24. Accordingly as follows: if he is painfully chastised, together with all his as yet fresh, youthful bones (xx. 11 *a*; acc. to the *Q'rî* רוב) upon his bed of sickness, and already loathes all food (now a parenthetical sentence to make the picture graphic, vv. 21, 22: his flesh wastes away מראי *from appearance*, form, comeliness, losing all appearance, then the *K'thîbh* שְׁפִּי: *and the leanness of his limbs* = his most wasted limbs *are not*

prayeth to God and He is favourable unto him,
causeth his face to behold joy,
giveth anew to the man his righteousness;
he singeth before men and saith:
"I have sinned and made the straight crooked,
yet the like was not rendered me,
He redeemed me from passing into destruction,
my life now enjoyeth the sight of the light."—
Behold, all this doeth God,
twice, thrice with a man,
30 to bring back his soul from destruction,
that he may give light in the light of life.
Attend, Job, hearken unto me!
hold thy peace, and I will speak!
if thou hast words, return me an answer,
speak, for I desire to justify thee:
if not, hearken *thou* unto me,
hold thy peace, and I will teach thee wisdom!

to be seen any more at all, have lost appearance and comeliness, so that he is already near to the *slayers* or angels of death; this definite distinction of angels of death and of life, occurs here for the first time): *if then one of the many* angels of life or *mediators* (מליץ in quite another sense than xvi. 20), whose work it is *to show to man his uprightness*, the way of uprightness which he must walk in, *is for him* (which can only be after man really follows the mediation which is offered to him acc. ver. 16) *and* God permits this mediator to redeem him (פרעהו appears to be acc. פדה, ver. 28, a false orthography for פדאהו), accepting the intercession of the angel and the prayer of repentance, ver. 26, as *ransom* of the lost man, then his sufferings have quickly fled, ver. 25, so that upon his prayer, being translated into circumstances of rejoicing and made again to share in the divine justification (צדקה is not in this sense found in the earlier book), he can in the presence of all men loudly proclaim his marvellous deliverance, as Ps. xxxii. Ver. 28 to be read acc. to the *K'thîbh*.— As if he already anticipated at the end that Job would be unable to make any reply, although he does not desire to hinder him, he requests at the close, vv. 31—33, at once silent attention to the following speech.

2. Ch. xxxiv.

1 And Elihu answered and said:

Hear, ye wise, my words,
  ye understanding, give ear unto me!
since the ear trieth words,
  as the palate tasteth for eating;
justice let us choose for ourselves,
  acknowledge amongst us what is good!—
5 But Job said: "I am right,
  yet God hath taken from me my right,
notwithstanding my right I must lie,
  my wound is incurable—without guilt!"
—Who is a man like Job,
  that drinketh blasphemy like water,
and walketh of one mind with evil doers,
  to go with men full of wickedness:
since he even saith, "a man hath no profit
  if he delighteth to be with God!"
10 Therefore, men of understanding, hearken unto me!
  far be from God a wickedness,
    from the Almighty an injustice!
for everyone's work He recompenseth to him,
  and as everyone doeth, He sendeth upon him.—

1. Vv. 2—16: again a somewhat long introduction. It begins already with increased confidence by the appeal to all wise men to hear the words of the man who is determined in their midst and with their help to seek what is most just and good, vv. 2—4, ver. 2 from xii. 11. He will now refute the notion of Job, that God is unjust towards him, vv. 5, 6 (ver. 5 *b* from xxvii. 2; ver. 6 עַל as x. 7, xvi. 17, *notwithstanding, in spite of my right I lie* according to God's sentence, therefore I may not maintain my right, and if I do so, I appear as guilty; חִצִּי after vi. 4, xvi. 9, xix. 11, but אָנוּשׁ after Mic. i. 9), with regard to which notion, so daringly expressed, Elihu cannot help uttering at once his horror, because according to it Job must like acknowledged blasphemers maintain that godliness is unprofitable, which could really be inferred from ch. xxi., xxiv., vv. 7—9 (ver. 7 *b* from xv. 16; וְלָלֶכֶת, ver. 8 *b*, acc. § 351 *c*), and with regard to which all wise men will agree with Elihu when he maintains the exact opposite, vv. 10, 11. Really, if the one consideration only is kept in view, that He is the one God who superintends and governs everything, who

Surely too! God doeth not wickedness,
  the Almighty perverteth not justice:
who inspecteth man upon the earth[1],
  and who then observeth the whole world?
should He give heed to Himself only,
  gather unto Himself His spirit and breath,
15 then all flesh would die together,
  man would return to dust!
so if there is yet understanding, hear this,
  give ear to the sound of my words:

Will also one that hateth right be able to control?
  or wilt thou condemn the powerful-righteous One?
Him who saith to a king, "thou worthless one!"
  and "wicked" to the nobles,

sustains the world not at the call of outward force and compulsion but from pure grace and mercy (inasmuch as all life flows from and returns to Him), then it appears clearly enough that it is impossible He should be unjust, inasmuch as from Him alone all life, law, and preservation proceed. Hence Elihu calls upon Job, if he supposes that he still possesses any intelligence, to further think out attentively this true proposition, vv. 12—16. The phrase ver. 13 *a* becomes plain from the exactly similar passage xxxvi. 22, 23, *who examineth against him* (man, ver. 11, in order to punish him if necessary) *the earth* and everything that is done by man upon it? some one else than God? ארצה therefore here and xxxvii. 12 acc. § 173 *h*; שום as ver. 23, iv. 20, xxiv. 12, hence the thought is continued immediately, ver. 14, with the same verb in this signification.

2. Vv. 17—37. It is intended therefore to prove here that God precisely as God, *i.e.*, from His inmost nature, cannot be unjust: and the further proof of this proceeds from the fundamental thought which had just been thrown out, in order then gradually to revert more particularly to Job's case. From the idea of God as the highest, ultimate ruler, follows of itself, vv. 17—20, that He cannot be unjust, because government is everywhere and always founded upon equal justice and is dissolved by the contrary; God is the righteous and mighty at the same time (צדיק כביר a kind of compound epithet, acc. § 270 *d*), inasmuch as He would not be able to exercise the highest power without the highest justice, nor the latter without the former, as we always see that He is both at once; He who without distinction of persons judges all men alike, in that He often quickly, as in one night, punishes the potentates of the earth also, so that they vanish not by an ordinary, visible, *i.e.*, merely human, hand and

[1] So in both editions; but see the comment. Tr.

who payeth no consideration to princes,
acknowledgeth not the rich before the poor,
because they are all the work of His hands:
20 suddenly they die at midnight,
they stagger in crowds and pass away;
the strong man is removed—not by a hand.—
For His eyes are upon everyone's ways,
and all his steps He seeth;
there is no darkness and no gloom,
that there evildoers might hide themselves:
for He payeth not first heed to one,
that a man should go to God for judgment:
He breaketh in pieces the mighty without examination,
and causeth others to stand in their stead!
25 Wherefore He knoweth their deeds,
and overturneth them at night, so that they are crushed,
as wicked men He putteth them to scorn
at the place where all see it,
—they who only therefore departed from Him
and considered not any of His ways,
in order to bring the complaint of the weak before Him,
that He might hear the complaint of the sufferers:

power, but by the invisible operation of the highest righteousness (comp. with ver. 20*c* Zech. iv. 6, Dan. ii. 34); ver. 18 הָאֹמֵר should be read.—If it is asked how this can be, the answer follows, vv. 21—30, that He thus judges because everything is seen by Him, vv. 21, 22, because He has no need first to observe whether the guilty person comes to judgment or not—to whom again but to Himself? (just as Job, in fact, always appealed to God), but with Him the examination and the judgment are one and the same, it being unnecessary in His case that a long and doubtful question and inquiry should be first put with regard to the guilt or innocence of a suspected person as is the case with human judges, vv. 22, 23; moreover, for the reason precisely that he knows everything, He also knows what is specially decisive—the deeds of the potentates—and punishes them quickly (*at night*, as ver. 20*a*) and publicly before the eyes of all, just as if they were common criminals who are executed under public scorn, vv. 25, 26 (תחת *instead* of them, as if they were such, comp. ver. 18), these infatuated potentates, who, when their fate is looked at from the point of view of this their end, seem to have departed from God and to have fallen into unrighteousness simply in order to bring the complaint of those who are unjustly tormented the more certainly before God's throne, vv. 27, 28: He

then He keepeth quiet—and who will condemn Him?
hideth His face—and who will behold Him?
both from a nation and a man,
30 that profane men may not reign,
nor snares of the people.—
For one saith to God even:
"I suffer what I do not transgress;
what I see not teach *Thou* me that;
if I did iniquity, I will not do it again!"
according to thy mind shall He recompense, that thou deniedst,
that *thou* choosest and not *I*?
—Yet what thou knowest speak!
understanding men will say to me,
the wise man that hearkeneth unto me:
35 "Job speaketh not with understanding,
and his words have no wisdom."—
O that Job might be tried to the utmost,
on account of the answers amongst bad men,

then indeed, taketh rest, *i.e.*, giving no more help (Ps. lxxxiii. 2, Zech. i. 12, 13) and turning His face away, coming with punishment both upon a nation and upon all persons of the earth—but who will condemn Him on that account, or who will hinder Him?—since He really is angry only in order to overthrow injurious potentates who mislead the people, therefore precisely for the sake of justice! vv. 29, 30.—And when the matter is looked at negatively from the other side, it is equally certain, that man as a creature may not speak to God as his equal, charging Him with injustice and demanding defiantly an account from Him (ver. 32 *a* בלעדי אחזה is the object of the verb הרני: *that which is beside what I see teach Thou me, i.e.*, what I do not see, what is unseen by me, comp. § 333 *b*, a similar construction to that of ver. 31 *b*), or promising amendment *if* he should have done wrong, as if that were doubtful! whence would follow really, that God would be compelled according to the man's own notion to treat him as he demanded in folly rejecting (God Himself!) or desiring! vv. 31—33 *b*: and here, as he discusses this supreme infatuation, Elihu is so profoundly moved by divine inspiration that he even uses *I* instead of God, ver. 33 *b*, as if God Himself spoke, and being unable to speak calmly further on this point he hastens to conclude, since Job's folly is now perfectly clear to all and nothing further can be desired than that God Himself should try him most thoroughly! vv. 33*c*—37. In this passage a late word is מעבד, ver. 25, as generally עבד in the sense of *to do*, Ecc. ix. 1, Dan. iii. 1; אָבִי, ver. 36, which can only be the expression of a strong desire, §§ 101 *c*,

that he addeth to his guilt further evil,
acteth scornfully in our midst,
and multiplieth his words against God.

358 *a* note, is rare. If the divine *I*, ver. 33 *b*, in Elihu's mouth does not owe its origin to an involuntary recollection of the language of the earlier prophets, we may also suppose that he here inserts some words of an ancient prophet which were at that time well known.

3. Ch. xxxv.

1 And Elihu answered and said:

Hast thou considered that as right
when thou thoughtest, "I am more right than God",
when thou sayest even, "what then doth it profit thee",
"what then do I gain more than if I sinned?"
I will reply to thee with words,
and to thy friends as well as thee!
5 Look unto the heavens, behold,
survey the skies, too high for thee!
if thou sinnest—what wilt thou do against Him?
if thy transgressions are many,—what doest thou to Him?
if thou art righteous,—what givest thou to Him?
and what will He receive from thy hand?
for men like thee is thy wickedness,
for mortals thy righteousness!—

In this case, almost without any introduction, as if already quite sure of his position against Job, he begins forthwith to quote the words which have now to be refuted, vv. 2—4: what has to be refuted is the idea that man gains nothing by godliness, an idea which easily follows from complaining of unrighteousness (ver. 2 *b*) and was also previously mentioned, xxxiv. 9, as arising therefrom: the proposition might be derived from ch. xxi., xxiv. (yet contrary to Job's meaning); and because this speech is intended only to refute this error, which had already been mentioned but not refuted in the previous one, xxxiv. 9, this its brief, abrupt opening is explained, since it is meant to have the appearance of a supplement to the previous speech. Ver. 3 *a* is an indirect quotation of another's speech, as xix. 28 *b*.—The refutation is: least of all can the idea of profit be applied to divine things, because man can neither injure the infinitely exalted One by sin nor profit Him by righteousness, on the contrary, simply injures or profits himself and his fellow men, vv. 5—8 (being very

On account of a multitude of wrong there is complaint,
a man crieth out on account of the violence of many:
10 and yet never thinketh, "where is God my Maker,
who giveth songs of gladness in the night,
who maketh us more instructed than the beasts of the earth,
and wiser than the birds of heaven!"
there they complain—and He answereth not—
because of the pride of evil men:
only vanity God heareth not,
and the Almighty regardeth it not.—
Well then, how sayest thou: "Thou regardest it not;
the contention is before Thee—but Thou waitest for it!"
15 therefore, because His wrath hath not yet punished,
He knoweth not of the foolishness quite well!
But Job—vanity his mouth spreadeth abroad,
without knowledge he heapeth up words.

similar to xxii. 2, 3, 12): if therefore man, as often happens, cries in vain for deliverance from violence, it comes therefrom that he wildly complains amid continual sin and the ignoring of the truth of Him, who really eternally (even in the darkest night, ver. 10, xxxiv. 25) delivers surprisingly, who has appointed man from the creation to know Himself vv. 9—13 (as to עשוקים, ver. 9, see § 179*a*; זעיק in the Hiph. acc. to later usage, Jon. iii. 7). How much less is therefore gain and deliverance possible, if Job charges God directly with the injustice of not being willing to regard the case which he has laid before Him, of waiting for it as if it had not yet been laid before Him (since God, surely, knows everything, long since therefore that which Job supposes He does not regard): whence would then follow that God does not at all regard it seriously, simply because He has hitherto not punished such folly! (but Job will soon see the contrary!). The suffix of the 3rd person in לפניו, ver. 14, is a too rapid variation from the direct quotation with the 2nd person, and ought probably to be corrected into ך–, or better still וַיִּתְחוֹלֵל, comp. Ps. xxxvii. 7, should be read, as חולל in this sense does not occur elsewhere. אַיִן, ver. 15, is used unexpectedly alone and before the verb, and is probably on that account to be taken so that together with the perf. it expresses our *not yet*, literally *it is not that He hath examined*, as otherwise the simple negative would have sufficed to express this idea. With פש comp. فس and فسفس, unless פשע *transgression* should be read with the LXX; ולא is the apodosis, § 345*a*.

4. CH. xxxvi., xxxvii.

1 And Elihu said further:

Wait for me a little, that I may teach thee:
for I have yet to speak of God;
I will lift my knowledge far hence [1],
and to my Maker ascribe what is due.
For truly, my words are not lies,
a man of perfect knowledge is with thee.

5 **B**ehold, God is mighty—but without contempt,
mighty in power of understanding:
He permitteth not the wicked to live,
but the right of the sufferers He granteth,
He withdraweth not from the righteous His eyes,
and the kings worthy of the throne,
them He causeth to reign ever exalted.

1. xxxvi. 2—4. Rising at last to the Highest Himself in his thought and speaking with great amplitude in the praise of God, Elihu seeks by that means also to remind Job at the same time of his errors, as he here announces with greatest confidence in his own knowledge. תְּמִים דֵּע', ver. 4, can only be understood acc. xxxvii. 16.

2. xxxvi. 5—25. The immediate aspect of God which is to be celebrated, as might be expected from the chief matter of Elihu's speeches, is that which refers purely to human affairs, accordingly His righteousness, vv. 5—15, with which is then connected the appropriate admonition and application to Job, vv. 16—25. The highest righteousness, which acc. ch. xxxiv. is associated with equally great power and wisdom, is inexorable towards sinners as such, but for all men who seek after it, although outwardly very despicable, already sunk in the deepest misery, it becomes the ever merciful, provident grace and redemption, ver. 5 *a* answers to ver. 6 *b* and ver. 7 *a*; and both aspects of the divine righteousness are exhibited in the case of all men without distinction, including the potentates of the earth: *the kings for the throne, i.e.*, who deserve the throne, them He causeth to reign perpetually [2], *that they may rule exaltedly*, ver. 7 *b*, *c*,

---

[1] In his Grammar, § 218 *b*, Ewald renders לְמֵרָחוֹק *von weitem her*, but here *fernhin*. Tr.

[2] According to the construction of יָשַׁב with לְ־ Ps. ix. 5, one might also consider as possible the meaning *and with kings upon the throne He causeth them* (the righteous) *to reign*. But this would be contrary to the accents, or

But if they are bound in fetters
  taken captive in the bands of affliction;
and He maketh known to them their doing
  and their sins, how they were defiant,
10 and openeth thus their ear to correction,
  saith that they must turn from evil:
if they hear and submit themselves,
  then they end their days in prosperity,
    and their years in pleasure;
if they hear not, then they rush upon the weapons,
  and die without knowledge,
who with reprobate heart put aside wrath,
  complain no more that He bindeth them;
though in youth their soul die,
  their life in the midst of the unchaste,
15 yet He delivereth the afflicted in his affliction,
  and openeth in distress their ear.—

yet the afflicted, and, precisely by their affliction, warned as by a divine voice which is then heard (vv. 9, 10 from xxxiii. 15—19), will if they only submit themselves to correction (עבד in a new meaning, from Ps. ii. 11) by following that voice, yet be gloriously delivered (נעימים see § 172 *b*), but in the reverse case must if they continue in their infatuation (iv. 20) perish, by their destruction itself laying aside their foolish defiance as well as their senseless complaint against God: although such an one may be bent on dying even in his strong youth under the greatest sufferings of the divine correction just like debilitated unchaste men (קְדֵשִׁים are καϑάρματα, purgamenta, offscourings; בְּ־ *amongst*, as one of their number, xxxiv. 36 *b*), he can nevertheless yet as a humble sufferer be warned and saved, vv. 14, 15; the two sentences therefore form at the same time antitheses, acc. § 357 *b*, and the similarity of the words xxxiii. 16, 20 is also in favour of this interpretation.—The application, vv. 16—25, proceeds upon the supposition that Job has been led astray to folly by too great prosperity and superabundance of outward possessions (which the three friends also thought, and generally Elihu is not much superior to them), as now the plain punishments showed: *And* (ואף somewhat more emphatic than וְ־, but peculiar to

---

rather to the entire structure of the clauses, as the strong emphasis on וַיּוֹשִׁ cannot then be explained; it would also be contrary to Elihu's way of thinking, and moreover something far too exalted and unexpected in this connection; besides, a thought likes this stands in quite another connection and is intelligible 1 Sam. ii. 8, and quoted thence Ps. cxiii. 7, 8. It is rather the words of Job xii. 13 which are present to Elihu's mind in vv. 7—13.

And thee also hath led astray more than biting need
the wide place, in which is no straitness,
the quietness of thy table, full of fat:
and with the judgment of the wicked thou art full,
judgment and sentence follow each other.
Yea violence may not lead thee astray through abundance,
let not the large ransom turn thee aside!
shall thy wealth set itself in array—without distress,
with all the means of force?
20 be not eager for the night,
that nations may vanish upon the spot!
O take heed, turn not to vanity:
for to this thou inclinest rather than to affliction.

these speeches) *there hath misled thee more than the mouth of need*, devouring need, *a breadth in which there is no straitness, i.e.*, an unlimited breadth (רחב appears as neut. with the fem., of the verb, which is rare, see § 174 *g*) as well as the *quietness*, or the undisturbed enjoyment *of thy sumptuous table;* and now *thou art full of judgment* or the punishments of a sinner, which even succeed each other in a long series, vv. 16, 17. Yea, may this not still further continue to be the case! vv. 18—21: *riches* (חמה would be used as xxix. 6 instead of חמאה *fat*, and the fem. would be construed as neut. with the masc. of the verb, which occurs in late writers; but it is probably better to read חמס *wrong*) *that they do not lead thee astray* (פן as Prov. v. 6, § 337 *b*) *through abundance!* (שפק as xx. 22, corresponding to the following רב; the signification *to scorn* of God, ספק xxxiv. 26, 37, does not readily adapt itself to this connection) *and let not the largeness of the ransom, i.e.*, the great wealth of outward power, wherewith at other times a man can generally purchase immunity from outward evils, *mislead thee!* comp. Ps. xlix.; how infatuated would that be! *shall thy wealth* (שׁוּעַ the abstract noun of שׁוֹעַ xxxiv. 19, another word not found in the earlier book) *prepare itself* with all other means of war with which defence is made against human enemies, *without distress*, with no external distress at hand, since the enemy that troubles thee is God against whom a man cannot arm himself, comp. ver. 16 *a*; surely, Job does not desire to provoke a great calamity, by not taking warning from a less serious one: *pant not after the night*, that the dark night of general calamity may come upon the earth (xxxv. 10 *b*), *that* whole *nations may perish* (lit. עלה, *tolli*, taken up, vanish, perish) *under themselves, i.e.*, where they stand, on the spot, since whole nations often suffer from the infatuated blindness of a great man, xxxiv. 29 *c*. בחר, ver. 21, does not occur elsewhere with על in the sense of *to choose*, if it is read we should then have to understand it thus: *thither* (to vanity) *thou turnest rather than to suffering*, ver. 15: but probably בֹּחֵר = בֹּחַן, as "Isa." xlviii. 10, is better, *for*

Behold, God worketh loftily in His power,
  who is like Him ruler?
who hath ever examined for Him His way,
  and who hath said, "Thou didst iniquity?"
remember thou to exalt His doing,
  which men have often sung:
25 all mortals admire it,
  men, as they behold it from afar!

Behold, God is more glorious—than we know,
  the number of His years—it is unsearchable:
thus He draweth up drops of water,
  which purify rain as His vapour,
with which the skies flow down
  and distil over many people:
still more, how can one understand the sails of wide clouds,
  crashing thunders of His tent,

that reason (that thou shouldst not turn to vanity) *wast thou tried by affliction*, although we should then expect בעני. The last reason for all this is, vv. 22—25, the infinite greatness of God (מורה, ver. 22, *Lord*, related to مَرْءٌ, *vir*, is quite Aramaic, δυνάστης in LXX correctly), which can so little be charged with an act of injustice, that, on the contrary, when only beheld and apprehended from a distance, it is universally celebrated and admired by every thoughtful man.

3. xxxvi. 26—xxxvii. 24. The praise of God with reference to nature, xxxvi. 26—xxxvii. 13, and the admonition likewise attached to it, xxxvii. 14—24, are still longer: the poet has here present to his mind evidently much that has been said in the speeches of Jahvé, ch. xxxviii. and xxxix., although his imitation falls far behind its model. After the general introduction, ver. 26, the speech starts with the rain, clouds, and thunderstorms, vv. 27—33, lingers then particularly by the thunder, xxxvii. 1—5, which to the mind of the ancients was the most divine of nature's phenomena (comp. Ps. xxix.), and reverts at last to the clouds xxxvii. 6—13, having referred to some other phenomena of the inanimate world. According to vv. 27, 28 even the creation of the ordinary rain is wonderful, in that drops of water, drawn up from the dirty earth, bring forth the pure rain, which serves at the same time as vapour, or a vapour-like cloud-covering, of God: but it is still more wonderful (אף אם is varied by אף כי, § 354 *c*) when in a tempest the clouds spread themselves like the broad sail of a great ship, in the mysterious centre of which crashes a deep voice, whilst He veils Himself primarily in light, which sometimes emits its flashes, but then

30 if He spreadeth His light around Him,
and thereupon covereth the foundations of the sea!
for by them He judgeth the nations,
giveth food also in great abundance:
both hands He covereth with light
and sendeth it forth against the adversary;
Him His thunder-call announceth,
xxxvii. the cattle even that He is approaching.
1 Yea truly at this my heart is alarmed
and leapeth up from its place:
hear hear attentively the commotion of His voice,
and the rumbling coming from His mouth;
forth under the whole heavens He sendeth it,
His light unto the wings of the earth:
after it roareth the voice,
He thundereth with the proud voice:
and should not find them, when His voice resoundeth?
5 God thundereth with His voice marvellously,
who doeth great things, more than we know!

further in the darkest water-clouds which seem to be drawn from the foundations of the sea, vv. 29, 30 (הן ver. 30 = if, comp. §§ 103 *g*, 355 *b*, is not the same as the הן before אל *God*, vv. 5, 22, 26, which begins a new description of His wonders); yet He must be in possession of this power in order that He may dispense life and nourishment no less than judgment and punishment, when He flings forth His light (lightning), vv. 31, 32, comp. xxxvii. 12, 13 (מפגיע appears to be equivalent to ἐναντίος, *adversarius*); even the cattle announce like the thunder the approach of Him who in His tempest maketh the earth tremble, *e.g.*, the peacock, as the poets of India often describe, ver. 33.[1] But it is particularly the thunder, with its strange, mysterious sound (xxvi. 14 *c*), which excites most intensely astonishment and agitation, xxxvii. 1—5, as like the light (lightning) it passes in a moment under the whole heaven to the ends of the earth, and resounds after the approaching God just as it had sounded before Him acc. xxxvi. 33: should not He, whose voice thus makes itself heard everywhere with terror, reach and find men, even if they flee from Him from fear of punishment? עִקֵּב is as in Syriac *to pursue*, *investigare* correctly in Vulg.,

---

[1] The אַף ver. 33 *b* is more loosely inserted, *the cattle indeed* (tell of Him) *that He . . .;* the poet uses this particle often, and the construction of it is in his case more than usually free.—The animals are likewise not passed over in a similar description xxxvii. 8.

Thus to the snow He saith: fall on the earth!
and to the heavy rain,
to the heavy rains of His splendour;
the hand of all people He sealeth,
for a sign to all men of His creation,
and wild beasts go into coverts,
and rest in their dens;
from the secret chamber cometh a storm,
and from the severe winds cold,
10 from the breath of God ice is given,
the breadth of the water is straitened;
with wet also He loadeth the clouds,
scattereth the cloud-mass of his lightning:
which turneth then round about,
—guided by Him as men do
whatsoever He commandeth them—
over the wide land and earth,
either for correction, if it is for the land,
or for mercy He causeth them to come.—
Give ear unto these things, Job,
stand still, consider God's wonders!

a new Aram. word, as is also שׁרה *to let go*, send forth, comp. ܫܪܐ. The commencement of ver. 6 like that of xxxvi. 27, specification after the same general proposition. The examples, vv. 6—13, are taken from the rainy and snow season of each year: snow and heaviest rain ver. 6 (where הֱוֵא stands in an unusual manner for *fall!*), in consequence of which both the labour of man is stopped, so that the hand which is at other times so active in the field now remains as it were shut up at home, as for a sign to men that they are only created beings, subject to a higher will, and also the wild animals seek their dens, vv. 6—8; then connected therewith stormy northwinds, blowing from hidden celestial chambers, cold, ice as if blown there by God's cold wind (xxxviii. 22, Ps. cxxxv. 7), vv. 9, 10; lastly the broad cloud of his light, laden with *wet* (רִי), through which His lightning flashes, which long guided by Him, according to the requirements of the divine conduct of human affairs, turns hither and thither over the earth, in order at last to empty itself either destructively for correction (*if* that is *for its land*, must fall upon the land belonging to the cloud), or fruitfully for mercy, vv. 11—13; comp. also *Jahrbb. der Bibl. Wiss.* IV. p. 66 sq.—The application to Job, vv. 14—24, refers ironically to the impossibility of contending with Him who is thus incomparably powerful in the creation, vv. 14—20, in order then to conclude the more em-

15 understandest thou how God giveth to them commands
and maketh the light of His clouds to shine?
understandest thou the sails of the wide clouds,
the wondrous works of the perfectly wise One?
thou, whose garments are warmed
when He quieteth the earth from the south:
dost thou with Him arch the skies,
which are firm as a molten mirror?
tell us what we shall say unto Him!
we cannot make preparation—from darkness!
20 will it be narrated to Him that I speak?
did anyone ever say, that he will be destroyed?
Accordingly, men never yet saw the light,
as it shineth in the clouds,
and the wind passing over hath purified them;
from the north cometh gold,
yet an awful splendour covereth God,

phatically with the proof of the necessity of man's submission to Him, vv. 21—24. Does Job really understand and can he at his pleasure (like God) manage either those terrible signs of the dark heavens (described at greater length above, xxxvi. 27—xxxvii. 12), vv. 15, 16 (מפלשי is evidently nothing more than a variation of מפרשי, xxxvi. 29), or the exactly contrary wonders of the perfectly bright, summer heavens (ver. 18 after Gen. i. 6)?—the creature who contributes nothing more to the summer than that he painfully feels the heat as soon as not he, but God makes the earth quite still and calm from the south by a sultry wind! vv. 17, 18. At all events Elihu with his friends does not arrogate to himself anything of this kind, he will not prepare himself for a struggle with Him—in the consciousness of his own weakness, darkness and defective understanding compared with the pure light (ver. 22 *b*), or Job would have first to tell him what he must say! no, if a man complain against God, he speaks to the wind, his words never reaching the desired place, ver. 20 *a*, as it is then foolish to lament that one is destroyed by God, ver. 20 *b*. Accordingly (ועתה as xxxv. 15), though all distant, splendid precious things of the earth can be beheld, ver. 22 *a*, comp. xxviii. 10, yet still less than the radiant sunlight, even when it has by the purifying winds become quite cloudless and is quite clearly to be seen in its bright skies, is man able to discern with the eye of sense Him whom the most awful splendour (נורא placed before its substantive acc. § 293 *c*) covers, who is equally powerful and righteous (ch. xxxiv): accordingly, as also the experience of history teaches, He cannot be rejected and condemned by men, but must be feared; and all who in imaginary wisdom speak proudly against Him, are not even regarded by Him and thus

Him the Almighty we find not,
Him who is of exalted power
and who perverteth not justice and all righteousness:
therefore mortals fear Him,
He overlooketh all the wise of understanding.

thereby suffer the worst punishment of their folly. In connection with ver. 22 *a* it must be noted, that the ancients often derived the best gold from the north and had many traditions and legends about it, comp. in addition to the passages before cited Plin. *Nat. Hist.* vi. 11, xxxiii. 4, Heeren's *Hist. Werke*, part xi. p. 310, and on Kuvêra's seat in the North the Hindoo Legends, *e.g.* in Rhode, *Hindus*, lib. II. p. 293, further A. v. Humboldt in the *Vierteljahrsschrift* 1838, part iv., and Sjögern in *Ausland* for 1840, p. 33. Neither may it be forgotten that this poet has evidently in his mind ch. xxviii., both in the case of this detached sentence and generally in that of this conclusion vv. 21—24.

FINIS.